Project Economics and Decision Analysis

Volume I: Deterministic Models

Project Economics and Decision Analysis

Volume I: Deterministic Models

M. A. Mian

Copyright © 2002 by
PennWell Corporation
1421 South Sheridan Road
Tulsa, Oklahoma 74112
1-800-752-9764

sales@pennwell.com
www.pennwell.com
www.pennwell-store.com

Managing Editor, Marla M. Patterson

Cover design and book layout by Joey Zielazinski

ISBN 0-87814-819-1

Printed in the United States of America

2   3   4   5   06   05   04

This book is dedicated to my brother, the late M. Rashid Mian, who passed away in a tragic car accident, and the memories that we shared together for more than 40 years. It was his idea to write this book with me. I have incorporated some of his handwritten notes on production-sharing economics in Chapter 5.

He was a warm, dynamic, vivacious, and fun-loving person. He was truly one of the most beloved and admired members of our family. We loved him deeply, and his loss leaves an enormous void in all our lives.

May God bless his soul in peace.

CONTENTS

3. BEFORE-TAX CASH-FLOW MODELS

4. AFTER-TAX CASH-FLOW MODEL

7. INVESTMENT SELECTION DECISION-MAKING

APPENDIX A

APPENDIX B

INDEX

PREFACE

The international oil and gas industry remains one of the most important, highly capital-intensive and risky industries at global, regional, and local levels. Capital and exploration spending in this sector average in excess of $40 billion/year (*Oil & Gas Journal* {*OGJ* }: June 10, 1996). Our profit margins are under real pressure from many factors, including the higher costs of developing new reserves, less oil found per foot drilled, rising inflationary costs of doing business, oversupply of crude, crude oil price volatility, competition for oil company investments, competition for acreage/concessions, competition for funds, and the overall business risk and uncertainty.

Therefore, it is crucial to carry out prudent economic evaluations of any capital investment before resources are committed. This, of course, requires a thorough understanding of the techniques available and their application by all those involved in decision-making. To assist in achieving this goal, the industry deserves a comprehensive guide to provide all the necessary concepts of capital investment evaluation, capital budgeting, and decision analysis. This book, *Project Economics and Decision Analysis*, will hopefully meet this requirement.

Objective

One goal in writing this book has been to provide students, practicing engineers, geologists, economists, planners, and managers with a solid foundation in the dynamic and growing field of capital investment evaluation with emphasis on the uncertainty aspect. It describes how investment decisions are currently made under different stages of uncertainty and prescribes techniques for making rational decisions. This two-volume set describes the philosophy, process, and methods of capital investment evaluation and decision analysis.

In summary, the main objectives of the book are to:

- Explain the ever-expanding role of economics in prudent capital investment decision-making.

- Assist readers in developing a knowledgeable vocabulary of the terms associated with economic analysis.

- Review the procedures used in preparing capital investment evaluations and decision analysis.

- Relate the new vocabulary and knowledge to some specific problems.

- Present ways of interpreting estimates that include uncertainty (i.e. converting probabilistic description into a measure of profitability).

- Provide solid hands-on experience with capital investment evaluation and decision analysis.

Emphasis and Style

The book presents a balanced blend of theoretical concepts and their practical utility. I prefer to focus less on extensive theoretical discussions than might be found in other books. Theory, I feel, distracts the reader from the most important concepts and their practical application. Moreover, theory can seem sterile and pointless unless its usefulness is made clear. Therefore, I have focused more on practical application. The underlying concepts are stressed and made concrete with liberal use of illustrations, many of them taken from actual real-life capital investment evaluations. Algebraic formulations and spreadsheets are used side-by-side to help readers develop conceptual thinking skills. Emphasis is placed on model formulation and interpretation rather than algorithms

The technical materials have been developed with considerable patience—assuming very little foreknowledge and proceeding in a step-by-step manner to minimize the possibility of the reader getting lost along the way. Moreover, I have resorted to a greater degree of informality in the presentation in the belief that *readability* should be an overriding consideration. Toward the same goal, intuitive and economic explanations are frequently provided to clarify the why of a particular concept/technique.

This book is primarily intended for use by economists, earth scientists, engineers, and students. It also is intended to serve as a refresher and perhaps as a self-study textbook. The problem-solving approach is instructive in nature, but the foundational principles show the practical application of the material. Its chief purpose is two-fold: (1) to render a systematic exposition of certain basic deterministic investment evaluation methods, and (2) to relate these to the decision analysis in such a way that the mutual relevance of the two is clearly brought out.

Therefore, the book is divided into two separate, yet complementary, volumes. This book, Volume 1, is essentially introductory and deals with the deterministic evaluation tools used for capital investment evaluations. These concepts are seldom covered as broadly or from the same viewpoints in economics and other courses, yet they are fundamental to the proper understanding of all evaluation work.

Volume 2 in this series deals with the concepts of decision analysis (i.e., incorporating risk and uncertainty as applied to capital investments). Generally, each topic is introduced by a brief practical or conceptual overview, followed by a brief discussion related to its application in practice and a solved example.

For optimum benefit, it is recommended that readers explore both volumes and benefit from their integrated instruction. Additionally, a CD is included with Volume 2 and provides helpful software, spreadsheets, and tables to enhance the practical application of this material.

Examples and Assignment Problems

Included in this book are an abundance of solved real-life examples (100+) and end-of-chapter assignment material (200+ questions and problems). Examples help reinforce the learning process. Each solved example is straightforward, fully explained, and avoids sudden leaps to conclusions that might confuse the reader. The assignment material is divided into questions and problems. The questions primarily address key concepts and terms in the chapter. The problems either consolidate a number of chapter topics or focus on a comprehensive analysis of a single topic.

The wide variety of assignment material offers practical knowledge since the assignments include various combinations of breadth and depth, theory and procedures, simplicity and complexity. For maximum benefit, the reader should work out as many of these problems as possible, if indeed not all.

Spreadsheet Applications

An additional unique feature of this book is embedded application of computers in solving investment evaluation and decision analysis problems. Rapid advancements in computer hardware and software are revolutionizing our working environment. Powerful computers are now available at affordable prices, and new state-of-the-art software makes it easy to do things much faster and efficiently. Much of this was not feasible several years ago. Today, most of us are using spreadsheet programs to build models of the decision problems we face as a regular part of our daily work activities. Spreadsheets also capture users' interest and add a new relevance to investment evaluation and decision analysis.

Examples are provided to show how computers can be used to help make better evaluations and, hence, better decisions. The Microsoft Excel spreadsheet is making it increasingly easy and practical to do sensitivity and scenario analysis. Its use has gained acceptance in the industry and makes it feasible to do a variety of analyses with a multitude of problems. The latest version of DecisionTools™ Suite (an Excel add-in) by Palisade Corp., including the award winning @RISK, PrecisionTree, BestFit, TopRank, and RISKview is used where applicable. Screen captures of the various menus of DecisionTools Suite are used. A copy of the software is included on the CD-ROM accompanying Volume 2 of this book. The CD-ROM also includes all the tables and spreadsheets incorporated in the book. This will greatly enhance the utility of the book and permit the quantification of project evaluation and risk analysis in a practical manner.

Reviewers' Comments

Many useful comments were received from PennWell's technical reviewers. These are incorporated wherever possible. Some reviewers noted that perhaps I may overkill some of the basic concepts, such as the Time Value of Money, etc. That may be true, but this is how I learned these concepts more than 20 years ago when I took a course from Dr. Franklin J. Stermole at Colorado School of Mines. These basic concepts had been of considerable help to me over the years, enabling me to visualize the investment problems and their time horizons. Therefore, I have decided to leave them as is. Similarly, the use of interest tables (in this modern age of computers) might be considered orthodox. The tables *may* not be used in practice, but they definitely add to understanding the concepts. I feel strongly that readers will benefit, therefore I have included them here.

Request for Suggestions

Considerable amount of dedication and investment (time and capital) goes into writing and publishing such a book. I have made every effort to introduce this two-volume set as a comprehensive desk reference. I sincerely welcome your thoughts as an end-user to help us further improve the contents, presentation, and utility of this book so as to make it a standard for the new generation of petroleum industry personnel. I will always be very grateful for your comments, suggestions, or corrections sent to me directly or through PennWell.

Acknowledgements

Many people are involved in the successful publication of a book. I wish to thank the following for making significant contributions to this book. Without their assistance, this project could not have been possible.

- All the people at PennWell who contributed their efforts to the production of this book, especially managing editor Marla Patterson and the PennWell production and editing staff, as well as Sue Rhodes Dodd, my project editor and president of Amethyst Enterprises in Tulsa, Oklahoma.

- Mr. Randy Heffernan of Palisade Corporation for sending me a copy of the latest version of their DecisionTools™ Suite and allowing me to include this tool on the CD-ROM accompanying Volume 2. This has significantly enhanced the utility of this book.

- I would like to thank James A. MacKay of Texaco, Houston, Texas, and Dr. Roger Eraj Ertefai (Petrochemical and Refining

Group Leader) at Qatar Petroleum for reviewing some parts of the manuscript. Their comments were very valuable.

- I would like to thank my wife, three daughters, and son for their continued patience, support, encouragement, love, and back rubs throughout this project. They contributed to this effort in ways I probably will never know or understand. Special thanks to my daughters at the University of Colorado at Boulder for being on the Dean's list; this has contributed a lot to my enthusiasm.

- Last but not least, I thank my parents for their continued support and inspiration and for being together for more than 50 years.

M. A. Mian, P.E.

chapter ONE

Introduction

This introductory chapter sets the stage for this book by presenting basic concepts and definitions for capital investment evaluation (also referred to as investment appraisal or economic evaluation) techniques presented in the following chapters. The chapter is divided into three sections:

1. Profit planning

2. Basic concepts of economics related to capital investments

3. Defining uncertainty and risk

Many terms, such as capital budgeting, inflation, supply, and demand, profit planning, etc., presented in this chapter are referred to in day-to-day decision-making process. However, many of us may not be fully aware of the theory behind them. These terms are often accepted as routine business jargon. The concepts presented in this chapter will assist in clarifying these terms and enabling us to relate them to the evaluation of capital investment projects.

The worldwide oil and gas industry applies advanced techniques of investment analysis. Because of the dynamics of high risk, highly capital-intensive investments, complexity of operations, and profit potential, companies are compelled to seek the most sophisticated investment methods.

In virtually every segment of the oil and gas industry, oil and gas reserves estimates and complete economic evaluations are vital requirements for sales, mergers, acquisitions, estate settlements, litigations, and financing of exploration, field development, and major facilities' projects. For the protection of the public, every public company in the United States is required to submit an annual 10-K report with the Securities and Exchange Commission (SEC). For the 10-K filing, every public company must update its reserves estimates and accompanying economics. Petroleum engineering techniques are used to estimate oil and gas reserves and to make these forecasts. The economics constitute the oil and gas revenues, capital expenditures, operating expenses, taxes, cash flow, and various investment profitability measures.

Corporate or investor success or failure is based on the correct evaluation of investment opportunities and the results of decisions. The economic evaluations also serve as a good communication tool between the technical staff and the management of the corporation. Most of the investment decisions are based on the overall financial impact of an investment opportunity rather than on any specific technical considerations.

It is not necessary for every investor or every person in the corporate orbit to be a petroleum engineer, geologist, or a financial analyst. Most of the time, specialists do investment evaluations. Personnel involved in evaluating the data, recommending a course of action, and making the final decision must exchange sufficient and appropriate information/data. This total awareness considerably increases the quality of the decision-making process.

PROFIT PLANNING

The term *profit planning* is broadly defined as a systematic and formalized approach for accomplishing the planning, coordination, and control responsibilities of management. By making a continuing stream of well-conceived decisions, management can plan and control the long-range destiny of the enterprise. The concept speaks to planned prosperity as opposed to unplanned happenstance. Thus, the essence of the profit-planning concept is management's decision-making process. For long-term success of an enterprise, a stream of these decisions must generate plans and actions. These will then provide the essential cash outflows required to support the planned cash inflows of the enterprise. This is necessary to ensure the organization earns realistic profits and return on investments, which are long-term objectives.[1]

Long-term planning projects specified objectives and goals of an enterprise beyond the short-term. Today's actions are influenced by increased consciousness of tomorrow's expected events. Therefore, management concentrates on those events that can produce the best and largest economic results. This is an important key to the success of the business. Peter Drucker defines planning as:

> *The continuous process of making present entrepreneurial (risk-taking) decisions systematically and with the greatest knowledge of their futurity; organizing systematically the efforts needed to carry out these decisions; and measuring the results of these decisions against the expectations through organized, systematic feedback.*[2]

The management decisions must be *purposive* (i.e., primarily concerned with the purpose of developing enterprise objectives and devising realistic strategies to attain these objectives). Decisions must also be *futuristic* (i.e., concerned with the long-term). This is called *strategic* planning. Objectives should be more than statements of good intentions; they should be specific strategic goals.

Typical Oil Company Objectives

The typical primary objectives of any oil company are:

1. Add to the reserves inventory through exploration efforts or purchase of reserves in the most cost efficient manner,

2. Maximize ultimate oil and gas recovery from the reserves inventory through research efforts, studies, and the use of sound reservoir development and production practices,

3. Maintain sustained optimum production levels in line with sound reservoir management principles,

4. Ensure reliability of fuel and feedstock supplies to industry (where applicable),

5. Sustain the highest degree of reliability and availability of production facilities,

6. Conduct all operations in the most efficient, cost effective, safe, and environmentally acceptable manner, and

7. Maximize return on investment and total worth of the company.

Once the objectives are set, these objectives are then converted into actual doing. The decision-making process is a work program and will result in implementing many projects. These projects have to be coupled with specific and concrete work assignments with defined goals, deadlines, milestones, and clear accountability. Unless converted into action, objectives are nothing more than dreams.

The achievement of these objectives requires diverse activities within each sector of the enterprise. Attaining some of these objectives entails high risks. It requires effort, and that means capital. Businesses have to make a profit in order to survive.

The Role of Management in Planning

The planning function is classified into long-term *strategic* plans and short-term *tactical* plans. Strategic plans provide broader view of activities focusing on objectives and goals over a longer time period, say, from 5 to 10 years. The tactical plans provide detailed view of the activities focusing on the means to attain goals.

After objectives are established, management must set goals and incorporate tactics to attain these goals. It will provide (a) time dimensions for attainment of the goals, (b) quantitative measurements, and (c) subdivision of responsibilities. The management now develops strategies to specify the operational plan of attack to be used in pursuing the goals.

Finally, management operationalizes the objectives, goals, and strategies into one or more detailed profit plans (or budget). The profit plan explicitly states the goals in terms of time expectations and expected financial result (present worth, return on investment, profit, and costs).

Profit planning is a continuous and iterative process, as opposed to a periodic endeavor. The plans must be revised as conditions change and new information becomes available.

Planning of Capital Expenditures

In line with the attainment of the typical oil company objectives, the long-term and short-term profit plans of an oil company will include activities such as:

- Oil and gas exploration,
- Infill drilling, including optimizing development of existing fields/reservoirs,
- Secondary and enhanced oil recovery,
- Gas processing requirements,
- Expansion and contraction of plants, buildings, and equipment,
- Preventive maintenance of production facilities and infrastructure, and
- Major renovations, upgrading, and replacements of equipment/ production facilities.

These and other similar investment decisions comprise the capital expenditure plans, also referred to as the *capital expenditure budget*. In the planning process, each capital budget item is an identifiable project with its unique time dimension and plan of implementation. Capital projects are normally capital intensive (a large commitment of funds), and their impact on the enterprise extends far into the future.

The addition of each one of these capital projects to the profit plan has to be fully justified in terms of their derived financial, technical, and strategic benefits. Considerable planning and control are necessary to prevent (1) idle operating capacity of plant and equipment, (2) over-investment in operating capacity of plant and equipment, and (3) investment in projects that will produce a low or marginal return on the committed funds.

The capital budget plans are normally comprised of a series of unique capital projects. Therefore, the overall plans include projects spread over three time dimensions:

1. Projects that extend the farthest into the future (more than five years).

2. Projects that extend from three to five years.

3. Projects that are part of the short-term profit plan i.e., a one-year period.

   The implementation of projects is scheduled according to operational priority, technical maturity, and financial rewards.

The capital expenditure plans normally include two principal types of projects. These are (1) major projects—each involving considerable funds, and (2) minor capital additions. The major capital projects normally cover more than one year. These projects will normally be considered and planned over a number of years before a final decision is reached. The minor capital additions comprise implementation of relatively low-cost machines and tools, computers, minor renovations to buildings, and other miscellaneous items. Most of the minor capital projects will be *service-producing* projects, while the major capital projects will be *revenue-producing* projects. Some projects will require much detailed analysis as compared to others. The techniques used for the economic analysis of both service-producing and revenue-producing capital investments are presented in the following chapters.

SOME BASIC PRINCIPLES OF ECONOMICS

Economics is a social science that studies the allocation of scarce resources among competing ends. The principles, theories, or models of economics are used to explain and predict economic events. Policies are developed to correct economic problems. Economics studies/models are subdivided into *macroeconomics* and *microeconomics*.

Macroeconomics is the branch of economics dealing with the aggregate level of (1) output and employment, (2) national income, and (3) the general price levels and the factors influencing it. Microeconomics, on the other hand, deals with the economic behavior of individuals such as consumers, resource owners and business firms in a system where the economic activity is not directly controlled by the government. For example, it deals with the questions of:

1. How the purchasing power of an individual is influenced by the price of a commodity.

2. How a firm optimally combines various resources for the production of goods and services, and

3. How the goods and services produced by the economy should be distributed.[3]

The purpose of this book primarily is to provide tools for capital investment evaluations and decision analysis. In order to correctly use the relevant concepts presented here, it is important to understand some basic concepts related to macroeconomics, microeconomics, and their impact on variables used in capital investment evaluation and decision analysis.

For example, inflation and recession in an economy will significantly affect returns from an investment. But most people are probably not aware of what causes inflation or recession, how they affect returns from investments, and how governments counteract these unfavorable economic trends. Similarly, many oil and gas companies invest in foreign countries where their investments are exposed to the risk of radical currency devaluation.

A brief exposure to the selected concepts and terms developed in economics (i.e., description of tools and concepts most useful in investment analysis) is therefore considered appropriate.

Demand, Supply, and Price Equilibrium

Supply and demand are terms used indiscriminately in casual discussions of economic events concerning services, commodities, and product prices. A comment such as "there are ample reserves of crude oil" may appropriately reflect the stock of oil in the ground. However, it does not say anything regarding the conditions under which producers will be willing or able to produce this stock of crude oil. Therefore, supply is defined in terms of the quantity of a specific commodity offered at a given price. Demand is referred to the consumption of that supplied quantity at that price.

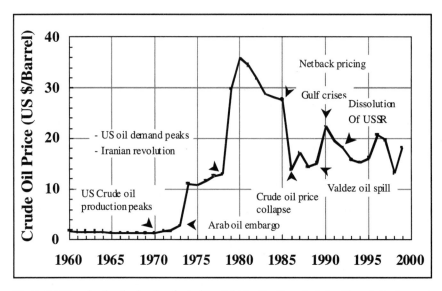

Fig. 1–1 FOB crude oil netback values for Arabian Light (ex Ras Tanura), derived from Rotterdam spot prices (Source: Oil Market Trends)

Figure 1–1 is an illustration of the historical crude oil prices and the events coinciding the periodic fluctuations in these prices. Careful analysis of history can explain reasons for the price fluctuation.

For example, when Iraq invaded Kuwait in August 1990 (the Gulf War), the crude oil prices jumped to a 5-year high level (from an average of $17/barrel to $33/barrel). This was due to the fear of oil supply disruption from the Gulf. However, the price fell back to an average of $18/barrel in March 1991 when the Allied forces freed Kuwait from Iraq, and an embargo was imposed on Iraq.

Similarly, on May 20, 1996, an agreement was signed by the United Nations and Baghdad (Iraq) allowing Iraq to export oil for the first time since Iraqi troops invaded Kuwait in August 1990. This event led to the following news headlines in the *Gulf Times*.

> *Iraq sends shivers through oil market and Brent crude prices fell by a dollar in London on the week. Dealers and analysts agreed that this extra oil would cripple the market already creaking under the strain of burgeoning supplies.*

Similar analysis appeared in the *Oil & Gas Journal* (December 9, 1985):

> *Even a small production rise or demand decline has a potential to force the price of crude oil sharply lower, some oil economists believe. Since very little oil is turned out at the highest direct production cost increment, a minor increase in the current supply surplus could cause prices to topple towards the next "cost plateau," which might be around $16 a barrel, says L.J. Deman, corporate economics manager for Texas Eastern.*
>
> *OPEC's present shutting-in of some 11 million barrels/day of the world's lowest cost capacity allows demand to currently intersect supply at a production cost around $24 a barrel, he notes. That props up prices well above the $8 to $10 level which full OPEC output might theoretically imply. Risks of a sharp price break could intensify debate in non-OPEC nations over whether to restrict internal output or impose an oil import tariff.*

Besides the crude oil prices, the cost of all other oil industry related services are subject to the law of supply and demand. In 1996, the demand for offshore rigs in the Gulf went up, resulting in increase of rig rentals from $21,000 per day to $29,000 per day, soaring to $60,000 per day in early 1997. This rise in rig demand was due to increased crude oil price to $19/barrel and triggered increased exploration and field development activities.

The imbalance of supply and demand for any commodity and/or services affects project economics. Therefore, it is essential to be fully aware of the mechanism of how *equilibrium market price* for commodities is achieved in a free-enterprise economy.

Demand. Demand refers to the willingness as well as the ability of consumers to buy a commodity. The existence of a need creates demand for a given commodity over a given time period. However, the need by itself is not a sufficient condition. The consumer must have the financial ability, i.e., money, to transform this need into effective demand for the commodity. Therefore, if price of a commodity is increased, its demand will go down. This is because some of the consumers who could afford the commodity at the lower price may not afford it at the higher price. At the lower product price, more of the product will be purchased because:

a) consumers can now purchase more with their unchanged money income,

b) the number of consumers who will be able to purchase the product at lower prices increases, and

c) consumers substitute this (now relatively cheaper) commodity for others in consumption.

Supply. On the other hand, supply refers to the ability and willingness of a *producer* to supply a commodity over a given period at various alternative prices. The unit price a producer receives for its product is independent from the volume of the producer's output. The producer's objective is to determine what output level will maximize the short-term profit. This output level for any one producer is based on how production costs vary with output for that producer. This in turn determines the market price.

Supply and Demand Curves. In models of free-enterprise economy (i.e., perfect competition) economists postulate the existence of two mathematical curves. These are the market demand curve and the indus-

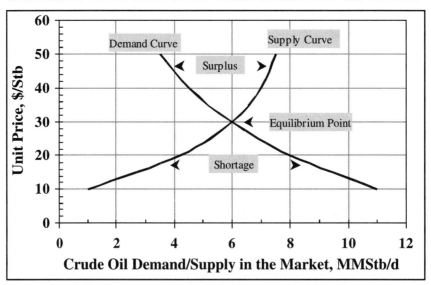

Fig. 1–2 Hypothetical crude oil supply and demand curves

try supply curve, both shown in Figure 1–2. The industry supply curve is the sum of all the individual producers' supply curves for a commodity. The market demand curve is the sum of the demand curves of *all* individuals in the market for a commodity.

The demand curve slopes downward (from left to right, or *negative sloping*). This trend implies a consumer will buy more of a commodity at lower prices. This is called the *law of demand*. On the other hand, the supply curve slopes up (from left to right) showing that higher prices must be paid to induce the producer to supply more of the commodity.

Equilibrium Price. The intersection of the supply and demand curves determines the *equilibrium price* and the *equilibrium quantity* of a commodity. The equilibrium price is the price consumers are willing to pay over a given period that exactly equals the quantity producers are willing to supply. At a price higher than the equilibrium price, the demand for the commodity drops, resulting in *surplus* supply of the commodity. The producers then have to push the price down towards its equilibrium level. On the other hand, at a price lower than the equilibrium price, the quantity demanded exceeds the quantity supplied, resulting in *shortage* of the commodity. The producers therefore have to push the price up towards its equilibrium level.

Shifts in Demand, Supply, and Equilibrium. The market demand curve for a commodity is based on these assumptions:

- The number of consumers in the market stays constant.
- The consumers' tastes, money income, and need stays the same.
- The prices of other related commodities remain unchanged.

Similarly, the market supply curve for a commodity is based on these assumptions:

- The number and size of producers of the commodity remain same.
- The technology used to produce the commodity is unchanged.
- The factor price (the cost involved in producing a commodity) is unchanged. The prices of other related commodities remain unchanged.

However, changes in one or more of these assumptions will shift the curves, resulting in new equilibrium price and equilibrium quantity for the commodity. For example, the market demand curve will *shift up* (commodity's equilibrium price and quantity will both rise as shown in Figure 1–3) if one or more of the factors *rises* (such as number of consumers, consumers' income, consumers' taste for the commodity, or the prices of related substitute commodities). Opposite changes will cause a downward shift in demand.

The market supply curve will *shift down* and to the right, i.e., increase, if one or more factors changes. Factors include increase in the number and/or size of the producers, improvement in technology, fall in factor price, or decrease in the prices of other commodities used in production. This will result in lower equilibrium price and a *higher* equilibrium quantity.

Elasticity of Supply and Demand. The elasticity of supply curve (ε_s) is the measurement of the average percentage change in the quantity of a commodity supplied because of an average percentage change in its price, expressed in absolute terms. The supply curve of a commodity is said to be *elastic* if $\varepsilon_s > 1$, *unitary elastic* if $\varepsilon_s = 1$, or *inelastic* if $\varepsilon_s < 1$.

Similarly, the elasticity of demand curve (ε_d) is the measurement of the average percentage change in the quantity of a commodity demanded because of an average percentage change in its price, expressed in absolute terms. The demand curve of a commodity is said to be *elastic* if $\varepsilon_d > 1$, *unitary elastic* if $\varepsilon_d = 1$, or *inelastic* if $\varepsilon_d < 1$.

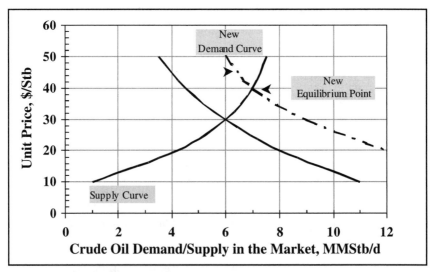

Fig. 1–3 Supply/demand curves, showing shift in the demand curve

Mathematically,

(1.1)

$$\varepsilon_s = \frac{Change\ in\ Quantity\ Supplied}{of\ Quantities\ Suplied\ /\ 2} \div \frac{Change\ in\ Price}{Sum\ of\ Prices\ /\ 2}$$

(1.2)

$$\varepsilon_d = \frac{Change\ in\ Quantity\ Demanded}{Sum\ of\ Quantities\ Demanded\ /\ 2} \div \frac{Change\ in\ Price}{Sum\ of\ Prices\ /\ 2}$$

The concept of elasticity shows whether an increase or decrease in price of a commodity will increase/decrease total revenue generated by the commodity. Therefore, if price of a commodity falls; the total revenue of producers from the commodity will (a) increase if the demand curve is elastic, (b) remain constant for a unitary demand curve, or (c) decrease if the demand curve is inelastic.

The numerical value of ε_d also shows how expenditures for the commodity will change with price changes, if no shift takes place in the demand curve. $\varepsilon_d > 1$ indicates an increase in price will result in decreased expenditure on the product while $\varepsilon_d < 1$ indicates if price is increased, total expenditure on the product will increase. The value of ε_d may be greater than 1.0 for some price ranges and be less than 1.0 for other ranges.

Example 1–1

Considering the demand curve of Figure 1–2, calculate the elasticity of demand if the oil price drops from $30/barrel to $20/barrel.

Solution. From Figure 1–2,

at $30/barrel   Demand = 6 MMStb/day
at $20/barrel   Demand = 8 MMStb/day

Using Equation (1.2)

$$\varepsilon_d = \frac{8-6}{(8+6)\ /\ 2} \div \frac{30-20}{(30+20)\ /\ 2} = 0.2857 \div 0.40 = 0.71$$

Since $\varepsilon_d < 1$, the demand curve in the \$20/barrel to \$30/barrel range is inelastic. Therefore, the total revenue of the producer will be decreased. This is because the percentage increase in quantity exceeds the percentage decline in price.

Inflation

Capital investment decision-making is affected by inflation. It will make investments with costs incurred earlier in the economic life look more attractive than investments costs for the same purpose incurred later.

Inflation occurs when there is an increase in general price level (i.e., when the price of a given quantity, basket, of goods and services increases). But not all prices rise. Even during acute inflationary periods, some specific prices may be relatively constant while others actually fall. Nor does inflation mean prices rise evenly or proportionately. If some prices rise and others fall, the price level may not change. Inflation reduces the purchasing power of a unit of money over time. It is typically reported as a percentage increase in prices from one time to another. The percentage increase is referred to as the rate of inflation.[3-4]

Inflation affects real income and wealth. Real income is the amount of goods and services that can be purchased with a given money income. For example, a worker's salary increases by 10%. If prices remain stable, the worker can purchase 10% more goods and services, meaning real income also increased by 10%. If prices increased more than 10%, the worker cannot buy as much as he or she previously could, meaning real income is less than money income. If the price level doubles while the money income is constant, the real income is cut in half, meaning only half the basket of goods can now be bought.

The so-called "rule of 70" provides a convenient formula for gaining a quantitative appreciation of inflation. The rule allows a quick calculation of the number of years required to double the price level, by dividing the number 70 by the annual rate of inflation. For example, 5% annual rate of inflation doubles the price level in about 14 (=70 ÷ 5) years.

There are three major causes of inflation (1) demand-pull inflation, (2) cost-push inflation, and (3) structural inflation. These three causes of inflation are related and not mutually exclusive (i.e., all three can be in action simultaneously).

Demand-Pull Inflation. The demand-pull inflation develops when economic resources are fully employed, and:

1. There is an increase in aggregate demand,

2. Aggregate demand grows at a faster rate than aggregate supply, or

3. Bottlenecks develop prior to full employment (i.e., some industries are fully utilizing their productive capacity before others and, therefore, unable to respond to further increases in demand for their products by increasing supply; so their prices rise).

Demand-pull inflation occurs because prices need to be increased in order to ration goods and services as the desire to purchase exceeds the ability of the producers to supply. The essence of demand-pull inflation is crudely expressed in the phrase, "too much money chasing too few goods."

Cost-Push Inflation. This type of inflation stems from the supply or cost side of the market. It may be due to the market power of labor unions, business firms or suppliers of raw materials, or to government regulation or taxation of business. In order to increase their profits, the firms with sufficient market control increase prices of goods and services they produce. Similarly, when (1) the government raises taxes on businesses, (2) labors' wages are increased, or (3) suppliers of raw materials increase their prices; the result will be higher cost of producing goods and services and passing those costs on to the consumer. Therefore, cost-push inflation results when monopolistic power permits supply prices to be influenced by the actions of firms, labor unions, raw material suppliers, or government.

The economy will also suffer from cost-push inflation if there is simultaneous increase in inflation and unemployment. This inflation/unemployment is supply driven in the sense that initially, producers will produce goods that are not purchased. In order to reduce their financial losses, producers increase prices and reduce their workforce. This will result in simultaneous increase in inflation and unemployment. This is called *stagflation*.

A typical example of the cost-push inflation is the rapid crude oil price level increases in the 1973–1975 period. In late 1973, the Organization of Petroleum Exporting Countries (OPEC) became effective and exerted its market power to quadruple the prices of oil.

Structural Inflation. This is also referred to as demand-shift inflation. In this case, the total demand is not excessive, but a sharp change in the structure or composition of total demand takes place. This results in increased prices and wages in those segments of the businesses where expanding demand occurred. However, the prices and wages do not fall in those businesses where demand declined. This results in net increase in price and wage levels, thus inflation occurs.

Impact of Inflation. Let's shift from the causes of inflation to the impact/effects of inflation. How does inflation redistribute income? What is the possible impact of inflation on financial management of capital investments? What are possible ways of accounting for the effect of inflation in capital investment decision-making? These will be more thoroughly addressed in Chapter 3.

1. *Fixed money income groups.* Inflation arbitrarily penalizes people receiving relatively fixed money incomes. The households whose money income is not keeping up with the pace of the rate of inflation will find their real incomes deteriorating because of inflation. The purchasing power of each dollar they receive in their pay envelopes will fall as prices rise, resulting in a decline of their standard of living.

2. *Savers.* As prices rise, the real value or purchasing power of savings will deteriorate if inflation is higher than the interest earned on the savings. For example, a person deposits his savings of $1,000 in a saving account earning 6% interest per year. After one year, he will have $1,060 in savings. However, if inflation is 8% during that year, the real value of the $1,060 is then only $981.48 (=$1,060/1.08). To put it another way, the basket of goods that could be bought for $1,000 a year ago is now costing $1,080 because of 8% inflation, while only $1,060 are available now.

3. *Debtors and Creditors.* Inflation tends to benefit debtors (borrowers) at the expense of the creditors (lenders). As the prices go up, the value of the dollar comes down. As a result, the debtor

gets dear dollars but pays back cheap dollars. However, this will happen only if the inflation is unexpected. If the rate of inflation is known or it can be anticipated, the lenders will add the percentage rate of inflation to the rate of interest charged on the loan. This analysis also implies that, rather than being a cause of inflation, high interest rates are a consequence of inflation.

4. *Planning Difficulties.* Businesses operate based on long-term plans. For example, a firm commits capital investment in a plant in anticipation of receiving certain revenue over the economic life of the plant. However, if the anticipated costs are not in line with the anticipated inflationary increase in costs, the investment may become marginal or uneconomical. Therefore, it is important to use improved forecasting techniques in order to include more flexibility in reflecting the increased level of uncertainty in the economy.

5. *Demand for Capital.* Inflation increases the amount of capital required to embark on a desired volume of business. The costs of expanding or replacing plants increase, while workers demand higher wages. All these require raising additional capital. On the other hand, the Federal Reserve System tends to restrict the supply of loanable funds in order to curb inflation. The ensuing scramble for limited funds drives interest rates higher (i.e., increase in cost of capital). High interest rates and shortage of capital are causing firms to be especially careful in planning long-term capital outlays.

6. *Depreciation.* In financial statements and cash flows, depreciation charges are based on yesterday's currency value. With the shrinkage in an inflationary economic environment, this depreciation will rapidly become inadequate. Eventually, the asset has to be replaced, at which time the replacement cost in depreciated currency will not be enough.

Expectations of long-term oil and gas prices, currency exchange rates, inflation rates, and financing and discount rates are, of course, critical in evaluating the potential rewards from a capital investment project.

UNCERTAINTY AND RISK

In Volume 1 of this series, it has been implicitly assumed the results and implications of investment decisions are known at the time of the decision (i.e., the future is known, and it is known with certainty). That is, the probability of success for each investment under evaluation is considered to be 100%. In reality, such conditions simply do not exist. In practice, different investment options will inherit different degrees of associated uncertainty and consequently different degrees of risk. Risk and uncertainty are complementary concepts.

> *Risk refers to situations where a project has a number of possible alternative outcomes, but the probability of each outcome is known or can be estimated. Uncertainty refers to a situation where these probabilities are not known or cannot be estimated.*

When faced with decision choices under uncertain conditions, we can use informal analysis methods and quantitative methods to ascertain risk and uncertainty associated with the available investment options. Informal analysis involves the decision-maker's experience, intuition, judgment, and gut feeling. The quantitative analyses use a logical and consistent decision strategy by incorporating the effects of risk and uncertainty into the analysis results. Several different approaches are available that can be used to quantitatively incorporate risk and uncertainty into investment analysis.[5]

Most methods of dealing with risk and uncertainty require assessments of probability of the uncertain outcomes. Therefore, the success of each method depends upon the accuracy of these probabilities. Thus, the importance of developing accurate probability estimates is the essential part of decision analysis.

Volume 2 of this series is devoted to outlining a number of approaches for analyzing degrees of risk and allowing for them when making investment decisions. The following topics are included in Volume 2.

1. *Introduction*

2. *Statistics and Probability Concepts.* This chapter is divided into two parts. The first part deals with the descriptive statis-

tics (i.e., calculating measures of central tendency and measures of variability from grouped and un-grouped data). The second part deals with the concepts of probability and theoretical probability distributions.

3. *Expected Value and Decision Trees.* In this chapter, the probability concepts and the deterministic concepts presented in this volume are combined to arrive at the expected value of investment alternatives under consideration.

4. *Incorporating Attitudes toward Risk.* In this chapter, the decision-maker's particular risk attitudes (risk preferences) are incorporated into decision analysis.

5. *Determining Venture Participation.* The concept of Gambler's Ruin is presented in this chapter, and it is used to determine the optimum working interest in a certain investment. In addition, the concepts of risk tolerance and risk aversion are used to arrive at a balanced portfolio of investments while optimizing the working interest carried in each investment of the portfolio.

6. *Simulation in Decision Analysis.* The concepts related to Monte Carlo simulation are presented in this chapter.

Volume 2 also includes Palisade Corporation's DecisionTools^{TM} suite on a CD-ROM. This powerful and versatile Decision Tools suite includes the following software.

- *PrecisionTree.* Used for constructing and solving decision trees.
- *BestFit and RISKview.* Used for fitting probability distributions to historical data and viewing distributions.
- *@RISK.* Used for simulation analysis.
- *TopRank.* Used for what-if analysis.

In addition to the DecisionTools suite, the spreadsheet solution of all the examples presented in Volume 1 and Volume 2 are also given on the CD-ROM. Three comprehensive economics analysis spreadsheets are also included on the CD-ROM, and a description of these is given in Appendix B of Volume 1.

QUESTIONS and PROBLEMS

1.1 Distinguish between strategic and tactical planning.

1.2 Briefly differentiate between objectives, goals, and strategies as applied to planning.

1.3 What is a profit plan? Why is planning a continuous and iterative process?

1.4 Contrast major and minor capital investments. Give examples of each.

1.5 What is meant by the term *capital budgeting*?

1.6 What is the significance of a demand curve and a supply curve? How are these curves determined?

1.7 What is a free-enterprise system? How is the market price of goods or services determined in a free-enterprise system?

1.8 Define the terms *elasticity of demand* and *elasticity of supply*. What are the conditions for a demand curve to be elastic, unitary elastic, or inelastic?

1.9 The total revenue of the producer rises when price falls, the demand curve is (a) elastic, (b) unitary elastic, (c) inelastic, (d) any of the above. Ans. (a)

1.10 The total revenue of the producer rises when price of his commodity rises, the demand curve is (a) elastic, (b) unitary elastic, (c) inelastic, (d) any of the above. Ans. (c)

1.11 Explain the basic causes of demand-pull and cost-push inflation.

1.12 What is the effect of inflation on (a) fixed income groups, (b) debtors, and (c) creditors? How can one be protected against the redistribution effect of inflation?

1.13 Explain the difference between money income and real income.

1.14 What is the difference between risk and uncertainty?

REFERENCES

[1] Welsch, G.A., *Budgeting: Profit Planning and Control, 4th Edition,* Prentice-Hall Inc., Englewood Cliffs, New Jersey, 1976.

[2] Drucker, P.F., *Management: Tasks, Responsibilities, Practices,* Harper and Row Publishers, Inc., New York, 1974.

[3] Salvatore, D., and Diulio, E.A., *Theory and Problems of Principles of Economics,* Schaum's Outline Series, McGraw-Hill Book Co., New York, U.S.A., 1980.

[4] McConnel, C.R., *Economics: Principles, Problems, and Policies, 8th Edition*, McGraw-Hill Book Co., New York, U.S.A., 1981.

[5] Stermole, F. J., and Stermole, J. M., *Economic Evaluation and Investment Decision Methods, Tenth Edition*, Investment Evaluations Corporation, 3070 South Newcombe Way, Lakeweed, CO 80227, U.S.A., 2000.

chapter TWO

The Time Value of Money

This chapter introduces simple concepts concerning the role of *interest* (cost of money) in investment evaluation (capital budgeting). The concepts presented in this chapter are essential in day-to-day personal finances and important for the understanding of many topics presented throughout this book, whether dealing with investment analysis involving risk and uncertainty or otherwise. Although the concepts are simple, they are frequently misinterpreted. Most of the problems involving the cost of money can be solved with only a few simple formulas.

Decision-making in investment analysis requires anticipated receipts (*revenues*) and disbursements (*costs*) of alternative investment proposals be placed on *equivalent* basis. The economic meaning of equivalence, methods used to arrive at the equivalent basis, and the consequences of not using the equivalent basis are discussed in this chapter.

It will be clear from the discussion in this chapter that interest is the *time value of money*. It must be taken into consideration in all investment analysis problems in order to arrive at valid decisions. Implementation of projects, besides technical know-how and manpower resources, requires financial resources. Two major forms of financial resources are used by business firms: (1) equity financing through common stock, and (2) various forms of debt. Financial markets include commercial banks, savings and loan associations, finance companies, investment bankers, and insurance companies, etc. Regardless of the source of financing, the financial resources cost money.

THE CONCEPT OF INTEREST

Interest is the price/rent paid for the use of money or loanable funds, expressed as a percentage of loaned or borrowed funds. The amount of loaned or borrowed funds is referred to as the *principal*. The rate of interest, rate of capital growth, is customarily stated on an annual basis. Thus, a 10% interest rate per year on $100 borrowed or invested for one year will yield $110. The $100 is referred to as *principal*, and the $10 is the interest charged or received. The gain of $10 is called the rate of *return* of 10% on the investment of $100. Due to this growth ability of capital over time, it is said, "money makes money."

The interest charged becomes cost to the borrower and revenue for the lender. Since it is a cost to the borrower, interest is considered an important element in investment decisions involving the acquisition of financial resources a firm must have. In this transaction between the borrower and the lender, both the borrower and the lender try their best to achieve their own profitability goals.

Interest rates in the market are linked to the *prime lending rate*. The prime lending rate is the interest rate charged by banks to their most creditworthy customers (usually the most prominent and stable business customers). The prime rate stems from the *discount rate* and the *federal funds rate*. These rates are fixed by the country's central banks. For example, the Federal Reserve (the Fed) of United States, European Central Bank (ECB) of the European Union, Bank of Japan, and so on. The *discount rate* is the interest rate the Fed charges banks to borrow reserves from the Fed. Banks borrow reserves from the Fed when it is impractical to borrow from other banks. The *federal funds* rate is the target interest rate for banks borrowing reserves among themselves.

Many consumer loans (including credit cards, home equity loans, and home equity lines of credit) are tied in some way to the prime rate. When it changes, so do the interest rates consumers must pay. When the Fed raises or lowers the federal funds rate and federal discount rate, banks typically raise or lower their prime rates by the same amount. Historically, the discount rate is lower than the Fed funds rate by 50 basis points (0.5%). Similarly, the prime rate is higher than the Fed funds rate by three percentage points. For example, in 2001 the Fed cut the discount rate to 1.25% and the Fed funds rate to 1.75%. Accordingly, the banks adjusted their prime rate to 4.75%. The rates were cut by 475 basis points (4.75%) from January to December of 2001.

Consequently, most interest rates in the market had to be cut. Such change by the Federal Reserve authorities implies a change in economic conditions has occurred. The new conditions call for tightening or easing of monetary conditions. Lower rates are needed to keep the economy from slipping into recession, and the rates are raised to curb inflation.

The observed prevailing interest rates in the financial markets usually vary, at any given time there is an array of different rates. This depends on the risk, maturity of loan, administrative costs of the loan incurred by the financial institution, and competition for loanable funds. In general, the interest rate on loans will be higher due to

- Lender's risk—which reflects the possibility that, for various reasons, the principal and the accrued interest may not be repaid by the borrower
- Longer period of loan—due to risk exposure for a longer period of time
- Smaller amount of loans—due to higher administrative costs
- A less competitive financial system
- The nature of investment—rates are higher for riskier investments

Therefore, the interest rate facing a saver is always less than the rate facing a borrower. In the market, the quoted interest rates range from 3% to 21% or even higher. For example, interest charged on home-mortgage loans may be 6.5%; credit unions may charge 10%; retailers and credit card companies typically charge 18% to 21%; and banks pay only around 2% on savings deposits.

The interest rate is also influenced by the demand and supply of *loanable funds*. A loanable fund is the actual amount of money available for lending to prospective borrowers. The *demand for loanable funds* depends on borrowing by

1. Firms in order to invest in various productive investments available to them

2. Consumers as home-mortgage loan, automobile loans, loans required for their other day-to-day requirements

3. Governments in order to finance their budgets

On the other hand, *supply of loanable* funds stems from the past and current savings of individuals and firms. The Central Bank, commercial banks, and the public are the major sources of money supply.

Simple and Compound Interest

Simple interest is calculated using *principal* only, which earns interest over a fixed period (loan period). At the end of the period, both the principal and the accrued interest are returned. A simple interest loan may be made for any length of time. The total interest can be computed using the following equation.

(2.1)

$$\text{Interest} = (\text{Principal}) \times (\text{Number of Periods}) \times (\text{Interest Rate, fraction})$$

When simple interest for a partial year is calculated; the year is commonly considered to be of 12 months, 30 days in each month, or 360 days.

Example 2–1

Suppose $2,000 is borrowed at a simple interest rate of 8%. Calculate (a) the principal plus interest at the end of the year, and (b) principal and interest if the loan has to be paid after 90 days.

Solution: (a) Using Equation 2.1

$$\text{Interest} = (2{,}000) \times (1) \times (0.08) = \$160.00$$
$$[\text{Principal} + \text{Interest}] = \$2{,}000 + \$160 = \$2{,}160$$
$$= (\$2{,}000) \times (1 + .08) = \$2{,}160$$

(b) Principal plus interest at the end of 90 days will be:

$$\text{Principal} + \text{Interest} = \$2{,}000 \times \left(1 + \frac{90}{360} \times 0.08\right) = \$2{,}040.00$$

Therefore, the interest in part (a) is \$160 while that in part (b) is \$40, which is simply (160 x 90/360).

Compound interest is the interest accrued on both the principal and the unpaid interest earned in the previous periods. At the end of one interest period, the principal and the earned interest are left to accrue interest for another period. The principal and accrued interest essentially becomes the principal sum for interest computation in the following period. The accumulated interest depends on the number of compounding periods per year and the number of years interest is earned on the money. This is the type of interest widely used in home-mortgage loans, automobile loans, credit card installments, and other installment loans. Interest compounding determines the future sum (at some specified time and interest rate) of a sum of money invested today. Compound interest is calculated using the following equation.

(2.2)

$$\text{Interest} = \left[\left(1 + \frac{i_n}{m}\right)^{tm} - 1\right] \times \text{Principal}$$

OR **(2.3)**

$$[\text{Principal} + \text{Interest}] = \left(1 + \frac{i_n}{m}\right)^{tm} \times \text{Principal}$$

where

i_n = the nominal interest rate, fraction per year

m = compounding or interest periods per year, $m = 1$ for yearly compounding

$m = 2$ for semiannual compounding, $m = 4$ for quarterly compounding,

$m = 12$ for monthly compounding, and so on

t = the loan period, years

If the interest is compounded once per year, then Equation (2.2) reduces to

(2.2a)

$$\text{Interest} = \left[\left(1 + \frac{i_n}{m} \right)^{tm} - 1 \right] \times \text{Principal}$$

Example 2–2

Suppose that $2,000 is borrowed for one year at an interest rate of 8%. Calculate the interest at the end of the year if the interest is compounded (a) yearly and (b) quarterly, and (c) what will be the interest at the end of three years if the interest is compounded semi-annually?

$$\text{Interest} = \left[\left(1 + \frac{0.08}{1} \right)^{1 \times 1} - 1 \right] \times \$2,000 = \$160$$

Solution: (a) If the interest is compounded yearly, using Equation (2.2), the interest is

The resulting interest is the same as that obtained in Example 2–1.

(b) If the interest is compounded quarterly, using Equation (2.2), the interest is

$$\text{Interest} = \left[\left(1 + \frac{0.08}{4} \right)^{1 \times 4} - 1 \right] \times \$2,000 = \$164.86$$

The same interest can be calculated without using Equation (2.2) as follows:

$$1\text{st Quarter's Interest} = \frac{0.08}{4} \times \$2{,}000 = \$40$$

Principal at the end of 1st Quarter is, therefore, $2,000 + $40 = $2,040.

$$2\text{nd Quarter's Interest} = \frac{0.08}{4} \times \$2{,}040 = \$40.80$$

Principal at the end of 2nd quarter amounts to $2,000 + $40.00 + $40.80 = $2,080.80

$$3\text{rd Quarter's Interest} = \frac{0.08}{4} \times \$2{,}080.80 = \$41.62$$

Similarly, the interest for the fourth quarter amounts to $42.45. Thus, the total interest at the end of the year (for four quarters) sums to

$$\$164.87 = \$40.00 + \$40.80 + \$41.62 + \$42.45,$$

which is the same, within rounding, as $164.86 calculated by using Equation (2.2).

(c) Using Equation (2.2), the interest after three years (with semi-annual compounding) will be

$$\text{Interest} = \left[\left(1 + \frac{0.08}{2} \right)^{3\times2} - 1 \right] \times \$2{,}000 = \$530.64$$

Example 2–3

Suppose an employee's monthly salary now is $4,000, and he receives merit increase of 5% every year. What will be his salary after five years from now?

Solution: Using Equation (2.3), salary after five years from now will be

$$\text{Salary} = (1 + 0.05)^5 \times \$4,000 \approx \$5,105$$

The effect of compounding at various interest rates over a period of 15 years is shown in Figure 2–1. The figure shows how a sum of $10 today grows with time and interest. Of course, at higher interest rates, the growth is faster relative to that at lower interest rates.

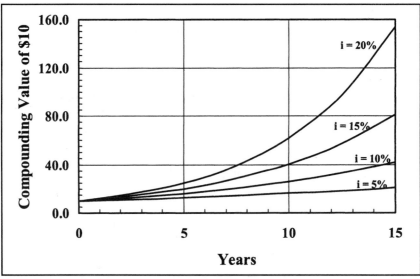

Fig. 2–1 Relationship between interest rates, time, and compound value

Nominal and Effective Interest Rate

Compound interest rate is further classified into *nominal* rate (i_n) and the *effective* annual interest rate (i_e). Compound interest is normally reported as nominal interest rate per year, compounded periodically, i.e., daily, monthly, quarterly, or semiannually, or continuously (infinite number of times per year, approximately equal to the daily compounding).

Effective interest is the rate when applied to a sum of money once per year will give the same amount of interest as will be given by a nominal interest rate compounded m periods per year. Effective and nominal interest rates are equal $(i_e = i_n)$ if interest is compounded annually; they are related to each other by the following equations.

For Periodic Compounding,

(2.4)

$$i_e = \left(1 + \frac{i_n}{m}\right)^{tm} - 1$$

Equation (2.4) is used for nominal annual interest rates compounded any number of times up to and including continuous compounding. However, as the frequency of compounding increases, m approaches infinity and the equation becomes equivalent to the continuous compounding as shown by Equation (2.5).

For Continuous Compounding,

(2.5)

$$i_e = e^r - 1$$

To differentiate between the periodic and continuous interest rates, the nominal continuous interest rate will be designated by r.

The use of effective interest rate reduces Equations (2.2) and (2.3) to

(2.6)

$$\text{Interest} = \left[(1 + i_e)^t - 1\right] \times \text{Principal}$$

(2.7)

$$[\text{Principal} + \text{Interest}] = (1 + i_e)^t \times \text{Principal}$$

Example 2–4

Suppose a sum of $2,000 is borrowed for one year at an interest rate of 8%. Calculate the total amount to be paid back to the bank after one year if the interest is compounded quarterly.

Solution: First calculate i_e, using Equation (2.4)

$$i_e = \left(1 + \frac{0.08}{4}\right)^4 - 1$$

$$= 0.08243 \; or \; 8.243\%$$

Now using Equation (2.7), we get

$$[\text{Principal} + \text{Interest}] = (1 + 0.08243)^1 \times \$2,000$$
$$= \$2,164.86$$

The same answer, as calculated in Example 2–2b, is obtained.

Example 2–5

A U.S. dollar currency account is maintained at a bank. The account is fixed for one month, starting 05/20/2002. After the expiration of one month, the account is either automatically renewed for another month or the money is withdrawn at the end of the month. The deposit receipt received from the bank gives the following details.

Current Principal = $50,000   Date of Deposit = 05/20/2002
Maturity = 06/20/2002   Interest Rate = 5.875%
Interest on maturity = $253.60

Determine the basis used by the bank to calculate interest on maturity. What effective interest rate is the bank paying?

Solution: The interest is either compounded monthly or daily. On a monthly basis, using Equation (2.3), the principal plus interest are:

$$[\text{Principal} + \text{Interest}] = \left(1 + \frac{0.05875}{12}\right)^{1/12 \times 12} \times \$50,000$$

$$= \$50,250.79$$

On daily basis for 31 days (from 05/20/2002 to 06/20/2002)

$$[\text{Principal} + \text{Interest}] = \left(1 + \frac{0.05875}{360}\right)^{31} \times \$50,000$$

$$\approx \$50,253.60$$

This presumes interest rate of 5.875%, compounded daily. The effective interest rate equivalent to nominal rate of 5.875%, compounded daily is:

Using Equation (2.4):

$$[\text{Principal} + \text{Interest}] = \left[\left(1 + \frac{0.05875}{360}\right)^{360} - 1\right] \times 100$$

$$= 6.051\%$$

or using Equation (2.5):

$$i_e = (e^{0.05875} - 1) \times 100 = 6.051\%$$

The preceding example shows one has to be very careful with the quoted interest rates.

CASH-FLOW DIAGRAM

Every capital investment project will typically have cash receipts (inward flow of cash) and cash disbursements (outward flow of cash) into or out of the treasury, respectively. Typical examples of cash flows are seismic acquisition, processing and interpretation costs; drilling and completion costs; production facility costs; lease operating costs; corporate overhead costs; and revenues from the sale of crude and natural gas; etc. Subtracting the cash disbursements from the cash receipts will generate net negative or positive cash flow. Mathematically:

$$\text{(2.8)}$$

$$\text{Net Cash Flow} = \text{Receipts} - \text{Disbursements}$$

Cash-flow diagrams graph net cash flows and cumulative net cash flows over time. The diagram typically shows (1) cash receipts at the end of each year generated by the investment, (2) cash disbursements of all costs (initial and subsequent costs) per year required for the operations, and (3) total time span of the investment in years. Therefore, the major point of the cash-flow diagram is to show that a capital investment is an amount paid to receive expected net cash inflows over the economic life of the investment.

For ease of recognizing the various elements of cash flow, cash receipts (positive) are shown as upward-pointing arrows while the cash disbursements (negative) are shown as downward-pointing arrows on the diagram. On the diagram, the beginning of Year 1 is considered *time zero* at which the equivalent (present value) of all the future cash flows is calculated. *Time zero shows* the beginning of the first year or period, time "1" shows the end of the 1st year (Year 1) or period and the beginning of 2nd year (Year 2) or period, and so on. Figure 2–2 shows a typical cash-flow diagram.

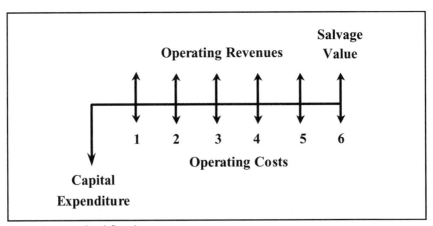

Fig. 2–2 A typical cash-flow diagram.

A clearly drawn cash-flow diagram serve as a valuable tool in problem solving because it provides a pictorial description of an investment problem. It helps in simplifying complicated descriptive problems. The cash-flow diagrams used throughout this book assist in solving investment alternatives.

THE TIME VALUE OF MONEY

If you were asked, would you rather have $100 today or $100 one year from today? Your obvious answer would most likely be that you would rather have $100 today. On the other hand, if one asked you to have $100 today or $110 one year from today, you would probably be indifferent.

Your replies intuitively involve the consideration of *time value of money*. The difference in the worth between the two amounts, one year apart, is *interest* (i.e., the growth potential of money over one year). You know in the back of your mind that if $100 is received today, you can invest it at 10% interest per year and have $110 ($100 x 1.1 = $110) one year from today. The trade-off involves length of time and the available earning power of the money. The concept of interest is key to accounting for time value of money.

You are indifferent to the second offer because you know both amounts are the same. However, if you know of an alternative investment that will make you $120, you will obviously again settle for the $100 today. On the other hand, if the timing of benefits with *comparable risk* and *uncertainty* vary widely, more immediate benefits may be preferable to those benefits that will be obtained further out in time.

In the same way, if you were asked, would you rather have $100 today or $130 one year from today? You will most likely settle for the $130. This is because you know you cannot find an investment that will yield 30% return if $100 is invested today. This is why it is important to consider time value of money in all investment evaluations and decision analysis.

By looking at the above example from another perspective, assume the $130 to be received one year from today has a higher associated risk. In this case, you will also assess the risk factor. Based on the risk involved, you may decide to take the immediately available funds ($100) and invest them at a profit commensurate with your *risk preference*. Your decision obviously will reflect your attitude to risk. Are you a person who prefers to select the least risky alternatives in a decision, i.e., risk averter, or are you prepared to tolerate some level of risk, i.e., risk seeker or indifferent to risk.

Capital investments are begun with an objective to generate a stream of positive net cash flows in the years ahead. Investing in oil and gas projects are typical examples—a well is drilled, completed (capital expenditure), and then put on production to generate revenue. The well may produce for 5, 10, 20 years, or even longer.

Besides the receipt of revenues in future periods, the pattern of receipts also varies from property to property, i.e., the pattern of how cash is generated. Some wells or fields produce at higher rates, decline severely in the early years, and then stabilize at a steady decline. Other wells or fields start at lower rates and keep a steady decline for a longer time period. Although both wells/fields may give the same ultimate recovery, the former is of more value due to the effect of the time value of money (higher revenue generated in the early years).

Therefore, to account for the time value of money, all future expenditures and revenues need to be converted to a *common denominator*, i.e., a common equivalent value of all the future cash flows is calculated at a common point in time. This common point in time may be the present, future, or even annual. Customarily, *analysts choose the present*. This "present" is also referred to as *time zero*. When comparing capital investments, time zero is the same for all alternatives subject to evaluation for decision analysis. This is achieved by *discounting* future cash-flow streams. Discounting is the mirror to the *compounding interest* calculations. The distinction is whether we are paying or receiving *interest*. Compounding converts a present sum of money into its *equivalent* future sum. Discounting converts a future sum of money into its *equivalent* present sum.

The rate used for discounting is typically referred to as the *discount rate*, i_d. The effect of discounting at various interest rates over a period of 15 years is shown in Figure 2–3. The figure shows how a sum of money received in the future deteriorates in value over time. Figure 2–3 shows how a sum of $10 received after 15 years is only worth $0.65 today, at an interest rate of 20%. The present value of a dollar available at some date in the future declines as the interest rate increases; if the interest rate is fixed, a dollar received farther out in the future is worth less today.

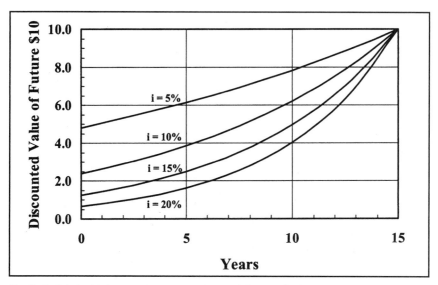

Fig. 2–3 Relationship between interest rate, time, and discounted value

As a result, the discounting of future cash flows favors earlier receipts from investments over longer-term alternatives. This increases the chances investors will be biased towards the short-term investment alternatives versus the long-term alternatives.

The "time value of money calculations" are achieved by using (1) interest tables, (2) mathematical equations, (3) financial calculators, or (4) computer (spreadsheets). The widely available spreadsheet programs (MS Excel and Lotus 1-2-3) have built-in financial functions to facilitate such calculations. Equations and interest tables may not be used in practice because of limited availability. However, understanding the basic concepts presented here helps knowing which equations are in use and why they are used.

Present Value of Future Sum

In the preceding section, it was mentioned that present point in time is customarily chosen at which the equivalent value of all the future cash flows is calculated. All the future values are converted to their equivalent of present value. This equivalent value is typically referred to as the *present* value or *present worth* of future cash flows.

Present value of a single sum of money, received at some future point in time, is calculated using the following equation:

(2.9)

$$P_v = F_v \left[\frac{1}{(1+i_e)^t} \right]$$

where

P_v = present value (at time zero) of future sum
F_v = future sum received at time t
i_e = effective interest rate (discount rate, fraction)

The present value of periodic cash flows is calculated with Equation (2.10).

(2.10)

$$P_v = (F_v)_1 \frac{1}{(1+i_e)^1} + (F_v)_2 \frac{1}{(1+i_e)^2} + (F_v)_3 \frac{1}{(1+i_e)^3} + \ldots\ldots + (F_v)_t \frac{1}{(1+i_e)^t}$$

OR

$$P_v = \sum_{t=1}^{n} (F_v)_t \left[\frac{1}{(1+i_e)^t} \right]$$

In Equations (2.9) and (2.10), the term $[1/(1 + i_e)^t]$ is referred to as the *present worth factor*, P/F. Tables are available to provide these factors for a sum of $1 at several i_e and t values. Interest factors (for i = 1% to i = 10%) for year-end payments and annual compounding/discounting are given in Appendix A. Additional tables are provided on the CD that accompanies Volume 2. Table 2–1 is an excerpt from Table A8 (Appendix A), showing interest factors for i_e=8%.

Although the interest tables are provided for annual compounding/discounting, they can be used in situations where the interest is compounded/discounted more than once a year. For example, when the interest rate is 8% compounded semiannually, the present value factor

	Single Payment		Equal Payment Series				Uniform
t	Compound Amount Factor, F/P	Present Worth Factor, P/F	Compound Amount Factor, F/A	Sinking Fund Factor, A/F	Present Worth Factor, P/A	Capital Recovery Factor, A/P	Gradient Series, A/G
1	1.0800	0.9259	1.0000	1.0000	0.9259	1.0800	0.0000
2	1.1664	0.8573	2.0800	0.4808	1.7833	0.5608	0.4808
3	1.2597	0.7938	3.2464	0.3080	2.5771	0.3880	0.9487
4	1.3605	0.7350	4.5061	0.2219	3.3121	0.3019	1.4040
5	1.4693	0.6806	5.8666	0.1705	3.9927	0.2505	1.8465
6	1.5869	0.6302	7.3359	0.1363	4.6229	0.2163	2.2763
7	1.7138	0.5835	8.9228	0.1121	5.2064	0.1921	2.6937
8	1.8509	0.5403	10.6366	0.0940	5.7466	0.1740	3.0985
9	1.9990	0.5002	12.4876	0.0801	6.2469	0.1601	3.4910
10	2.1589	0.4632	14.4866	0.0690	6.7101	0.1490	3.8713
11	2.3316	0.4289	16.6455	0.0601	7.1390	0.1401	4.2395
12	2.5182	0.3971	18.9771	0.0527	7.5361	0.1327	4.5957
13	2.7196	0.3677	21.4953	0.0465	7.9038	0.1265	4.9402
14	2.9372	0.3405	24.2149	0.0413	8.2442	0.1213	5.2731
15	3.1722	0.3152	27.1521	0.0368	8.5595	0.1168	5.5945
16	3.4259	0.2919	30.3243	0.0330	8.8514	0.1130	5.9046
17	3.7000	0.2703	33.7502	0.0296	9.1216	0.1096	6.2037
18	3.9960	0.2502	37.4502	0.0267	9.3719	0.1067	6.4920
19	4.3157	0.2317	41.4463	0.0241	9.6036	0.1041	6.7697
20	4.6610	0.2145	45.7620	0.0219	9.8181	0.1019	7.0369

Table 2–1 Excerpt from Table A8 (Appendix A) – 8% interest factors for annual compounding.

will be read as $P/F = 0.9246$ from Table A4 for $i = 4\%$ at $t = 2$. Similarly, the compound factor F/P will be 1.0816.

The interest factor tables in Appendix A are provided for whole interest rates (such as 8% or 9%). The interest factors for intermediate interest rates (such as 8.25%) between two consecutive interest factors tables can be estimated using *linear interpolation*. The following relationship is used for interpolation.

(2.11)

$$(P/F) = \left[\frac{i_e - (i_e)_L}{(i_e)_H - (i_e)_L} \right] \left[(P/F)_H - (P/F)_L \right] + (P/F)_L$$

where

$\quad (P/F)$ = the present worth factor

$\quad i_e$ = the desirable interest rate

$\quad (i_e)_L$ = the lower than desired interest rate

$\quad (i_e)_H$ = the higher than desired interest rate

$\quad (P/F)_L$ = interest factor at lower interest rate

$\quad (P/F)_H$ = interest factor at higher interest rate

Similarly, if the time period t, or the number of interest periods tm are beyond the values listed in the available interest factor tables, the desired factor can be obtained from a combination of various tables. For example, if a value of $(P/F)_{i=10,\ t=50}$ is desired that is not in Table A10 (interest factors table for $i = 10\%$), then the following relationship can be used to obtain the desired factor.

$$
\begin{aligned}
(P/F)_{i=10,t=50} &= (P/F)_{i=10,t=40} \times (P/F)_{i=10,t=10} \\
&= (0.0221) \times (0.3856) \\
&= 0.00852
\end{aligned}
$$

Example 2–6

In six years, it is estimated \$5,000 (future value) will be required to purchase a piece of equipment. What amount should be deposited in a bank today, at an effective interest rate of 8% to accumulate \$5,000 at the end of the sixth year?

Solution: The cash-flow diagram for this example is shown in Figure 2–4. Using Equation (2.9), the present value is

$$
P_v = \$5,000 \times \left[\frac{1}{(1+i_e)^6} \right]
$$
$$
= \$3,150.85
$$

Using Interest factor (P/F), value at the intersection of column P/F and row $t=6$, from Table 2–1:

$$
(P/F)_{i_e=8\%,t=6} = 0.6302
$$
$$
P_v = \$5,000(0.6302) \cong \$3,151
$$

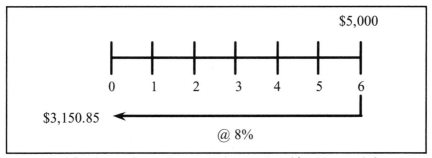

Fig. 2–4 Cash-flow diagram showing the present value equivalent of $5,000 received after six years (Example 2–6)

Example 2–7

Suppose that a landowner receives annual royalty payments of $2,000; $2,200; $1,900; $2,500 and $1,500 over the next five years. Calculate the present worth of these payments at an interest (discount) rate of 8%.

Solution: The cash-flow diagram for the problem is shown in Figure 2–5. Using Equation (2.10)

$$P_v = \$2,000 \left[\frac{1}{(1+0.08)^1}\right] + \$2,200 \left[\frac{1}{(1+0.08)^2}\right] + \$1,900 \left[\frac{1}{(1+0.08)^3}\right]$$

$$+ \$2,500 \left[\frac{1}{(1+0.08)^4}\right] + \$1,500 \left[\frac{1}{(1+0.08)^5}\right]$$

$$= \$1,851.85 + \$1,886.15 + \$1,508.28 + \$1,837.57 + \$1,020.87$$

$$= \$8,104.72$$

The same problem is solved by using the (P/F) factor at $i_e = 8\%$, $t = 1$ to 5 from Table 2–1 as shown in Figure 2–5.

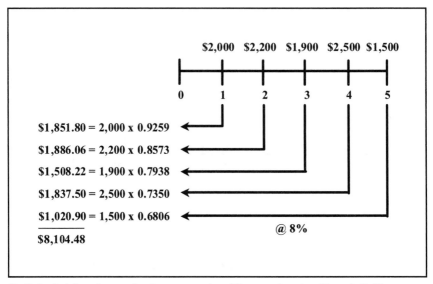

Fig. 2–5 Cash-flow diagram showing present value of five annual receipts (Example 2–7)

Example 2–8

Rework Example 2–6 for an effective interest rate of 8.5%. Use interest tables of Appendix A.

Solution: Since an interest factor table for 8.5% is not provided, the factor is obtained by linear interpolation between interest factors from Table A8 and Table A9.

From Table A8:

$$(P/F)_{i=8\%,\ t=6} = 0.6302$$

From Table A9:

$$(P/F)_{i=9\%,\ t=6} = 0.5963$$

Using Equation (2.11)

$$(P/F)_{i=8\%,t=6} = \left(\frac{0.085-0.08}{0.09-0.08}\right)(0.5963-0.6302)+0.6302$$
$$= (0.50)(-0.0339)+(0.6302)$$
$$= 0.61325$$

Therefore:

$$P_v = F_v(P/F)_{i=8.5\%,t=6}$$
$$= \$5,000(0.61325)$$
$$= \$3,066.25$$

Using Equation (2.9), the present value is

$$P_v = \$5,000\left[\frac{1}{(1+0.085)^6}\right]$$
$$= \$3,064.73$$

Note the small difference between the P_v calculated by using Equation (2.9) and the P_v calculated by using the interpolated interest factor. The difference is due to the non-linear relationship between interest compounding and time as shown in Figures 2–1 and 2–3. Therefore, the linear interpolation gives approximate interest factor of 0.61325 versus 0.61295 from equation.

Example 2–9

Calculate the present value of $5,000 received at the end of sixth year (Example 2–6), if the interest rate is 8% per year compounded quarterly. Note that compounding frequency is quarterly, i.e., four times ($m = 4$) per year.

Solution: In this example, $t=6$, $i_n=0.08$, and $m=4$

Therefore

$$i = \frac{i_n}{m} = \frac{0.08}{4} = 0.02$$
$$t = tm = 6 \times 4 = 24$$

The interest factor (P/F) at $i = 2\%$, and $t = 24$ is obtained from Table A2 as 0.6217. Thus:

$$P_v = \$5,000 \times 0.6217$$
$$= \$3,108.50$$

Using Equation (2.3) in terms of discounting, the present value is

$$P_v = F_v \frac{1}{\left(1+\dfrac{i_n}{m}\right)^{tm}}$$
$$= \$5,000 \times \frac{1}{\left(1+\dfrac{0.08}{4}\right)^{6 \times 4}} = \$3,108.61$$

Future Value of Present Sum

As it has been previously mentioned, future value of a present sum is a reciprocal of the present value of future sum. Here interest is added to the cash flows, i.e., compounding versus discounting. Thus Equation (2.9) becomes:

(2.12)

$$F_v = P_v (1 + i_e)^t$$

The factor $(1+i_e)^t$ is referred to as the *single payment compound amount factor*, represented by the factor F/P in interest tables. The problem-solving methodology is the same as discussed in the previous section.

The future value of a single sum received/invested (at a compound interest) at present is the original sum plus the compound interest thereon, stated as of a specific future reference date. The future value of several periodic receipts or disbursements between the present and future value reference dates can be calculated by using Equation (2.12). This is done by calculating the future value of each year's cash flow and then added together. The receipt/disbursement at each interval is treated as a single sum at present. The following equation is used to achieve this.

(2.13)

$$F_v = (P_v)_1 (1+i_e)^{t-1} + (P_v)_2 (1+i_e)^{t-2} + (P_v)_3 (1+i_e)^{t-3} + \ldots\ldots + (P_v)_n (1+i_e)^{t-n}$$

OR

$$F_v = \sum_{t=1}^{n-1} (P_v)_t (1+i_e)^t$$

where

n = number of periods, years

$(P_v)_t$ = present value at time t, t=1 to n

Example 2-10

Calculate the equivalent future value of $3,150.85 invested today at 8% interest for a period of six years.

Solution: The cash-flow diagram for Example 2–10 is shown in Figure 2–6.

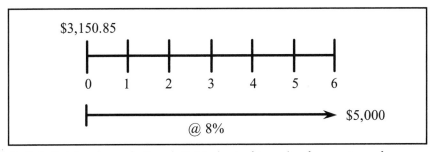

Fig. 2–6 Cash-flow diagram for Example 2–10, showing future value of a present sum of money

Using Equation (2.12), the future value is

$$(F_v)_{t=6} = \$3,150.85(1 + 0.08)^6$$
$$= \$5,000$$

Using the interest factors, the single payment compound amount factor $F/P = 1.5869$ is obtained from Table 2–1 at the intersection of Column F/P and Row $t=6$. Thus:

$$(F_v)_{i=8\%,\, t=6} = \$3,150.85(1.5869) \cong \$5,000$$

Example 2–11

Using the royalty payments in Example 2–7, calculate the future value of these payments at 8% effective interest.

Solution: The cash-flow diagram for Example 2–11 is shown in Figure 2–7. Using Equation (2.13):

$$
\begin{aligned}
F_v &= \$2,000(1+0.08)^4 + \$2,200(1+0.08)^3 + \$1,900(1+0.08)^2 + \$2,500(1+0.08)^1 \\
&\quad + \$1,500(1+0.08)^0 \\
&= \$2,000(1.3605) + \$2,200(1.2597) + \$1,900(1.1664) + \$2,500(1.08) + \$1,500 \\
&= \$11,908.50
\end{aligned}
$$

The present value of this amount is calculated by treating it as a single future sum,

$$P_v = \$11,908.50 \, \frac{1}{(1 + 0.08)^5}$$

$$= \$8,104.73$$

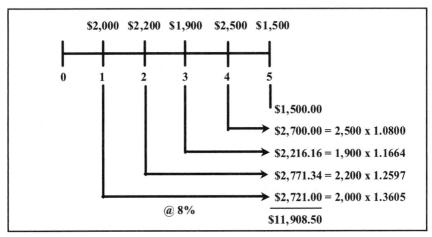

Fig. 2–7 Cash-flow diagram for Example 2–11, showing future value of periodic receipts

which is the same value as calculated in Example 2–7. Similarly, the future value of $8,104.73 (obtained in Example 2–7) could have been calculated by treating it as a single payment present sum.

Assuming the payments are received at the end of each year, the payment received at the end of the fifth year is already at future value. The payment received at the end of the first year earns interest for four periods; receipt at the end of second year earns interest for three years, and so on, except for the fifth payment, which does not earn any interest.

The future value of present sum at nominal interest rate may be calculated by using Equation (2.12) and (2.13) while replacing the i_e by i_n/m and t by t_m, where m is the number of compounding periods per year.

Present Value of an Annuity

A series of equal periodic payments or disbursements at regular intervals, normally at the end of a period, over a period of time while the interest is compounded at a certain rate is called *annuity*. Typical examples of annuity are (1) home-mortgage payments, (2) automobile loans, (3) salaries and social security receipts, (4) insurance premiums, (5) payment into pension funds, and (6) other installment loans. The concept is helpful in calculating the equivalent present value of alternative annuities for comparison.

Present value of a series of cash flows (annuity) determined *one peri-od before* the receipt or payment of the first sum of money, is referred to as an *ordinary annuity*. If the present value of an annuity is determined on the date when the first cash flow occurred, the present value is referred to as the present value of *annuity due*.

Thus, the present value of an annuity is the single sum of money invested today at a certain interest rate in order to withdraw equal amounts each year. At the end of the annuity period, with the withdrawal of the last amount, the bal-ance is equal to zero. To qualify cash flows for annuity, it is required that

1. The periodic payments or disbursements are of equal amount
2. The interest rate is constant throughout the annuity period under consideration
3. The time intervals between each payment must be of the same length
4. The interest rate is compounded at the end of each time period

In Example 2–7, the present value of unequal annual royalty receipts was calculated. The present value of an annuity is determined in a similar way. However, the condition of equal periodic cash flows simplifies the solution that can be achieved by using a single equation. The following equation is used to calculate the present value of an annuity.

(2.14)

$$P_v = A_v \left[\frac{(1+i_e)^t - 1}{i_e(1+i_e)^t} \right]$$

The resulting factor, $[(1 + i_e)^t - 1/i_e(1 + i_e)^t]$, is referred to as the equal payment series present worth factor for ordinary annuity. The fac-tor is represented by the P/A factor in the interest tables.

Example 2–12

An oil company has to pay $10,000 per year, starting one year from today, on a loan obtained for five years at an effective interest rate of 8%. Calculate the equivalent present value of these five yearly payments. The payments include both principal and interest.

Solution: The cash-flow diagram for Example 2–12 is shown in Figure 2–8. Using Equation (2.14), the present value of annuity is

$$P_v = \$10,000 \left[\frac{(1+0.08)^5 - 1}{0.08(1+0.08)^5} \right]$$
$$= \$10,000(3.9927)$$
$$= \$39,927$$

The *equal payment series present worth factor* (*P/A*) in Table 2–1 is found at the intersection of Column *P/A* and Row *t*=5 as 3.9927.

To calculate the present value of an *annuity due* while only the *ordinary annuity* interest tables are available (such as the tables in Appendix A), use the following steps:

1. Obtain the *P/A* factor from the ordinary annuity interest tables for the desired interest rate and for *t*=*n*–1, where *n*= number of payments.

2. Add one to the factor obtained in Step 1.

3. Calculate the present value by multiplying the periodic cash flow by the factor calculated in Step 2.

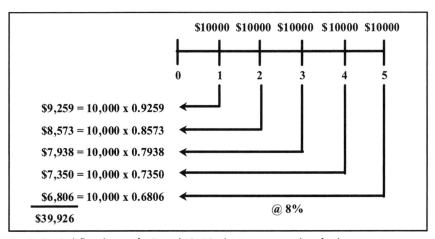

Fig. 2–8 Cash-flow diagram for Example 2–12, showing present value of ordinary annuity

Example 2–13

An oil producer acquired production equipment by paying $10,000 as down payment and agreed to pay the balance in four year-end installments of $10,000. Calculate the present value of the annuity due at an interest rate of 8%. Note that the total number of payments (including the down payment) is five.

Solution: The cash-flow diagram for Example 2–13 is shown in Figure 2–9.

Step 1. The P/A factor from Table 2–1 for "n–1" and i = 8% (i.e., four payments) is 3.3121.

Step 2. Add 1 to the P/A factor in Step 1, i.e., 3.3121+1=4.3121.

Step 3. Therefore:
$$P_v = \$10,000 \times (4.3121) = \$43,121$$

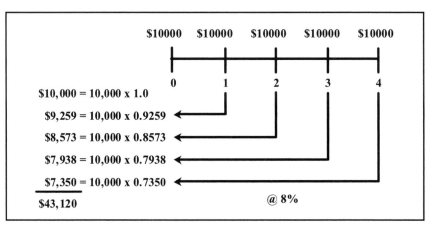

Fig. 2–9 Cash-flow diagram for Example 2–13, showing present value of annuity due

Future Value of an Annuity

If it is desired to calculate the equivalent single future value that will result from an annuity, a series of equal periodic cash flows occurring at the end of succeeding periods, the following equation is used.

(2.15)

$$F_v = A_v \left[\frac{(1+i_e)^t - 1}{i_e} \right]$$

The resulting factor, $[(1 + i_e)^t - 1]/i_e$, designated by F/A factor in the interest tables is referred to as the *equal payment compound amount factor.* If the future value of an annuity is determined at the point when last payment of an annuity is made, such a series of cash flows is called *ordinary annuity.* If the future value of an annuity is calculated at the end of a period following the last cash flow in the series, this is referred to as the future value of an *annuity due.* The following modification of Equation (2.15) is used to calculate the future value of annuity due.

(2.15a)

$$(F_v)_{t+1} = A_v \left[\frac{(1+i_e)^{t+1} - 1}{i_e} - 1 \right]$$

Example 2–14

Calculate the future value of the annuity given in Example 2–12, by treating it as (a) an ordinary annuity and (b) an annuity due.

Solution: The cash-flow diagram for the ordinary annuity is shown in Figure 2–10.

(a) Using Equation (2.15), the future value of ordinary annuity is:

$$(F_v)_5 = \$10,000 \left[\frac{(1+0.08)^5 - 1}{0.08} \right] = \$58,666$$

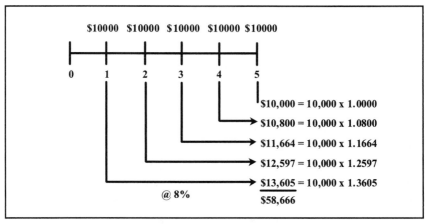

Fig. 2–10 Cash-flow diagram for Example 2–14, showing future value of ordinary annuity

The same answer can be obtained by using the *F/A* factor from Table 2–1. Similarly, the *F/P* factor or Equation (2.12) can be applied to the P_v calculated in Example 2–12 to get F_v.

(b) The cash-flow diagram for the annuity due is shown in Figure 2–11. Using Equation (2.15a)

$$F_v = \$10,000 \left[\frac{(1+0.08)^{5+1} - 1}{0.08} - 1 \right]$$

$$= \$10,000(6.3359) = \$63,359$$

In order to use the ordinary annuity interest factors for determining future value of annuity due, the following steps should be followed.

1. Look up the value of *t*+1 payments at an interest rate i_e in interest tables as

$$(F/A)_{i_e=8\%,\, t=6} = 7.3359.$$

2. Subtract 1.00 from the factor obtained in Step 1, as 7.3359–1 = 6.3359.

3. The factor 6.3359 is now the equal payment compound amount factor for an annuity of 5 periodic payments at an interest rate of 8%. Thus, the future value

$$(F_v)_{5+1} = \$10,000 \times 6.3359 = \$63,359$$

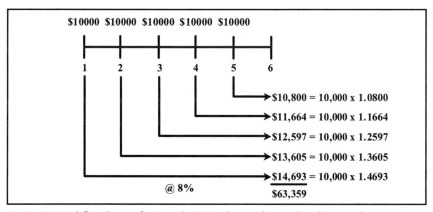

Fig. 2–11 Cash-flow diagram for Example 2–14, showing future value of annuity due

Present Value of Deferred Annuity

In some cases, the series of equal periodic cash flows, i.e., annuity, will not start until some time in the future, meaning the annuity will be postponed by a number of periods from the present time (time zero). There is no exclusive equation or interest factor for calculating the present value of deferred annuity. The concepts presented in the preceding sections are used in combination to arrive at the present value. Example of a deferred annuity is schematically shown in Figure 2–12.

The present value of deferred annuity may be calculated in any one of the following three ways. Refer to the annuity presented in Figure 2–12.

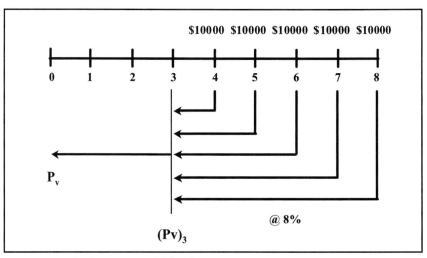

Fig. 2-12 Graphical presentation of deferred annuity

1. Calculate the present value of year three, $(P_v)_3$, treating the cash flows as ordinary annuity by using Equation (2.14) or interest factor (P/A). Then calculate the present value by treating the $(P_v)_3$ as the future value at end of year three and using Equation (2.9) or (P/F) factor.

2. Calculate the future value by treating the cash flow as ordinary annuity and using Equation (2.15) or factor (F/A). Then calculate the present value of this future value by using Equation (2.9) or factor P/F.

3   Calculate the present value of the entire series by treating the problem as if the annuity started from year one. Then subtract the present value of the annuity of the deferred period, i.e., the first three years. Note that by calculating the present value of deferred annuity in this way, it is understood the same cash flow occurs over the entire period including the deferred period. Thus, the present value calculation using this method involves a combination of two ordinary annuities.

The practical utility of such equivalence calculations is applicable to deferred loan amortization. For example, money is borrowed for a period of five years. However, the loan is paid back in three equal annual installments with the first installment due at the end of third year.

Example 2–15

Calculate the present value of the deferred annuity presented in Figure 2–12. Use the three methods presented for calculating the present value of deferred annuity. Presume an interest rate of 8%.

Solution: Using Equations (2.14) and (2.9):

$$P_v = \$10,000\left[\frac{(1+0.08)^5-1}{0.08(1+0.08)^5}\right] \times \left[\frac{1}{(1+0.08)^3}\right]$$

OR

$$= \$10,000(P/A)_{i=8\%,t=5}(P/F)_{i=8\%,t=3}$$
$$= \$10,000(3.9927)(0.7938)$$
$$= \$31,694.05$$

Using Equations (2.15) and (2.9)

$$P_v = \$10,000\left[\frac{(1+0.08)^5-1}{0.08}\right] \times \left[\frac{1}{(1+0.08)^8}\right]$$

OR

$$= \$10,000(F/A)_{i=8\%,t=5}(P/F)_{i=8\%,t=8}$$
$$= \$10,000(5.8666)(0.54027)$$
$$= \$31,695.48$$

Using the third method, using Equation (2.14)

$$P_v = \$10,000\left[\frac{(1+0.08)^8-1}{0.08(1+0.08)^8} - \frac{(1+0.08)^3-1}{0.08(1+0.08)^3}\right]$$

OR

$$= \$10,000\left[(P/A)_{i=8\%,t=8} - (P/A)_{i=8\%,t=3}\right]$$
$$= \$10,000(5.7466 - 2.5771)$$
$$= \$31,695$$

Annuity from Present Value

This is a useful concept of equivalence and can be applied in our day-to-day activities. The periodic installments on home-mortgage loans, automobile loans, or other fixed installment loans are typical examples of this type of calculation. The concept is also applicable in situations where a certain amount is deposited at an annual interest rate, and you wish to withdraw the principal plus earned interest in a series of equal year-end amounts over the following t years. Thus, in such cases the present value, interest rate, and number of periods are known while the annuity needs to be calculated. The following equation is used for such calculations.

(2.16)

$$A_v = P_v \left[\frac{i_e (1 + i_e)^t}{(1 + i_e)^t - 1} \right]$$

The term, $[i_e (1 + i_e)^t / (1 + i_e)^t - 1]$, is referred to as the *equal payments series capital recovery factor*, designated by the *A/P* factors in Appendix A. The calculated annuity (series of equal periodic cash flows) includes both the principal and the accrued interest thereon. In debt payment situation, as each periodic payment is made on the due date, a portion of it goes to the accrued interest on the outstanding principal balance and a portion reduces the principal. Therefore, on home-mortgage loans only a small amount of the actual borrowed principal reduces in the first few years of the mortgage period. A considerable portion of the monthly mortgage payment in the beginning pays for the accrued interest on the outstanding principal.

Example 2-16

Suppose $20,000 is borrowed from a bank at an interest rate of 8% in exchange for a promise the loan will be paid off through a series of five equal year-end installments. Calculate the yearly installment, if the first payment is due one year from the day money is borrowed.

Solution: The cash-flow diagram for Example 2–16 is shown in Figure 2–13. Using Equation (2.16), the annual installment is

$$A_v = \$20,000\left[\frac{0.08(1+0.08)^5}{(1+0.08)^5-1}\right]$$
$$= \$20,000(0.2505)$$
$$= \$5,010 \text{ per year}$$

Note that over the five-year period $25,050 will be paid instead of $20,000 borrowed. The $5,050 is the interest charged by the bank.

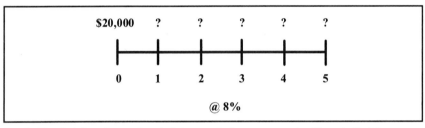

$20,000   ?   ?   ?   ?   ?

0   1   2   3   4   5

@ 8%

Fig. 2–13 Cash-flow diagram for calculating annuity from present value (Example 2–16)

Example 2–17

A piece of equipment is acquired for $50,000. The anticipated useful economic life of the equipment is 10 years. Calculate the equivalent annual cost of the equipment if the market interest rate is 8%.

Solution: Using the $(A/P)_{i=8\%, t=10}$ factor from Table 2–1:

$$A_v = \$50,000(A/P)_{i=8\%, t=10}$$
$$= \$50,000(0.14903)$$
$$= \$7,451.50 \text{ per year}$$

Example 2–18

On January 1, 2002 a sum of $20,000 is deposited in a bank account paying 8% interest per year. The money stays in the account for three years. Starting at the end of year 4, the money will be withdrawn in five equal year-end installments. How much money should be withdrawn each year in order to have five equal year-end withdrawals?

Solution: The problem is similar to the case of deferred annuity. First, the future value of the deposit is calculated at the end of year three. Then treating this future value as a present value, the annuity for the remaining five years is calculated. The cash-flow diagram for this problem is shown in Figure 2–14.

Using Equations (2.12) and (2.16) in combination

$$A_v = \$20,000\left\{(1+0.08)^3\left[\frac{0.08(1+0.08)^5}{(1+0.08)^5 - 1}\right]\right\}$$

OR

$$A_v = \$20,000\left[(F/P)_{i=8\%,t=3} \times (A/P)_{i=8\%,t=5}\right]$$
$$= \$20,000(1.2597)(0.2505)$$
$$= \$6,311.10 \text{ per year starting end of year 4}$$

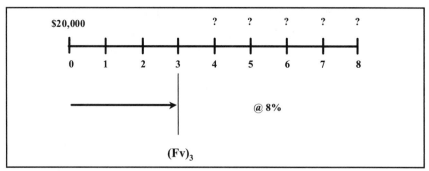

Fig. 2–14 Cash-flow diagram for Example 2–18

Annuity from Future Value

An annuity to generate a desired future value is determined using the following equation.

$$A_v = F_v \left[\frac{i_e}{\left(1 + i_e\right)^t - 1} \right]$$

The factor, $i_e / [(1 + i_e)^t - 1]$, in Equation (2.17) is referred to as the *equal payment series sinking fund factor*, designated by the interest factor (A/F) in the interest factor tables. Equation (2.17) or the factor A/F may be used to find the required year-end payments for the accumulation of a desired future amount.

Example 2–19

An oil producer plans to replace certain equipment at a cost of $100,000 five years from today. If the interest rate is 8%, how much money must the oil producer keep aside per year in order to generate $100,000?

Solution: The cash-flow diagram for Example 2–19 is shown in Figure 2–15.

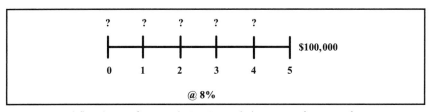

Fig. 2-15 Cash-flow diagram for Example 2–19, to calculate annuity from given future sum.

Using Equation (2.17), annual value is

$$A_v = \$100,000 \left[\frac{0.08}{\left(1 + 0.08\right)^5 - 1} \right]$$

OR

$$A_v = \$100{,}000(A/F)_{i=8\%, t=5}$$
$$= \$100{,}000(0.1705) = \$17{,}050 \text{ per year}$$

Present Value of Uniform Gradient Series

In the preceding sections, annuities and how to calculate the present value or future value of an annuity were discussed. An annuity, however, requires the series of periodic cash flows are equal in value. In many cases, the series of periodic cash flows may not be equal but may increase or decrease at a certain uniform rate per period.

In general, a uniformly increasing series of cash flows may be expressed as A_1, A_1+G, A_1+2G . . . . . $A_1 + (t-1)G$. Similarly, a uniform decreasing series of cash flows may be expressed as A_1, A_1-G, A_1-2G, ... $A_1- (t-1)G$.

As previously shown, first calculating the present value of each payment and then adding them all together will calculate the present value of a uniform gradient series. However, this method is tedious and time consuming for hand calculations. Another recommended, method is to first convert the uniform gradient series into its equivalent annuity. This annuity is then used to calculate its present or future value using Equation (2.14) or Equation (2.5), respectively. The following equation is used to convert the uniform gradient series into its equivalent annuity.

(2.18)

$$A_v = A_1 \pm G\left[\frac{1}{i_e} - \frac{t}{(1+i_e)^t - 1}\right]$$

where
    G = annual change, positive or negative
    A_1 = cash flow at the end of the first year

The factor, $[1 / i_e - t / (1 + i_e)^t - 1]$, in Equation (2.18) is referred to as the uniform gradient series factor, designated by the A/G factor in the interest factors tables. The A_v calculated by using Equation (2.18) is then used to calculate the present or future value.

Example 2–20

Suppose an oil well produces 2,000 barrels per year in the first year of production. The production declines by 200 barrels per year for each of the following five years. If the market rate of interest is 8%, calculate the equivalent uniform annual production rate. If the price of oil is $16 per barrel, calculate the present value of the production.

Solution: The cash-flow diagram for the problem is shown in Figure 2–16. Using Equation (2.18)

$$A_v = 2,000 - 200 \left[\frac{1}{0.08} - \frac{6}{(1+0.08)^6 - 1} \right]$$

OR

$$A_v = 2,000 - 200(A/G)_{i=8\%,t=6}$$
$$= 2,000 - 200(2.2763)$$
$$= 1,544.74 \quad \text{barrels/year}$$

and

$$A_v = 1,544.74 \times \$16 = \$24,715.84 \text{ per year}$$

Using Equation (2.14) or interest factor $(P/A)_{i=8\%,t=6}$
$$P_v = \$24,715.84(P/A)_{i=8\%,t=6}$$
$$= \$24,715.84 \, (4.6229)$$
$$= \$114,258.86$$

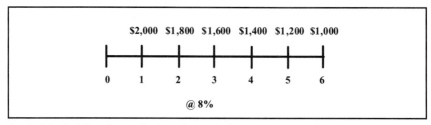

Fig. 2–16 Cash-flow diagram for Example 2–20, showing negative gradient series

Present Value of Shifted Gradient Series

In the previous section, the uniform gradient series and how to calculate the present value of such a series was discussed. There, it was presumed the gradient occurs in the second year of the series of payments and continues throughout the entire period under evaluation. In some cases, the gradient series may start to occur at any time during the series of payments and may not continue for the entire period under evaluation. Such a series of cash flows is referred to as the *shifted gradient.*

In order to calculate the present value of shifted gradients, a combination of various interest factors will be required. No single interest factor or equation is available to solve such gradients. The following example provides the steps required to calculate the present value of shifted gradients.

Example 2–21

Calculate the present value and annuity of the cash flows illustrated in the cash-flow diagram in Figure 2–17.

Step 1: Calculate the P_v of the three uniform cash flows of $100.
Using $(P / A)_{i_e = 8\%, \, t = 3}$

$$P_v = \$100(2.5771)$$
$$= \$257.71$$

Step 2: Calculate the equivalent annuity A_v of the gradient series at year 4 using $(A/G)_{i_e = 8\%, \, t=5}$

$$(A_v)_{t=4} = \$100 + 50(1.8465) = \$192.33$$

Step 3: Calculate the P_v at year 3 of the annuity in Step 2 using $(P/A)_{i_e = 8\%, \, t=5}$

$$(P_v)_{t=3} = \$192.33(3.9927) = \$767.92$$

Step 4: Calculate the $(P_v)_0$ of the $(P_v)_{t=3}$ in Step 3 using $(P/F)_{i_e = 8\%, \, t=3}$

$$P_v = \$767.92(0.7938) = \$609.57$$

Step 5: Now add the present value calculated in Step 1 and Step 4

$$P_v = \$257.71 + \$609.57 = \$867.28$$

To calculate the equivalent annuity, use $(A/P)_{i_e = 8\%, \, t=8}$ and the P_v calculated in Step 5.

$$A_v = \$867.28(0.1740)$$
$$= \$150.91 \text{ per year}$$

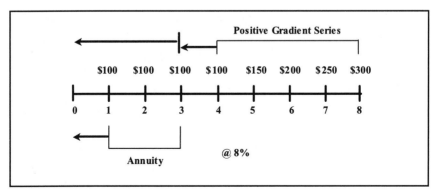

Fig. 2–17 Cash-flow diagram for Example 2–21

Note very carefully how the various conversions took place in Example 2–21. The most critical part of the problem is the proper placement of P_v, A_v or F_v. The same problem can be solved in several other ways. Therefore, a clear understanding of the various equivalence relationships presented in this chapter is important.

Calculation of Unknown Interest Rate

In all examples presented in this chapter, a certain interest rate is presumed. In some cases, however, the series of cash flows and the timing of the occurrence of these cash flows will be given but the interest rate, which has impacted these cash flows, may be unknown.

For example, a person has borrowed $20,000 today with a promise to pay back to the lender $30,037.13 five years from today. In this example, the P_v, F_v and t are known, and we need to calculate the interest rate charged by the lender. The unknown interest rate may be calculated using one of the following methods.

1. Using the interest tables: setting up the P/F or F/P relationship and solving for the factor value can find the interest. For example:

$$\left(F/P\right)_{i=?,t=5} = \frac{\$30,073.13}{\$20,000} = 1.5037$$

   From the interest tables, F/P factor of 1.5037 for t=5 lies between the 8% and 9% tables. The F/P value from the 8% table is 1.4693 and from the 9% table is 1.5386. Interpolating between these values:

$$i = 8 + \left(\frac{1.5386 - 1.5037}{1.5386 - 1.4693}\right) \times (9 - 8)$$
$$= 8.5\%$$

2. The following equation may be used to directly calculate the interest rate.

$$i = \exp\left[\frac{\ln(F/P)}{t}\right] - 1$$

$$= \exp\left[\frac{\ln(30,073.13/20,000)}{5}\right] - 1$$

$$= \exp(0.08158) - 1$$

$$= 0.085 \ or \ 8.5\%$$

Similarly, if P_v, F_v, and interest rate are known, the unknown number of years may be determined by interpolation of the interest tables.

LOAN AMORTIZATION SCHEDULE

Loan amortization means paying off a debt, normally gradual retirement of debt with a series of equal periodic payments. The series of payments include interest accrued on the outstanding loan balance and some portion of the principal.

As previously mentioned, with each payment the interest portion of the total payment for the following period decreases and the principal portion increases. The loan payment is calculated using the *equal payment series capital recovery factor*, *A/P*, or Equation (2.16). As each periodic payment is made, the payment is split between interest on the outstanding balance and principal amount by using the concept of simple interest, Equation (2.1).

In granting the loan, the lender is buying an opportunity to receive a certain periodic cash flow over a certain period. In negotiating the loan, the lender establishes the following information in consultation with the borrower. Based on this, the periodic payment and amortization schedule is calculated.

1. The amount of the loan requested,

2. The number of years and times per year payments of interest and principal are made, and

3. The rate of interest charged.

Example 2–22

An oil producer borrows $100,000 at an interest rate of 8% for a period of three years. The loan has to be paid back quarterly over the three-year period, with the first payment due exactly three months from the date money is borrowed. Calculate the quarterly payment and show the loan amortization schedule.

Solution: Using Equation (2.16), the quarterly payment is

$$A_v = \$100,000 \left[\frac{\dfrac{i_n}{4}\left(1+\dfrac{i_n}{4}\right)^{t \times 3}}{\left(1+\dfrac{i_n}{4}\right)^{t \times 3} - 1} \right]$$

$$= \$100,000 \left[\frac{0.02(1+0.02)^{12}}{(1+0.02)^{12} - 1} \right]$$

$$= \$100,000(0.09456)$$

$$= \$9,456 \quad \text{per quarter}$$

The amortization schedule is given in Table 2–2. The $92,544, outstanding loan balance at the end of the first quarter (after the first payment has been made) becomes principal owed during the second quarter, and so on. *Simple interest* calculations are used at the end of each payment to calculate the interest and principal for that payment. The first quarter's calculations are shown below.

Column 2 = Outstanding loan = $100,000
Column 3 = First payment = $9,456
Column 4 = Column 2 x 0.08/4= $100,000 x 0.02 = $2,000
Column 5 = Column 3 – Column 4 = $9,456 – $2,000 = $7,456
Column 6 = Column 2 – Column 5 = $100,000 – $7,456 = $92,544

End of Quarter	Principal Owed During Quarter	Loan Payment	Interest	Principal	Balance Principal Owed
1	$100,000	$9,456	$2,000	$7,456	$92,544
2	92,544	9,456	1,851	7,605	84,939
3	84,939	9,456	1,699	7,757	77,182
4	77,182	9,456	1,544	7,912	69,270
5	69,270	9,456	1,385	8,071	61,199
6	61,199	9,456	1,224	8,232	52,967
7	52,967	9,456	1,059	8,397	44,570
8	44,570	9,456	891	8,565	36,005
9	35,005	9,456	720	8,736	27,269
10	27,269	9,456	545	8,911	18,358
11	18,358	9,456	367	9,089	9,269
12	9,269	9,456	185	9,271	0

Table 2–2 Loan amortization schedule for Example 2–22

FUNDS FLOW AND COMPOUNDING/DISCOUNTING

Throughout this chapter, it was assumed the cash flows, regardless of their actual frequency of occurrence, occurred at the end of the year or interest period in which they occurred. In addition, it was assumed that the interest is compounded/discounted at the end of the year or interest period. This is referred to as *discrete period* interest compounding/discounting and *end of period* cash flows.

It should be kept in mind that all the equivalence factors presented in the preceding sections are applicable only in case of the above assump tions. Variations to the above assumptions that have practical applications and are frequently used in the industry are

1. Continuous *interest compounding/discounting and* discrete *period cash flows*: The continuous interest compounding/discounting (i.e., compounding/discounting interest an infinite number of times per year) closely approximates daily compounding/discounting. To differentiate between the periodic interest rate, i_e, and the continuous interest rate, the later is designated by r. Equations for the continuous compounding/discounting and discrete period cash flows are given in Table 2–3.

    The continuous interest rate r may be converted to effective interest rate by using Equation (2.5). This effective interest rate can then be used in the equations for discrete period interest compounding/discounting and end of year cash flows.

2. Continuous *interest compounding/discounting and* continuous *flow of funds*: In many instances, it may be reasonable to presume cash flows occur on a relatively continuous basis throughout the year or interest period. Such situations involve a *funds-flow* process. In this case, an infinite number of cash flows (received or disbursed continuously) per year to match the interest rate with an infinite number of compounding/discounting periods. Equations for the continuous interest compounding/discounting and continuous flow of funds are given in Table 2–3.

3. Discrete *period interest compounding/discounting and* mid period *cash flows*: The use of this assumption in handling time value of money problems has gained considerable popularity in the oil industry. According to this assumption, all cash flows are presumed to occur at the middle of the interest period instead of at the end. Consequently, all cash flows after time zero occur half a period sooner than the end of period convention.

    The equivalent values obtained by using the end-of-year cash-flow convention may be converted to conform to the mid-period convention. This is done by multiplying the former value by the factor $(1 + i)^{0.5}$ or by replacing the t in Equations (2.9) through (2.17) by $t - 0.5$.

	Continuous Interest Discrete Cash Flow	Continuous Interest Continuous Cash Flow
Single payment compound amount factor, F/P	$F_v = P_v(e^{rt})$	$F_v = P_v\left[\dfrac{re^{rt}}{e^r - 1}\right]$
Single payment present worth factor, P/F	$P_v = F_v\left[\dfrac{1}{e^{rt}}\right]$	$P_v = F_v\left[\dfrac{e^r - 1}{re^{rt}}\right]$
Uniform series compound amount factor, F/A	$F_v = A_v\left[\dfrac{e^{rt} - 1}{e^r - 1}\right]$	$F_v = \overline{A}_v\left[\dfrac{e^{rt} - 1}{r}\right]$
Sinking fund factor, A/F	$A_v = F_v\left[\dfrac{e^r - 1}{r^{rt} - 1}\right]$	$\overline{A}_v = F_v\left[\dfrac{r}{e^{rt} - 1}\right]$
Uniform series present worth factor, P/A	$P_v = A_v\left[\dfrac{e^{rt} - 1}{(e^r - 1)e^{rt}}\right]$	$P_v = \overline{A}_v\left[\dfrac{e^{rt} - 1}{re^{rt}}\right]$
Capital recovery factor, A/P	$A_v = P_v\left[\dfrac{(e^r - 1)e^{rt}}{e^{rt} - 1}\right]$	$\overline{A}_v = P_v\left[\dfrac{re^{rt}}{e^{rt} - 1}\right]$
Uniform gradient series factor, A/G	$A_v = A_1 \pm G\left[\dfrac{1}{e^r - 1} - \dfrac{1}{e^{rt} - 1}\right]$	

$\overline{A}_v$ = the single total amount of funds flowing continuously during a period, in a uniform series of equal payments

Table 2–3 Equations for two different types of funds flow and continuous interest compounding/discounting.

For example, recalculating the present value of the $5,000 in Example 2–6 using the mid-year convention as

$$P_v = \$5,000\left[\frac{1}{(1 + 0.08)^{5.5}}\right]$$

$$= \$3,274.46$$

OR,
from Example 2–6:

$$P_v = \$3,150.85(1 + 0.08)^{0.5}$$
$$= \$3,274.46$$

The selection of the type of compounding/discounting (i.e., annual, monthly, daily, continuous, etc.) and the assumption of the pattern of cash flows (i.e., year-end, mid-year, monthly, uniform, etc.) used in cash-flow analysis should be representative of the fiscal practices of the firm's treasury and the projects being considered.

In general, the year-end cash flows and the mid-year discounting are widely used in the industry. The year-end cash flows and year-end discounting at a certain discount rate will give conservative present value, followed by mid-year discounting and continuous discounting. Some analysts argue that continuous cash flows and discounting more closely reflect reality. However, (1) the cash-flow reinvestment may not be as efficient as implied by the calculations, and (2) the cash-flow projections are not accurate enough to warrant the extra accuracy.

The analysts are also advised that before using any canned economic analysis models or calculators with built-in financial functions, they should check the assumptions to make sure they are in accordance with your requirement and standards used.

SPREADSHEET APPLICATION

The use of computers, specifically spreadsheets (Lotus 1-2-3 and Microsoft Excel) have revolutionized the working environment of engineers, geologists, economists, financial/investment analysts, accountants, stockbrokers etc. The use of spreadsheets greatly simplifies the calculations covered in the preceding pages.

The Microsoft Excel's financial =*functions* and their equivalents in Lotus 1-2-3 are invaluable tools for answering important financial questions. There are some financial calculations that the spreadsheets do not handle directly. However, with a little effort, the scope of these spreadsheets can be expanded to handle such calculations by combining functions or building straightforward formulas. This section explains how, with a little finesse, the spreadsheets can be used to calculate

1. The term of a present value, or how long it will take to pay off a loan at a given payment schedule and interest rate

2. The future value of an initial lump-sum payment

3. The present value of a future lump-sum payment

4. Balloon loan payments

5. The interest and principal parts of a payment

6. The present value of a constantly changing annual receipts/payments

7. The future value of constantly changing annual receipts/payments

8. How to calculate periodic interest rates

Solving the data given in Examples 2–1 through 2–22 covers these topics. Many tips not normally shown in the user manuals of the spreadsheets are introduced. These assist in solving a variety of real-life problems. Microsoft Excel is utilized to carry out the calculations. Table 2–4 presents the Examples 2–2 to 2–19.

The following Excel commands are used in the calculations performed in Table 2–4. The interest rate in all relationships is used as a fraction. If a nominal interest rate is given and the compounding periods per year are more than one (1), then the nominal interest rate is divided by the number of compounding periods per year and the years are multiplied by the compounding periods per year. For example, to make monthly payments on a four-year car loan at 12% nominal interest rate, use 12%/12 for the interest rate and 4 x 12 for the *periods (time)*.

1. *=EFFECT(Nominal Interest Rate, Compounding Periods per year):* Returns the effective annual interest rate when the nominal annual interest rate and the compounding frequency per year are given.

2. *=FV(Interest Rate, Periods, Payment, Present Value, Type):* Returns the future value of an annuity or a lump-sum present value. If the future value of an annuity is required, the Present Value is input as zero (0) and vice versa. Type is the number zero (0) or one (1) and indicates when payments are due (i.e., zero is used for end of period payments like in ordinary annuity and one is used when payments are made at the beginning of the periods like in annuity due).

3. *=INTRATE(Settlement, maturity, investment, redemption, basis):* Returns the interest rate when the present value, future value, date of present value, and date of future value are given.

	A	B	C	Cell Formulae
1	Example 2–2	Money invested	2,000.00	
2		Interest rate	0.08	
3	a.	Annual compounding	1.00	
4	b.	Payment after 1 year	1.00	
5		Quarterly compounding	4.00	
6	c.	Payment after 3 years	3.00	
7		Semi-annual compounding	2.00	
8				
9	a.	Interest	160.00	=FV(C2,C3,0,–C1,0)–C1
10	b.	Interest	164.86	=FV(C2/C5,C5*C4,0,–C1,0)–C1
11	c.	Interest	530.64	=FV(C2/C7,C6*C7,0,–C1,0)–C1
12				
13	Example 2–3	Current salary	4000.00	
14		Merit increase per year	0.05	
15		Periods	5.00	
16				
17		Salary after 5 years	5,105.13	=FV(C14,C15,0,–C13,0)
18				
19	Example 2–4	Money borrowed	2,000.00	
20		Payback period, years	1.00	
21		Nominal Interest Rate	0.08	
22		Compounding periods	4.00	
23				
24		Effective interest rate	8.24%	=EFFECT(C21,C22)
25		Money to be paid back	2,164.86	=FV(C24,C20,0,–C19,0)
26				
27	Example 2–5	Current principal	50,000.00	
28		Principal at maturity	50,253.60	
29		Date of deposit	5/20/2002	
30		Date of Maturity	6/20/2002	
31				
32		Interest paid	5.890%	=INTRATE("5/20/2002","6/20/2002",C27,C28,2)
33		Effective interest rate	6.066%	=EFFECT(C32,360)
34				
35	Example 2–6	Future value	5,000.00	
36		Years	6.00	
37		Effective interest rate	0.08	
38				
39		Present value	3,150.85	=PV(C37,C36,0,–C35,0)
40				

Table 2–4 Excel spreadsheet representing Examples 2–2 to 2–19

	A	B	C	Cell Formulae
41	Example 2–7	Royalty, year 1	2,000.00	
42		Royalty, year 2	2,200.00	
43		Royalty, year 3	1,900.00	
44		Royalty, year 4	2,500.00	
45		Royalty, year 5	1,500.00	
46		Effective interest rate	0.08	
47				
48		Present value	8,104.73	=NPV(C46,C41:C45)
49	Example 2–9	Future value	5,000.00	
50		Nominal interest rate	0.08	
51		Quarterly compounding	4.00	
52		Years	6.00	
53				
54		Present value	3,108.61	=PV(C50/C51,C51*C52,0,–C49,0)
55				
56	Example 2–10	Present value	3,150.85	
57		Effective interest rate	0.08	
58		Years	6.00	
59				
60		Future value	5,000.00	=FV(C57,C58,0,–C56,0)
61				
62	Example 2–11	Royalty, year 1	2,000.00	
63		Royalty, year 2	2,200.00	
64		Royalty, year 3	1,900.00	
65		Royalty, year 4	2,500.00	
66		Royalty, year 5	1,500.00	
67		Effective interest rate	0.08	
68		Years	5.00	
69				
70		Future value	11,908.50	=FV(C67,C68,0,-NPV(C67,C62:C66),0)
71				
72	Example 2–12	Annual payments	10,000.00	
73		Effective interest rate	0.08	
74		Years of payment	5.00	
75				
76		Present value	39,927.10	=PV(C73,C74,–C72,0,0)

Table 2–4 continued . . .

	A	B	C	Cell Formulae
77	Example 2–13	Annual payments	10,000.00	
78		Effective interest rate	0.08	
79		Number of payments	5.00	
80				
81		Present value	43,121.27	=PV(C78,C79,–C77,0,1)
82				
83		Annual payments	10,000.00	
84		Down payment	20,000.00	
85		Effective interest rate	0.08	
86		Number of payments	4.00	
87				
88		Present value	53,121.27	=C84+PV(C85,C86,–C83,0,0)
89				
90	Example 2–14	Annual payments	10,000	
91		Effective interest rate	0.08	
92		Number of payments	5.00	
93				
94	a.	Future value (Ordinary)	58,666	=FV(C91,C92,–C90,0,0)
95	b.	Future value (deu)	63,359	=FV(C91,C92,–C90,0,1)
96				
97	Example 2–15	Annual payments	10,000	
98		Effective interest rate	0.08	
99		Deferred period, years	3.00	
100		Number of payments	5.00	
101				
102		Present value	31,695.42	=PV(C98,C99,0,–PV(C98,C100,–C97,0,0),0)
103				
104	Example 2–16	Present value	20,000.00	
105		Effective interest rate	0.08	
106		Equal year-end payments	5.00	
107				
108		Annual Payments	5,009.13	=PMT(C105,C106,–C104,0,0)
109				
110	Example 2–17	Present value	50,000.00	
111		Effective interest rate	0.08	
112		Useful economic life, yrs	10.00	
113				
114		Annual equivalent cost	7,451.47	=PMT(C111,C112,–C110,0,0)
115				

Table 2–4 continued . . .

	A	B	C	Cell Formulae
116	Example 2–18	Deposit, 1/1/2002	20,000.00	
117		Effective interest rate	0.08	
118		Deposit duration, years	3.00	
119		Withdrawals over, years	5.00	
120				
121		Amount of Withdrawals	6,310.06	=PMT(C117,C119,–FV(C117,
122				C118,0,–C116,0),0,0)
123	Example 2–19	Future value of equipment	100,000.00	
124		Effective interest rate	0.08	
125		Sinking fund period, years	5.00	
126				
127		Yearly deposits required	17,045.65	=PMT(C124,C125,0,–C123,0)
128				

Table 2–4 continued . . .

4. *=NPV(Interest Rate, Value 1, Value 2, ... Value n):* Returns the net present value of a series of equally spaced periodic cash flows at a certain discount rate.

5. *=PMT(Interest Rate, Periods, PV, FV, Type):* Calculates the payment for a loan based on constant payment and a constant interest rate when the present value of a loan is given. The payment calculated by PMT includes principal and interest payment but no taxes. The PMT can also be used to calculate a sinking fund that will accumulate to some required future value. In the former case, FV=0 and in the later case PV=0.

6. *=PV(Interest Rate, Periods, Payment, Future Value, Type):* Returns the present value of an annuity or a lump-sum future value. If the future value of an annuity is required, the Future Value is input as zero (0) and vice versa. Type is the number zero (0) or one (1) and indicates when payments are due (i.e., zero is used for end of period

payments like in ordinary annuity and one is used when payments are made at the beginning of the periods like in annuity due).

Table 2–5 duplicates the amortization schedule of Example 2–22 similar to the one shown in Table 2–2. In this table, three spreadsheet's commands (=PMT, =IPMT, and =PPMT) are used. The IPMT calculates the interest payment for a given period on an investment based on periodic, constant payments and a constant periodic interest rate. The PPMT calculates the principal payment corresponding the IPMT. The following steps are used to set up the amortization schedule of Table 2–5.

1   Input the loan parameters in Cells C1 to C4.

2. In Cell C6, input the formula =PMT(C4/C3,C3*C2,C1,0,0).

3. In Cells A10 to A21, input the quarters 1 to 12.

4. In Cell B10, input the formula
    =IPMT(C$4/C$3,A10,C$3*C$2,C$1,0,0). Copy the Cell B10 all the way from Cell B11 to B21.

5. In Cell C10, input the formula
    =PPMT(C$4/C$3,A10,C$3*C$2,C$1,0,0).
    Copy the Cell C10 all the way from Cell C11 to C21.

6. In Cell D10, input =C1+C10.

7. In Cell D11, input =D10+C11. Copy Cell D11 all the way from Cell D12 to D21.

	A	B	C	D
1	Money Borrowed		100,000	
2	Payment Periods, Years		3	
3	Payments per Year		4	
4	Nominal Interest Rate		0.08	
5				
6	Quarterly Payment		(9,456.0)	
7				
8	**End of**			
9	**Quarter**	**Interest**	**Principal**	**Balance**
10	1	(2,000.0)	(7,456.0)	92,544.0
11	2	(1,850.9)	(7,605.1)	84,939.0
12	3	(1,698.8)	(7,757.2)	77,181.8
13	4	(1,543.6)	(7,912.3)	69,269.5
14	5	(1,385.4)	(8,070.6)	61,198.9
15	6	(1,224.0)	(8,232.0)	52,966.9
16	7	(1,059.3)	(8,396.6)	44,570.3
17	8	(891.4)	(8,564.6)	36,005.7
18	9	(720.1)	(8,735.8)	27,269.9
19	10	(545.4)	(8,910.6)	18,359.3
20	11	(367.2)	(9,088.8)	9,270.5
21	12	(185.4)	(9,270.5)	(0.0)

Table 2–5 Amortization schedule of Example 2–22

QUESTIONS and PROBLEMS

2.1 What is meant by the term *time value of money*? Explain the concept of *equivalence*.

2.2 What is meant by the terms *discounting* and *compounding*? Why are these important in investment analysis?

2.3 What is the difference between *simple* and *compound interest*, *nominal* and *effective interest* rates?

2.4 What are the necessary conditions for an ordinary annuity?

2.5 What are the cash-flow assumptions with respect to (a) periodic discounting and year-end cash flows, (b) periodic discounting and mid-year cash flows, (c) continuous discounting and periodic cash flows, and (d) continuous discounting and continuous cash flows?

2.6 Calculate the effective interest rate for the following nominal interest rates.
a) Interest rate of 12% compounded annually.
b) Interest rate of 12% compounded semi-annually.
c) Interest rate of 12% compounded quarterly.
d) Interest rate of 12% compounded daily.
e) Interest rate of 12% compounded continuously.

2.7 Compare the interest earned on $1,500 over:
a) 10 years at an interest rate of 8%, compounded yearly, and
b) 10 years at an interest rate of 8%, compounded quarterly.

2.8 Calculate the future value of the following investments.
a) $1,000 in 10 years at an interest rate of 8%, compounded annually.
b) $15,000 in 8 years at an interest rate of 8%, compounded monthly.

2.9 Calculate the present value of $15,000 to be received 10 years from today. Assume an interest rate of 10%, compounded annually.

Errata for
Project Economics & Decision Analysis (Vol. I)

Equation (3.3)

$$EL_{oil} = \frac{WI \times LOE}{NRI\left[P_o(1-T_o) + P_g(1-T_g)\left(\dfrac{GOR}{1,000}\right)\right](1-T)}$$

Equation (3.8)

$$d_y = 1 - (1 - d_m)^{12}$$

OR

$$d_m = 1 - (1 - d_y)^{1/12}$$

Equation (3.25)

$$C_c = C_r \left(\frac{Q_c}{Q_r} \right)^m$$

2.10 The annual amount of a series of payments to be made at the end of each of the next 10 years is $500. What is the present worth of the payments at 7% interest compounded annually?

2.11 Calculate the future value of the following investments at an effective interest rate of 12%.
a) $800 invested at the end of each of the next 8 years.
b) $800 invested every 6 months for the next 4 years.
c) $800 received at the end of each of the following 4 years and $1,000 per year for the following 4 years.
d) $1,000 invested monthly for the next 4 years.

2.12 Calculate the present value of the cash flows in Problem 2.11.

2.13 Calculate the equal series of annual payments, which will accumulate to $20,000 in 5 years at an effective interest rate of 8%.

2.14 A piece of machinery costs $20,000 and has an estimated life of 8 years and a scrap value of $2,000. What uniform annual amount must be set aside at the end of each of the 8 years for replacement if the interest rate is 6% compounded annually?

2.15 If $15,000 is put in a bank account today at an interest rate of 8%, what annual amount of money can be withdrawn every year over the next 7 years?

2.16 What equal series of payments must be paid into a sinking fund to accumulate the following?
a) $5,000 in 7 years at an effective interest rate of 8% when payments are made annually.
b) $20,000 in 5 years at an interest rate of 12% when payments are made quarterly.

2.17 An oil company employs a petroleum engineer on his 45th birthday at a salary of $60,000 per year, which is expected to increase by an average of $1,500 at the end of each year until his retirement age of 65. The company's retirement package pays one-half the average salary over the last three years of the employment. Since vesting is required after 10 years, he may leave the company at that time and begin drawing retirement on his 65th birthday. The company invests its employees' pension fund at 8%, and assumes a life expectancy of 75 years. It pays half the cost of the retirement system. What fraction of this employee's pay (on an annual basis) must be withheld in order to ensure an adequate fund for his retirement at any time after 10 years?

2.18   A property costs $12,000 today. If it is appreciating at a rate of 5%, calculate its price in 50 years.

2.19   The operating cost of a new machine is $500 for the first year. Starting the second year, the operating cost increases by $200 per year for the next 10 years. Calculate the equivalent annual operating cost of the machine. What will be the present and future value of the operating costs over the 11-year period? Assume the market interest rate of 8.5%.

2.20   Calculate the rate of interest compounded annually if:
a)   An investment of $8,000 today accumulates to $20,750 in 10 years.
b)   A series of 5 year-end payments of $5,000 results in an accumulated amount of $30,525.

2.21   A person wins $10,000 in a state lottery. He plans to deposit this money in a savings account to earn 8% annual interest for 6 years. If he wants to withdraw equal annual amounts from the account for 6 years, starting with the first withdrawal one year from the date of deposit, what will be the amount of each withdrawal?

2.22   Calculate the equal quarterly series equivalent to the decreasing gradient series given below. Assume the interest rate is 8%.
a) $10,000 at the end of 1st quarter
b) $9,500 at the end of 2nd quarter
c) $9,000 at the end of 3rd quarter

d) $8,500 at the end of the 4th quarter
e) $8,000 at the end of the 5th quarter
f) $7,500 at the end of the 6th quarter
g) $7,000 at the end of the 7th quarter
h) $6,500 at the end of the 8th quarter
i) $5,000 at the end of the 9th quarter
j) $4,000 at the end of the 10th quarter
k) $3,000 at the end of the 11th quarter, and
l) $2,000 at the end of the 12th quarter.

2.23 What is the present value of the following continuous fund flow.
a) $5,000 per year over 8 years at an interest rate of 8% compounded continuously.
b) $5,000 per month for 8 years at an interest rate of 8% compounded continuously.

2.24 How many years will it take $5,000 to double at an interest rate of 8%, compounded annually?

2.25 An oil producer has borrowed $100,000 at an interest rate of 12% for a period of three years. Calculate (a) the quarterly payment, and (b) monthly payment. If the loan has to be paid back using quarterly payments, show the amortization schedule for the first two years.

2.26 If $100,000 is borrowed by an oil producer right now at 6% interest per annum (compounded annually) to be paid back in 8 yearly installments, how much of the principal will remain to be paid after a $30,000 payment is made 4 years from now?

2.27 An oil producer has purchased a pumping unit for $30,000, and the loan is to be paid back for in 24 equal monthly installments of $1,773 per month. Calculate the nominal interest rate charged for this financing arrangement. Calculate the effective interest rate.

2.28 An engineer has generated an oil production forecast for a group of wells. According to this forecast, the wells produce 30,000 barrels in the first year. Starting the second year, production declines by 2,000 barrels per year for 4 years. Starting the sixth year, production declines by 3,000 barrels per year for another 4 years. Calculate the present value of the revenues if the oil price is $15 per barrel for the first 5 years and $16 per barrel thereafter. Also, calculate the equivalent annual value of these revenues. Assume interest rate of 8%.

2.29 An oil company has installed an offshore production facility for $10 million. The annual maintenance cost of the facility is $60,000 per year for the first year, increasing by $10,000 per year for the next 9 years. In the 11th year, a major overhaul is conducted at a cost of $500,000. The overhaul has helped in keeping the maintenance costs fixed at $150,000 per year for the remaining 10 years. At the end of 20 years, the facility is sold for a sum of $2 million. If the market interest rate is 8%, calculate the present value of all the costs over the 20 years period. Also, calculate the equivalent annual cost of the facility.

chapter THREE

Before-Tax
Cash-Flow Models

Capital investment analysis is the analytic process of reaching a decision between alternative investment projects. The decision process, in general, is based on the following three steps:

1. Data gathering about each investment alternative through estimation and forecasting of relevant variables,

2. Combining the quantitative information gathered in Step 1 into profitability measures (also referred to as decision criteria or profitability yardsticks), and

3. Making the final decision based on the criteria calculated in Step 2 and judgment on the non-quantified information.

The variables required to arrive at the Before Federal Income Tax (BFIT or BTAX) project cash flow (Step 1) are discussed in this chapter. The discussion of Step 2 and Step 3 is presented in Chapters 6 and 7, respectively. Therefore, this chapter is intended to provide groundwork for the decision analysis methods presented in the following chapters.

Before embarking on the sophisticated decision analysis methods, awareness of the process of converting the available investment project description into a series of realistic estimates of future cash flows is essential. These cash flows incorporate initial costs of project implementation and the resulting long-term net benefits.

Forecasting cash flow is the foundation of almost all economic analysis carried out for investment decision-making. Some cash-flow forecasts are simple (merely involving estimate of future cost and timing of a single well or lease equipment). Others may be complicated (estimating cash flows of full field development over a longer period of time, together with detailed fiscal calculations for each year).

The most important—and the most difficult—step in capital investment analysis is estimating its cash flows—both the investment outlays required and the annual net cash inflows after the project is implemented. Cash-flow forecasts consist of many variables, and many individual departments participate in the process. For example:

1. Reservoir engineers, together with geologists and geophysicists, generate production forecasts and the wells required to achieve this forecast.

2. The drilling department generates drilling cost forecast of the wells required for the project.

3. The production department identifies facilities required for the project, and engineering department estimates cost of these.

4. Economists, together with marketing staff's knowledge of price elasticity, advertising effects, and the state of economy forecast product prices.

The project evaluators' or economists' role in this process includes:

- Coordinating the efforts of other departments
- Ensuring all involved in generating the forecasts use a consistent set of economic assumptions
- Noting and resolving any anomalies in the information received from other departments
- Making sure no biases are inherent in the forecasts

The last point is important, because division managers often become emotionally involved with pet projects. This leads to cash-flow forecasting biases in order to make bad projects look good on paper. If estimation bias occurs, the project cash flows and the resulting project profitability could be either too optimistic or too pessimistic.

Some people argue that the decision analysis (risk analysis) tools take care of any inherent biases. This is not true. The unbiased point estimates of the key variables are not sufficient, therefore data on appropriate probability distributions or other indications of the likely range of errors are also essential.

There are several basic principles of cash-flow analysis vital to the correct analysis of available investment alternatives. These include basic definitions, the treatment of depreciation and depletion, capital costs, intangible and tangible drilling costs, incorporating inflation, concepts of nominal and real cash flow, the treatment of interest on loans and loan payments (financing mix), and the tax treatment of various costs. Each of these principles is discussed in this and the following chapter in order to arrive at a clear understanding. The after federal income tax (AFIT or ATAX) cash-flow model is discussed in Chapter 4. Chapter 5 deals with the cash-flow model required for international production-sharing contracts. The focus of this chapter is on

- Information required for arriving at project cash flows
- Practical tips on how to generate estimates of various variables required
- Measures used in determining investments' profitability, etc.

In this chapter, it is temporarily assumed the generated cash flows are known with certainty—an unrealistic presumption to be certain, but a useful one for expository purposes.

The difficulties one may encounter in generating cash-flow forecasts and the importance of these forecasts are duly acknowledged. However, forecast errors can be minimized if the principles discussed and the practical tips presented in the following sections are observed.

A prerequisite for generating the inputs in a cash flow is to know the past, and based on this knowledge, to forecast the future. A wise man once said, "Those who do not study the past are destined to repeat it." Those who study the past are more likely to know what to expect in the future than those who do not. Therefore, using statistical forecasting to "study the past" helps in making better plans for the future.

CASH-FLOW MODEL

As stated in Chapter 2 (Equation 2.8), in its basic form, *cash flow* of an investment is simply the cash expanded over a defined period. *Net cash flow* is simply *cash received* less *cash spent* during a period. The period is usually one year, and the net cash-flow projections are made over the economic project life (i.e., several periods, maybe 20 to 25 years in the future until abandonment). In its simplest form, the cash-flow projection would be as shown in Table 3–1. In this table, year 1 is the first year of projected cash flow.

		Year 1	Year 2	Year 3	Year 4	Year 5
	Cash Received	$	$	$	$	$
Less	Cash Expanded	$	$	$	$	$
Equals	Net Cash Flow	$	$	$	$	$

Table 3–1 Simple net cash-flow projection

The cash received is the product stream times the projected price of the product. The product streams could be crude oil, natural gas, liquefied petroleum gas [LPG—propane and butane), natural gas liquids (NGL—propane, butane, and pentane [C5+]), liquefied natural gas (LNG), heating oil, petrochemicals, and sulfur, etc. The crude oil is reported in stock tank barrels (STB) or standard cubic meters, gas in million standard cubic feet (MMSCF) or cubic meters, heating oil in barrels, and the other products in metric tonnes.

The cash expanded is further divided into three main categories as capital expenditure (CAPEX), operating expenditure (OPEX), abandonment costs, production taxes, and sunk costs. The CAPEX is further classified into geological and geophysical (G&G), drilling, and facility costs. The estimate of the costs (capital as well as operating) is not only of prime importance for the required economic analysis, but it also plays an important role in the preparation of the company's budgets.

Underestimating these costs may lead to projects cost overruns that result in disappointing profitability, not to mention the painful justification of budget increases. On the other hand, if the estimate is set too high, it may result in either prematurely killing a project or unnecessary freezing (or even spending) of funds that could have been usefully employed elsewhere in the company's program.

The estimation of costs depends on the cost of a commodity or service that fluctuates with time and varies from location to location, for example:

1. General inflation.

2. Market conditions, (i.e., worldwide or regional peak of oilfield construction activity) that temporarily drive up costs of equipment and services due to the law of supply and demand.

3. Escalation, which is the combined effect of items 1 and 2. Sometimes this term is also used to indicate the overall cost increases of a project as compared to its original estimates.

4. Local wage levels and productivity.

5. Cost of transportation from source.

6. Taxes and import duties.

7. Climatic and terrain conditions.

The combined effect of items 4 to 7 on project costs is usually expressed in estimate as a *location factor*, referenced to a standard location, such as Gulf of Mexico, the Middle East, or North Sea, etc.

In addition to capital and operating costs, major items of cash flow for most projects are royalties, profit sharing (international contracts), severance and ad valorem taxes, and income taxes, etc. These costs are collectively referred to as *State* or *Government Take*.

The economic evaluation of each project as a whole consists of multiple sub evaluations. For example, the type of (a) drilling contract to use; (b) drilling fluid to use; (c) drilling bits to use; (d) equipment to use— lease equipment or buy equipment; etc. In the following pages, each one of the revenue and expense items and how they are estimated is further explained. Putting the forecasts of all these variables together and calculating profitability yardsticks from these is called a cash-flow model.

DATA REQUIRED FOR PROJECT EVALUATION

To make sound economic evaluation of a given investment project, certain basic data is required. The following check list serves as a guide for collecting appropriate data for projects (wells, fields, upstream and downstream facilities, etc.) under evaluation.[1]

1. Ownership maps, geological structure maps, isopach maps, and geological cross sections, etc.

2. Lease location data.

3. Complete suite of well logs.

4. Core analysis data for the zones cored and analyzed.

5. Reservoir fluid sample analysis data.

6. Chronological history of all well operations including original drilling and completion.

7. Tabulation of monthly oil, water, and gas production by lease, by wells, and by pay zones since original completion along with tabulation of any bottomhole pressure surveys, etc.

8. Summary of allowable formula and current daily allowable rates for each well.

9. Gross oil and gas prices accompanied by a summary of the oil and gas sales contract agreement with the respective purchasers and the term of agreement.

10. Severance and local taxes actually paid to the local authorities accompanied by randomly selected payment vouchers for confirmation.

11. Tabulation of actual historical gross operating expenses per well per month for each property. Identify the routine OPEX versus the non-routine expenditure, such as, equipment replacement, workover, and stimulation, etc.

12. In case of undeveloped or non-producing reserves, provide an estimate of completed well costs or recompletion costs for reserves behind the casing.

13. Tabulation of the ownership interests including reversionary interests and the latest payout amounts or status.

14. A copy of all previously prepared geological or engineering reports/studies containing data pertinent to the current evaluation of the property.

15. A summary of lease and assignment provisions, lease facilities, operating agreements, and unitization agreements, etc.

FORECASTING PRODUCT STREAM

Petroleum engineers, together with geologists and geophysicists, use several methods to forecast future oil and/or gas production resulting from the development of a field. Process engineers and chemical engineers forecast the products generated by petrochemical plants by using the oil and/or gas forecasts generated by the reservoir engineers.

An oil and/or gas property goes through several development stages. Most likely, at each stage, a different reserve estimate is developed with a different degree of confidence. The first stage in the development of any oil and/or gas property is the exploratory stage when a wildcat well is drilled. The reserve estimates at this stage are based on analogy with other similar prospects and geologic settings. If the estimates are favorable, the drilling of a wildcat is approved.

Once the first well is drilled and productive horizon identified, more physical information about the rock and fluid properties is obtained with the help of well logs, core analysis, PVT analysis, drill stem test, transient well test (pressure test) analysis, etc. Based on this information, the reserve estimates are revised appropriately.

After the first well starts producing oil and/or gas, reservoir pressure and production performance become available. This information may further warrant revision of the reserve estimates. With the passage of time, the data on the property accumulates and the estimates revised accordingly. At different stages, more appropriate techniques may be used to obtain better estimates.

The drilling of every new well into the same productive horizon (reservoir) provides added information (such as the aerial extent of the reservoir, the type of oil and/or gas accumulation, and the reservoir producing mechanism, etc). The reserves numbers remain an estimate until the abandonment of the well/lease. Unfortunately, the reserve estimates are no longer estimates when the property is abandoned; they are exact amounts.

Several techniques, depending on the type of data available (i.e., stage of field/reservoir development), are in common use for estimating oil and/or gas reserves. These techniques include:

- Volumetric calculations
- Historical production and reservoir pressure performance analysis (decline curve analysis)
- By analogy to similar reservoirs in the close vicinity of the area under evaluation
- Material balance calculations
- Reservoir simulation and process simulation

In this chapter, reserves estimated by (a) volumetric calculations, (b) analogy, and (c) from historical production performance of the reservoir are discussed. An in-depth study of material balance calculations and reservoir simulation is beyond the scope of this book; these topics are covered in detail in many other technical books.[2]

In dealing with oil and/or gas reserve estimates, the following most commonly used terminology are used:

1. *Original oil and/or gas in place (OOIP and/or OGIP) or initial oil and/or gas in place (IOIP and/or IGIP) or gas initially in place (GIIP) and stock tank oil initially in place (STOIIP).* These terms refer to the total estimated volume of hydrocarbon accumulation.

2. *Ultimate oil and/or gas recovery or reserves.* This refers to the total volume of hydrocarbons eventually produced/recovered over the economic productive life of the reservoir. Having determined the original oil and/or gas in place, some empirical correlations and/or experience are applied in order to predict the percentage of the total hydrocarbons volume economically and technically producible. This producible volume is referred to as the ultimate oil and/or gas recovery or reserves, also referred to as recoverable oil and/or gas reserves.

3. *Cumulative oil and/or gas production.* When a property starts producing, the production of oil, gas, and/or water is accumulated on a daily, monthly, and yearly basis. These accumulated amounts are referred to as cumulative production of oil, gas, and/or water at a specific point in time, i.e., as at 12/31/2001.

4. *Remaining oil and/or gas reserves.* The reserves produced after a certain point in time are referred to as the remaining oil and/or gas reserves (or just reserves) as of that time, i.e., as at 01/01/2002. These estimates assume existing economic conditions, established operation practices, and current government regulations.

The sum of the *cumulative* production and the remaining reserves at a point in time is again referred to as the *ultimate* oil and/or gas reserves or recovery.

Volumetric Calculations

Volumetric estimates of oil and gas reserves are generally used at early times in the life of a field. These estimates are considered preliminary as compared to the estimates obtained from using historical performance of wells/fields. Reservoir heterogeneities are a commonly overlooked factor, which makes the volumetric estimates often different from those obtained by evaluating performance.

The data required for estimating OOIP are (a) formation thickness (h, feet), (b) drainages area (A, acres), (c) porosity (ϕ, fraction), (d) formation oil saturation (S_o, fraction), and (e) oil formation volume factor (B_o, RB/STB). The following equation is used to estimate OOIP (N) in STB.

(3.1)

$$N = \frac{7,758\,\phi\,(1 - S_w)\,hA}{B_o}$$

The porosity and water saturation (S_w, fraction) are obtained from well logs or core analysis or both. The formation thickness is estimated from resistivity logs or from geologic maps if the well is in a developed reservoir. The drainage area is estimated based on experience, type of reservoir producing mechanism, analogy to wells producing from similar horizons in the other areas, and from geologic maps. The oil formation volume factor is either determined in the laboratory from fluid analysis, or it is estimated from empirical correlations. The constant 7758 in Equation (3.1) is a constant used to convert acre-feet into reservoir barrels. The B_o is used to convert reservoir barrels into their equivalent STB.

The OOIP is then multiplied by a recovery factor (E_r, fraction) to estimate the recoverable oil. The recovery factor is selected based on experience, reservoir drive mechanism, analogy, and rock and fluid properties. The primary recovery factor, depending upon the type of reservoir drive, ranges from 12% to 30%.

The volumetric calculation of gas reserves require about the same information as what is used for oil volumetric reserve calculations. The following equation calculates OGIP (*G*).

(3.2)

$$G = 43,560 \, \phi \left(1 - S_w\right) hAB_g$$

The B_g(SCF/CF) in Equation (3.2) is called gas formation volume factor, used to convert reservoir gas into its equivalent volume at the standard conditions. The constant 43,560 converts acre-feet into cubic feet. The recovery factor for gas wells may be based on experience or it may be calculated from an estimated abandonment pressure. Since gas flows more readily than oil, usually a higher percentage (70–90%) of the OGIP is recoverable. At the same time, a larger area could be drained by each well. For this reason, the spacing of oil wells is usually denser than the spacing of gas wells.

Example 3–1

An oil well has been drilled and completed. The productive zone has been encountered at a depth of 7815–7830 feet. The log analysis showed an average porosity of 15% and an average water saturation of 35%. The oil formation volume factor is determined in the laboratory to be 1.215 RB/STB. Experience shows other reservoirs of about the same properties drain 80 acres with a recovery factor of 12%. Compute the OOIP and the ultimate oil recovery.

Solution: Using Equation (3.1), the OOIP is

$$N = \frac{7,758 \, \phi \left(1 - S_w\right) hA}{B_o} = \frac{7,758 \times 0.15 \left(1 - 0.35\right) \times 15 \times 80}{1.215}$$
$$= 747,000 \text{ STB}$$

The ultimate recovery is given by

$$N_{ul} = N \times E_R$$
$$= 747{,}000 \times 0.12 = 89{,}600 \text{ STB}$$

Decline Curve Analysis

The purpose of decline curve analysis is to determine future production and therefore ultimate recovery for wells/fields with some production history. Since decline curve analysis depends on a curve-fit of past performance, the accuracy is expected to be higher for a well/field with several months or years of production history than for a well with only a limited history. Decline curve analyses are based on the following assumptions.

1. Sufficient past production performance is available in order to make a reasonable match of this performance and extrapolating its future performance.

2. The past production history is based on capacity (unrestricted) production with no changes in operational policy such as artificial lift, stimulation, etc. It is assumed the property will continue to be operated in the same manner in the future.

In its simple form, decline curve analysis can be performed by finding a curve that approximates the past production history and extrapolating this curve into the future. A more rigorous procedure is to fit the past performance with a mathematical curve (represented by a mathematical equation). Once the characteristics (parameters) of this curve are known, they can be used to predict future performance.

Three rate-time decline curves (1) exponential decline, (2) hyperbolic decline, and (3) harmonic decline (special case of hyperbolic decline) are discussed in this section. In addition to these rate-time curves, several other decline curves used in the industry, such as, rate–cumulative production plot, cumulative oil–cumulative gas curves, water cut versus cumulative production curve, and (gas–oil ratio) GOR versus cumulative oil production curve are also discussed. The rate-time curves are commonly plotted on semi-logarithmic graph paper as log q vs. t.

To work with rate-time curves, monthly or daily production is first plotted on semi-logarithmic graph paper (monthly is most common). After production is plotted, a declining pattern is observed and the future trend is forecasted. This future trend is extrapolated to the *economic limit* (EL) of the property. Production is abandoned before it would cease due to natural causes (depletion), because it declines to a rate where it costs more to produce the hydrocarbons than those hydrocarbons are worth.[3]

Therefore, the EL is the production rate below which the net cash flow is negative. The EL is computed as follows.

(3.3)

$$EL_{oil} = \frac{WI \times LOE}{NRI\left[P_o(1-T_o) + P_g\left(\dfrac{GOR}{1,000}\right)\right](1-T)}$$

(3.4)

$$EL_{gas} = \frac{WI \times LOE}{NRI\left[P_g(1-T_g) + P_o(Y)(1-T_o)\right](1-T)}$$

where

EL_{oil} = economic limit for oil well, bbls/month
EL_{gas} = economic limit for gas well, Mscf/month
P_o, P_g = oil and gas prices, \$/Stbl and \$/Mscf
LOE = lease operating expenses, \$/well/month
WI = working interest, fraction
NRI = net revenue interest, fraction
GOR = gas–oil ratio, Scf/Stb
Y = condensate yield, Stbs/Mscf
T_o, T_g = oil and gas severance/production taxes, fraction
T = Advalorem tax, fraction

Exponential Decline. Exponential decline is also referred to as *constant percentage decline.* The mathematical expression that defines this type of decline is an exponential equation of the form $y=ae^{bx}$. The exponentially declining production plots as a straight line on semi-logarithmic graph paper (production on log scale and time on linear scale). The following equations are used to interpret exponential decline curve.

Oil produced during interval $t=0$ and t_o

(3.5)

$$\Delta N_p = \frac{(q_i - q_o) \times 12}{a}$$

Time required to produce ΔNp

(3.6)

$$t = \frac{\ln\left(\dfrac{q_i}{q_o}\right)}{a}$$

Rate at time t_o

(3.7)

$$q_{ot} = q_i e^{-at_o}$$

$$d = \frac{(q_i - q_o)}{q_i} = 1 - \frac{q_i}{q_o} = 1 - e^{-at}$$

$$a = -\ln(1-d) = \frac{\ln(q_i) - \ln(q_o)}{t}$$

where
 q_i = rate at the beginning of time period, Stb/month
 q_o = rate at end of time period or EL, Stb/month
 t = time period between qi and qo, years
 ΔN_p = cumulative production during time period, Stb
 a = nominal decline rate, fraction
 d = effective decline rate, fraction

Changing effective monthly decline rate to effective yearly decline rate, and vice versa:

$$d_m = 1 - (1 - d_y)^{1/12}$$ **(3.8)**

OR

$$d_m = 1 - (1 - d_y)^{1/12}$$

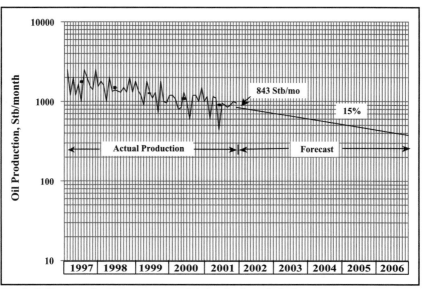

Fig. 3–1 Rate-time plot showing exponential decline for Example 3–2

Example 3–2

In Figure 3–1, there is a rate-time plot of actual oil production for years 1997 through 2001 and the forecasted oil production thereafter. The cumulative oil production (N_p) on 12/31/2001 is 78,044 Stb. Calculate:

a. Effective and nominal decline rate, $q_{1/1/2002}$ and $q_{1/1/2003}$ are read from the graph as 843 Stb/month and 717 Stb/month, respectively.
b. Remaining oil reserves from 1/1/2002 to EL of 200 barrels per month.
c. Time required producing the oil calculated in (b).

d. Production rate at the end of year 2004.

e. Ultimate oil recovery (N_{ul}).

Solution: Calculate effective decline rate/year:

(a)
$$d = \frac{843 - 717}{843} \times 100 = 14.94\% \cong 15\%$$

$$a = -\ln(1 - 0.15) = 0.1625$$

(b)
$$N_r = \frac{(q_i - q_{EL})}{a}$$

$$= \frac{(843 - 200) \times 12}{0.1625} = 47,483 \text{ Stb}$$

(c)
$$t = \frac{\ln\left(\dfrac{843}{200}\right)}{0.1625} = 8.85 \text{ years}$$

(d)
$$q_{ot} = q_i e^{-at_o}$$

$$= 843 e^{(-0.1625 \times 3)} = 518 \text{ Stb/month}$$

(e) Ultimate Recovery, $N_{ul} = N_p + N_r$

$$= 78,044 + 47,483 = 125,527 \text{ Stb}$$

The raw production data plot may normally exhibit wild fluctuations. To make the data easier to extrapolate into the future, it can be smoothed by calculating averages for periods of time and plotting the averages at the middle of the time period used for averaging (yearly averages shown in Figure 3–1). For steeper decline rate, averages over a shorter period, say 3 or 6 months, should be used because the average rate for the period does not represent true logarithmic average rate. This is particularly true for steeply declining production.

Hyperbolic Decline. The hyperbolic decline curve is a concave upward curve when plotted on semi-logarithmic graph paper. As a consequence, the decline characteristic, a, is not a constant value but rather is the slope of the tangent to the rate–time curve at any point. The slope of this tangent to the curve may be evaluated graphically in the same manner as the exponential decline. The decline characteristic a, however, changes with producing time. The curvature of the curve is defined by hyperbolic exponent, b (also denoted by n in some books). The hyperbolic exponent is constant with time. A typical hyperbolically declining production curve is shown in Figure 3–2.

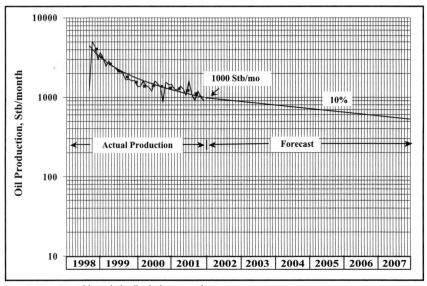

Fig. 3–2 A Typical hyperbolically declining production curve

In normal petroleum operations, the value of b ranges between 0 and 1.0 with $b=0$ being an exponential decline and $b=1$ being harmonic decline (special case of hyperbolic decline). However, it is found that in fractured tight (low-permeability) formations, exponents in excess of 1.0 may be calculated. Care should be exercised in these cases, as a large value of b will result in an unrealistically low decline rate late in the well life. The following equations are used to interpret hyperbolic decline curves.

Several methods are available in literature to evaluate the hyperbolic exponent b. Three of the most commonly used methods are (1) French curve method, (2) shifting the curve on log–log graph paper, and (3) type-curve fitting method. Only the first two methods are presented here.[4–8]

$$\Delta N_p = \frac{(q_i)^b}{(1-b)a_i\left[q_i^{(1-b)} - q_o^{(1-b)}\right]} \tag{3.9}$$

$$t = \frac{\left(\dfrac{q_i}{q_o}\right)^b - 1}{ba_i} \tag{3.10}$$

$$q_{ot} = q_i\left(1 + ba_it_o\right)^{-1/b} \tag{3.11}$$

$$a_t = a_i\left(\frac{q_t}{q_i}\right)^b = \frac{1}{b}\left[\left(1-d_t\right)^{-b} - 1\right]$$

$$d = \frac{q_i - q_o}{q_i}$$

$$d_t = 1 - \left(1 + ba_t\right)$$

French curve method: The French curve is usually a plastic template made in the shape of a hyperbolic curve. This is a preferred method because it is easy to use, it gives comparable results, and is not time consuming. The following steps should be followed:

1. Plot the monthly production data on a semi-logarithmic graph paper.

2. With the help of a French curve, draw a best-fit curve through the plotted data.

3. Select a point q_i on this curve and draw tangent to the curve at this point.

4. Compute the effective decline rate, d, per year and compute $a_i = -ln(1-d)$.

5. Select another point q_t at some point t from the initial rate q_i and try different values of b in equation (3.11) until a value of b is found that gives a q_t value close to the one selected. This trial-

and-error calculation can be easily done with the help of a pro-grammable calculator.

These values of b, a_i, and q_i are then used to forecast production per-formance. If the q_i is different from the q_i at effective date of evaluation, a new value of a_i must be calculated by using the following equation.

(3.12)

$$(a_i)_{new} = \frac{(a_i)_{old}}{[1 + n(a_i)_{old} \Delta t]}$$

Curve shift on log–log paper. This method involves a log–log trial-and-error plot of the rate versus time data until a straight line is obtained. The pro-cedure involves plotting the log of the rate versus the log of the time plus some constant, $(t + A)$. The constant A is varied until a straight line is obtained. Over-shifting the curve to the right shows upward curvature. The hyperbolic expo-nent b is then given by the reciprocal of the slope ($b = -1/\text{slope}$) of the straight line. The method is illustrated in Figure 3–3 for the data in Table 3–2.

Trying to find the constant A in the term $(t + A)$ by hand is tedious and time consuming. Therefore, a Newton-Raphson iteration technique is utilized to simplify the computation of the constant A. The following relationship is used.

The iteration is carried out by guessing the initial value of $A_i = 0$ and calculating $f(A)$ and $f'(A)$. If $f(A_i)$ is significantly different from zero, A_{i+1} is calculated using Equation (3.15) and the process repeated until the function converges to zero (or close to zero).

No.	Month	Q_o, Stb	No.	Month	Q_o, Stb	No.	Month	Q_o, Stb
1	1	28,200	4	19	6,635	7	37	2,850
2	7	15,680	5	25	4,775	8	43	2,300
3	13	9,700	6	31	3,628	9	49	1,905

Table 3–2 Hyperbolically declining production data

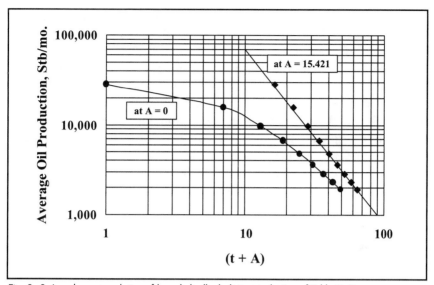

Fig. 3–3 Log–log extrapolation of hyperbolically declining production of Table 3–2

(3.13)

$$f(A) = \frac{\log Q_2 - \log Q_1}{\log(t_2 + A) - \log(t_1 + A)} - \frac{\log Q_3 - \log Q_1}{\log(t_3 + A) - \log(t_1 + A)}$$

(3.14)

$$f'(A) = \frac{(\log Q_1 - \log Q_2)\left[\dfrac{1}{t_2 + A} - \dfrac{1}{t_1 + A}\right]}{[\log(t_2 + A) - \log(t_1 + A)]^2}$$

$$- \frac{(\log Q_1 - \log Q_3)\left[\dfrac{1}{t_3 + A} - \dfrac{1}{t_1 + A}\right]}{[\log(t_3 + A) - \log(t_1 + A)]^2}$$

(3.15)

$$A_{i+1} = A_i - \frac{f'(A)}{f(A)}$$

The above equations require only three data points on the curve. The two end points and the median or central point from the given set of data points give sufficient data to compute the constant A, provided the data are correct and smooth. If the data are not smooth, a best-fit curve is first drawn through the data points. The two end points on the curve (x_1, x_3, and the corresponding y_1 and y_3) and the median point is chosen at $x_2 = (x_1 + x_2)/2$ with the corresponding y_2 read from the curve.

An Excel spreadsheet can be used to perform the above iterative process in order to compute the variable A. The following systematic instructions help in developing the model on Excel as shown in Table 3–3 and Table 3–3.xls on the CD that accompanies Volume 2 in this series.[9]

1. Select three data points from Table 3–2 at $t = 1$, 25, and 49 months and the corresponding production rates as $Q_3 = 28,200$; $Q_2 = 4775$; and $Q_1 = 1905$ Stb/month.

2. Enter the t in Cells B5 to B7 and the corresponding Q_o in Cells C5 to C7.

3. Enter A=0 (initial guess) in Cell A10.

4. Enter the following formula in Cell B10
   = (LOG(C6) - LOG(C7))/(LOG(B6+A10)-LOG(B7+A10))
   -(LOG(C5)- LOG(C7))/(LOG(B5+A10)- LOG(B7+A10))

	A	B	C	D	E	F	G
4	Point	t, month	Q_o		t	Qo	(t + A)
5	3	1	28,200		1	28,200	16.421
6	2	25	4,775		7	15,680	22.421
7	1	49	1,905		13	9,700	28.421
8					19	6,635	34.421
9	Est. A	f(A)	b		25	4,775	40.421
10	15.421	0.0000	0.5072		31	3,628	46.421
11					37	2,850	52.421
12					43	2,300	58.421
13					49	1,905	64.421

Table 3–3 Spreadsheet to calculate hyperbolic exponent b and constant (t+A) for curve shifting

5. To calculate the hyperbolic exponent b, enter the following formula in Cell C10.

    $= -1/((\text{LOG}(C6)-\text{LOG}(C7))/(\text{LOG}(B6+A10)-\text{LOG}(B7+A10)))$

6. In Cells E5 through E13, input the t(s) from Table 3–2 and input the corresponding production rate in Cells F5 through F13. Enter the formula "=E5+A$10" in Cell G5 and then copy it all the way to Cell G13. The data thus calculated has shifted the curve (plot of F5:G13) by the variable A, as shown in Figure 3–3.

7. Now click on **Tools** ⇨ **Solver** in the Excel toolbar menu. In the Solver dropdown menu select the following:
    a. Set Target Cell: B10
    b. By Changing Cells: A10
    c. Equal to: click on **Value of**: 0

8. Now click **OK**, and the solver will perform the iterations. The final value of A will appear in Cell A10 by setting Cell B10 = 0.

Harmonic Decline. Harmonic decline is a special case of hyperbolic decline with hyperbolic exponent $b=1.0$. The rate-time relationship, in this case, can also be straightened out on log–log graph paper after shifting and assumes a slope of 45° (unit slope line). In this specific case, a plot of the inverse of the production rate versus time on a linear scale should also yield a straight line. The following equations are used in the same way as with hyperbolic decline.

(3.16)

$$\Delta N_p = \frac{q_i}{a_i} \ln \frac{q_i}{q_o}$$

(3.17)

$$t = \frac{\left(\dfrac{q_i}{q_o}\right) - 1}{a}$$

(3.18)

$$q_{ot} = \frac{q_i}{1 + a_i t}$$

Low-Permeability (Tight) Gas Reservoirs. The Federal Energy Regulatory Commission (FERC) classifies low-permeability gas reservoirs (tight gas sands) as those reservoirs with an average in-situ permeability to gas of 0.1 md or less. These tight reservoirs must be hydraulically fractured to achieve economical production rates. Massive hydraulic fracturing (MHF) treatments have made it possible to economically produce these reservoirs. The MHF treatments improve production by exposing larger surface areas of these low-permeability formations to flow into the wellbore through the creation of vertical fractures.

Gas production from the tight sands in the early life of the well experiences a sharp initial decline (linear flow characteristics) followed by a long transition (pseudosteady-state) into exponential decline. If the well's production history indicates it has passed the linear flow regime, then the evaluation is relatively simple (i.e., the conventional exponential decline forecast can be applied).

Most of the performance prediction methods discussed in the previous sections do not give good results when applied to tight sand gas production. The use of hyperbolic decline curves, discussed earlier, is not recommended because these curves do not account for the transformation of fracture production into matrix production. Further, most wells show a hyperbolic exponent between 0 and 1, while a majority of the tight sands production shows value of b greater than 1.0. In case of high capacity wells showing longer productive lives, the use of higher exponent (greater than 1.0) makes the forecasted lives even longer and unrealistic. The hyperbolic decline curves, in general, have a tendency to flatten with time, making the forecasts optimistic in the latter part of the life of the well.

There are several techniques for evaluating reserves and predicting future performance of tight sand gas wells. Some techniques yield excellent results but are time consuming or require data that may not be available. The method presented here is easy to use, requires the routinely recorded production data, and yields good results. This author has used this method, and in a majority of the cases, it has provided excellent results. However, exceptions are always there, and engineers are advised to test the method in each particular case and then use it. The best way to check the accuracy is to determine whether the method gives a reasonable match with the actual production used.

Production from these low-permeability fractured reservoirs when plotted on semi-logarithmic graph paper exhibits hyperbolic decline characteristics with hyperbolic exponent greater than 1.0. The same production data when plotted on log–log paper (rate vs. time) generally shows a decline slope of -0.50. Formation damage reduces the early flush production rates but has diminishing effect. So the slope will be less than -0.50 initially and then will approach -0.50 after three to six months. Sometimes, early time slope is greater than -0.50, which indicates the depletion of thin lenses of high permeability near the wellbore. This typical behavior is observed in many low-permeability reservoirs.[10–12]

The following equations can be used to forecast the past production performance of these reservoirs:

(3.19)

$$\log q_g = -\frac{1}{2}\log t + \log C$$

which gives

(3.19a)

$$q_g = \frac{C}{\sqrt{t}}$$

and

(3.20)

$$\frac{1}{q_g} = m\sqrt{t} + C_1$$

Equation (3.19) is used with the production plotted on log–log paper (rate q_g vs. elapsed time t) and a half unit slopeline is drawn through the data points to give intercept C at $t=1$ month. This intercept is then used in Equation (3.19a) to forecast future performance. This method can be used on wells with at least 12 months of production or when sufficient data fall on half unit slope.

The second equation, Equation (3.20), can be used with as little as four months of initial production. The reciprocal production rate $(1/q_g)$ is plotted versus the square root of time $(\sqrt{t})$ on coordinate graph paper. The method of linear regression is usually used to determine the values of C_1 and m. Feeding these values into Equation (3.20) generates production rates at any given time, t.

In most low-permeability gas reservoirs, the linear flow characteristics can last for up to three or four years. When using these methods, the production should be scheduled for up to this period and then switched to an average exponential decline (draw a line tangent to this forecast) to EL. This incorporates the boundary effects into the long-term production. Failing to do this will result in unrealistically long productive life and very high gas recovery. The exponential declines in tight sands are usually in the range of 6% to 10% per year.

An example from a tight sand formation is presented to clarify the use of the technique and the limitations of using it. Remember, if the forecast generated by the given method does not match (say within 5%) with the actual production, do not use it. Always plot the forecast back on the rate-time plot showing the actual production and make sure the forecast is reasonable based on the actual production and experience with the formation.

Example 3-3

Use the technique presented in this section to forecast the future production of a well producing from the Pictured Cliff formation in the San Juan County of New Mexico. The monthly production for the last 20 months is reported in Table 3–4.

Month	Production Mscf	Month	Production Mscf	Month	Production Mscf
1	10,106	8	4,667	15	3,693
2	9,240	9	4,396	16	2,641
3	6,738	10	3,512	17	3,528
4	6,138	11	4,230	18	3,250
5	5,608	12	3,918	19	3,209
6	3,957	13	3,834	20	2,038
7	3,943	14	3,712		

Table 3–4 Production data for Example 3–3

Solution:

    a. Plot the production data of Table 3–4 on log–log graph paper as shown in Figure 3–4.

    b. Draw a half unit slope line through the data points.

    c. Read the value of C at t=1 month as C=14,000.

    d. Forecast the future production rate at 12, 24, 36, and 48 months as follows:

$$Q_{12} = \frac{14,000}{12^{0.50}} = 4,041 \text{ Mscf}$$

$$Q_{24} = \frac{14,000}{24^{0.50}} = 2,858 \text{ Mscf}$$

$$Q_{36} = \frac{14,000}{36^{0.50}} = 2,333 \text{ Mscf}$$

$$Q_{48} = \frac{14,000}{48^{0.50}} = 2,021 \text{ Mscf}$$

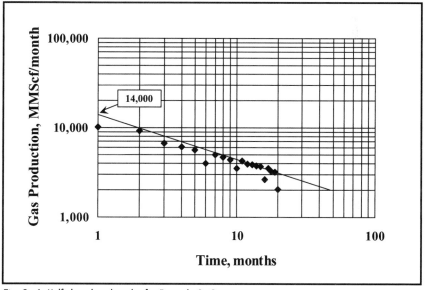

Fig. 3–4 Half slope log–log plot for Example 3–3

Example 3–4

Rework the data in the previous example in order to compare the forecast with the actual production. The actual yearly production from the same well is given in Table 3–5. Plot the actual production and forecast on a rate-time plot. Compute the cumulative production for the first four years (48 months) and compare it with the actual 48 months of production.

Year	Production Mscf	Cumulative Mscf	Year	Production Mscf	Cumulative Mscf
1	67,453	67,453	7	20,947	233,422
2	38,831	106,284	8	21,215	254,637
3	30,744	137,028	9	17,751	272,388
4	28,396	165,424	10	15,633	288,021
5	24,512	189,936	11	15,014	303,035
6	22,539	212,475			

Table 3–5 Production Data for Example 3–4

Solution: The rate-time curve for the actual production and the forecast is shown in Figure 3–5.

$$\text{Cumulative, 4 Years} = 2 \times 14,000(12 \times 4)^{0.50}$$
$$= 193,990 \text{ MScf (Actual} = 165,424 \text{ MScf)}$$

This method usually gives higher cumulative because the first few months of production do not fall on the half-unit slope line while the forecast is accounting for it as it is on the half-unit slope line. However, this method gives a good forecast as shown in Figure 3–5.

Rate-Cumulative Production Plot. The rate–cumulative plots can be used for estimating the ultimate recovery of oil from a well, or a producing lease. These types of plots have an advantage over *rate-time* plots, because any interruptions due to mechanical or other failures or downtime do not affect the plotting coordinates. The evaluation of workovers and remedial treatments tends to be directly evident on these plots, and any change in recovery can be read easily by extrapolating the plotted data. These plots have the following characteristics.

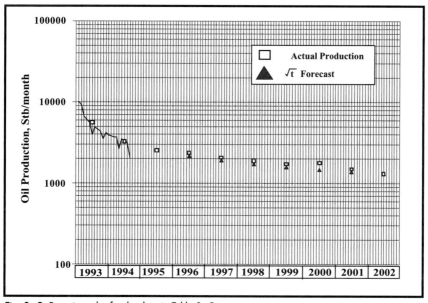

Fig. 3–5 Rate-time plot for the data in Table 3–5

1. The rate–cumulative data forms a straight line on *Cartesian coordinate* graph paper if the rate-time plot of the same data shows a straight line on semi-logarithmic graph paper, i.e., exponential decline with $b = 0$. Theoretically, the slope of the rate–cumulative curve should be the same as the nominal decline rate calculated from the rate-time plot. However, because of the difference in "eyeballing'" the curves and data smoothing, some differences may exist. A typical rate–cumulative plot corresponding to the rate-time plot in Figure 3–1 is shown in Figure 3–6. Note the slope of the rate–cumulative curve is 15%, same as the 15% decline of the rate-time curve. Also the ultimate recovery from the rate–cumulative plot at EL=200 STB/month is 125,000 barrels versus 125,527 barrels from the rate-time curve.

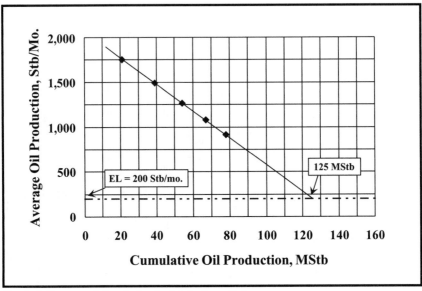

Fig. 3–6 Rate–cumulative plot for the data in Figure 3–1

2. The rate–cumulative data forms a straight line when plotted on *semi-logarithmic* graph paper (with rate plotted on log scale) if the rate-time plot of the same data shows a harmonic decline with $b = 1.0$.

3. If the rate-time plot of the data exhibit hyperbolic decline with $0 < b < 1.0$, then the rate–cumulative data forms a straight line after being shifted (in the X direction) on a log–log graph paper, i.e., to plot *log q* versus $\log(A - N_p)$. The value of A can be found by trial-and-error, using different values until one is found that gives a straight line plot on log–log graph paper with a *slope* = $[1/(1 - b)]$. Also for a hyperbolically declining production, the rate–cumulative plot is a straight line as a special graph paper with the rate scale marked off so it is linear in q^{-b} and the cumulative scale is linear.

Cumulative Gas (G_p)—Cumulative Oil (N_p) Plot. The projection of associated gas in oil production or condensate in gas production is not as straightforward as the projection of the primary product. There are several methods of projecting associated gas production from solution gas drive reservoirs. The material balance techniques (Tarner, Tracy, etc.,) can be used to predict gas–oil ratio versus cumulative oil production. However, these methods require produced fluid's properties and relative permeability data that are often not available.

Another frequently used method of projecting associated gas is to assume constant GOR throughout the productive economic life of the property. This assumption is correct as long as the reservoir is producing at above the bubble-point pressure. However, the GOR increases dramatically as the reservoir pressure drops below the bubble point. In this case, a pessimistic gas rate is predicted. On the other hand, near abandonment, the GOR trends downward so a constant GOR assumption at this stage may be too optimistic.

A log–log plot of cumulative gas production (G_p) versus the corresponding cumulative oil production (N_p) is most often utilized to project the associated gas production. On this plot, G_p and N_p plot as a straight line as shown in Figure 3–7, with unit slope until the reservoir pressure is above the bubble-point pressure. Below the bubble-point pressure, the GOR increases and the slope on log–log plot increases as shown in Figure 3–7.

Another plot of G_p versus N_p, which according to this author's experience is a better forecasting tool, is to plot log of G_p versus N_p (on semi-logarithmic graph paper) as shown in Figure 3–8. On this plot, the data plots as a straight

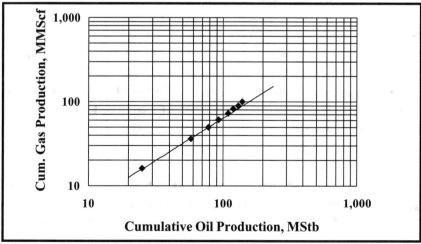

Fig. 3–7 Cumulative gas (G_p) versus cumulative oil (N_p) plot

line after shifting it by a constant A, $(G_p + A)$ in the direction of y-axis. Knowing the cumulative oil production at a particular point in time, its associated cumulative gas production can be projected using this plot.

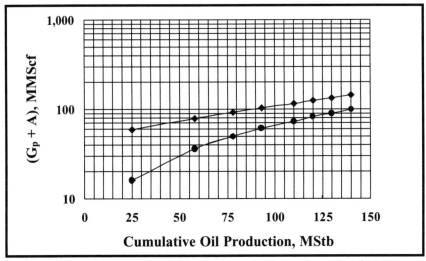

Fig. 3-8 Semi-logarithmic plot of cumulative gas production versus cumulative oil production.

Water Cut Versus Cumulative Oil Plot. This plot is most often used in water-drive reservoirs and reservoirs producing under waterflood. However, its use is not limited only to these two types. The method can be applied to any reservoir showing increasing water production. In the case of water-drive or waterflood, the oil production is consistent and maintains a shallow decline while the water production increases relatively faster.

Since the disposal of produced water costs money, the variable monthly operating expenses increase, hence raising the EL, which in turn limits the oil production. The wells showing increasing water production, if forecasted with the regular rate-time curves or rate–cumulative curves without accounting for water production and the associated cost, may not provide realistic results.

To determine the ultimate oil recovery, the water cut that is the percentage of water produced per total fluid produced [$q_w/(q_o + q_w)$], is plotted versus N_p on semi-logarithmic graph paper. The plot usually provides a straight line or shows some relationship between the two variables. After the trend is defined, the cumulative oil production limit is obtained from the trend at about 98% water cut.

But arbitrarily choosing the 98% water cut may not always provide a true EL of cumulative oil production. At this percentage, one does not know the EL. Therefore, it is suggested to use a companion plot of total fluid versus water cut, plotted on semi-logarithmic graph paper. This plot gives an idea of the specific ratio of water and oil at certain water cut. Now it can be determined if the percentage of oil in the total fluid is above or below the EL. These curves may also be used to forecast the water production and hence the associated variable cost.

A water cut–cumulative oil production plot and a water cut–total fluid production plot for a well producing from Mission Canyon formation in North Dakota are shown in Figures 3–9 and 3–10, respectively. The cumulative oil production at 98% water cut is read from Figure 3–9 as 47,250 barrels. At 98% water cut, the total monthly fluid production is read from Figure 3–10 as 3610.6 barrels/month. This gives oil production of approximately 72 barrels [3,610.6 x (1 - 0.98)], which meets the requirement of the estimated EL.

If the EL was more than 72 barrels/month, then one would have to determine the cumulative at a percentage lower than 98%, and so on. In fact, one would first determine the water cut percentage giving the forecasted EL and then determine the ultimate oil recovery at this percentage.

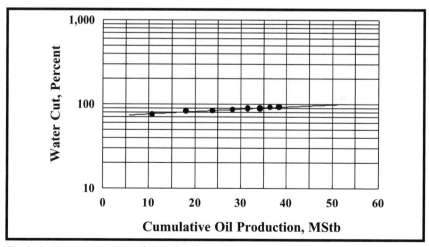

Fig. 3–9 Water cut versus cumulative oil production plot

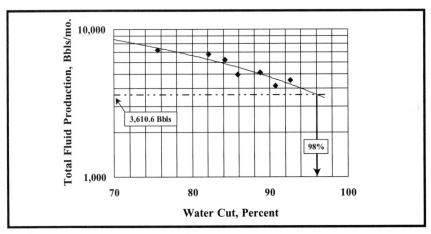

Fig. 3–10 Water cut versus total fluid production plot for the data in Figure 3–9

Gas Reservoir Material Balance

The gas material balance calculations are relatively simple as compared to oil material balance and therefore, they are used routinely. The relative simplicity is because unlike saturated crude oil and condensate, natural gas does not undergo phase changes upon reduction in reservoir pressure (i.e., below bubble point, at bubble point, and above bubble-point pressure).

The gas material balance is of interest especially in situations when gas production is severely curtailed due to market demand. The production performance (rate-time performance) in this case cannot be relied upon for calculating gas reserves. Using material balance, gas in place and reserves may be estimated from pressure performance history. The gas material balance calculations are based on the following assumptions:

1. No large pressure gradients exist across the reservoir at any given time (i.e., pressure equilibrium exists throughout the reservoir).

2. Reliable production, injection, and periodic reservoir pressure measurements are available.

3. Laboratory PVT data apply to the reservoir gas at the average pressure used.

4. The change in volume of interstitial water and the change in porosity with pressure are negligible.

In practice, the most common way for performing gas material balance calculations is to plot (p/z) versus G_p on Cartesian coordinate graph paper (i.e., p/z on y-axis and G_p on x-axis. Where p is the periodic measurement of reservoir pressure, z is the corresponding gas deviation factor, and G_p is the corresponding cumulative gas production. Theoretically, the plot should be a straight line. A best-fit line drawn through the points and extended to the $p/z=0$ gives gas-in-place. The ultimate recovery can also be read from the curve at (p_a/z_a), i.e., the reservoir pressure at abandonment and its corresponding z-factor.

(3.21)

$$\frac{p}{z} = a + b(G_p)$$

where

$$a = \frac{p_i V_i T_{sc}}{z_i p_{sc} T_R}$$

and

$$b = \frac{V_i T_{sc}}{p_{sc} T_R}$$

In Equation (3.21), p/z is the dependent variable, Gp is the cumulative at p_i/z_i, and a and b are the coefficients of the equation, corresponding to the intercept and slope, respectively. The coefficients a and b may be found by using the method of *least squares (regression)*. The following equations are utilized.

(3.22)

$$b = \frac{n\sum_{i=1}^{n}(p/z)_i(G_p)_i - \sum_{i=1}^{n}(p/z)_i\sum_{i=1}^{n}(G_p)_i}{n\sum_{i=1}^{n}(G_p)_i^2 - \left[\sum_{i=1}^{n}G_p\right]^2}$$

(3.23)

$$a = \overline{p/z} - b\overline{G_p}$$

$$G_p = \frac{a}{-b}$$ (3.24)

Recoverable Gas at $p_x / z_x = \dfrac{a - p_x / z_x}{-b}$ (3.24a)

where

n = the number of p/z vs. G_p pairs

$\overline{p/z}$ = average p/z value, $(\Sigma\ p/z)/n$

$\overline{G_p}$ = average G_p value, $(\Sigma G_p)/n$

In addition, a plot of $G_p B_g$ versus $B_g - B_{gi}$ on a Cartesian coordinate graph paper should result in a straight line going through the origin, with G being the slope of this straight line.

Example 3–5

Following is the gas well test information on a Morrow formation gas well in Clark County, Kansas. Compute (a) the OGIP, (b) the recoverable gas (G_{ul}) at an abandonment p_a=200 psi, and (c) the remaining gas reserves at p/z=800. Other pertinent reservoir gas PVT data are given below.

T_{pc} = 370.88° R P_{pc} = 671.24 psi
γ_g = 0.64 (air=1.0) T_R = 123° F

Date	p_{ts}, psi	G_p, MMscf
01/01/85	1,422	166.406
01/01/86	1,208	293.967
01/01/87	980	406.317
01/01/88	847	490.43

Solution: The following steps are required:

1. Convert wellhead shut-in pressure to bottomhole shut-in pressure.

2. Determine gas deviation factor z at each bottomhole shut-in pressure.

3. Compute p/z value for each pressure.

4. Plot p/z versus G_p.

The calculations are tabulated in Table 3–6 and plotted in Figure 3–11. The p_i/z_i from Figure 3–11 is approximately equal to 2460. The OGIP G is also calculated individually at each pressure and presented in Table 3–6. The calculated Gs are in good agreement.

a. The OGIP at $p/z=0$ in Figure 3–11, $G \approx 881$ MMscf.

b. To find recoverable gas at $p_a=200$ psi, first find z at 200 psi.

$$p_{pr} = \frac{p_a}{p_{pc}} = \frac{200}{671.24} = 0.298 \text{ psi}$$

$$T_{pr} = \frac{T_R + 460}{T_{pc}} = \frac{123 + 460}{370.88} = 1.572° R$$

Therefore,

$$z = 0.975 \text{ and } p_a/z_a = 205.13$$

G_p @ $p_a = 200$ psi ≈ 807 MMscf (From Figure 3–11)

G_p @ $p/z = 800 \approx 600$ MMscf (From Figure 3–11)

G_{ul} @ $p/z = 800 = G_{p205} - G_{p800}$

$= 807 - 600 = 207$ MMscf

Date	p_{ts} (psi)	p_{ws} (psi)	z	p/z	G_p (MMscf)	$G_p \times p_i/z_i$ $p_i/z_i - p/z$
01/01/85	1,422	1,661	0.8287	2,004	166.406	897.717
01/01/86	1,208	1,406	0.8456	1,663	293.967	907.351
01/01/87	980	1,135	0.8687	1,307	406.317	866.904
01/01/88	847	978	0.8841	1,106	490.430	891.032

Table 3–6 p/z Data for Example 3–5

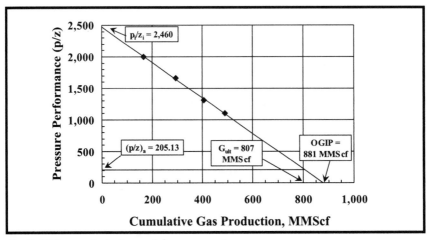

Fig. 3–11 Pressure-Production graph for gas reservoir

Example 3–6

Rework the data in Example 3–5 to calculate OGIP and recoverable gas at *p/z*=800, using regression analysis.

Solution: The data for regression analysis are tabulated in Table 3–7.

Using Equation (3.22)

$$b = \frac{4(1,895,816.644) - (6,080)(1,357.120)}{4(519,722.644) - (1,357.120)^2} = -2.817$$

$$\overline{p/z} = \frac{6,080}{4} = 1,520$$

$$\overline{G_p} = \frac{1,357.120}{4} = 339.280$$

Using Equation (3.23)

$$a = 1,520 - (-2.817)(339.280)$$
$$= 2,475.752$$

Using Equation (3.24)

$$G = \frac{2,475.752}{-(-2.817)} \cong 879 \text{ MMscf}$$

$$G_p \text{ @ } p/z = 800 = \frac{2,475.752 - 800}{-(-2.817)} \cong 595 \text{ MMscf}$$

p/z	G_p, MMscf	(p/z)(G_p)	$(G_p)^2$
2,004	166.406	333,477.624	27,690.957
1,663	293.967	488,867.121	86,416.597
1,307	406.317	531,056.319	165,093.505
1,106	490.430	542,415.580	240,521.585
6,080	1,357.120	1,895,816.644	519,722.644

Table 3–7 Regression analysis of *p/z* data

Production Forecast by Analogy

This is a useful way of determining reserves and the associated production forecast, specifically for the fields/wells with insufficient information. The method is widely used on new wells drilled in a developed field and/or exploratory wells (wildcats). The analogy used for wells drilled in a developed field is expected to constitute the reservoir characteristics in the wells producing in the adjacent sections. For wildcats, the analogy can be used from other fields producing from the same type of expected hydrocarbon accumulations. The closer the analogous properties are to the properties to be evaluated, the better and more reliable the estimates will be.

Analogous information can be used to determine average recovery factor, ultimate oil and/or gas reserves, and the most likely production behavior. The data used are the production, completion reports, well logs, fluid properties, structure maps, isopach maps, and isovolume maps. The more information is available, the better the analogy will be.

The recovery factor is determined by determining reserves using the performance prediction methods, and these reserves are then compared with volumetric calculations. The ultimate oil and/or gas recovery is estimated from the average performance trends of the analogous reservoirs. In new wells, a major problem is finding out how they will perform. This is important because it assists in forecasting the pattern of revenue generation. The forecast is based on the average performance of the wells producing from the same type of reservoirs.

Note that analogy must be from the same type of reservoirs with approximately the same geological age, reservoir drive mechanism, and petrophysical properties. For example, one should not apply the properties of J-Sand gas wells in Colorado to the Austin Chalk wells in Texas and vice versa. The following example clarifies the use of production forecasting by analogy.

Example 3–7

In Figure 3–12, there is an acreage plat with four producing wells in Section 11, 13, and 23. All four wells are producing from the Pictured Cliff formation in San Juan County, New Mexico. A company proposes to drill another infill well in Section 14 as shown on the plat. What reserves and production behavior would be expected if the well is successfully drilled into the same formation? The yearly production data of the four producing wells is given in Table 3–8.

The average production per well per month is then plotted on the rate-time plot as shown in Figure 3–13. The cumulative for the seven years of production is an average of 261,608 Mscf/well. The initial rate is 1900 Mscf/month and the expected EL is 800 Mscf/month. The production is forecasted to decline exponentially at 10% per year.

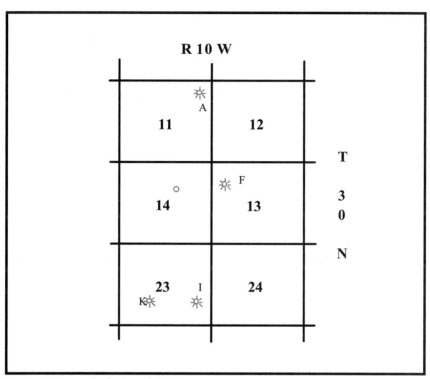

Fig. 3–12 Acreage plat for Example 3–7

Year	Sec. 11A	Sec. 13F	Sec. 23K	Sec. 23I	Average
1	48,612	54,678	73,236	111,992	72,130
2	30,365	27,487	44,601	65,050	41,876
3	26,420	23,987	36,847	55,711	35,741
4	21,889	20,783	34,973	51,513	32,290
5	21,639	19,908	30,798	46,378	29,681
6	23,158	16,795	28,550	41,901	27,601
7	9,451	15,238	26,435	38,030	22,289

Table 3–8 Production (Mscf) data for example 3–7

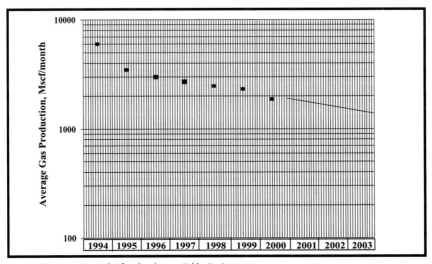

Fig. 3–13 Rate–Time plot for the data in Table 3–8

$$\text{Remaining Reserves} = \frac{(1,900 - 800) \times 12}{-\ln(1 - 0.10)}$$

$$= \frac{13,200}{0.10536} = 125,284 \ \text{MScf}$$

$$\text{Ultimate Recovery} = 261,608 + 125,284$$

$$= 386,892 \ \text{Mscf}$$

The undeveloped location therefore, will be assigned an ultimate gas recovery of 386,892 Mscf and the forecast as presented in Figure 3–13, with an expected initial rate of 10,000 Mscf/month.

In reality, some companies may assign some risk factor to the undeveloped reserves. The above analysis could have been further refined if isopach and isovolume maps are available. Since the isovolume map shows the $h\phi(1 - S_w)$ of each well, it can be used to determine the approximate value of volumetric reserves for the undeveloped location. In practice, the engineers/geologists prorate the reserves according to this value and any other known parameters from the analogous wells. For example, if an analogous well has $h\phi(1 - S_w)$=50 and its reserves are estimated at 500 MMscf, then the well to be drilled at $h\phi(1 - S_w)$=25 contour will be assigned 250 MMscf. Doing this is valid only if such correlation has been demonstrated by other producing wells. Averaging always works well or some definite valid correlation may be looked at. Remember, $h\emptyset(1 - S_w)$ is not the only parameter controlling the recoverable reserves.

If there is a wide variation in the reserves of the analogous properties, then the simple averaging of reserves or production forecast will not be valid (i.e., it will give higher mean). In this case, the median (not the mean) of the reserves or production forecast should be determined. Alternatively, the concepts of risk analysis presented in Volume 2 of this series can be used to arrive at expected reserves and production forecast.

PRODUCT PRICING

Prices of crude oil in international trade are universally quoted in U.S. dollars per API barrel of 42 U.S. gallons at 60° F and atmospheric pressure, i.e., STB. Crude oils differ in quality. Consequently, the products extracted and manufactured from crude oil also differ significantly from one crude to another.

Crude oils from different sources are categorized primarily according to their API gravity and then the sulfur content (percent by weight) in the crude. The API gravity of crude oils varies from 5° to 55°. Average crude oils have a 25° to 35° range. Light oils are 35° to 45° and heavy oils are below 25°. The price of crude oil is dependent on these two factors at any particular market conditions. The lighter crudes (higher API gravity) receive a higher price as compared to the heavier crude (lower API gravity). This is because the lighter crudes tend to have more gasoline by volume than the heavier crudes while the heavier crudes have proportionately more gas–oil (diesel) and residue cracking stock.

In addition to the refining yield of the crude, its sulfur content is an important factor in reducing its value. Sulfur content tells the refiner the amount of basic impurity in the crude oil. Even though the API gravity figure might be attractively high, this might reflect high sulfur content. The sulfur content for most crude oils falls between 1% and 2.5%, where 1% sulfur content is considered *sweet* crude and 2.5% sulfur content is considered *sour* crude. Besides discounting the price due to sulfur, some refiners would simply not purchase sour crude (high sulfur content) at any price because they may not be equipped to process such crude.

For example, a benchmark price is applied to crudes with gravity between 40 and 45 °API, having sulfur content of 0.5% or less. A typical quality deduction by a refiner is then $0.15 per °API for crudes between 30 and 40 °API gravity. For crudes below 30 °API, the deduction is $3.0 plus $0.10 per °API less than 30 °API. For crudes with gravity greater than 45 °API, the price is reduced by $0.075 per °API. The sulfur deduction is $0.05 per 0.1% sulfur over 0.5% sulfur, with no sulfur penalty for crudes of less than 30 °API.

The amount of entrained water is an additional factor for discounting the price. The salt-water contamination is generally expressed in pounds of salt per barrel. All of these factors impact on the actual price the refiner is willing to pay for each barrel of crude oil, regardless of where in the world it is produced.

There is no single benchmark-pricing source for crude oil. The high volume of trading in crude oils has resulted in the following major price references/benchmarks. All the trading in the world is done in reference to these price references (i.e., adjusted for quality from one of these several marker crudes).

1. *West Texas Intermediate (WTI):* based on 38 to 40 °API and 0.3% sulfur. West Texas sour, a secondary benchmark, has 33 °API and 1.6% sulfur. All the crudes produced in the United States are traded in reference to these benchmarks.

2. *Saudi Arabian (Arab light):* based on 33.4 °API and 1.8% sulfur.

3. *Brent crude from the North Sea:* based on 38.3 °API while Ekofisk crude is based on 42.8 °API.

4. *Dubai Fateh field's crude.*

5. *Urals-Mediterranean* for the Russian production entering the western markets.

6. *Singapore* quotations are also increasingly employed as a reference for crude oil pricing in the Far East.

WTI in the United States, Dubai's Fateh crude from the Persian Gulf, and the highly important Brent from the United Kingdom have become the principal marker, or reference, crudes. Their prices are considered the most indicative of the world's market conditions. Since WTI is traded on the New York Mercantile Exchange (NYMEX), it has gained higher visibility resulting in its becoming the industry's principal reference crude.

According to the current practice of crude oil pricing in the international market, constant price differentials are maintained between the different marker (reference) crudes. For example, the Brent crude may be quoted as $0.95 – $1.00 below WTI. Similarly, Dubai has traditionally been quoted as $2.10 – $2.05 under Brent. The Brent market is mainly determined by the WTI prices on the NYMEX, and the prices of Dubai crude are also indirectly determined from the daily closing prices for WTI.

Historical FOB crude oil spot selling prices of various crudes are shown in Figure 3–14 for reference.

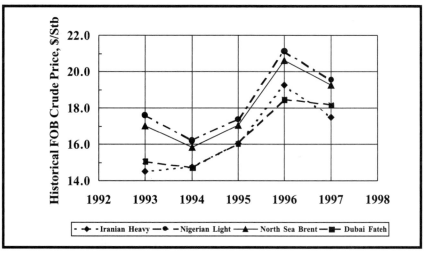

Fig. 3–14 Historical FOB crude oil spot selling prices of various crudes

Oil prices are influenced by many other independent factors. These include items such as conservation incentives/practices, the overall state of the global economy (recession versus growth), exploration efforts and the success of exploration activities, production in non-OPEC countries, political stability of OPEC members, alternate fuels, and so on. The crude oil price volatility will exist for as long as there is excess oil production capacity available in the world (i.e., supply is more than the demand).

There is a strong likelihood crude oil prices will remain weak, despite strong growth in oil demand. The basic reason for this is the shear volume of additional oil supplies likely to be available from the non-OPEC and

OPEC countries alike. This author forecasts the crude oil prices to remain in the range of $18/barrel to $30/barrel for another decade. The $30/barrel level is possible only if the crude oil supply by the OPEC members is curtailed.

Therefore, at present the uncertainties of crude oil price forecasting are so high, it is imprudent to base one's cash-flow projections on a single price scenario. Sensitivity analyses have to be conducted at a range of pricing scenarios. Use of decision analysis techniques to account for the crude oil price volatility will be discussed later in this book.

The price of natural gas is based on $ per million BTU, one million BTUs are taken as 1000 Scf (1 Mscf) of 1000 BTU gas. If the price of a certain gas is $2/MMBTU and the gas is 1200 BTU, then the price translates into $2 x 1.2 = $2.4 per Mscf. Refined product prices for a specific location are developed in relation to projected prices for these products in the major price-setting markets, which are the United States, Western Europe (Rotterdam), and Asia (Singapore). Refined product prices for these primary locations are developed based on each market's expected crude and product slate, operating costs, and profit margins for typical refinery configurations.

CAPITAL EXPENDITURES (CAPEX)

The main characteristic of CAPEX is they are one-off costs, usually incurred at the beginning of a project (also referred to as front-end costs). These usually large expenditures must be incurred, often several years before any revenue is obtained. CAPEX typically consists of G&G costs; drilling costs; tankers; offshore platform construction and installation, process facilities; wellheads, flowlines and trunk lines to transport oil and gas; supply bases; camps and accommodation; storage tanks or vessels; etc. The capital costs may also occur during the economic life of a project, for example:

- Recompletion of wells into another formation.
- Sidetracking an existing well with a horizontal well.
- Installing artificial lift facilities if the wells were initially on natural flow.

- Major upgrading/replacement of existing facilities.
- Installing facilities for secondary recovery (waterflood or gas injection) or enhanced oil recovery (EOR), etc.

Geological and Geophysical (G&G) Costs

G&G costs are pre-drilling exploration costs. These costs include topographical, geological, and geophysical studies. The geophysical costs include rights of access to properties, acquisition of seismic lines (seismic surveys), processing of seismic surveys, and interpretation of these surveys. These costs may incur either before or after acquisition of working interest in the property (lease). G&G costs are considered inherently capital in nature and must be added to costs of property acquired or retained. *For tax purposes, these costs are expensed in the year the costs incurred.*

Seismic acquisition, in most cases, is done by outside contractors who specialize in providing this service to the industry. The company's geophysical staff can either do the processing and interpretation of the acquired data in-house or it may be contracted out to the same contractor who has acquired the data.

The cost estimate is made based on the type of acquisition (i.e., onshore versus offshore, 2D seismic versus 3D seismic surveys, and many other parameters involved in acquisition and processing of data). The best way to arrive at a cost estimate is to either (1) approach various contractors for quotation, or (2) compare your current requirements with some of the analogous surveys conducted in the past. Remember, the costs of seismic acquisition, processing, and interpretation depend on supply and demand for these services in the industry. Therefore, obtaining fresh quotations from contractors are recommended.

Estimating Drilling Costs

Preparation of drilling cost estimates may require as much engineering work as the actual well design. The cost estimate is heavily dependent on the technical aspects of the well to be drilled. Therefore, these aspects have to be first established. These aspects include the following:

1. *The type of wells to be drilled* (i.e., exploration, appraisal, delineation, or development wells). Exploration and appraisal wells generally cost more because of extensive testing and coring, etc. In addition, since exploration wells are drilled in wildcat or rank wildcat areas, optimization of drilling parameters is difficult.

2. *The configuration of wells to be drilled* (i.e., vertical, deviated, horizontal, multilateral, new well or sidetrack, water disposal well or injection well).

3. *The type of drilling contract to be used and the rig type.* Rig cost constitutes a major percentage of the total drilling cost. The onshore rig costs range from $10,000 to $15,000 per day while the offshore rig costs range from $25,000 to $100,000 per day. The rig costs in a particular area depends on the supply and demand of the rigs available, i.e., local drilling activity.

4. *The depth of the well and the complexity of the formations the well is drilled through.* For example, the cost of drilling increases in high pressured, sloughing shale, unconsolidated formations and formations with thief zones etc.

5. *The casing scheme to be used and the type of casing required.*

6. The drilling muds rheology and the type of bits to be used.

7. Testing and coring requirements.

8. Completion equipment; etc.

Once the technical aspects are established, the expected time required to drill the well is determined. The actual well cost is then obtained by integrating the anticipated drilling and completion times with the well design.

As is obvious from the daily rig costs given above, the time required to drill a well has a significant impact on many items in the well-cost estimate. These items may include the following:

- Type of drilling contract
- Drilling rig
- Drilling fluid
- Offshore transportation (helicopter and marine)
- Rental tools
- Time dependent support services

The drilling time can be estimated based on the data available on analogous wells in the same or similar area. Numerous sources are available to enable estimating drilling time of a well. These include bit records, mud records, and operator's well histories on offset or analogous wells. The following several factors affect the amount of time spent in drilling a well. Each factor may vary with drilling geology, geographical location, and operator philosophy and efficiency.

- *Drilling rate:* dependent on rock type, bit selection, mud type and properties, weight on bit, and rotary speeds.
- *Trip time:* dependent on well depth, amount of mud trip margin, hole problems, rig capacity, and crew efficiency. As a rule of thumb, trip time is estimated as 1 hr/1000 ft of well depth.
- *Hole problems:* hole sloughing, lost circulation, and slower drilling rates are considered as standard hole problems
- *Running casing:* dependent on casing size, depth of well, hole conditions, efficiency of crew, and use of special equipment
- *Logging, coring, and pressure (DST, drawdown or buildup) surveys*
- *Directional/Horizontal drilling:* directional control of a well requires increases in the drilling time
- *Well completion:* dependent on the complexity of well completion (i.e., single completion, dual completion, commingled completion, gravel pack, acidizing, fracturing, and other forms of well treatments). The use of completion rig versus drilling rig, for completion operations, should be considered where technically and economically feasible. A completion rig is a smaller workover rig that costs significantly less than a large drilling rig.

The well-cost estimate is usually divided into several cost categories for engineering and accounting purposes (i.e., dry hole versus completed well costs and tangible versus intangible costs). General summaries of typical well costs are given in *Authority for Expenditure (AFE)* as shown in Table 3–9.

Facility Costs

A typical lease service installation (onshore) is shown in Figure 3–15. Many different elements of surface facilities are required to produce crude oil and/or gas. Some of these facilities are required from day one of the production; others may be required later during the economic life of a well. For example, the free-water-knockout tanks may not be required in

ITEMS AND DESCRIPTION	Quantity	Unit Price	Total Cost	
			Dry Hole	Producer
INTANGIBLE DRILLING COST				
Labor, Company, and Contract			x	
Fuel, Water, Power, and Lubricants			x	
Hauling			x	
Permit, Survey, etc.			x	
Roads, Location, and Contract			x	
Contract Drilling			x	
Day Work			x	
Drilling Bits			x	
Compressor and Tool Rentals			x	
Pulling Unit or Cable Tools			x	
Mud and Chemicals			x	
Mud Logger			x	
Cement and Cementing			x	
Coring			x	
Well Surveys (Deviation)			x	
Well Surveys (Logging)			x	
Drill Stem Test			x	
Perforating			x	
Acidizing, Fracturing, and Gravel Pack			x	
Supplies and Miscellaneous			x	
TOTAL INTANGIBLE DRILLING COSTS				
TANGIBLE DRILLING COSTS				
Casing (Conductor)			x	
Casing (Surface)			x	
Casing (Intermediate)			x	
Casing (Production)				x
Tubing				x
Packer (s)				x
Rods, Sucker				x
Pumping Unit				x
Electric Motor				x
Engine				x
Subsurface Pump				x
Christmas Tree				x
Miscellaneous Completion Equipment				x
TOTAL TANGIBLE DRILLING COSTS				
LEASE EQUIPMENT AND INSTALLATION				
Tanks, Storage				x
Treater				x
Heater				x
Meter Run				x
Separator				x
Line Pipe				x
Miscellaneous Connections				x
Trucking and Labour				x
TOTAL LEASE EQUIPMENT, ETC.				
TOTAL AFE COST				

Well Name: ___ Date: ___
County/State: ___ AFE No.: ___
Location: ___ Operator: ___

Table 3–9 Authority for Expenditure (AFE)

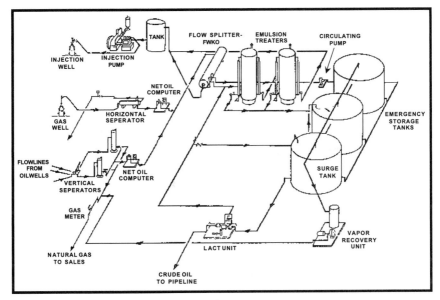

Fig. 3-15 A typical lease service installation (onshore).

the beginning. Similarly, artificial lift facilities (sucker rod pumping unit, electrical submersible pumps, or hydraulic pumps, etc.) may not be required from the beginning.

The facilities requirement in offshore fields is even complex and expensive. The offshore production facilities require (1) various platforms (process, flare, utilities, etc.), (2) wellhead jackets with topsides and flowlines, and (3) crude oil and/or gas lines from offshore production stations to the storage facilities onshore, etc. Facilities such as heat exchangers, compressors, desalination units, sea water pumps, power generation units, etc. are required on offshore platforms.

The facilities have to be planned and designed in such a way that benefit is achieved due to economies of scale. For example, installation of nine single-slot wellhead jackets with flowlines to drill nine wells in a field may cost $12 million. In this case, the possibility of drilling the nine wells from three three-slot wellhead jackets shall be looked at because installing these jackets with flowlines will cost $7 million. This option, if technically feasible, will save $5 million due to economies of scale. However, since longer reach wells have to be drilled from each of these three jackets, the incremental drilling cost may increase. The net benefit should therefore be considered. The same applies to compressors, separation facilities, and flowlines, etc. Therefore, it is necessary for a long-term assessment of the requirements rather than a short-term assessment.

Using the power law and sizing model can often accomplish equipment cost estimating. The power law model requires that the equipment must be similar in type and vary only in size. The economies of scale are in terms of size expressed in the relationship, which is given as:

(3.25)

$$C_c = \left(\frac{Q_c}{Q_r}\right)^m$$

where
C_c = cost of design size Q_c
C_r = known cost of reference size Q_r
Q_c = design size
Q_r = reference design size
m = correlation exponent, $0 < m < 1$

If $m = 1$, a linear relationship exists and the economies of scale do not apply. For most equipment, m is approximately 0.5, and for chemical processing equipment it is approximately 0.6. The determination of correct exponent is essential to the estimation process.

OPERATING EXPENDITURE (OPEX)

The main characteristic of OPEX, also referred to as lease operating expenditure (LOE), is they occur periodically and are necessary for the day-to-day operations of the field. In cash-flow analysis, operating costs are usually expressed in terms of expenditure per year or expenditure per barrel or per MScf. The operating costs typically consist of five elements (1) fixed cost, (2) variable cost per unit of production (determined as a function of production rate), (3) maintenance of facilities, (4) maintenance (workover) of wells, and (5) overheads. The breakdown of various cost categories is as follows:

1. *Feedstocks:* In economic analysis, required feedstocks have to be costed at their fair market value. In the absence of a fair market value, costs should fairly reflect the economic cost of manpower, materials, capital, and the values of co-product credits should be used. For downstream project evaluations, intermediate products are transferred from upstream to downstream plants at the cash cost of production. The value of this transfer cost has no effect on the net cash flow for an integrated complex (i.e., internal transfer revenue for one plant is a production cost for another). Using cash cost as a basis of transfer is, however, convenient for the calculation of inventory values.

2. *Utilities:* Utilities are estimated, based on the economic cost of energy (gas and electricity), manpower, materials, and capital.

3. *Maintenance:* Maintenance comprises material costs and manpower (skilled and unskilled) costs. These costs are associated with keeping the oilfield equipment in good working order. The total maintenance costs are related to the cost of the equipment to be maintained. The maintenance costs can be subdivided into
   a. Inspection costs
   b. Preventative maintenance costs (i.e., lubricants, periodic replacement of small parts, painting, and minor repairs)
   c. Remedial costs (i.e., replacement and major parts)

4. *Administrative and General Overhead:* General overhead comprises (a) labor (administration, laboratory, stores, medical, security, etc.), (b) materials and supplies (electricity, stationary, food, lodging, miscellaneous consumables, etc.), and (c) services (communications, insurance, travel, training, etc.). The corporate overheads cover company costs not related directly to the production site. These include corporate R&D, financial administration, and head

office and policy functions. Corporate overheads are normally estimated from previous projects at two percent of gross revenue.

Some companies prefer to subdivide the employee benefits category. Items such as employee health plans, life insurance, etc. are separated from the expense providing offices, motor pool, berths aboard ship, offshore catering, and other per employee support costs.

5. *Production Costs:* These costs can be subdivided into
   a. Lifting costs—related to bringing the oil and/or gas to the surface.
   b. Treatment costs of dehydration and oil/gas separation.
   c. Workover costs of well stimulation and downhole repairs.
   d. Secondary recovery costs related to the injection of water, gas, steam, or chemicals, and
   e. Water disposal costs.

6. *Evacuation Costs:* These costs are related to the transport of oil and/or gas from the field to a refinery or gas processing facility, an export terminal or any other point of sale. The costs depend strongly on the throughput, the distance to be covered, and the means of transport. Typical evacuation cost items are
   a. Pump and compressor fuel and losses.
   b. Tanker rentals according to world scale rate, which depends on the voyage and are indexed monthly.
   c. Pipeline tariffs, and
   d. Cost of operating terminals and jetties.

7. *Insurance Costs:* Particularly in the early phases of the lifetime of the field the oilfield equipment is insured. The rates vary from 0.5% to 4% of the replacement cost, in accordance with the vulnerability of the insured unit.

Although the economic effect of the last years of the project is rather small due to the discounting procedure, an overestimate of the late operating expenses will result in an underestimate of the economic lifetime of the project. This underestimated lifetime may have engineering consequences in the design of the oilfield equipment. The percentage of each of the above elements in the total OPEX varies from company to company and location to location. However, the following breakdown should be kept in mind.

- Production Costs—35% of total OPEX
- Evacuation Costs—23% of total OPEX
- Insurance Premium—21% of total OPEX
- Maintenance Costs—17% of total OPEX
- Overhead—4% of total OPEX

Another rule of thumb this author has used in the Middle East is given below. The total OPEX arrived through this combination is then checked with the actual historical unit OPEX in $/barrel.

- 5% of engineering CAPEX
- $1/barrel of oil production for offshore and $0.60/barrel for onshore field
- workover 10% of the wells every year, each workover on the average costs $130,000 for offshore and $22,000 for onshore wells

Both fixed and variable cost items are important to arrive at a realistic projection of operating expenses for a given project. Some of the expenses may be on monthly per barrel or per well basis. Individual well workover maintenance or production stimulation treatments occur less frequently. These are projected on statistical basis over the economic life of the project. For example, it may be assumed that each well will be worked over on the average once every five years. This, however, does not mean expenses are assigned on 5-year intervals (5-year bumps), rather they should be spread on yearly basis throughout the economic life of the wells. The spread may be estimated on the basis that a certain percentage of the total wells may require an annual workover.

Operating cost data generally must be developed from historical records for the project or from analogous operations. Some elements of direct operating expense (onshore and offshore) and allocated operating expense are summarized in Tables 3–10 and 3–11, respectively.

Onshore Operations	Offshore Operations
Pumper wages, benefits	Supply boats, marine
Pumper transportation	Helicopters
Purchased power, fuel, and water	Standby vessels
Field power, fuel, water	Docking charges
Treating chemicals	Shore base expense
Small tools, supplies	Underwater inspectors
Teaming, trucking, heavy equipment	- Platforms and pipelines
Gas gathering, compression	Communications and data transmission
Salt water disposal	Personnel
Roustabout gang wages, benefits	- Process maintenance
Roads, bridges, docks	- Process operators
Flowlines, tank batteries	Warehouse
Wells—pulling, clean-out	Pipeline tariffs
- Tubing and casing repair	Fuel
- Plug back in zone	Equipment standby
- Stimulation zone	- Cementing pumps
- Gas shut-off	- Wireline services
Outside labor and equipment	Food and lodging for personnel
- Service company personnel equipment	
- Service company deliveries	
- Contractor services	
Crop damage	
Pipeline gauging	

Table 3–10 Elements of direct operating expense

Abandonment Costs and Sunk Costs

Abandonment costs are a special category of CAPEX associated with the environmentally safe abandonment of the wells and facilities at the end of the economic life of the project. These costs may constitute a significant

| Office expenses, including rent and utilities |
| Lease supervision wages, benefits |
| Engineering salaries, benefits |
| Clerical, accounting wages, benefits |
| Toolroom, warehouse, shop wages, benefits |
| Motor pool expense, not recovered as direct charge on mileage basis |

Table 3–11 Elements of allocated operating expense

component of cash flow, particularly in offshore operations. Abandonment costs may be as high as the original development costs in real terms.

There are companies who specialize in abandonment of wells and facilities. In some cases, these companies take care of the abandonment in environmentally safe manner, in exchange for the salvage value of the facilities to be abandoned and some additional charge.

Sunk costs are costs incurred before the first period of a cash-flow projection. They are usually historic costs—for instance, previous exploration costs incurred before a development being analyzed gets underway. It is important for prior costs or sunk costs not to appear directly in a projection of future cash flow. Investment decisions are based on future costs and revenues because we can choose whether or not to incur them. We cannot do anything about sunk costs. By definition, they have already been spent and therefore cannot directly affect the future decisions in a financial sense.

For example, consider an oil company deciding whether to drill new oil wells on a lease in 2002. The company conducted a seismic survey on the lease in 1996 at a cost of $10 million, which showed a small oil accumulation. Given the results of this, the firm estimates capital investment of $55 million. This results in net cash flow (after OPEX and taxes) of $10 million each year for the next 10 years. If the firm's cost of capital is 10%, should the company develop the lease? Based on this information, the net present value (NPV) of the lease is $6.45 million (i.e., the investment is profitable), drilling should take place. However, if the cost of the seismic test is taken into consideration, the NPV of this project would be negative of –$3.55 (i.e., the project should be aborted). Since the firm has already spent the $10 million whether it drills or not, this sum represents a sunk cost and the investment decision should be independent of it. In other words, the firm would be better off taking the investment (drilling) since, on an incremental basis, the NPV is positive. Another way of looking at it is that taking the investment will reduce the loss from $10 to $3.55 million.

As discussed in the previous paragraphs, the sunk costs should be ignored when evaluating a subsequent investment opportunity. However, frequently there are tax credits generated by these costs and they should not be ignored. For example, tax deductions due to depreciation, depletion or investment tax credits yet to be accounted for should be included where appropriate. Such credits affect the after-tax economics and may have a significant impact on decision alternatives. For example, the tax credit available on the surrender of a non-producing lease and the write-off of its cost (sunk) may be greater than the value of developing a marginal producing property. Similarly, the depreciation tax benefits due to the seismic sunk costs (presented in the previous paragraph) may actually result in positive after-tax net cash flow.

Opportunity Costs

Opportunity cost is defined as the potential benefit lost or sacrificed when the choice of one course of action requires giving up an alternative course of action. When estimating the cash flow of a proposed capital investment project, the opportunity or alternative costs, and not just the direct outlay costs, must be taken into consideration.

A lease under evaluation, among other things, requires five sucker rod-pumping units at a total installed cost of $125,000. The company already has five idle units in the yard that can be used. Under the circumstances, what should be the cost of the pumps (if any) assigned to the proposed project? Remember in this case, it is a sunk cost. If one adopts the incremental cash-flow principle, it would appear on the surface at least, the cost of pumps should not be charged to the project. However, suppose the company can sell the pumps in the open market for a total price of $75,000. In such a case the opportunity cost of using the pumps, which is $75,000, should be accounted for in the cash flow. In the absence of an alternative use, (i.e., opportunity cost is zero); no cost should be charged to the new project.

Similarly, opportunity cost of using limited services of key personnel may have to be estimated, especially if their involvement in the new project creates a need to hire additional people elsewhere in the company. Despite the difficulties involved, a careful analysis of the opportunity costs of transferring existing assets to the new project must be made to ensure the overall return to the firm as a whole is reflected in the calculations.

TYPES OF COST ESTIMATES

During the life of a project, four types of estimates are typically made. Each type is linked to a certain stage in the development of the project and is based on the available design and planning information at the respective stage. The different types of these estimates, their purpose, and accuracy are discussed in this section.

Order of Magnitude Estimate

This estimate is based on general information. For example, the information available immediately after the discovery well is drilled. The design base, on which the cost-engineering study is then based, could for example cover the following data:

- Location
- Prevailing weather conditions
- Water depth in case of offshore discovery
- Terrain conditions in case of onshore discovery
- Distance to export terminal or refinery
- Recoverable reserves estimate
- Well potential, number and type of wells required
- Most probable reservoir mechanism
- Crude oil or gas properties (gravity, gas–oil ratio, sulfur or H_2 content, etc.)

For this type of estimate, analysts use known costs from existing similar projects and apply the appropriate scaling rules to downsize or upsize the facilities as required by the project on hand. These include the following:

- Drilling and completion
- Flowlines and trunklines
- Facilities for separation, compression, gas treatment, water injection, etc.
- Platform structure(s) in case of offshore development
- Storage facilities
- Evacuation system (pipeline, tanker, rail, jetty, trucking, etc.)

The *order of magnitude* estimate can be generated in a short time period with the resulting accuracy in the range of 25%–40%. These estimates are used for the earliest economic appraisals and ranking of prospects/alternatives. A promising subsequent economic analysis may result in an appraisal campaign.

Because of the appraisal campaign, well production data and detailed maps are made available. Based on this information, specialists are able to decide on the most likely production mechanism; this results in one or more production scenarios. These plans with detailed information allow the engineers to create a *conceptual* development plan(s). These development plans are then used for the *optimization study estimates*, one for each of the alternatives put forward by the engineers.

Optimization Study Estimate

The costing method used to generate these estimates mostly depends on scaling rules. However, this time they are applied to individual parts (as these are now better defined) of the various development units mentioned in the preceding paragraph. The costing study is far more detailed than in the order of magnitude case. It therefore takes more time with the resulting accuracy in the range of 15%–25%.

The results of this *optimization study* estimates are used in the economic analysis in order to select the most economically attractive development option. If that is not possible, another appraisal campaign may be necessary and the process is repeated.

Budget Estimate

Once the development plan has been selected and approved by the management of the company, the *design base* is considered *frozen*. This decision has important consequences for the engineering department. A team of engineers create the *basis of design (BOD)*, using preliminary surveys, process and instrument diagrams, and weight breakdowns, etc. System and equipment specifications are agreed on, and vendors and contractors are invited to bid on the required specifications. By freezing the BOD and the timing of the project, the largest potential for uncertainty is removed.

At this stage, the material and manpower requirements become clear; and the resulting *budget estimate* is based on the price of equipment, steel, man-hour rates, barge-day-rates and contractor bids, etc.

This cost estimate requires considerable amount of time to create with the resulting accuracy in the range of 10%–15%. This phase is terminated with either the approval or abandonment of the project. In the first case, the budget is firmed up and formally presented to the company's executive management for approval.

Control Estimate

Once the management approval is granted, the project execution phase commences, and contracts can be awarded. During this phase, the actual expenditure is continuously monitored versus the budget estimate. In this comparison, use is made of the so-called *S-Curve*, a graph of the cumulative expenditure versus time. By using this method, one obtains a forewarning of any possible expenditure overruns.

When new information becomes available during this phase (i.e., from new well data), the development plan is updated accordingly and new control estimates prepared. In case of large discrepancies (i.e., more than 10%) between the original budget estimate and the control estimate, the budget is revised upward and downward as warranted.

Cost Overrun

Costs may exceed the original budget for several reasons:

1. In order to induce contractors to deliver in time, they are often paid by *milestone payments* as soon as a certain agreed milestone is reached. If progress is still slow, the subsequent development steps are delayed and possibly more expensive according to inflation clauses in the contracts. This type of cost overrun need not necessarily be sanctioned by a separate management approval.

2. Contractors may encounter unforeseen difficulties such as extreme weather conditions or worker strikes. This often leads to increased costs, which if more than some 10%, may be subject to management approval.

3. New information may induce the petroleum engineers to change the BOD or scope of the project. Such scope changes can lead to delays and large cost increases, which are subject to management approval. To prevent this embarrassing situation, one is often tempted to leave the options open and build some flexibility into the project. But this flexibility can be costly. For an offshore development, it can result in an increased weight of the topside facilities, leading to a disproportionate increase in the weight and thus the price of the substructure. Cost overruns are often combined with an extended development period. Both are harmful on sound economics. Therefore, a CAPEX-overrun sensitivity without a corresponding extended development period yields optimistic results.

The Accuracy of the Estimates

Due to the nature of the business (i.e., too many unknowns), even using perfect estimating skills, methods, and data bases, an estimate can be only as good as the available definition of the project. Figure 3–16 shows qualitatively how the accuracy of the estimates generally improves with time. An estimate prepared at the earlier stage of the project often is less accurate, but as time passes, the project definition improves and so do the corresponding accuracy of cost estimates. A major improvement occurs when the BOD is frozen. This freezing reduces the amount of uncertainty, which simplifies the project planning, reduces the costs for uncertain elements (contingency), and thus improves the accuracy of the estimate.

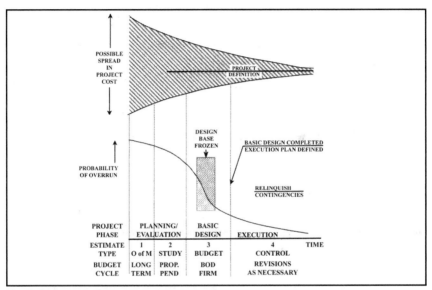

Fig. 3–16 Accuracy of cost estimate improves with time

Contingencies and Allowances

Probably no other single element in an estimate is subject to as much conflict and confusion as contingency. Despite its importance, contingencies are rarely well planned for or analyzed in detail. The purpose of contingency is to provide budget for uncertain (i.e., expected but undefined elements in an estimate). It is linked to the estimate's accuracy and should thus cover:

- Estimate omissions due to incomplete project definition,
- Inadequacies in the estimating method,
- Design and construction changes within the agreed project scope, and
- Variances in inflation and escalation rates, etc.

Whereas contingencies cover the *unknown unknowns* relating to the total project or a large portion of it, allowances are supposed to cover the *known unknowns* relating to individual aspects of the project. Allowances can be defined as the probable extra costs (probability of occurrence more than 50%) related to specific activities or cost elements and can be identified and quantified (usually from statistical data). Examples of allowances are:

- Material take-off allowances (i.e., 3% extra line pipe for a pipeline scaled from a map)
- Identified risks (i.e., buckle allowance, trenching allowance for an offshore pipeline)
- Foreseeable market conditions
- Foreseeable weather downtime
- New technology (in certain parts of the project)
- Growth (normal extra work), etc.

The value of the estimating contingency should be such, that the probability of cost overrun of the *median estimate* equals 50% (by definition). The *base estimate* equals the modal cost of the project. The relationship between these two statistical quantities is shown in Figure 3–17. The contingency is supposed to cover the difference between the mode and the median estimate. The contingency factor therefore depends on the skewness of the distribution curve in Figure 3–17. In practice, the contingency factor is about 2/3 of the accuracy shown in the section on types of cost estimates.

The resulting median estimate is used for the *Base Case* economic analysis. For the CAPEX *overrun* sensitivity, the budget proposal estimate should also include an overrun *allowance*, which should be selected in such a way that the probability of cost overrun of the budget estimate is only some 10% for a large project or some 20% for a small project.

This procedure implies more funds are reserved or frozen for the project than is probably necessary. It is, therefore, important to unfreeze these extra funds as soon as it becomes clear that certain expected cost overruns are not going to be realized and the funds will not be required.

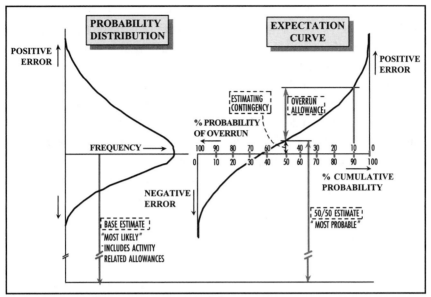

Fig. 3–17 A statistical view on contingencies and allowances

TRANSFER PRICING

Special problems can arise when evaluating projects in integrated companies, i.e., when one division or profit center of a company supplies goods and services to another division or profit center. The problems revolve around the question of what *transfer price* to charge for the transfer of goods or for the exchange of services.

Suppose a major, vertically integrated, oil company has three divisions. These three divisions are:

- Upstream, oil, and gas production (Division A)
- Downstream, gas processing (NGL) facility (Division B)
- Downstream, petrochemical facility (Division C)

Division A develops a gas field and strips liquids (condensate and raw NGL) from the gas in a stripping plant located in the field. The condensate is spiked into the company's crude oil line passing through the field, the stripped gas is injected back into the reservoir for pressure maintenance, and the raw NGL is sent to the company's Division B, where the C_2, C_3, C_4, and C_5+ are separated from the raw NGL. The C_3 and C_4 are sold; the C_5+ is combined with the condensate from Division A and spiked into the crude oil line. Division C takes the C_2 for producing petrochemical and related products. Ethane (C_2) is used to produce Ethylene, Low Density Polyethylene (LDPE), High Density Polyethylene (HDPE), Propylene, Ethylene glycol, etc. The above activities are schematically shown in Figure 3–18.

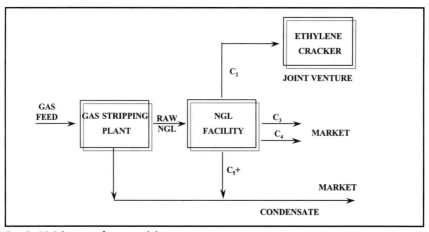

Fig. 3–18 Schematic of integrated divisions

In this example, there are two product transfers between divisions within the same company. The question is what price should control these transfers. Should the price be set to include some *profit* element for the transferring division, or should it be set to include only the accumulated costs to that point? Alternatively, should it be set at still some other figure? The choice of a transfer price can be complicated by the fact that each division may be supplying portions of its output to outside customers, as well as to sister divisions. A further complication is the selling price of one division becomes a cost expense to the other division. For example, an ethylene cracker takes 1000 tons of ethane from Division A at a price of $20/Ton, so the $20,000 becomes revenue for Division A and an expense (part of OPEX) for the Ethylene cracker. The higher this cost, the lower the purchasing division's profitability. Thus, the purchasing division would like the transfer price to be low, whereas the selling division would like it to be high. Perhaps the transfer could be at *market* price, so the same price is charged internally as charged to outside customers.

All three projects are set up from scratch and presented for evaluation. The problem is further compounded if the company owning Divisions *A* and *B* do not solely own Division C (i.e., it is a joint venture with another company). In practice, the following three general approaches are used in setting transfer prices for project evaluation and then later for the performance evaluation of each division, i.e., profit center.

1. Set transfer prices at cost using:
   a. Variable cost
   b. Full (absorption) cost
2. Set transfer prices at market price.
3. Set transfer prices at a negotiated market price.

Transfer Price at Cost

Many companies make transfers between divisions based on accumulated cost of the goods being transferred, thus ignoring any profit element to the selling division. A transfer price computed in this way might be based only on the variable costs involved, or fixed costs might also be considered and the transfer price thus based on full (absorption) costs accumulated to the point of transfer. In our example above, the transfer price for raw NGL is $/ton of NGL transferred to Division *B* and $/ton of C_2 transferred to Division C.

The cost approach to setting transfer prices, however, has the following disadvantages:

1. This approach has no built-in mechanism for telling when transfer should or should not be made between divisions (i.e., if the product can be sold outside the company for higher price than the cost).

2. The only division to show any profits is the one making the final sales to an outside party. The transferring division will not show any profit, thus evaluation of setting up this division by itself will be difficult.

3. The mechanism does not provide any incentive for the transferring division to control costs. If the costs of one division are simply passed on to the next, then there is little incentive for anyone to control costs. Therefore, the final selling division is simply burdened with the accumulated waste and inefficiency of intermediate processors, and the division will be penalized with a rate of return that is deficient in comparison to its competitors.

General Formula for Computing Transfer Price

A general formula exists in use by the engineers/economists as a starting point in computing the appropriate transfer price between projects, divisions, or segments of a multidivisional company. The formula is: *the transfer price should be equal to the unit variable costs of the good/services being transferred, plus the contribution margin per unit lost to the transferring division because of giving up outside sales.* The formula can be mathematically expressed as:

Transfer Price = Variable cost per unit + Lost contribution margin per unit on outside sales

A transfer price computed by the above formula is based on competitive market conditions.

Transfer at Market Price

This transfer price mechanism is based on some form of competitive *market price* and is considered the most appropriate approach to the transfer-pricing problem. The mechanism dovetails well with the profit center concept and enables the engineers to make profit-based performance evaluation feasible at many levels of an organization. By using this mechanism for transfer pricing, all projects/divisions/segments of a company are adequately evaluated for their respective profitability (economic viability).

The idea in using this type of transfer price mechanism is to create competitive market conditions that would exist if the various divisions were indeed separate firms and engaged in arm's length, open-market bargaining. The market price depends on (1) if a well-defined intermediate market exists for the product, or (2) the price changes in the intermediate market.

1. *Well-defined intermediate market exists:* The market conditions may differ from division to division, project to project, and company to company. If no intermediate market exits for the product, then the only customer a division has for its output is a sister division. If an intermediate market exists for part or the division's entire product, then it has a choice between selling to outside customers or selling to other divisions within the same company. The existence of intermediate market price represents an upper limit on the charge that can be made on transfers between divisions. In many situations, a lesser price can also be justified due to reduction in administrative and marketing expenses when inter-company sales are involved.

2. *Price changes in the intermediate market:* Here it becomes a problem of opportunity cost as discussed in the preceding sections. For example, if a division is already selling all it can produce to outside customers, then the division's opportunity cost is the purchase price paid by the outside customers. Therefore, if the inside business is accepted, it will be at a cost of giving up the outside business. Thus, when the selling division is at full capacity, the transfer price inside should never be less than this opportunity cost, or the selling division suffers.

However, the situation will change if the selling division is not at full capacity. Under this condition, the opportunity costs may be zero (depending on what alternative uses the seller has for the excess capacity). Under such situations, so long as the selling division can receive a price greater than its variable costs, all parties will benefit by keeping business inside rather than having the buying division go outside. Some type of *negotiated market price* can best serve such situation.

Similarly, one of the divisions may require a product unavailable from outside sources and must be produced internally by a sister division. In such situations, the buying division negotiates with the selling division to arrive at a mutually agreed transfer price sufficiently attractive for the economic viability of both divisions.

ASPECTS OF LEASING

Note that nowhere in the world do the companies involved in exploration and oil and gas production activities own the land or the underneath minerals. In some areas of the world both the land (surface) and the underneath minerals belong to the state/government. In other places the surface rights may belong to one party (individual) while the mineral rights belong to another (state or individual). In the United States and Canada, individuals may own rights to both the land and the underneath minerals. In other parts of the world, both the land and the mineral rights belong to the government. If the surface owner also owns the minerals (ownership in fee), he will usually be just as interested as the producer in bringing about the oil and gas production. An owner in fee may sell his surface ownership of the land while retaining the mineral rights. A legal instrument called a *mineral deed* accomplishes transfers of mineral ownership.

Before an oil and gas company can start drilling activities on a prospective piece of land, permissions to conduct such operations must be obtained from both the surface and mineral owners. Usually a *landman*, whose job is to seek out the owners of both estates and negotiate leases with them on behalf of the intended oil and gas company, takes care of the required legal formalities.

In the United States, there are also vast stretches of federal land usually associated with the American West. Here the government owns both the land and the minerals. If an oil and gas lease on federal land is successful and produces petroleum in commercial quantities, the U.S. Minerals Management Service collects the royalties and then divides them evenly with the state where the tract is situated. Joint federal/state mineral income sharing may also occur from offshore leases.[13]

In Canada, the surface and mineral rights may be owned separately. Owners may be individuals, the federal government (Crown land), or the provincial government. For example, in Alberta 80% of the mineral rights belong to the provincial government. In eastern Canada, individuals or private enterprises own almost all mineral rights. In southern Ontario, minerals are mostly privately owned while in northern Ontario almost all minerals belong to the provincial government. In Manitoba, about 80% of the mineral rights are owned by freeholders. The other provinces also have a higher percentage of freeholder mineral owners than Alberta.

The land department provides appropriate ownership interest rates for each property for economic evaluation. However, the mechanism of how the interests of each partner in an oil deal are derived have to be understood.

System of Land Ownership Identification

Just as every person has to have a name for identification, the lands are also assigned some identification so ownership rights and privileges can be easily identified. Most of the land in the United States has been surveyed by the General Land Office of the U.S. government and each state divided into small squares based on the survey. The system of survey is referred to as the USGS (United States Geological Survey) system or rectangular survey system.

According to this survey system, a *principal meridian* and a *base line* were established. The principal meridians run in a true north-south direction and the base lines run east and west at right angles to the meridians.

The General Land Office surveyed the states with a system of north-south and east-west coordinates, which divided the states into squares called *townships*. The squares were consecutively arranged into *north-to-south* townships and *east-to-west* ranges as shown in Figure 3–19(a). Each township is further divided into 36 sections, each of which contains 640 acres (1 acre = 43,560 sq. ft) and is one-by-one mile square. The numbering of the sections start as section 1 (one) in the NE corner of the township, consecutively numbered with section 6 (six) in the NW corner. Section 7 (seven) then starts with the section below section 6 and consecutively numbered towards the east, and so on. The 36 sections per township are shown in Figure 3–19(b).

In Canada, the same system is used but there the sections in a township are numbered in a different way. The section 1 starts in the SE corner of the township as shown in Figure 3–19(c). Each section is then further divided into 40-acre tracts (16 sub-sections) as shown in Figure 3–19(d). Similarly, in New Mexico, each section is further divided into 40-acre tracts and each tract is identified by a letter as shown in Figure 3–19(e).

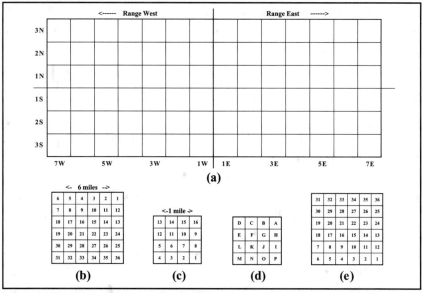

Fig. 3–19 The system of land ownership identification

Another land survey method is used in some states and offshore, this method is referred to as the *metes and bounds*. In this system, the ownership is irregular and unsystematic and the land is divided into blocks. This system is mostly applied in the state of Texas and most of the offshore.

It is extremely important to identify the exact legal location of the oil and gas wells in oil and gas property evaluation. The wells are assigned names but there may be repetitions and therefore it is recommended to use both the name of the well as well as the legal location. The wells are also assigned API numbers. By including the legal location, it is also easier to locate the well on the acreage map, which is then used for constructing structure map, isovolume map, isopach map, etc.

The wells are identified either by a corner-corner location or by certain distances from the boundaries of the section. For example, in Figure 3–20(a), the well is located in the southwest quarter (SW–1/4) of the southeast quarter (SE–1/4) of Section 15, Township 1 North Range 65 West; this description is abbreviated as SWSE–15–T1N–R65W. Similarly, in Figure 3–20(b), the well is located 2640 feet from the east line and 1760 feet from the north line of Section 15, Township 1 North Range 65 West. As mentioned above, each section is a one-by-one mile square (5280 ft x 5280 ft). If the section is drawn with a scale of 3 inches to a mile, then the well is located $1\frac{1}{2}$ inches (2640/5,280 x 3 in = 1.5 in) from the east line and 1 inch (1760/5,280 x 3 = 1.0 in) from the north line of Section 15, T1N R65W. This is abbreviated as 2640 FEL and 1760 FNL–15–T1N–R65W.

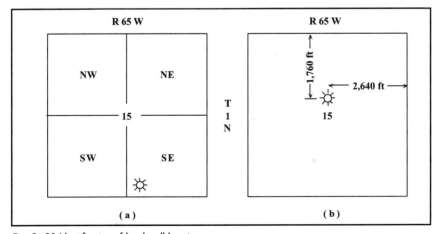

Fig. 3–20 Identification of legal well locations

Ownership Interest Computation

The mineral interest in a property is divided into *working* (operating) interests and *non-operating interests*. A working interest (WI) can be classified as a basic, joint, pooled, or unitized interest. A non-operating interest can be classified as a royalty, overriding royalty, production payment, or net profits interest. Associated with each working interest there is a *net revenue interest* (NRI) reduced proportionately by *non-operating working interest*. For an investor in an oil and gas deal, NRI is the key economic figure, which measures the percent of profits earned by investor. This NRI is earned by a specific working interest.

When a lease is obtained, a royalty, commonly *one-eighth* (12.5%) is retained by the land owner/mineral interest owner (*lessor*). The working interest owner at this stage earns a maximum of only 87.5% of any oil and gas revenues from the lease while paying 100% of the costs. On the other hand, the lessor receives 12.5% of the oil and gas free of any costs accept for the severance, ad valorem, and any other surcharge taxes levied by the state. The various types of interest arrangements and oil deals are defined below:

1. *Leasehold interest:* The interest owner (lessor) conveys leasehold interest to the lessee. The leasehold interest owner has the right to explore for and produce minerals.

2. *Primary term:* Leases are usually in effect for a period of 1 to 10 years and as long thereafter as hydrocarbons are produced. When hydrocarbons are produced on a lease, the lease is referred to as held by production.

3. *Lease bonus:* Upon acquiring mineral rights, the lessee pays a sign-up bonus to the lessor. The amount ranges from $1 per acre to $3000 per acre, depending on the exploration activity within or nearby the leased property.

4. *Delay rental:* Unless operations are commenced on or before one year from the effective date of the lease, the lease terminates regardless of the length of the primary term of the lease, unless the lessee pays a previously agreed delay rental, which enables the lessee to defer operations for one more year.

5. *Overriding royalty interests (ORRI):* This type of non-operating interest is similar to a landowner's royalty in that the ORRI owner receives a portion of the production free and clear of all costs. An override is often said as being *carved out* of the WI since it is created from the leasehold's share of the revenue.

6. *Joint working interest:* When more than one working interest owners are involved, each own an individual fraction of the WI in a single lease. A joint WI may result from leases, purchases or exchanges, or sharing arrangements. One party known as the operator (usually the party with the largest interest) in the property has the responsibility for developing and operating the property.

7. *Pooled working interest:* When two or more properties are combined that may have the same or different WI owner. The NRIs are combined separately at the same time. Pooling may be voluntary or mandatory; it will usually result in operations that are more efficient and a greater recovery of hydrocarbons.

8. *Unitized working interest:* When two or more WIs in different properties are combined, the resulting WI is referred to as unitized WI. Unitizations usually occur after production starts because the WIs and the associated NRIs are prorated based on the ultimate recovery of hydrocarbons dedicated to each lease. On the other hand, pooling usually occurs before development is started.

9. *Production payment (PPI):* Non-operating interest normally created out of the WI and usually expressed as a certain amount of money, a certain period, or a certain quantity of oil or gas. The PPI reverts to the WI from which it was created after the specified amount of money, period of time, or oil or gas are recovered. It is often used to pay down debt since the amount of money going for debt services is proportional to the producing rate.

10. *Carried interest:* It is a form of deal in which an interest owner does not receive any revenue and does not pay any costs until a certain condition is met. Carried interests are more often carried to the *casing point* or through the tanks of the first well. A farmout could be expressed as a carried interest. If a company has an X% WI to the casing point, then the carrying party pays all of

the dry hole costs. At the casing point, the carrying party may decide to put up X% of the completion costs to gain the X% of WI with its associated NRI. A 1/3 for 1/4 is a typical farmout agreement in which the farmee pays 1/3 of the costs to some pre-determined point in order to receive 1/4 WI.

The computation of ownership interest in oil and gas deals ranges from a simple two-owner arrangement (landowner and investor) to a complex multiple owner arrangements. The best way to determine these interests is to always flowchart the investors and their associated interests in a systematic manner. The following example clarifies the computations.

Example 3–8

Suppose a lease is obtained by Company X for a 12.5% landowner's royalty. To reduce the risk exposure in development, Company X further sells 30% of the deal to Company Y. Compute the NRI of each company.

Solution: Ownership interests of each party are given in Table 3–12.

	Working Interest Amount Spent (%)	Revenue Interest Amount Earned (%)
Lessor	0	12.50
Company X	70	61.25
Company Y	30	26.25
Total	100	100.00

Net Lease = $1.0 - 0.125 = 0.875$

Company X = $0.70 \times 0.875 = 0.6125$

Company Y = $0.30 \times 0.875 = 0.2625$

Table 3–12 Working and net revenue interest computation for Example 3–8

Example 3-9

A lease broker, Z, obtains a lease for a 12.5% landowner's royalty. He sells 100% of the deal to A retaining a 2.5% ORRI. A sells 100% of the deal to B retaining 2.5% ORRI. B sells 50% of the deal to C and 25% to D. Compute the ownership interests of each party in the deal.

Solution: Ownership interest computations are shown in Table 3–13.

	WI (fraction)	NRI (fraction)
Landowner	0.00	0.125
Broker Z	0.00	0.025
Broker A	0.00	0.025
Company B	0.25	0.206
Company C	0.50	0.413
Company D	0.25	0.206
TOTAL	1.00	1.000

Table 3-13 WI and NRI Computation for Example 3–9.

Example 3-10

A lease is obtained for a 12.5% landowner royalty. A geologist is retained to study the lease and retaining 2% ORRI. A promoter who sells the deal to investors keeps 5.5% ORRI with 25% back-in working interest after payout (after the WI participants have recovered all their costs from a successful producing well). Compute the before and after payout ownership interests for each party.

Solution: The various interests are shown in Table 3–14.

	Before Payout (%)		After Payout (%)	
	WI	**NRI**	**WI**	**NRI**
Lessor	0	12.50	0	12.500
Geologist	0	2.00	0	2.000
Promoter	0	5.50	25.00	21.375
Investor	100	80.00	75.00	64.125
TOTAL	100	100.00	100.00	100.000

Table 3–14 WI and NRI Comparison for the deal in Example 3–10

SEVERANCE AND AD VALOREM TAXES

In addition to CAPEX and OPEX, major items of cash outflow for most petroleum projects are royalties and taxes deducted from the pre-tax (Federal Income Tax) cash flow. In the oil and gas industry, besides the federal and state income taxes, each state has its own surcharge on oil and gas production. This surcharge is referred to as ad valorem and severance taxes. These taxes, collectively referred to as production taxes, are usually applied on a percentage basis or on a dollar per unit basis of the gross value at the point of production.

Production taxes are levied upon the owner of oil and gas interests by a state or local government. The tax is determined from the volume (or value) of production (or sales). State oil and gas taxes are quite simple in some states and extremely complicated in others. Several U.S. states impose ad valorem taxes that may or may not be significant.

Many states have tax incentive programs. These programs are constantly being revised. Many programs with time limits are being extended while others have expired. Many states allow tax exemptions to qualified wells and projects but stipulate unique criteria for "qualification" or "certification." No attempt has been made to describe all of the various qualifications or, for that matter, to include all special tax exemptions, especially those exceptions so specific that they require more knowledge than the date of first production and the producing rate of the property being evaluated.

These taxes range anywhere from zero in some states to as high as 15% of the gross value in other states. Therefore, it is extremely important to allow for the proper amount of these taxes in oil and gas property evaluations. The states with higher taxes will have a significant financial impact on the profitability of the property.

If two field development alternatives are available that are comparable in reserves, investment lives, and initial and ongoing costs, then the tax environment applicable to each alternative will have a significant influence on which alternative is chosen for further development. Obviously, the alternative with lower production taxes yields better economics.

As previously mentioned, many states have complicated exemptions, limits, or sliding scales. In order to provide a quick reference, a summary of the severance and ad valorem taxes is presented in Table 3–15 and Table 3–16, respectively. American Petroleum Institute's publication "TC–10 State and Local Oil and Gas Severance and Production Taxes" provides a 26-page summary of these taxes. The production taxes, by state, are also listed on the website of Society of Petroleum Evaluation Engineers (SPEE)—**http://spee.org/tax.htm**. The taxes presented here are given as a sample. The tax laws are constantly changing; therefore for further and more accurate details, individual state departments of revenue should be contacted.

The following descriptions, additional limitations or concessions levied by each state, relates to the notes in Table 3–15.[14]

1. For wells producing less than 25 Stb/d or 200 Mscf/d in unitized fields and all wells commencing production after September 1, 1979. Baldwin County has an additional 1% severance tax.

2. For wells producing more than 25 Stb/d or 200 Mscf/d commencing production on or before September 1, 1979. Baldwin County has an additional 1% severance tax.

3. For oil wells commencing production after June 30, 1981. For first five years only and subject to oil gravity and EL.

4. For oil wells commencing production on or before June 30, 1981. Rate is affected by oil gravity and EL.

Note	State	Oil	Gas	No	State	Oil	Gas
1	Alabama	0.06	0.06	17	Louisiana	0.03125	$0.07
2		0.10		18		0.0625	
3	Alaska	0.1225	0.10	19		0.125	
4		0.15		20		Note	
	Arizona	0.025	0.025	21	Michigan	0.066	0.05
5	Arkansas	0.04	$0.003	22		0.04	
6		0.05			Mississippi	0.06	0.06
		5 mill/Stb		23	Montana	0.05	0.0265
7	California	varies	varies	24		0.06	
8	Colorado	0.02	0.02	25		0.0002	
9		0.03	0.03	26	Nebraska	0.02	0.02
10		0.04	0.04	27		0.03	0.03
11		0.05	0.05	28		0.0004	0.0005
12		0.0006		29	Nevada	$0.005	$0.0001
13		0.0009		30	New Mexico	0.0375	$0.152
14	Florida	0.05	0.05	31		0.0019	
15		0.08	0.05	32		0.0255	
	Georgia	$0.005	$0.0005		New York	None	None
	Idaho	0.02	0.02	33	N. Carolina	$0.005	$0.0005
	Indiana	0.01	0.01	34	N. Dakota	0.05	0.05
16	Kansas	0.08	0.08	35		0.115	
	Kentucky	0.045	0.045	36		0.001875/b	
	Oklahoma	0.07085	0.07085		Ohio	$0.10	$0.03
	Oregon	0.06	0.06	37	Utah	0.04	0.04
	S. Dakota	0.045	0.045		Virginia	None	None
	Tennessee	0.03	0.03	38	W. Virginia	0.0434	0.0863
	Texas	0.046	0.075	39	Wyoming	0.06	0.06
				40		0.04	
				41		0.0001	
$ taxes are based on $/Stb and $/Mscf.							

Table 3–15 Severance and ad valorem taxes by state[14]

State	Oil	Gas	State	Oil	Gas
Alabama	None	None	Nebraska	0.06	0.06
Alaska	0.002	0.002	Nevada	0.06	0.06
Arizona	0.05	0.05	New Mexico	0.05	0.05
Arkansas	0.04	0.04	New York	0.10	0.10
California	0.09	0.09	North Carolina	0.05	0.05
Colorado	0.03	0.03	North Dakota	None	None
Florida	0.02	0.02	Ohio	0.07	0.07
Georgia	0.05	0.05	Oklahoma	None	None
Idaho	0.05	0.05	Oregon	None	None
Illinois		0.08	Pennsylvania	0.08	0.08
Indiana	0.07	0.07	S. Carolina	0.05	0.05
Kansas	0.08	0.08	S. Dakota	0.02	0.02
Kentucky	0.06	0.06	Tennessee	None	None
Louisiana	None	None	Texas	0.04	0.04
Maryland	0.07	0.07	Utah	0.05	0.05
Michigan	0.02	0.02	Virginia	None	None
Minnesota	0.05	0.05	W. Virginia	None	None
Mississippi	None	None	Wyoming	0.07	0.07
Montana	0.09	0.09			

Ad valorem taxes are often based on assessed value of equipment and property and are administered on county/parish/township basis.

Table 3–16 Approximate ad valorem tax rates (fraction of gross value)[14]

5. Oil production is 10 Stb/d or less during any calendar month.

6. Production is greater than 10 Stb/d during any calendar month.

7. Varies, depending on needs of the Oil and Gas Division. Usually small when compared to the estimated ad valorem tax rate. 1983 rate = $0.0144/Stb.

8. For gross income under $25,000. Wells averaging less than 10 Stb/d for taxable year are exempt.

9. For gross income greater than $25,000 and less then $100,000. Wells averaging less than 10 Stb/d for taxable year are exempt.

10. For gross income greater than $100,000 but less than $300,000. Wells averaging less than 10 Stb/d for taxable year are exempt.

11. For gross income $300,000 and over. Stripper production is exempt.

12. A conservation tax, for production on or after January 1, 1982.

13. A conservation tax, for production after January 1, 1979 and before July 1, 1981.

14. For wells producing less than 100 Stb/d and by tertiary methods.

15. For wells producing more than 100 Stb/d and not utilizing tertiary methods.

16. Any ad valorem taxes paid may be used as credit against the severance tax up to 3.67% of the gross value. Thus, the effective severance tax rate may only be 4.33% if the ad valorem taxes paid are at least 3.67% of the gross value.

17. For 10 Stb/d or less.

18. For 25 Stb/d or less and at least 50% salt water.

19. For wells producing more than 25 Stb/d and any condensate production.

20. A working interest in newly discovered fields is exempt from 50% of the severance tax for 24 months on the first 100 Stb/d. The 24-month period starts when regular production begins.

21. All production except stripper production.

22. Stripper production as per definition of the State of Michigan.

23. After April 1, 1985.

24. Until March 31, 1985.

25. Conservation tax. Montana also has a Resource Indemnity Trust tax of $25 + 0.5% of gross value more than $5,000.

26. Wells producing 10 Stb/d or less.

27. Wells producing more than 10 Stb/d.

28. Conservation tax.

29. Conservation tax.

30. Severance tax, gas rate changes yearly.

31. Conservation tax.

32. Emergency school tax.

33. Conservation tax.

34. Production tax on all crude oil and gas.

35. Extraction tax of 6.5% on all crude oil except stripper production and royalty interests on first 100 Stb/d in addition to 5% production tax.

36. Oil conservation tax.

37. Occupation tax effective 1/1/84. Wells producing less than 20 Stb/d are exempt. Production for the first six months is also exempt. The state has a conservation tax of 0.002.

38. The 0.0434 tax is the business and occupation tax. The gas tax is on the value more than $5,000 per year.

39. For production, where average daily rate is in excess of 10 Stb/d for preceding calendar year.

40. For production where average daily rate is less than or equal to 10 Stb/d for preceding calendar year.

41. Oil and gas conservation tax. Rate varies, with maximum 0.0004.

CASH-FLOW ESTIMATION BIAS

As stated at the beginning of this chapter, cash-flow estimation bias is the most critical—and the most difficult—part of the capital investment (project evaluation) process. Cash-flow components must be forecasted many years into the future, and estimation errors are bound to occur.[15]

Input into project economics is contributed by many departments. It is likely that, in the process, some departments will provide conservative estimates while some others will provide optimistic estimates. In totality, the end-result should balance out. Similarly, since large companies evaluate and accept many projects every year, and as long as the cash-flow estimates are unbiased and the errors are random, the estimation errors may tend to cancel out each other.

Several studies indicate capital budgeting cash-flow forecasts are biased. Many departments tend to be overly optimistic in their forecasts and as a result, revenues tend to be overstated and costs tend to be understated. The result is an upward bias in net operating cash flows and thus an upward bias in estimating the profitability of the proposed project. This practice could be dangerous in evaluating projects with borderline profitability.[16]

Many times, division managers/engineers become emotionally attached to their proposed projects, and hence unable to objectively assess their project's potential negative factors. Realizing biases may exist, economists or project evaluators should develop historical data on the forecast accuracy of the projects already completed. This information should then be considered in the project evaluation process. The data highlights the departments consistently providing either optimistic or pessimistic data. The economists can then adjust this situation, or at least it will provide the highs and lows. This information can be incorporated into the decision analysis process (to be discussed in Volume 2 of this series).

A first step in recognizing cash-flow estimation bias, especially for projects estimated to be either extraordinarily profitable or below expectation profitability, is to ask this question: What is the underlying cause of the project's unexpected profitability (high or low)? If the company has some inherent advantage, such as patent protection, unique project execution methods, unique manufacturing advantage, or marketing expertise, then the projects utilizing such an advantage may truly be extraordinarily profitable. At the end of the day, the project evaluators need to have experience in identifying the right information and/or anomalies in the data provided to them for evaluation.

CASH-FLOW ANALYSIS OF FOREIGN INVESTMENTS

Cash-flow analysis is much more complex when capital investments are being made in a foreign country. The relevant cash flows from a foreign investment are the dollar equivalent cash flows to be returned, or repatriated, to the parent company. Since in most cases, the cash flows are earned in the currency of the foreign country, they must be converted to dollars, and thus they are subject to future currency exchange rate fluctuations.

Fortunately, in the oil and gas industry, most transactions are done in U.S. dollars. However, many cash-flow items are either paid or received in local currency. Most of the operating expenses are paid in the local currency. Some of the locally produced capital equipment to be used in the project is billed in local currency. The services provided locally (i.e., helicopter and marine service for offshore operations) are billed in local currency, and so on. Similarly, if the product produced by the project are predominantly absorbed in the local market, the demand for this product is affected if the local currency is weakened/devalued. Since the company has to maintain its return in dollars, the product price in local currency will be increased to compensate for the devaluation. Thus, the consumers have to pay more for the same product. The revenue generated from the sale of the product in the local market when converted into the U.S. dollars at the weaker local currency results in fewer dollars than forecasted, even if the demand for the product stays the same. Therefore, the dollar cash flows and hence the value of the investment would decline.

The currency exchange rates change daily, and long-term trends associated with inflation and other fundamental factors occur though not in a predictable manner. The currency crises of Malaysia, Indonesia, Turkey, Korea, and Taiwan are typical examples. Therefore, over the economic life of a project, substantial changes could occur, but it is exceedingly difficult to predict what they will be. These exchange rate changes, beside other factors, make international capital investment quite complex, thus increasing the riskiness of foreign investments.

This is called a *true/real* investment situation. An American investor made a $12,500,000 real estate investment in a foreign country on

01/01/1990. At the time the local currency equivalent amounted to LC250,000,000. At the end of 1996, the property was sold for LC575,000,000 at which time $1 was equal to LC40. Do you think it was a sound investment? Not at all! By analyzing the investment, we find the investor made some 12.65% return [250,000,000 x (1 + 0.1265)7 @ 575,000,000] in the local currency. However, when the funds were repatriated, he ended up with $14,375,000 (575,000,000 ÷ 40 = 14,375,000), which is a return of only 2%. On the other hand, if the $12,500,000 were invested in a bank at an average interest rate of 5% (net of income tax), his net worth at 12/31/1996 would have been $17,588,755 (i.e., a net opportunity loss of $3,213,755).

Similarly, different countries have different local tax regimes to be incorporated into the project cash flow. On the other hand, in the United States, the taxes paid in the foreign country are deductible against the taxes to be paid in the United States.

CASH-FLOW ANALYSIS AND INFLATION

It is a usual practice to incorporate estimates of future inflation in cash-flow projections of revenues and costs. This reflects an expectation that the different elements discussed in the preceding section, which form the basis of the project cash flow, will be larger in the future years than they are now because of inflation. Note any reserves evaluation reports submitted to Securities and Exchange Commission (SEC) are required to be in constant (un-escalated or un-inflated) terms.

In cash-flow projections, simple assumptions about the general anticipated level of inflation are normally acceptable. For example, it may be assumed that the capital cost, OPEX, and product prices will all inflate (escalate) at 5% per year or so. Each stream may be subjected to a different escalation factor (i.e., product prices escalating at 2% per year, capital cost escalating at 5% per year, and OPEX escalating at 3% per year). Depending upon the assumptions made, the escalations may be applied from start of the project to end. They may be kept constant for some years and then escalated onward, and they may be subject to a ceiling. For example, oil price may be kept constant at $28/barrel until year 2005;

from 2006, it is escalated at a rate of 3% to a maximum of $35/barrel (i.e., the price will be $28.84 in 2006, $29.71 in 2007, and $35 in 2013).

Therefore, the cash-flow analysis starts by making estimates of capital, OPEX, and product prices in today's terms (that is, as if they were all incurred in the current year) and then inflating or escalating them year-by-year based on the inflation projection.

The escalated costs, prices, and cash flow discussed above are referred to as *inflated*, *nominal*, or *money-of-the-day* costs, prices, and cash flow. These are distinguished from today's *real, un-escalated, constant*, or *deflated* costs, prices, and cash flow. Real or deflated quantities represent a measure of the purchasing power of a future amount of money in today's terms.

If the inflationary expectations are embedded in the cash-flow model, the resulting net cash flow is called *nominal net cash flow*. On the other hand, if the inflationary expectations are not embedded in the cash-flow model, the resulting net cash flow is called *real net cash flow*. The nominal net cash flow can be converted to real net cash flow by deflating it by the projected inflation rate, provided each element has been escalated at the same rate.

It is important each element of the cash flow is escalated separately, rather than escalating the net cash flow. This is because the bottom line economics are dependent on the sensitivity of each element to the escalation rate. For example, a high capacity oil producer will respond differently to a 2% escalation than a low capacity producer at the same rate. Similarly, a project with high unit operating cost will be more sensitive to escalation compared to a low unit operating cost project.

The escalation rates might correspond to the general levels of inflation as measured, for instance, by the Consumer Price Index or some similar indicator.

THE COST OF CAPITAL

As mentioned in the previous chapters, most companies today use discounted cash-flow (DCF) techniques for project evaluation. The method involves forecasting the future cash flows, choosing the appropriate cost of capital (also referred to as the discount rate), and finding the present value of the forecasted net cash flows. The NPV is defined as the present value of receipts less the present value of disbursements. If the NPV at the project's cost of capital is positive, then accepting the project adds value to the firm and vice versa.

Assume that estimates on the future cash flows of a proposed project are sound. The success of the discounted cash-flow technique then depends on how well the analysts choose the discount rate. If a picked rate is too high, projects that add value to the firm will be unnecessarily rejected. On the other hand, if the discount rate is too low, projects that do not add value to the firm will be accepted. Therefore, choosing the appropriate discount rate is as important as the estimation of appropriate future cash flows. For detailed discussion, the reader is referred to an excellent book by Michael C. Ehrhardt.[17]

There are several different types of discounted cash flow approaches, and each has a different specification of cash flows and a different appropriate discount rate. In literature, the *weighted average cost of capital* approach is highly recommended. To implement this approach, one has to first estimate the costs of the various sources of financing (including equity). In general, these costs are a function of (1) the riskiness of the project being financed, and (2) the amount of debt used to finance the project. The technique involves

- *Estimating the current cost of each source of funds.* This is not the historical cost of the capital raised. It is the marginal cost of the incremental funds required for the project.

- *Finding the weighted average of the costs.* These separate sources of capital are based on the market values of the sources of financing. The result is the weighted average cost of capital.

The different sources of financing include the cost of (1) common equity (i.e., the return the shareholders expect the project to earn on their money), (2) preferred stock, (3) debt, and (4) other elements in the capital structure. The mixture of these elements is known as *capital structure*. The ratio of borrowed funds to either total funds or shareholders' equity is termed as *gearing* ratio. A firm is *highly geared* when it has a larger proportion of funds borrowed from intermediaries in relation to its share capital. Alternatively, *low gearing* occurs when a large bulk of the borrowed funds is in the form of share capital. The higher the level of capital gearing, the greater the risk associated with the project.

It is important to differentiate between two types of risks (1) project risk, and (2) financial risk. Project risk is the inherent uncertainty surrounding the level of pre-tax profits that will be generated by the project. It arises because it is usually impossible to forecast several variables that form the project cash flow accurately. Financial risk is the additional risk introduced because of gearing in the capital structure. The level of fixed interest financing in the capital structure determines the financial risk. The probability of cash insolvency increases with the level of gearing used by the firm, as does the variability of the earnings available for ordinary shareholders. The fixed interest loans have to be paid regardless of whether the company is making profit, but paying dividends to the providers of share capital can be avoided in poor years.

Determining the appropriate cost of each source is beyond the scope of this book and analysts will not normally be required to do so. The finance department of the firm normally specifies the appropriate discount rate. In the oil and gas industry, the general trend is to use a discount rate of 10%–12%.

Suppose there are X different sources of capital used to finance the project. If M_j is the market value of the the source of financing, then the market-weighted percentage of the project financed by source j, w_j, is defined as

(3.26)

$$w_j = \frac{M_j}{\displaystyle\sum_{j=1}^{X} M_j}$$

If r_j is the marginal cost source j, the weighted average cost of capital, r_c, is

(3.27)

$$r_c = \sum_{j=1}^{X} w_j r_j$$

To show the calculation of the weighted average cost of capital, assume the following capital structure for a project:

1. Ordinary shares with a market value of $3,000,000,
2. That 9% debenture (commitment to paying interest to debenture holders for a number of years, debentures may or may not be redeemable) stock with a market value of $200,000,
3. Long-term loans of $500,000 at 8% interest, and
4. A $300,000 overdraft at an interest rate of 11%.

The rate of corporation tax is 50% and the assumed cost of equity after tax is 12%. From this information, Table 3–17 can be developed for the relevant details.

	A	B	C	D
	Market Value	**Weighting**	**Cost after Tax**	**Weighted Cost (B x C)**
	$ 000	**%**	**%**	**%**
Equity	3,000	75.0	12.0	9.000
Debentures	200	5.0	4.5	0.225
Long-term Loan	500	12.5	4.0	0.500
Overdraft	300	7.5	5.5	0.413
	4,000	100.0		10.138

Table 3–17 Computing weighted average cost of capital

THE CASH-FLOW SPREADSHEET

Once all the data is collected, it is put together in a certain interpretive form to enable the analysts and management easily comprehend the profitability of the project. Many commercial software packages are available to take care of this task. Typical software are

- OGRE—Oil and Gas Reserve Evaluation
- EUREKA 5.13—Oil & Gas Economic Evaluation (Richard J. Miller and Associates, Inc.)
- WHAT-IF2—Oil and Gas Economic Analysis (T&E Garland, Inc.)
- PETROCALC3—Reservoir Economics and Evaluation (Gulf Publishers)

In addition to these commercially available economic evaluation softwares, many major oil companies have their own software. Nevertheless, there are situations when the analysts have to generate their own tools for analysis. One basic approach used by many analysts is to develop economic evaluation spreadsheets (or worksheets as they are sometimes called) on Lotus or Excel. Table 3–18 shows a cash flow for a typical North American producing lease, covering a simulated span of 16 years.

The output can be formatted in many different ways to adapt the spreadsheet to particular needs.

The cash flows typically shows project identification information (such as well/lease name, API number, location, field name, county, state, operator, and reserve category, etc.). Description of the various columns of the spreadsheet in Table 3–18 is given below.

1. Columns (B & C) list the gross (wellhead) oil and gas (or other products, i.e., propane, butane, ethane, sulfur, etc.) production forecast to EL. Using the methods discussed in this chapter helps to generate the forecast.

2. Columns (D & E) list the net product forecast, net to the interest owner whose interest is evaluated or net to the total lease (net revenue interest).

3. Columns (F & G) list the oil and gas prices.

4. Columns (H through J) list the CAPEX, LOE, and taxes (severance and ad valorem), respectively. The CAPEX and OPEX correspond to the working interest (WI) under evaluation. The CAPEX column may be further subdivided into drilling CAPEX, facility CAPEX, and so on. Similarly, the LOE column may be further subdivided into fixed cost, variable cost, workovers' cost, and so on.

    State and local taxes, which are directly related to the property under evaluation, are itemized in Column J. In North America, these are normally severance taxes (also referred to as production taxes). This is a form of sales tax applied to oil and gas sales (revenues) levied by the state and ad valorem taxes assessed by other local jurisdictions. In western Canada, where the government is both the royalty owner and the taxing authority, the royalty (referred to as crown royalty, normally sliding scale) and taxes are normally lumped together under the term Government Take.

    The practice of including the state and local taxes as part of the direct operating expenditure as is done in Column J is quite common. Income and other general taxes pertaining to the corporation as a whole are generally not recognized (in the before income tax cash flows) specifically as part of the operating costs at the well/lease level.

5. Column K lists the total cash outflow, which is the sum of Columns H, J, and I.

RESERVES AND ECONOMICS
AS OF JANUARY 1, 2002

Ref: Well #2-25 (Sec. 25-T5N-R65W), Weld County, Colorado

Proved Undeveloped — Sun Oil Company

Year	Gross Production Oil (MStb)	Gross Production Gas (MMScf)	Net Production Oil (MStb)	Net Production Gas (MMScf)	Product Prices Oil ($/Stb)	Product Prices Gas ($/MScf)	Expenditure Capital (M$)	Expenditure LOE (M$)	Expenditure Taxes (M$)	Expenditure TOTAL (M$)	Operating Revenue Gross (M$)	Operating Revenue Net (M$)	Cum. NCF (M$)	Cum. NCF Disc. @10% (M$)
2002	-	-	-	-			185.00	0.00	0.00	185.00	0.00	(185.00)	(185.00)	(176.39)
2003	5.174	43.432	4.527	38.003	22.00	2.25		14.40	14.81	29.21	185.11	155.90	(29.10)	(41.26)
2004	2.393	22.880	2.094	20.003	22.00	2.25		14.40	7.29	21.69	91.07	69.39	40.28	13.41
2005	1.820	16.407	1.593	14.356	22.00	2.25		14.40	5.39	19.79	67.34	47.55	87.83	47.48
2006	1.207	10.801	1.066	9.451	22.00	2.25		14.40	3.56	17.96	44.50	26.54	114.37	64.76
2007	0.971	8.625	0.850	7.547	22.00	2.25		14.40	2.85	17.25	35.67	18.42	132.79	75.66
2008	0.812	7.181	0.711	6.283	22.00	2.25		14.40	2.38	16.78	29.77	12.99	145.78	82.65
2009	0.698	6.152	0.611	5.383	22.00	2.25		14.40	2.04	16.44	25.55	9.10	154.88	87.11
2010	0.650	5.381	0.569	4.708	22.00	2.25		14.40	1.85	16.25	23.11	6.86	161.74	90.16
2011	0.631	5.048	0.552	4.417	22.00	2.25		14.40	1.77	16.17	22.09	5.92	167.66	92.55
2012	0.591	4.728	0.517	4.137	22.00	2.25		14.40	1.65	16.05	20.69	4.63	172.29	94.25
2013	0.572	4.576	0.501	4.004	22.00	2.25		14.40	1.60	16.00	20.02	4.02	176.31	95.60
2014	0.569	4.552	0.498	3.983	22.00	2.25		14.40	1.59	15.99	19.92	3.92	180.23	96.79
2015	0.567	4.536	0.496	3.969	22.00	2.25		14.40	1.59	15.99	19.85	3.86	184.09	97.85
2016	0.560	4.480	0.490	3.920	22.00	2.25		14.40	1.57	15.97	19.60	3.63	187.72	98.76
2017														
Sub	17.215	148.759	15.063	130.164			185.00	201.60	49.94	436.54	624.26	187.72		
Rem	0.000	0.000	0.000	0.000			0.00	0.00	0.00	0.00	0.00	0.00		
Total	17.215	148.759	15.063	130.164			185.00	201.60	49.94	436.54	624.26	187.72		

Initial WI Fraction	1.00000	Lease Operating Exp. ($/Month)	1200
Final WI Fraction	1.00000	Production Start Date	01/01/03
Initial Net Oil Fraction	0.87500	Oil Severance Tax (Percent)	8.00
Initial Net Gas Fraction	0.87500	Gas Severance Tax (Percent)	8.00
Final Net Oil Fraction	0.87500	Advalorem Tax (Percent)	0.00
Final Net Gas Fraction	0.87500	Reversion Point	0
		MScf to BOE	9.778

Net Present Value @10% (M$)	98.76
Rate of Return (ROR)	37.00%
Profitability Index	1.560
Payout (Disc. @ 10%), Years	2.75
Technical Cost, $/Stb	27.90
Technical Cost, $/BOE	14.81
Technical Cost, $/Stb (Disc.)	30.68
Technical Cost, $/BOE (Disc.)	16.23

NPV Profile

Percent	NPV (M$)
5%	136.26
15%	70.37
20%	48.22
25%	30.52
30%	16.10
35%	4.19
40%	(5.77)

Table 3–18 Typical (before federal income tax) cash flow

6. Column L lists the gross revenue (i.e., before any expenses are deducted), corresponding to the net production in Columns D & E (i.e., 100% WI and 87.5% NRI in this particular case). This is the sum of Column D times Column F and Column E times Column G.

7. Column M lists the net revenue (also referred to as the net cash flow), which is Column L less Column K. The net cash flow (in this case, before income tax) is an important indicator of how the operation is progressing year-by-year from a business standpoint.

8. Column N lists cumulative cash flow, the cumulative of Column M by year.

9. Column O lists the cumulative discounted net cash flow. As discussed in Chapter 2, the net cash flow generated in each year has to be brought to its equivalent of present value. This is obtained by multiplying the entries in Column M by $[1/(1 + 0.1)^{(n - 0.5)}]$, where 0.1 (10%) is the discount rate as discussed in the preceding section.

The cash-flow of Table 3–18 is included on the CD-ROM included with Volume 2 in this series. In addition, a more detailed cash-flow model is also included as a part of ECON-PAC on the CD-ROM.

QUESTIONS and PROBLEMS

3.1 Calculate the EL in barrels per month for an oil lease with WI=100%, NRI=87.5%, lease operating expense=$5000/month, price of oil=$15/stb, price of associated gas= $2.25/Mscf, gas–oil ratio=500 Scf/stb, and the severance tax for oil and gas is 7.085% each.

3.2 Calculate the EL in Mscf per month for a gas lease with WI=100%, NRI=87.5%, condensate price=$15/stb, gas price=$2.25/Mscf, condensate yield=5 stb/Mscf, and the severance tax for gas and condensate is 4.5% each.

3.3 An oil well has been drilled and completed. The productive zone has been encountered at a depth of 7815–7830 feet. The log analysis showed an average porosity of 15% and an average water saturation of 35%. The oil formation volume factor was determined from empirical equations to be 1.215 RB/Stb. Experience shows that other reservoirs of about the same properties drained 80 acres with a recovery factor of 12%. Compute the STOIIP and the ultimate recovery.

3.4 The initial rate and EL of the well in Problem 3.3 is 1680 Stb/month and 200 Stb/month, respectively. At what exponential decline rate will it recover the reserves calculated in Problem 3.3? How long it will take the well to reach the EL?

3.5 A gas well is completed at a depth of 8550 feet. The log analysis showed total formation thickness of 12 feet of 16% porosity and 30% water saturation. On potential test, the well produced dry gas with a specific gravity of 0.75. The reservoir pressure was determined from a drill stem test (DST) to be 3850 psi and the log heading showed a reservoir temperature of 155° F. The gas will be produced at the surface where the standard pressure is 14.65 psi and the standard temperature is 60° F. The study of the offset wells producing from the same formation has shown that the wells are capable of draining 160 acres at a recovery factor of 85%. Compute the GIIP and the recoverable gas reserves. The gas formation volume factor is 259.89 SCF/CF.

3.6   In Problem 3.5, if the abandonment pressure has been determined to be 800 psi below which no gas could be economically produced. Based on this information, compute the ultimate gas recovery and the recovery factor. The formation volume factor at abandonment pressure is 51.88 SCF/CF.

3.7   An oil well is producing consistently for the last five years. The monthly oil production for each year is given as follows. It costs $2,000 per month to operate the well, the current oil price is $27 per barrel, and the severance tax is 7.085% of the gross value. The well is not producing any associated gas. Compute (a) the EL based on 100% WI and 87.5% NRI, (b) plot the production versus time on an appropriate graph paper and compute the exponential decline, (c) the remaining oil reserves as of 1/1/1999, (d) production rate at the end of 2001, (e) the remaining life of the well, (f) ultimate oil recovery, and (g) production for 1999, 2000, and 2001.

3.8   Confirm the reserves obtained in Problem 3.7 by using rate–cumulative oil production plot.

Month	Oil Production, Stb				
	1994	1995	1996	1997	1998
January	2,399	1,882	1,637	1,334	1,151
February	2,059	1,621	1,265	1,177	1,028
March	1,808	1,536	1,386	1,208	1,151
April	1,627	1,551	1,310	1,191	1,075
May	1,699	1,526	1,300	1,370	1,081
June	1,575	1,553	1,241	1,315	983
July	1,618	1,514	1,289	1,268	1,037
August	1,660	1,428	1,299	1,312	959
September	1,575	1,320	1,240	1,224	989
October	1,538	1,534	1,290	1,229	897
November	1,541	1,309	1,240	1,202	1,044
December	1,702	1,474	1,348	1,229	996

3.9   In Problem 3.7, generate the cash flow to the EL of the lease.

3.10 A gas well is producing from the Morrow formation at a depth of 6462 feet in Camrick gas area, Texas County, Oklahoma. The productive interval is perforated from 6462 to 6593 feet. The reservoir temperature is 162° F and the gas gravity is 0.70. Based on the following pressure test data: compute (a) IGIP; (b) recoverable gas reserves, assuming an abandonment p/z of 500 psi; (c) recovery factor; and (d) remaining gas reserves as of 06/04/1998 to an abandonment pressure of 243 psi (p/z = 250 psi).

	Cumulative to Test, BSCF	BHP/z, psi
07/15/1986	1.774	1,546
07/15/1989	2.305	1,366
07/15/1992	3.151	1,102
07/19/1995	4.071	862
06/04/1998	4.808	612

3.11 A lease owned by Company XYZ has to be evaluated. The lease is currently producing at a rate of 4000 Stb/month. It is estimated that production will be constant for one year, and then decline exponentially at a rate of 30% per year. Current operating expenses are $15,000 per month and are expected to increase by 10% per year in a step rate manner. Oil price is $15/Stb, and severance tax is 12% of gross revenue. The company has a 50% working interest and a corresponding net revenue interest (NRI) of 40%. Determine:
a. EL.
b. Remaining 8/8ths reserves.
c. Remaining net reserves (your company's share).
d. The economic productive life of the lease.
e. The cash flow to the EL.

3.12   A 320-acre lease has to be evaluated. Data on the lease are as follows:

Average Porosity	= 15%
Net pay	= 15 ft
Water saturation	= 30%
Reservoir Oil Formation Volume Factor	= 1.2
Initial Producing Rate	= 1,714 Stb/m
Economic Limit	= 200 Stb/m
Recovery Factor	= 20%

Determine by calculations the following:
a.   STBs initially in place.
b.   Recoverable reserves.
c.   Exponential decline rate required to recover the reserves.
d.   Life of field, years.
e.   Average producing rate after five years, Stb/month.

3.13   Calculate the cost of a 9-slot wellhead jacket if 3-slot wellhead jacket for the same location costs $6 million. The correlation exponent in the area is 0.50.

3.14   The XYZ oil company acquires an oil and gas lease from a landowner Mr. A. The mineral deed shows Mr. A will be entitled to Landowner's royalty interest (LORI) of $1/8^{th}$. The geologist who found the area retains an ORRI of 1.5%. Calculate the NRI of the XYZ Oil Company assuming the company has a 100% working interest.

3.15   If the XYZ Oil Company in Problem 3.14 shares the working interest with three other investors as follows, compute the NRI of each investor assuming the same LORI and ORRI are applicable.

Investors	WI Share, %
A, XYZ Oil Company	50
B, ABC Oil Company	25
C, Gas Producers, Inc.	15
D, Dome Oil and Gas, Inc.	10

3.16 The XYZ Oil Company has successfully completed an oil well for a total cost of $900,000. The well will produce 30,000 barrels of oil in the first year, 18,000 barrels in the second year and 10,800 barrels in the third year. The selling price of oil is $25 per barrel, and the gross operating expenses for the first year are $36,000, $24,000 for the second year, and $16,000 for the third year. The XYZ oil company has a 50% WI with a net lease of 80%. The ABC oil company has a 25% WI in the lease that reverts to 30% WI after the XYZ oil company recovers its share of the drilling and completion costs. What is the payout amount at the beginning of the first year? After how long will the interest of ABC Oil Company revert? Assume the operating costs include the applicable production taxes.

3.17 Generate a cash flow for the data in Problems 3.3 and 3.4. Assume (a) the price of oil to be $20/Stb, (b) severance tax is 7%, (c) working interest is 100%, (d) net revenue interest is 87.5%, and (e) monthly lease operating cost is $3,700. The total cost of drilling and completing the well is $450,000.

REFERENCES

[1] Mian, M. A., "Creating Quality, Cost-Effective Property Reports," *World Oil*, September 1985, pp. 71–74.

[2] Mian, M. A,. *Petroleum Engineering Handbook for the Practicing Engineer, Vol. I*, PennWell Publishing Co., Tulsa, Oklahoma, 1992.

[3] Allen, Fraser H. and Seba, Richard D., *Economics of Worldwide Petroleum Production*, Oil & Gas Consultants International (OGCI), Inc., Tulsa, Oklahoma, 1993.

[4] Arps, J. J., "Analysis of Decline Curves," *Trans.*, AIME, 160, 1944, pp. 228–247.

[5] Fetkovitch, M. J., "Decline Curve Analysis Using Type Curves," *Journal of Petroleum Tech.*, June 1980, pp. 1065–1077.

[6] Rowland, D. A. and Lin, Cheng, "New Linear Method Gives Constants of Hyperbolic Decline," *Oil & Gas Journal*, Jan 14, 1985, pp. 86–89.

[7] Luther, L. C., "Linearization and Regression Analysis Technique Predicts Hyperbolic Decline in Reserves," *Oil & Gas Journal*, Aug. 26, 1985, pp. 78–79.

[8] Long, D. R. and Davis, M. J., "A New Approach to the Hyperbolic Curve, *Journal of Petroleum Tech.*, July 1988, pp. 909–912.

[9] Mian, M. A., "Program Quickly Solves Trial-and-Error Problems," *World Oil*, September 1990, pp. 67–75.

[10] Neal, D. B. and Mian, M. A., "Early-Time Tight Gas Production Forecasting Technique Improves Reserves and Reservoir Description," *SPE Formation Evaluation*, March 1989, pp. 25–32.

[11] Mian, M. A., "J-Sand (Tight) Performance Predicted by Type Curves," *Oil & Gas Journal*, May 30, 1983, pp. 109–112.

[12] Mian, M. A., "Predicting the Performance of Tight Gas Reservoirs," *World Oil*, August 1, 1984, pp. 47–50.

[13] Berger, Bill D. and Anderson, Kenneth, E. *Modern Petroleum, 3rd Edition*, PennWell Publishing Co., Tulsa, Oklahoma, 1992.

[14] Thompson, R. S. and Wright, J. D., *Oil Property Evaluation*, Thompson-Wright Associates, Golden, Colorado, 1984.

[15] Pohlman, R.A., Santiago, E.S., and Markel, F.L., "Cash Flow Estimation Practices of Large Firms," *Financial Management*, spring 1987, pp. 46–51.

[16] Pruitt, S.W., and Gitman, L.J., "Capital Budgeting Forecast Biases: Evidence from the Fortune 500," *Financial Management*, Spring 1987, pp. 46–51.

[17] Ehrhardt, Michael C., *The Search for Value: Measuring the Company's Cost of Capital*, Harvard Business School Press, Boston, Massachusetts, 1994.

chapter FOUR

After-Tax Cash-Flow Model

To this point it has been emphasized that investment decisions should be based on cash flows. In Chapter 3, a cash-flow model without any reference to corporate taxation is presented. Federal income tax is a disbursement that must be included in the economic evaluations. However, its inclusion in investment analysis increases their complexity. On the other hand, performing economic evaluations without accounting for tax effects is misleading. In some cases, incorporating taxes in economic evaluation may reverse the decisions based on the before-tax cash flows.

The interest payments on debt, depreciation, depletion, and amortization (DD&A) expenses do influence the value and timing of the taxable income and the resulting tax payment (actual cash *outflows*). These items are known as tax-deductible items. Corporate taxes may not affect all investments to the same degree. Therefore, for meaningful comparisons, project cash flows must always be expressed on an after-tax basis. The variables required, in addition to the ones discussed in Chapter 3, to arrive at After Federal Income Tax (AFIT or ATAX) cash flow are discussed in this chapter.

The tax laws vary considerably from country to country due to small business allowances, investment tax credits, adjustments for double taxation, and so on. Tax rates also vary with time. It is worth noting, however, that the corporate tax structures of many countries are similar, and for most countries range between 30% and 40%.

The net after-tax cash flow equals the pre-tax cash flow minus the applicable taxes (a specified percent of the firm's taxable income), mathematically expressed as:

(4.1)

$$NCF_{AFIT} = NCF_{BFIT} - T_c\left(NCF_{BFIT} - DD \& A - I\right)$$
$$= \left(1 - T_c\right)NCF_{BFIT} + T_c\left(DD \& A + I\right)$$

where
$\quad\quad T_c$ = the corporate tax rate, fraction
$\quad NCF_{AFIT}$ = the after corporate income tax net cash flow
$\quad NCF_{BFIT}$ = the before corporate income tax net cash flow
$\quad\quad DD\&A$ = depreciation, depletion, and amortization
$\quad\quad\quad I$ = interest payment on debt (loan)

The after-tax cash flow is central to all financial decision problems and can be derived as follows:

1. Calculate the project's net income by subtracting the operating costs, severance and ad valorem taxes, depreciation, intangible drilling costs (IDCs), and interest on debt to arrive at the taxable income before depletion. The concept of interest deduction is further discussed in the following pages. There are different ways of handling interest payments in cash flows; these will be discussed in Chapter 6.

2. Subtract the allowable depletion (cost depletion or percent depletion) allowance (discussed in the following sections) to arrive at the taxable income after allowable depletion. If the taxable income is negative (i.e., there is no tax payment), the loss is carried forward to the following years.

3. Calculate the tax liability by multiplying the positive taxable income by the applicable corporate tax rate.

4. Calculate the after-tax income by subtracting the tax payable from the taxable income.

5. Add the DD&A, IDCs, and interest to the after-tax income in Step 4 to arrive at the net after-tax cash flow.

The topics that form the basis for tax liability calculations and the after-tax cash flow are discussed in this chapter. The discussion is intended to be brief and not an exhaustive analysis of the more complex tax laws. Specific tax questions should be addressed to tax professionals. In its simplest form, the after-tax cash-flow projection would be as shown in Table 4–1. A framework for the development of AFIT cash-flow model is illustrated in Figures 4–1 through 4–3.

		Year 1	Year 2	Year 3	Year 4
	Cash Received	$	$	$	$
Less	Cash Expanded	$	$	$	$
	Depreciation	$	$	$	$
	IDCs	$	$	$	$
	Interest	$	$	$	$
Equals	Taxable Before Depletion	$	$	$	$
Less	Depletion Allowance	$	$	$	$
Equals	Taxable Income	$	$	$	$
Less	Tax at 30%	$	$	$	$
Equal	Net After Tax Income	$	$	$	$
Plus	Depreciation	$	$	$	$
	Depletion Allowance	$	$	$	$
	Interest	$	$	$	$
	IDCs	$	$	$	$
Equals	Net After Tax Cash Flow	$	$	$	$

Table 4–1 Simple ater-tax net cash-flow projection

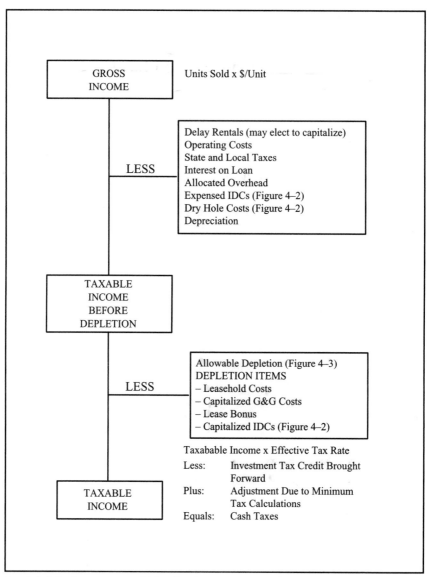

Fig. 4–1 Federal income tax model for oil and gas transactions (after Thompson and Wright)[1]

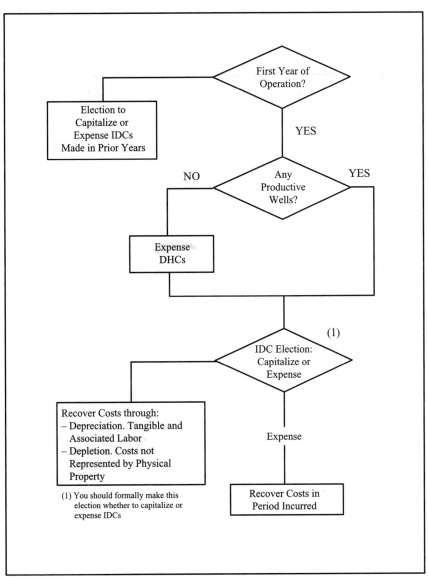

Fig. 4–2 Recovery of drilling and completion costs (after Thompson and Wright)[1]

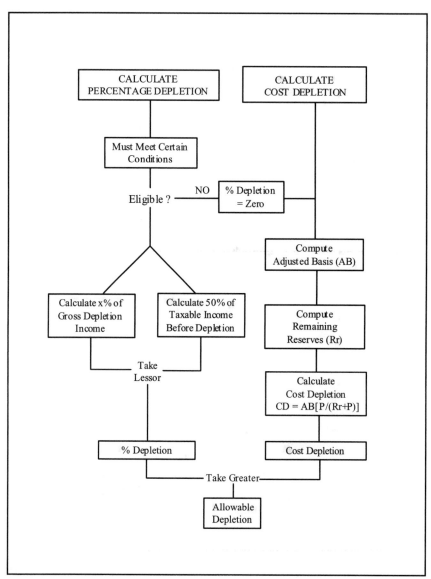

Fig. 4–3 Depletion allowance calculation (after Thompson and Wright)[1]

Depreciation

Depreciation is a deductible *non-cash* expense for income tax purposes. The higher the depreciation allowance being deducted in any given year, the lower the taxable income and the cash disbursements (cash outflow) in the form of income tax. As noted earlier, *depreciation is not an actual cash outflow and therefore is not subtracted from the annual cash flow as an expense.* However, the tax deductibility of depreciation decreases the firm's tax liability. Therefore, its inclusion in calculating the projects' after-tax cash flow is essential.

Depreciation is defined as a loss in the value of asset over the time it is being used. Events that can cause property to depreciate include wear and tear, age, deterioration, and obsolescence. The asset subject to depreciation can be either a *tangible property,* or *intangible property*.

Depreciation of a property begins from the time the property is placed in service for use in trade or business or for the production of income. Depreciating a property is stopped when the cost or other basis of the property is recovered or when it is retired (i.e., permanently withdrawn from use in trade or business) from service. The property is retired from service by selling or exchanging it, abandoning it, or destroying it. The cost of a property is fully recovered when its depreciation deductions are equal to the cost or investment in the project.

Tangible Property

Tangible property is that which can be seen or touched. Tangible property includes two main types (1) real property and (2) personal property. Real property is land and buildings, and generally, anything built or constructed on land or anything growing on or attached to the land. Land by itself can never be depreciated because it does not wear out or become obsolete and it cannot be used up. Personal property includes cars, trucks, machinery, furniture, equipment, and anything that is tangible except real property.

Intangible Property

Intangible property is generally any personal property that has a value but cannot be seen or touched. It includes items such as copyright, franchises, patents, trademarks, and trade names. Intangible property must either be amortized or depreciated using the straight-line method.

Unless the costs of patent or copyright are amortized, the costs can be recovered through depreciation. The useful life of a copyright or patent is the life granted to it by the government. If it becomes valueless in any year before its useful life expires, the remaining cost can be deducted in full for that year. If patents or copyrights are acquired as part of the acquisition of a substantial portion of a business after August 10, 1993 (or after July 25, 1991, if elected), the cost must be amortized over 15 years. If these are not acquired as part of an acquisition of a substantial portion of a business, the costs shall be depreciated as mentioned above.

A franchise can be depreciated only if it has a determinable useful life and cannot be amortized. If a franchise has been acquired after August 10, 1993 (after July 10, 1991, if elected), the cost must be amortized over 15 years.

For property to be depreciable, it must first meet all of the following basic requirements:

1. The property must be used in business or held to produce income.
2. The property must have a determinable useful life longer than one year.
3. The property must be something that is subject to wearing out, decaying being used up, becoming obsolete, or losing its value from natural causes.
4. If a repair or replacement increases the value of a property, makes it more useful, or lengthens its life, the repairs or replacement cost must be capitalized and depreciated. If the repair or replacement does not increase the value of a property, make it more useful, or lengthen its life, the cost of the repair or replacement is deductible in the same way as any other business expense.

For additional details on depreciation and how to depreciate property, reference is made to Publication 946 of the Internal Revenue Service.

Modified Accelerated Cost Recovery System

The Modified Accelerated Cost Recovery System (MACRS) is the name given to tax rules for getting back (recovering) through depreciation deductions the cost of a depreciable property. These rules generally apply to tangible property placed in service after 1986. MACRS consists of two main systems that determine how a property can be depreciated. The main system is called *General Depreciation System* (GDS) while the second system is called *Alternative Depreciation System* (ADS). Unless law specially requires ADS or you elect it, GDS is generally used. The main difference between the two systems is that ADS generally provides for a longer recovery period and uses straight-line method of depreciation.

If a property is depreciated under a method not based on a term of years, such as the *unit-of-production* method, you can elect to exclude that property from MACRS. Once it is determined that a property can be depreciated under MACRS and whether it falls under GDS or ADS, the following information is required to figure out depreciation.

1. Its basis (i.e., the cost paid for the property).

2. Its property class and recovery period. Under MACRS, property is assigned to one of several property classes. These property classes establish the recovery periods (number of years) over which the basis of the property can be recovered. The list of class lives and recovery periods for various oil and gas related properties are given in Table 4–2.

    Under GDS, most tangible property is assigned to one of the following eight main property classes.

    a. *3-year property.* This class includes tractor units for over-the-road use and any racehorse more than two years old when placed in service.

    b. *5-year property.* This class includes automobiles, taxis, buses, trucks, computers and peripheral equipment, office machinery (such as typewriters, calculators, copiers, etc.., and any property used in research and experimentation. It also includes breeding cattle and dairy cattle.

    c. *7-year property.* This class includes office furniture and fixtures such as desks, files, safes, etc. Any property that does not have a class life and that has not been designated by law, as being in any other class is also a 7-year property.

    d. *10-year property.* This class includes vessels, barges, tugs, similar water transportation equipment, any single purpose agricultural or horticultural structure, and any tree or vine bearing fruits or nuts.

			Recovery Periods (in years)	
	Description of Assets Includes	Class Life (in years)	GDS MACRS	ADS
1.	**Office Furniture, Fixtures, and Equipment** Includes furniture and fixtures that are not a structural component of a building. Includes such assets as desks, files, safes, and communication equipment. Does not include communication equipment that is included in other classes.	10	7	10
2.	**Information Systems** Includes computers and peripheral equipment used in administering normal business transactions and the maintenance of business records, their retrieval and analysis. Information systems are defined as: a) **Computers:** A computer is a programmable electrically activated device capable of accepting information, applying prescribed processes to the information, and supplying the results of these processes with or without human intervention. It usually consists of a central processing unit containing extensive storage, logic, arithmetic, and control capabilities. Excluded from this category are adding machines, electronic desk calculators, etc., and other equipment described in Class 3 below. b) Peripheral equipment consists of the auxiliary machines designed to be placed under control of the central processing unit. Non-limiting examples are: card readers, card punches, magnetic tape feeds, high speed printers, optical character readers, tape cassettes, mass storage units, paper tape equipment, keypunches, data entry devices, teleprinters, terminals, tape devices, disc drives, disc files, disc packs, visual image projector tubes, card sorters, and collators. Peripheral equipment may be used on-line or off-line. Does not include equipment that is an integral part of other capital equipment that is included in other classes of economic activity.	6	5	5
3.	**Data Handling Equipment; Except Computers** Includes only typewriters, calculators, adding and accounting machines, copiers, and duplicating equipment	6	5	6
4.	**Light General Purpose Trucks** Includes trucks for use over the road (actual weight less than 13,000 pounds).	4	5	5
5.	**Heavy General Purpose Trucks** Includes heavy general-purpose trucks, concrete ready mix-trucks, and ore trucks over the road (actual unloaded weight 13,000 pounds or more).	6	5	6
6.	**Offshore Drilling** Includes assets used in offshore drilling for oil and gas such as floating, self-propelled and other drilling vessels, barges, platforms, and drilling equipment and support vessels such as tenders, barges, towboats and crew boats. Excludes oil and gas production assets.	7.5	5	7.5
7.	**Drilling of Oil and Gas Wells** Includes assets used in the drilling of onshore oil and gas wells and the provision of geophysical and other exploration services; and the provision of such oil and gas field services as chemical treatment, plugging and abandoning of wells and cementing or perforating well casings. Does not include assets used in the performance of any of these activities and services by integrated petroleum and natural gas producers for their own account.	6	5	6
8.	**Exploration for and Production of Petroleum and Natural Gas Deposits** Includes assets used by petroleum and natural gas producers for drilling of wells and production of petroleum and natural gas, including gathering pipeline and related storage facilities. Also includes petroleum and natural gas offshore transportation facilities used by producers and others consisting of platforms (other than drilling platforms classified in Class 6 above), compression or pumping equipment and gathering and transmission lines to the first onshore transshipment facility. The assets used in the first onshore transshipment facility are also included and consists of separation equipment (used for separation of natural gas, liquids), and liquid holding or storage facilities (other than those classified in Class 12). Does not include support vessels.	14	7	7
9.	**Petroleum Refining** Includes assets used for the distillation, fractionation, and catalytic cracking of crude petroleum into gasoline and its other components.	16	10	16

Table 4–2 Class lives and recovery periods for various oil and gas properties

Description of Assets Includes	Class Life (in years)	Recovery Periods (in years)	
		GDS MACRS	ADS
10. **Pipeline Transportation** Includes assets used in the private, commercial, and contract carrying petroleum, gas, and other products by means of pipes and conveyers. The trunk lines and related storage facilities of integrated petroleum and natural gas producers are included in this class. Excludes initial clearing and grading land improvements but includes all other related land improvements.	22	15	22
11. **Natural Gas Production Plant**	14	7	14
12. **Liquefied Natural Gas Plant** Includes assets used in the liquefaction, storage, and re-gasification of natural gas including loading and unloading connections, instrumentation equipment and controls, pumps, vaporizers and odorizers, tanks, and related land improvements. Also includes pipeline interconnections with gas transmission lines and distribution systems and marine terminal facilities.	22	15	22

Table 4–2 Continued . . .

e.   *15-year property.* This class includes certain depreciable improvements made directly to land or added to it, such as shrubbery, fences, roads, and bridges.

f   *20-year property.* This class includes farm buildings (other than agricultural or horticultural structures).

g.   *Residential rental property.* This class includes real property such as rental home or structure (including a mobile home) if 80% or more of its gross rental income for tax year is for dwelling units. The recovery period for this property is 27.5 years.

h.   *Nonresidential real property.* The recovery period for nonresidential real property is 39 years if it is placed in service after May 12, 1993 otherwise it is 31.5 years.

3.   Its placed-in-service date.

4.   Which convention to use. To figure out the depreciation deduction under GDS or ADS, one of the following three conventions is used.

a.   *The Half-Year Convention.* This convention is generally used for property other than nonresidential real and residential rental property. Under this convention, all depreciable property placed in service or disposed of during a tax year is treated as placed in service or disposed of at the midpoint of the year regardless of when during the year. First, figure out the depreciation for a full tax year using the method you select. Then apply the half-year convention by taking only half of the total amount calculated for the first year.

b. *The Mid-Month Convention.* This convention is used for (i) non-residential real property, and (ii) residential real property. Under this convention, all depreciable property placed in service or disposed of during a month is treated as placed in service or disposed of at the midpoint of the month, regardless of when during the month. First, figure out the depreciation for a full tax year using the straight-line method for residential rental or nonresidential real property. Then multiply this amount by a fraction. The numerator of the fraction is the number of full months in the tax year that the property is in service plus 1/2 (or 0.5). The denominator is 12.

c. *The Mid-Quarter Convention.* This convention can apply to any depreciable property (other than nonresidential real property and residential rental property) in certain circumstances. These circumstances occur during any tax year when the total depreciable bases of your MACRS property placed in service during the last three months of that tax year are more than 40 percent of the total depreciable bases of all MACRS property placed in service during the entire tax year. When that happens, you must use this convention. To figure the MACRS deduction using this convention, first figure your depreciation for the full tax year. Then multiply by the percentages (i) 87.5%, (ii) 62.5%, (iii) 37.5%, and (iv) 12.5% for the first, second, third, and fourth quarter, respectively, of the tax year the property is placed in service.

5. Which depreciation method to use. Under MACRS, five methods can be used to depreciate a property.

a. The 200% declining-balance method over the GDS recovery period (for non-farm property in the 3-, 5-, 7-, and 10-year property classes), which switches to the straight-line method when that method provides a greater deduction.

b. The 150% declining balance method over the GDS recovery period (for property in the 15- and 20-year property classes and property used in farming businesses), which switches to the straight-line method when that method provides a greater deduction.

c. The straight-line method over the GDS recovery period used for nonresidential real property and residential rental property, and if you elect it, property in the 3-, 5-, 7-, 10-, 15- and 20-year classes.

d. The 150% declining balance method over fixed ADS recovery periods, which switches to the straight-line method when that method provides a greater deduction.
e. The straight-line method over fixed ADS recovery periods.

Accelerated Cost Recovery System

The Accelerated Cost Recovery System (ACRS) applies to property placed in service after 1980 and before 1987. For the property placed in service after 1986, the MACRS method is used. Property depreciated under ACRS was called *recovery property*. The recovery class of property determined the recovery period. Generally, the class life of property placed it in a 3-year, 5-year, 10-year, 15-year, 18-year, or 19-year recovery class.

Under the ACRS, prescribed percentages were used to recover the unadjusted basis of recovery property. The depreciation deduction is figured out by multiplying the prescribed percentage for the recovery class by the unadjusted basis of the recovery property.

ACRS also provided an alternative ACRS method that could be elected. This alternate ACRS method uses recovery percentage based on a modified straight-line method. Under the ACRS method, only the half-year of depreciation was deducted for the year a property was placed in service. This applied regardless of when in the tax year the property was placed in service. For each of the remaining years in the recovery period, full deduction is taken. If the property is held for the entire recovery period, a half-year of depreciation is allowable for the year following the end of the recovery period.

Straight-Line Depreciation

Before 1981, one could use a reasonable method for every kind of depreciable property. One of these methods was the straight-line method. In this method of depreciation, the depreciable cost or cost basis of the property is equally distributed over the useful life of the asset. The following equation is used.

(4.2)

$$D_n = \frac{C - S_v}{n}$$

where D_n is the depreciation in nth year, C is the total cost of the depreciable asset, S_v is the salvage value, and n is the useful life of the asset. Salvage value, also referred to as residual value, terminal value, or scrap value is the estimated value of property at the end of its useful life. It is what one would expect to get for the property if it is sold after it can no longer be used productively. The difference between the total acquisition cost of the asset and its predicted salvage value is sometimes called *depreciable value*.

It should be remembered that if a depreciable asset is expected to have any salvage value at the end of the project's economic life and this value exceeds the equipment's book value (original prices less accumulated depreciation at that time), a corporate tax liability would be incurred on the profit (net of abandonment costs) from the sale of such equipment. Starting with the 1986 tax year, corporate long-term capital gains are to be taxed as ordinary income, and are subject to 34% tax rate. The tax and sales proceeds appear in the last year of the project's cash flow. Similarly, if equipment is replaced at the beginning or in the middle of a planned project, the transaction should be reflected in the cash flow in the respective period. Tax payments generated by such transactions can be crucial to the investment decision.

Example 4–1

Compute the straight-line depreciation for a pumping unit acquired at a cost of $35,000 with a salvage value of $5,000 at the end of its useful life of 5 years.

$$D_n = \frac{\$35,000 - \$5,000}{5}$$

$$= \$6,000 \text{ per year}$$

Declining Balance Depreciation

This method is also referred to as the accelerated depreciation method. The method is appropriate when it can be reasonably estimated that the benefits derived from an asset will decline with time. The declining balance depreciation is also used under the MACRS method of depreciation. A fixed value of percentage is applied to the book value (total value of asset less accumulated depreciation of previous years) of the asset each year.

The declining balance depreciation is further divided into different percentages, such as the 200% declining balance method (also referred to as the *double declining balance depreciation*), 175% declining balance, 150% declining balance, and 125% declining balance. The fixed percentage is calculated by dividing the above-mentioned percentages by the recovery period assigned to the asset. The following example clarifies the computations.

Under this method, the salvage value is not subtracted when figuring yearly deductions. However, the property may not be depreciated below its reasonable salvage value. In addition, it is allowed to switch to the straight-line depreciation in the year when this method provides greater deduction over the declining balance method.

Example 4–2

For the pumping unit in Example 4–1, calculate 200% declining balance depreciation and switching to straight line when feasible. Assume zero salvage value at the end of 5 years.

Solution: Fixed Percentage $= \dfrac{200\%}{5} = 40\%$ *or* 0.40

The depreciation schedule is shown in Table 4–3. The book value at the beginning of the 2nd year (adjusted basis) is $21,000 (i.e., $35,000 – $14,000 = $21,000), and so on. The straight-line depreciation is calculated by dividing the book value at the beginning of the year by the remaining life of the asset.

Sum-of-the-Years'-Digits Depreciation

This method produces a declining depreciation charge each year by applying a declining charge to the total cost of asset (depreciation base). The declining charge is determined each year by dividing the remaining

Year	Book Value of Asset at Beginning of Year	Rate	D_n Declining Balance	D_n Straight Line	Deduction Taken
1	$35,000	0.4	$14,000	$7,000	$14,000
2	21,000	0.4	8,400	5,250	8,400
3	12,600	0.4	5,040	4,200	5,040
4	7,560	0.4	3,024	3,780	3,780
5	3,780	0.4		3,789	3,780
			Total		35,000

Table 4–3 200% declining balance with switch to straight-line depreciation.

life of the asset by the sum of the years' digits. For an asset with a 5-year life, the sum of years' digits is 5+4+3+2+1 = 15, and the declining charge for the 1st year is 5/15, and so on. The following equation is used to calculate the sum of years' digits.

(4.3)

$$SYD = \frac{n(n+1)}{2}$$

(4.4)

$$SYD = \frac{Number\ of\ Remaining\ Years\ of\ Life}{SYD} \times (C - S_v)$$

where *SYD* is the sum of years' digits, and n is the useful life of the asset to be depreciated.

In this method of depreciation, the depreciation rate is equal to the years remaining divided by the sum of the years. Clearly, the annual depreciation is higher towards the beginning of the project because this is when the remaining life is longer.

Example 4-3

Rework Example 4–2 using the half-year convention. In this convention, the deduction taken is half of the calculated depreciation. For the 5-year property, the final year is the *6th* year because of applying the half-year convention in the 1st year. For the straight-line depreciation in the 2nd and 3rd year, the adjusted basis is be divided by 4.5 and 3.5 years, respectively, and so on. The rate for the final year need not be determined because the remaining recovery period is less than 1 year.

Solution: The calculations are shown in Table 4–4.

Year	Book Value of Asset at Beginning of Year	Rate	D_n Declining Balance	D_n Straight Line	Depreciation Taken
1	$35,000	0.4	$14,000	$3,500	$7,000
2	28,000	0.4	11,200	6,222	11,200
3	16,800	0.4	6,720	4,800	6,720
4	10,080	0.4	4,032	4,032	4,032
5	6,048	0.4	2,419	4,032	4,032
6	2,016	0.4	806	2,016	2,016
				Total	$35,000

Table 4–4 Depreciation Calculation Using Half Year Convention (Example 4-3).

Example 4-4

Compute the sum of years' digits depreciation for the asset in Example 4–2.

Solution: $SYD = \dfrac{5(5+1)}{5} = 15$

The depreciation schedule for Example 4–4 is shown in Table 4–5.

Year	Depreciation Base	Fraction	Depreciation Charge	Book Value at Year End
1	$35,000	5/15	$11,667	$23,333
2	$35,000	4/15	9,333	14,000
3	$35,000	3/15	7,000	7,000
4	$35,000	2/15	4,667	2,333
5	$35,000	1/15	2,333	0

Table 4–5 Depreciation schedule for Example 4–5

Units of Production Depreciation

When physical wear and tear is the dominating factor in the useful life of the asset, depreciation may be based on units of service rather than on the units of time. Therefore, this method is used when it is determined that the life of the asset is dependent on how much the asset is used or it produces, rather than the passage of time. The activity may be measured in hours, days, months, years, or the number of items produced, etc. The following equation is used to establish units of production depreciation rate. The depreciation charge for each year is calculated by multiplying the activity per period by the depreciation rate.

(4.5)

$$\text{Depreciation Rate} = \frac{Cost - Salvage\ Value}{Total\ Lifetime\ Activity}$$

Example 4–5

A drilling rig is purchased for $1,300,000. It is estimated that the rig will be able to drill a total of 10,000,000 feet. After drilling that many feet, the rig can be sold for $150,000. In the 1st year of service, the rig drills 155,000 feet, and in the 2nd year, it drills 100,000 feet. What is the depreciation deduction for the 2 years?

Solution:

$$\text{Depreciation Rate} = \frac{\$1,300,000 - \$150,000}{10,000,000}$$

$$= \$0.115 \text{ per foot}$$

$$\text{Depreciation for Year 1} = 155,000 \times 0.115$$

$$= \$17,825$$

$$\text{Depreciation for Year 2} = 100,000 \times 0.115$$

$$= \$11,500$$

Depreciate an asset

Amortize an investment

Deplete a resource

AMORTIZATION AND DEPLETION

A part of a certain business capital expenditure may be amortized (deducted) each year. Amortization generally allows a write-off of costs that are not ordinarily deductible. On the other hand, if you have an exhaustible natural resource or timber, you are allowed a depletion allowance.

Amortization

All costs incurred to get a business started are treated as capital expenditure and are part of your basis in the business. If you elect to amortize, these costs are deducted in equal amounts over a period of 60 months or more.

Business startup costs and organizational expenses for a corporation or partnership are capital expenditures. To be amortizable, the costs must be paid or incurred before the day the active trade or business begins. However, startup costs do not include deductible interests, taxes, and research and experimental costs.

Startup costs include cost of items such as survey of potential market; analysis of available facilities, labor supply, etc.; initial advertisements; salaries and wages for training employees and their instructors; and salaries and fees for executives, consultants, and other professional services.

Organizational costs include the cost of temporary directors; organizational meetings; incorporation fee; accounting services; and legal services for drafting the charter, bylaws, terms of the original stock certification, and minutes of organizational meeting. However, costs of issuing and selling stock or securities, such as commissions, professional fees, and printing costs, are not amortizable.

The amortization deduction each year is figured out by dividing the total of startup and organizational costs by the number of months in the amortization period. The resulting amount can be deducted each month.

Depletion

Natural exhaustible resources such as minerals, oil, natural gas, and timber, etc. are sometimes called wasting assets. Depletion is the gradual exhaustion of the original amounts of the resources acquired. Depletion differs from depreciation and amortization because the former focuses mainly on a physical phenomenon and the later focuses more broadly on any cause of the reduction of the economic value of fixed asset, including physical wear and tear plus obsolescence.

The depletion deduction is available to you as an owner and operator only if you have a legal interest in the oil and gas in place and you have the right to income from the extraction and sale of these. Typical in oil and gas deals, more than one party may have an economic interest in the reserves (or mineral deposit). Therefore, each interest owner accounts for his/her portion of the depletion deduction against his share of the costs paid for the acquisition of these reserves and the proportionate share of the reserves and production. Depletion is figured separately for each mineral property (i.e., each separate interest you own in each mineral deposit in each separate tract or parcel of land).

There are two ways of calculating depletion on mineral property (1) *cost depletion* and (2) *percentage depletion*. However, percentage depletion generally is not allowed for any oil or gas wells. However, an exemption from this rule applies to certain oil and gas producers. These are the independent producers and royalty owners (small producers).

The independent producers and royalty owners are those whose average daily oil production is up to 1000 barrels of oil equivalent (6000 standard cubic feet of natural gas is the equivalent of a barrel of oil). This is the small producer exemption.

Depletion allowed or allowable each year is the greater of percentage depletion (if allowed) or cost depletion. However, the adjusted basis may never be less than zero.

Cost Depletion. Cost depletion is figured out by dividing the adjusted basis of the mineral property by the total recoverable units in the property's natural deposit. Then multiply the resulting rate per unit by:

1. The units sold for which you receive payment during the tax year, if you use the cash method of accounting, or

2. The units sold, if you use the accrual method of accounting.

The total recoverable units is the number of units of mineral remaining at the end of the year (including units recovered but not sold) plus the number of units sold during the tax year. The recoverable units in place in a natural deposit are mainly an engineering problem to be determined by using generally accepted industry practice.

The adjusted basis of your mineral property is your original cost or other basis plus any capitalized costs, minus all the depletion allowed or allowable on the property. The basis for depletion would therefore be the same adjusted basis you would use in determining gain on the sale or other disposition of property but not including:

1. The amounts recoverable:

    a. Through depreciation deductions

    b. Through deferred expenses (including deferred exploration and development costs), and

    c. Through deductions other than depletion.

2. The residual value of land and improvements at the end of operations, and

3. The cost or value of land acquired for purposes other than mineral production.

In equation form, cost depletion can be represented by:

(4.6)

$$\text{Cost Depletion} = AB \left(\frac{Q}{R_r + Q} \right)$$

where AB is the adjusted basis for the taxable year, Q is the number of units sold during the year, and R_r is the number of remaining reserves at the end of the taxable year. This means that each year the remaining reserves have to be determined. The remaining reserves may not necessarily be the previous year's remaining reserves less the production during the year (i.e., the reserves may have been revised upward or downward due to additional studies, etc). Items included in the depletable basis for cost depletion are geological and geophysical (G&G) costs, lease bonus paid by the lessee, and capitalized intangible costs not represented by physical property.

Percentage Depletion. Percentage depletion is figured out by multiplying a certain percentage, specified for each mineral, by your gross income from the property during the tax year. Gross income from oil and gas property is the amount you receive from the sale of the oil or gas in the immediate vicinity of the well. The depletion deduction under this method cannot be more than 50% of your taxable income from the property, figured without the depletion deduction.

When figuring your percentage depletion and the taxable income limit, an amount equal to any rents and royalties (which are depletable income to the payee) paid or incurred for the property is excluded from the gross income from the property. Also, reduce your gross income from the property by the allocable part of any bonus paid for a mineral lease or an oil and gas lease.

If you are a qualified independent producer or royalty owner of oil and gas, your deduction for percentage depletion cannot be more than the smaller of:

1. Your taxable income from the property figured without the deduction for depletion, or

2. 65% of your taxable income from all sources figured without the depletion allowance, any net operating loss carryback, and any capital loss carryback. Any amount that cannot be deducted because of the 65% limit can be carried over and added to your depletion allowance (before applying any limits) for the following year.

The use of percentage depletion for oil and gas is not allowed, except for certain domestic oil and gas production. In general, the percentage depletion is 15% of the gross income from the *qualifying* production from oil and gas property. Gross income from the property does not include lease bonuses, advance royalties, or other amounts payable without regard to production from the property received or occurred after August 16, 1986. Independent producers and royalty owners (small producers) qualify for the 15% depletion rate for a maximum daily average production of 1000 barrels of oil equivalent (6000 ft^3 of natural gas are considered equivalent to a barrel of oil). This is the small producer exemption.

Percentage depletion is allowed for regulated natural gas and for gas sold under a fixed contract or produced from geopressured brine, regardless of whether you qualify for the small-producer exemption. *Income from natural gas sold under a fixed contract qualifies for percentage depletion at 22%.* Natural gas sold under a fixed contract is the domestic gas sold by the producer under a contract in effect on February 1, 1975, and at all times thereafter before the sale.

If you qualify for percentage depletion and it is less than the cost depletion for any year, you must use cost depletion for that year. To figure your depletion allowance for mineral properties, you should calculate it under both depletion methods for each property, and claim a deduction for the greater of the two amounts if the percentage depletion is less than the 50% of the taxable income before depletion.

Example 4–6

It is estimated that a taxpayer has remaining reserves (net to his interest) at the end of his tax year of 50,000 barrels of oil. His production share in the year was 6000 barrels sold at $18 per barrel. His net taxable income before depletion from the property was $80,000 and the taxpayer's total taxable income was $450,000. Compute the appropriate depletion charge for the year. The adjustable bases of the capitalized leasehold costs are $45,000.

Solution:
Using Equation (4.6):

$$\text{Cost Depletion} = \$45,000\left(\frac{6,000}{50,000+6,000}\right)$$
$$= \$4,821$$

Percentage depletion computation and limitation check:

- Percentage Depletion = 0.15 (6,000 × 18) = $16,200
- 50% Net Income Limitation = $40,000
- 65% Taxable Income Limitation = $292,500

Therefore, the allowable percentage depletion is $16,200 since the percentage depletion is greater than the cost depletion of $4,821. Note that the adjusted basis (AB) for the next year's cost depletion calculations is reduced by $16,200, i.e., AB for the next year is $28,800 ($45,000 – $16,200) and R_r is 44,000 (50,000 - 6000) barrels.

INTANGIBLE DRILLING COSTS (IDCs)

The pre-1986 tax laws allow taxpayers to expense domestic IDCs. Under this law, the amount that the integrated producer can expense is 80% of its IDCs with the difference being amortized over 36 months, beginning in the month costs are incurred. The independent producer may elect to expense IDCs in the year incurred. The Tax Reform Act of 1986 changes the rules as summarized below

1. The independent producer may elect to expense 100% of IDCs in the year incurred for domestic wells. For foreign IDCs, the cost may be recovered over a 10-year period using straight-line amortization or may be added to its depletable basis.

2. The integrated producer may elect to expense 70% of IDCs in the year they were incurred and amortize the remaining 30% over 60 months for domestic wells. The foreign IDCs must be capitalized over a 10-year period using straight-line amortization or may be added to its depletable basis.

Dry hole costs may be expensed in the year incurred, regardless of the way the IDCs are treated. This is applicable to both the integrated and independent producers. The breakdown of various expenditures involved in drilling a well and their respective tax treatment is shown in Table 4–6.[1]

There are a number of other tax items (i.e., Alternative Minimum Tax) that affect the oil and gas business, but these are not included here because they are not directly applicable to project evaluations and a large amount of assumptions are necessary for their calculations.

Example 4–7

An independent oil company acquired mineral rights for $500,000 in 2002. The company drilled and completed a well on the lease for a total of $3,000,000 from which $1,000,000 was depreciable completion costs. The drilling cost of $2,000,000 is expensed for tax purposes and deducted against income in 2003. Initial well tests show an estimated daily production of 750 barrels per day, declining at a rate of 50 barrels per day in each succeeding year. Lease operating costs are projected at $400,000 per year, escalating by $50,000 per year in each succeeding year. The crude oil will be sold at $10 per barrel. Recoverable oil reserves are estimated to be 1,500,000 barrels. Assume that the company has 100% WI and 87.5% NRI in the lease, salvage value is zero, the income tax rate is 30%, and there is no production tax. Use double declining balance depreciation where applicable. Calculate the net after-tax cash flow for the 1st four years.

	Tax Treatment	
	Dry Hole Costs	**Completion Costs**
Administrative Costs	E	IDC
Location—Stake, Permit, Damages	E	IDC
Rig Tariff	E	IDC
Rig Transportation	E	IDC
Company Labor—Drilling	E	IDC
Cementing—Surface Casing	E	IDC
Cementing—Production Casing	E	IDC
Bits and Reamers	E	IDC
Logging	E	IDC
Coring Services	E	IDC
Mud Logger	E	IDC
Engineering while Drilling	E	IDC
Mud, Water, and Fuel	E	IDC
Drillstem Tests	E	IDC
Casing Crew—Surface Casing	E	IDC
Casing Crew—Production Casing		IDC
Completion Unit		IDC
Completion Costs		IDC
Swabbing Costs		IDC
Company Labor—Completion		IDC
Perforating		IDC
Surface Casing		Tangible
Production Casing		Tangible
Tubing		Tangible
Wellhead Equipment		Tangible
Float Equipment, Centralizers		Tangible
Packers		Tangible
Line Pipe		Tangible
Tanks and Fittings		Tangible
Separators and Fittings		Tangible
Pumping Unit		Tangible

Table 4–6 Breakdown of various expenditures involved in drilling a well and their respective tax treatment[1]

Solution: First calculate cost depletion for the four years as

$$CD_{2003} = 500,000 \left[\frac{273,750}{(1,500,000 - 273,750) + 273,750} \right] = \$91,250$$

$$CD_{2004} = (500,000 - 91,250) \left[\frac{255,500}{(1,500,000 - 529,250) + 255,500} \right] = \$85,167$$

$$CD_{2005} = (500,000 - 176,417) \left[\frac{237,250}{(1,500,000 - 766,500) + 237,250} \right] = \$79,083$$

$$CD_{2006} = (500,000 - 255,500) \left[\frac{219,000}{(1,500,000 - 985,500) + 219,000} \right] = \$73,000$$

The percent depletion is calculated as follows:

$$PD_{2003} = 273,750 \times 10 \times 0.875 \times 0.15 = \$359,297$$
$$PD_{2004} = 255,500 \times 10 \times 0.875 \times 0.15 = \$335,344$$
$$PD_{2005} = 237,250 \times 10 \times 0.875 \times 0.15 = \$311,391$$
$$PD_{2006} = 219,000 \times 10 \times 0.875 \times 0.15 = \$287,438$$

The cash flow for Example 4–7 is shown in Table 4–7. The before-tax cash flow for the same example are – $3,500,000; $1,995,312; $1,785,625; $1,575,937; and $1,366,250 with a total, for the period from 2002 to 2006, of $3,223,124 versus the after-tax cash flow of $2,455,348. The difference between the two cash flows is the tax deduction of $767,776.

	2002	2003	2004	2005	2006
Production, Stb	0	273,750	255,500	237,250	219,000
Gross (8/8ths) Revenue	0	2,737,500	2,555,000	2,372,500	2,190,000
Royalty at 12.5%	0	–342,188	–319,375	–296,563	–273,750
Net Operating Revenue	0	2,395,313	2,235,625	2,075,937	1,916,250
Operating Costs	0	–400,000	–450,000	–500,000	–550,000
Depreciation	0	–400,000	–240,000	–144,000	–86,400
IDCs	–2,000,000	0	0	0	0
Taxable Before Depletion	0	1,595,313	1,545,625	1,431,938	1,279,850
Allowable Depletion	0	–359,297	–335,344	–311,391	–287,438
Percent Depletion (15%)	0	359,297	335,344	311,391	287,438
50% Limit	0	797,656	772,813	715,969	639,925
Cost Depletion	0	91,250	85,167	79,083	73,000
Taxable after Depletion	–2,000,000	1,236,016	1,210,281	1,120,547	992,413
Loss Forward	0	–2,000,000	–763,984	0	0
Taxable Income	–2,000,000	–763,984	446,297	1,120,547	992,413
Tax @ 30%	0	0	–133,889	–336,164	–297,724
Net Income	–2,000,000	–763,984	312,408	784,383	694,689
+ Depreciation	0	400,000	240,000	144,000	86,400
+ Allowable Depletion	0	359,297	335,344	311,391	287,438
+ Loss Forward	0	2,000,000	763,984	0	0
+ Acquisition Cost	–500,000	0	0	0	0
+ Tangible Drilling Costs	–1000,000	0	0	0	0
After Tax Net Cash Flow	–3,500,000	1,995,313	1,651,736	1,239,773	1,068,526

Table 4–7 After-tax cash flow for Example 4–7

Example 4–8

A gas field development project is proposed. The drilling of wells in 2002 at a total cost of 185 M$ from which 111 M$ is intangible drilling cost and 74 M$ is tangible drilling cost. The tangible drilling costs are subject to depreciation with annual recovery of 14.28% in 2003, 24.49% in 2004, 17.49% in 2005, 12.49% in 2006, 8.93% in 2007 to 2009, and 4.46% in 2010. The interest of an integrated company is to be evaluated, therefore, the 70% of the IDCs will be expensed and the remaining 30% will be amortized over 60 months. The oil and gas produced from the lease will be sold at $14/Stb and $2.25/MScf, respectively. Severance and ad valorem taxes are 8% for oil and gas. The NRI is 80% against a WI of 100%. The lease operating expenses are $700 per month. Develop an after-tax cash flow for this example. The oil and gas production is given in Table 4–8. Assume a corporate tax rate of 34%.

Solution: The cash flow for Example 4–8 is shown in Table 4–8.

Example 4–9

A gas field is proposed to be acquired in 2002 for total cost of 12,000 M$, which includes 2400 M$ worth of tangible costs. Most of the field is already developed except for one well that will be drilled in 2003 at a total cost of 910 M$, which consists of 673 M$ as IDC and 273 M$ as tangible costs. Calculate the after-tax net cash flow for the proposal at an oil price of $16/Stb and gas price of $2.00/MScf. Severance and ad valorem taxes equal 8% of gross income. The NRI against 100% WI is 80%. The production forecast and operating expenditures are listed in Table 4–9. Assume a corporate tax rate of 34%.

Solution: The after-tax cash flow for Example 4–9 is shown in Table 4–9. Note that oil and gas property acquisition is different from other oil and gas deals in that there are almost no preferential tax treatments. The acquisition cost must be recovered through cost depletion except for that portion allocated to tangible equipment and recovered under ACRS. Percentage depletion on an acquired oil and gas property is not allowed.

Year	Gross Production Oil MStb	Gross Production Gas MMScf	Net Production Oil MStb	Net Production Gas MMScf	Product Prices Oil $/STb	Product Prices Gas $/Mscf	Bonus (M$)	Expenditure Itangible (M$)	Expenditure Tangible (M$)	Expenditure LOE (M$)	Expenditure Taxes (M$)	Expenditure Total (M$)	Operating Revenue, BFIT Gross (M$)	Operating Revenue, BFIT Net (M$)	Cum. NCF (M$)	Cum. NFC Disc. (M$)
2002	-	-	-	-			-	111	74	-	-	185.00	-	-	(185.00)	(176.39)
2003	5.174	43.432	4.527	38.003	14.00	2.25	-	-	-	8.40	11.91	20.31	148.89	128.58	(56.42)	(64.94)
2004	2.393	22.860	2.094	20.003	14.00	2.25				8.40	5.95	14.35	74.32	59.97	3.55	(17.68)
2005	1.820	16.407	1.593	14.356	14.00	2.25				8.40	4.37	12.77	54.60	41.83	45.38	12.28
2006	1.207	10.801	1.056	9.451	14.00	2.25				8.40	2.88	11.28	36.05	24.77	70.15	28.41
2007	0.971	8.625	0.850	7.547	14.00	2.25				8.40	2.31	10.71	28.88	18.17	88.31	39.16
2008	0.812	7.181	0.711	6.283	14.00	2.25				8.40	1.93	10.33	24.08	13.76	102.07	46.57
2009	0.698	6.152	0.611	5.383	14.00	2.25				8.40	1.65	10.05	20.66	10.61	112.68	51.76
2010	0.612	5.381	0.536	4.708	14.00	2.25				8.40	1.45	9.85	18.09	8.24	120.92	55.43
2011	0.544	4.782	0.476	4.184	14.00	2.25				8.40	1.29	9.69	16.08	6.39	127.31	58.01
2012	0.491	4.303	0.430	3.765	14.00	2.25				8.40	1.16	9.56	14.49	4.93	132.24	59.82
2013	0.447	3.911	0.391	3.422	14.00	2.25				8.40	1.05	9.45	13.18	3.72	135.96	61.07
2014	0.410	3.585	0.359	3.137	14.00	2.25				8.40	0.97	9.37	12.08	2.71	138.68	61.89
2015	0.378	3.309	0.331	2.895	14.00	2.25				8.40	0.89	9.29	11.15	1.85	140.53	62.40
2016	0.352	3.072	0.308	2.688	14.00	2.25				8.40	0.83	9.23	10.36	1.13	141.66	62.69
2017	-	-	-	-									-	-	141.66	62.69
2018															141.66	62.69
2019															141.66	62.69
2020															141.66	62.69
2021															141.66	62.69
Sub	16.309	143.801	14.270	125.826			-	111	74	117.60	38.63	341.23	482.89	141.66		
Rem.	-	-	-	-			-	-	-	-	-	-	-	-		
Total	16.309	143.801	14.270	125.826			-	111	74	117.60	38.63	341.23	482.89	141.66	141.66	62.69

Table 4–8 Typical AFIT cash flow for drilling deal, iIntegrated oil company

TAX CALCULATIONS

Year	Cost Depl. (M$)	Percent Depl. (M$)	50% Limit (M$)	Allowable Depl. (M$)	Dep. (M$)	Expensed IDC (M$)	Capitalize IDC (M$)	Loss Forward (M$)	Taxable Income (M$)	Income Tax (M$)	After Tax NCF (M$)	After Tax Cum. (M$)	A-Tax Disc. @ 10% NCF (M$)	A-Tax Disc. @ 10% Cum. NCF (M$)
2002	-	-	-	-	-	-	-	-	-	-	------		(176.39)	(176.39)
2003	-	-	16.82	-	10.57	77.70	6.66	-	33.65	11.44	117.14		101.53	(74.86)
2004	-	-	17.60	-	18.12	-	6.66	-	35.19	11.97	48.01		37.83	(37.03)
2005	-	-	11.11	-	12.94	-	6.66	-	22.23	7.56	34.27	14.42	24.55	(12.48)
2006	-	-	4.43	-	9.24	-	6.66	-	8.86	3.01	21.75	36.17	14.17	1.69
2007	-	-	2.45	-	6.61	-	6.66	-	4.90	1.66	16.50	52.67	9.77	11.46
2008	-	-	3.57	-	6.61	-	-	-	7.15	2.43	11.33	64.00	6.10	17.55
2009	-	-	2.00	-	6.61	-	-	-	4.00	1.36	9.25	73.25	4.53	22.08
2010	-	-	2.47	-	3.30	-	-	-	4.94	1.68	6.56	79.81	2.92	25.00
2011	-	-	3.20	-	-	-	-	-	6.39	2.17	4.22	84.03	1.71	26.70
2012	-	-	2.46	-	-	-	-	-	4.93	1.68	3.25	87.28	1.20	27.90
2013	-	-	1.86	-	-	-	-	-	3.72	1.27	2.46	89.74	0.82	28.72
2014	-	-	1.36	-	-	-	-	-	2.71	0.92	1.79	91.53	0.54	29.26
2015	-	-	0.93	-	-	-	-	-	1.85	0.63	1.22	92.75	0.34	29.60
2016	-	-	0.57	-	-	-	-	-	1.13	0.38	0.75	93.50	0.19	29.79
2017	-	-	-	-	-	-	-	-	-	-	-	93.50	-	29.79
2018	-	-	-	-	-	-	-	-	-	-	-	93.50	-	29.79
2019	-	-	-	-	-	-	-	-	-	-	-	93.50	-	29.79
2020	-	-	-	-	-	-	-	-	-	-	-	93.50	-	29.79
2021	-	-	-	-	-	-	-	-	-	-	-	93.50	-	29.79
SubTot.	-	-	70.83	-	74.00	77.70	33.30	-	141.66	48.17	93.50	-	29.79	-
Rem.	-	-	-	-	-	-	-	-	-	-	-	-	-	-
Total	-	-	70.83	-	74.00	77.70	33.30	-	141.66	48.17	93.50	93.50	29.79	29.79

Initial WI Fraction	1.00000
Final WI Fraction	1.00000
Initial Net Oil Fraction	0.87500
Initial Net Gas Fraction	0.87500
Final Net Oil Fraction	0.87500
Final Net Gas Fraction	0.87500

Lease Operating Exp. ($/Month)	700
Production Start Date	01/01/03
Oil Severance Tax (% or -$/Stb)	8.00
Gas Severance Tax (% or -$/Mscf)	8.00
Ad Valorem Tax (%)	-
Tax Rate (%)	34.00
Independent or Major (1 or 2)	2
Acquisition = 1 Else 2	1
Reversion Point	
1 BOE of Mscf of Gas	

	BFIT	AFIT
Net Present Value @ 10%, M$	62.69	29.79
Rate of Return (ROR), %	26.00	17.80
Present Value Ratio	1.355	1.169
Payout (Disc. @ 10%), years	3.59	4.88
Technical Cost, $/Mscf	2.71	3.09
Technical Cost, $/BOE	9.68	11.05
Technical Cost (Disc.), $/Mscf	3.10	3.64
Technical Cost (Disc.), $/BOE	11.05	12.97

Table 4–8 Continued . . .

Year	Oil MStb	Gas MMScf	Oil MStb	Gas MMScf	Oil $/STb	Gas $/Mscf	Bonus (M$)	Intangible (M$)	Tangible (M$)	LOE (M$)	Taxes (M$)	Total (M$)	Gross (M$)	Net (M$)	Cum. NCF (M$)	Disc. (M$)
2002							9,600	-	2,400	-	-	12,000	-	(12,000)	(12,000)	(11,442)
2003	77	3,394	67.38	2,970	16.00	2.00		637	273	155	561	1,626	7,018	5,391	(6,609)	(6,769)
2004	81	4,205	70.88	3,679	16.00	2.00				306	679	985	8,493	7,507	898	(853)
2005	69	3,619	60.38	3,167	16.00	2.00				319	584	903	7,299	6,396	7,295	3,729
2006	56	2,880	49.00	2,520	16.00	2.00				332	466	798	5,824	5,026	12,321	7,002
2007	47	2,385	41.13	2,087	16.00	2.00				346	387	733	4,832	4,099	16,420	9,429
2008	40	2,002	35.00	1,752	16.00	2.00				361	325	686	4,064	3,377	19,797	11,247
2009	35	1,686	30.63	1,475	16.00	2.00				376	275	651	3,441	2,789	22,587	12,611
2010	30	1,445	26.25	1,264	16.00	2.00				392	236	628	2,949	2,321	24,908	13,644
2011	11	1,100	9.63	963	16.00	2.00				324	166	490	2,079	1,589	26,496	14,286
2012	6	673	5.25	589	16.00	2.00				188	101	289	1,262	973	27,469	14,644
2013	4	468	3.50	410	16.00	2.00				119	70	189	875	686	28,155	14,873
2014	2	280	1.75	245	16.00	2.00				68	41	109	518	409	28,564	14,997
2015	2	259	1.75	227	16.00	2.00				68	39	107	481	375	28,938	15,101
2016	2	240	1.75	210	16.00	2.00				68	36	104	448	344	29,283	15,187
2017	2	224	1.75	196	16.00	2.00				68	34	102	420	318	29,601	15,260
2018															29,601	15,260
2019															29,601	15,260
2020															29,601	15,260
2021															29,601	15,260
Sub Tot.	464	24,860	406.00	21,753			9,600	637	2,673	3,490	4,000	20,400	50,001	29,601	-	-
Rem.	-	-					-	-	-	-	-	-	-	-	-	-
Total	464	24,860	406.00	21,753			9,600	637	2,673	3,490	4,000	20,400	50,001	29,601	29,601	15,260

Table 4–9 Typical AFIT cash flow for acquisition, integrated oil company

TAX CALCULATIONS

Year	Cost Depl. (M$)	Percent Depl. (M$)	50% Limit (M$)	Allowable Depl. (M$)	Dep. (M$)	Expensed IDC (M$)	Capitalize IDC (M$)	Loss Forward (M$)	Taxable Income (M$)	Income Tax (M$)	After Tax NCF (M$)	After Tax Cum. (M$)	A-Tax Disc. @ 10% NCF (M$)	A-Tax Disc. @ 10% Cum. NCF (M$)
2002	-	-	(171)	-	343	-	-	(343)	(343)	-	(12,000)	(12,000)	(11,442)	(11,442)
2003	1,339	-	2,595	1,339	627	446	38	-	3,508	1,193	4,198	(7,802)	3,639	(7,803)
2004	1,629	-	3,491	1,629	487	-	38	-	5,353	1,820	5,687	(2,115)	4,481	(3,321)
2005	1,401	-	3,005	1,401	348	-	38	-	4,610	1,567	4,829	2,714	3,459	138
2006	1,117	-	2,370	1,117	248	-	38	-	3,623	1,232	3,794	6,509	2,471	2,609
2007	926	-	1,911	926	239	-	38	-	2,896	985	3,115	9,623	1,844	4,453
2008	779	-	1,569	779	239	-	-	-	2,360	802	2,575	12,198	1,386	5,839
2009	658	-	1,329	658	131	-	-	-	1,999	680	2,109	14,308	1,032	6,871
2010	564	-	1,154	564	12	-	-	-	1,744	593	1,728	16,035	769	7,639
2011	405	-	794	405	-	-	-	-	1,184	402	1,186	17,222	480	8,119
2012	246	-	486	246	-	-	-	-	727	247	726	17,947	267	8,386
2013	171	-	343	171	-	-	-	-	515	175	511	18,458	171	8,557
2014	101	-	204	101	-	-	-	-	307	104	304	18,762	92	8,649
2015	94	-	187	94	-	-	-	-	281	95	279	19,042	77	8,726
2016	88	-	172	88	-	-	-	-	257	87	257	19,299	65	8,791
2017	82	-	159	82	-	-	-	-	236	80	238	19,537	54	8,845
2018	-	-	-	-	-	-	-	-	-	-	-	19,537	-	8,845
2019	-	-	-	-	-	-	-	-	-	-	-	19,537	-	8,845
2020	-	-	-	-	-	-	-	-	-	-	-	19,537	-	8,845
2021	-	-	-	-	-	-	-	-	-	-	-	19,537	-	8,845
SubTot.	9,600	-	19,600	9,600	2,673	446	191	(343)	29,258	10,064	19,537	-	8,845	-
Rem.	-	-	-	-	-	-	-	-	-	-	-	-	-	-
Total	9,600	-	19,600	9,600	2,673	446	191	(343)	29,258	10,064	19,537	-	8,845	-

Parameter	Value	Parameter	Value
Initial WI Fraction	1.00000	Lease Operating Exp. ($/Month)	
Final WI Fraction	1.00000	Production Start Date	01/01/03
		Oil Severance Tax (% or -$/Stb)	8.00
Initial Net Oil Fraction	0.87500	Gas Severance Tax (% or -$/Mscf)	8.00
Initial Net Gas Fraction	0.87500	Ad Valorem Tax (%)	-
Final Net Oil Fraction	0.87500	Tax Rate (%)	34.00
Final Net Gas Fraction	0.87500	Independent or Major (1 or 2)	2
Reversion Point		Acquisition = 1 Else 2	1
		1 BOE of Mscf of Gas	

	BFIT	AFIT
Net Present Value @ 10%, M$	15,260	8,845
Rate of Return (ROR), %	44.78	31.00
Present Value Ratio	2.248	1.723
Payout (Disc. @ 10%), years	3.19	3.96
Technical Cost, $/Mscf	0.94	1.40
Technical Cost, $/BOE	5.06	7.56
Technical Cost (Disc.), $/Mscf	1.21	1.86
Technical Cost (Disc.), $/BOE	6.48	9.99

Table 4–9 Continued . . .

REFERENCES

[1] Thompson, R. S. and Wright, J. D., *Oil Property Evaluation*, Thompson-Wright Associates, Golden, Colorado, 1984.

chapter FIVE

International Petroleum Economics

In Chapters 3 and 4, cash-flow models applicable to the oil and gas exploration and production in the United States or to any other related investment projects are discussed. In the international oil and gas business, financial and contractual arrangements for the exploration and production of oil and gas are different from these. These arrangements are typically referred to as the *fiscal regime*. The fiscal regime or fiscal system includes all aspects of legislative, taxation, contractual, and fiscal elements. The major difference is that in the United States, the mineral rights belong to individuals or the state. Ownership of minerals in places outside the United States is vested almost entirely in a national government. Federal petroleum law is the basis for all petroleum operations. Such laws often vest important discretionary powers in federal administrative or legislative bodies.

The basic cash-flow variables, such as the ones discussed in Chapters 3 and 4, are still applicable to the economic evaluations of international oil and gas investments. For example, production forecast, reserves, expenditure forecast (CAPEX and OPEX), depreciation, depletion, and income tax calculations are still applicable.

In the United States, an oil company (lessee) acquires mineral rights from the state government or private landowner (lessor). In the international oil and gas exploration and production operations, a host government grants *license* or enters into a *contract* with a contractor for a given *contract area*. The terms *license, concession, acreage position, lease,* or a *block* are used interchangeably. The *host government* is represented by either a national oil company, an oil ministry of the country, or both. The contractor or operator refers to an international oil company, contractor group, or consortium of these.

The prime objectives of the host government are sovereignty, economic growth, and environment (quality of life). The sub-objectives are the optimal exploitation and use of mineral resources, satisfying domestic demand, fostering direct and indirect employment, accumulating expertise, and so forth. To meet these objectives, the host government may have the following constraints.[1]

1. It finds it difficult to gain access to risk capital,

2. It may lack the expertise needed for the exploration and development of the natural resources, or

3. Governments may be unwilling to take the risks associated with the above.

The international companies are able to provide risk capital and the necessary expertise in return for a reward if the exploration is successful. Therefore, a government as the owner of mineral resources engages a foreign oil company as a contractor to provide technical and financial resources for exploitation of these resources. Two basic forms of fiscal arrangements are (a) Concessionary Systems and (b) Contractual Systems. These arrangements are used when a government engages the foreign oil company. Each form can be used to accomplish the same purpose.

Petroleum laws and requirements vary widely from country to country. The most common provisions and regulations have to do with the following:

1. Type of permit, contract, or concession.

2. Size, shape, and geographic limits of area to be explored and developed.

3. Initial or primary term and extensions. If exploration efforts are successful, typical contract terms are for 20 to 30 years.

4. Fees and bonuses.

5. Relinquishment or surrender.

6. Selection and convertibility of acreage.

7. Assignment or transfer of acreage, lease, or concession.

8. Royalty payments, sharing of profits, and cost recovery.

9. Tax obligations.

10. Obligation to supply domestic markets first and building local refineries.

11. Employment and training of nationals.

12. Equity participation by government and repatriation of capital by the contractor.

Details relevant to the economic evaluation of various fiscal systems are discussed in this chapter. In their books, Kirsten Bindemann and Daniel Johnston provide a comprehensive overview of the international petroleum fiscal systems and production-sharing contracts.[1-2]

TYPES OF CONTRACT ARRANGEMENTS

There are two basic types of petroleum fiscal systems (1) concessionary system, also referred to as tax/royalty system and (2) contractual system. The concessionary system allows private ownership of mineral resources as in the United States. In the contractual system, the state/government retains ownership of minerals. The contractual systems are further reclassified into *service contracts* and *production-sharing contracts (PSC)*. The primary difference here is whether the fee is taken in cash (service) or in kind (PSC). The production-sharing contract is also referred to as the *production-sharing agreement (PSA)*. The service contracts are further reclassified into *pure service contracts* and *risk service contracts*. The difference is primarily based upon whether the fees are based upon a flat fee (pure) or profit (risk). Some countries offer both concessionary arrangements as well as service or production-sharing contracts. The bottom line in either case is a financial issue (i.e., how costs are recovered, risks shared, and profits divided).

Under a concessionary system and production-sharing agreement, the contractor bears all exploration costs, field development costs, operating costs, and risks in return for a stipulated share in the resulting production from the field. The risk and reward under each of the above contract types are summarized in Table 5–1.

The Concessionary System

The cash flow generated in the concessionary system is similar to the cash flows presented in Tables 3–18, 4–8 and 4–9. The provisions of royalty/tax regimes are normally laid down in the country or state's legislation and regulations and are the same for all companies. In the concessionary system, the hydrocarbons extracted by the companies normally belong to them, and they pay royalties and taxes to the government of the country where they operate. This fiscal system may range from a simple one royalty and one tax system to more sophisticated formulas

Contract Type	Contractor	Host Government
Concession	All risk/all reward	Reward is function of production and price
Production-Sharing Agreement	Exploration Risk/Share in Reward	Share in Reward
Joint Venture	Share in Risk and Reward	Share in Risk and Reward
Pure Service Contract	No Risk	All Risk

Table 5–1 Risk and reward of main contract types[2]

with various layers of royalties and taxation. The flow diagram in Figure 5–1 shows the revenue distribution under a simple concessionary system. Table 5–2 is a cash-flow projection for a concessionary system. Sample calculations are also shown in Example 5–1. Typical mathematical calculations in the concessionary system involve the following steps.

1. The royalty comes right off the top (i.e., deducted from the gross/wellhead revenue). This arrangement is similar to the landowner's royalty and/or overriding royalty of most lease arrangements in the United States.

2. The operating costs, applicable depreciation, depletion if allowed, amortization, and intangible drilling costs are deducted from the revenue left after the royalty deductions. The deductions are subject to respective tax rules as stipulated in the agreement. In many systems, the intangible capital costs are expensed in the year incurred. Bonuses are not always deductible for tax purposes.

3. The revenue remaining after royalty and deductions is called taxable income, which is subject to the tax deduction. In some cases, there are two or three layers of taxation. For example, provincial taxes are deducted from the taxable income before it is subjected to the federal income tax. In other cases, there are windfall profits taxes deducted before the provincial and federal tax.

Example 5–1

A 30-million-barrel field is developed with a total cost (tangible and intangible) of $129 million. The operating cost over the productive life of the field is estimated at $110.50 million. Calculate the contractor and government share, if the royalty is 12.5% and the tax rate is 35%. Assume the crude oil price of $18/Stb.

Solution: The following calculations are summarized from a detailed cash flow. In the cash flow, the tangible costs are depreciated (straight line) over a period of five years. The intangible costs are expensed in the year incurred.

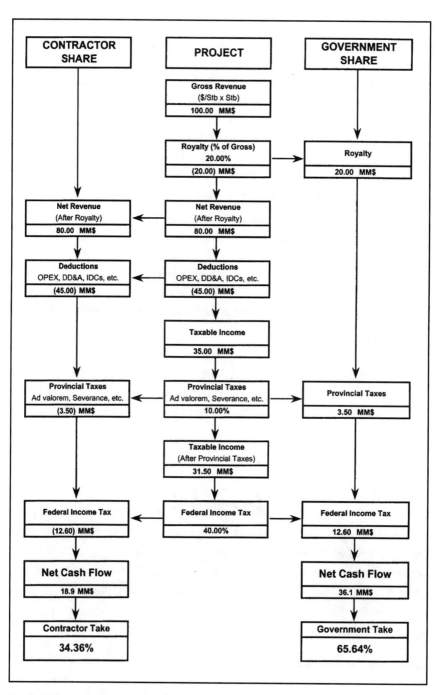

Fig. 5–1 Concessionary system flow diagram

Sample Concessionary System Cash Flow Projection

Year	Oil Production (MStbls)	Oil Price ($/Stb)	Gross Revenue (M$)	12.5% Royalty (M$)	Net Revenue (M$)	CAPEX Intangible (M$)	CAPEX Tangible (M$)	Operating Cost (M$)	DD&A (M$)	Total Deductions (M$)	Tax Loss C/F (M$)	Taxable Income (M$)	35.0% Income Tax (M$)	NET CASH FLOW Contractor (M$)	NET CASH FLOW Government (M$)
2002	-	18.00	-	-	-	15,000	12,000	-	-	15,000	(15,000)	(15,000)	-	(15,000)	-
2003	-	18.00	-	-	-	10,000	10,000	-	-	10,000	(15,000)	(25,000)	-	(10,000)	-
2004	-	18.00	-	-	-	7,000	45,000	-	-	7,000	(25,000)	(32,000)	-	(7,000)	-
2005	5,405	18.00	97,290	12,161	85,129	-	30,000	19,418	19,400	38,818	(32,000)	14,311	5,009	41,302	17,170
2006	4,594	18.00	82,697	10,337	72,359	-	-	16,560	19,400	35,960	-	36,380	12,733	23,647	23,070
2007	3,905	18.00	70,292	8,787	61,506	-	-	14,168	19,400	33,568	-	27,938	9,778	18,159	18,565
2008	3,319	18.00	59,748	7,469	52,280	-	-	12,118	19,400	31,518	-	20,762	7,267	13,495	14,735
2009	2,821	18.00	50,786	6,348	44,438	-	-	10,375	19,400	29,775	-	14,663	5,132	9,531	11,480
2010	2,398	18.00	43,168	5,396	37,772	-	-	8,894	-	8,894	-	28,878	10,107	18,771	15,503
2011	2,036	18.00	36,693	4,587	32,106	-	-	7,635	-	7,635	-	24,472	8,565	15,907	13,152
2012	1,733	18.00	31,189	3,899	27,290	-	-	6,565	-	6,565	-	20,726	7,254	13,472	11,153
2013	1,473	18.00	26,511	3,314	23,197	-	-	5,655	-	5,655	-	17,542	6,140	11,402	9,454
2014	1,252	18.00	22,534	2,817	19,717	-	-	4,882	-	4,882	-	14,836	5,192	9,643	8,009
2015	1,064	18.00	19,154	2,394	16,760	-	-	4,224	-	4,224	-	12,535	4,387	8,148	6,782
	30,003		540,061	67,508	472,554	32,000	97,000	110,512	97,000	239,512		161,042	81,565	151,477	149,072

	Contractor	Government
Net Present Value, M$ @ 10.0%	64,742	72,121
Internal Rate of Return 10.0%	46.4%	
Discounted Take	47.3%	52.7%
Un-Discounted Take	50.4%	49.6%

Table 5–2 Sample concessionary system cash-flow projection

	Contractor Share	Government Share
Production, MStb	30,000	
Crude Oil Price, $/Stb	x 18.00	
Gross Revenue, M$	540,000	
Less Royalty @ 12.5%	-	67,500
Gross Revenue after Royalty, M$	472,500	
Capital Expenditure, M$	-129,000	
Operating Expenditure, M$	-110,500	
Taxable Income, M$	233,000	
Income Tax @35%, M$	-81,550	81,550
Net Cash Flow, M$	151,450	149,050

The Production-Sharing System

Production-sharing systems are more common now as compared to the concessionary system. The first PSA was signed in 1966 between the Indonesian National Oil Company and IIAPCO. Many aspects of the government/contractor relationship under a PSA may be negotiated but some are fixed. The basic structure is effectively predetermined by the legislation of the host government. Typically, model PSAs are put forward by the host government as a basis for bidding and negotiations. Once a contract is signed, the fiscal terms remain fixed for the contract period of 25 to 30 years. The PSAs now are not limited to exploration only. In order to avail the technical expertise of international oil companies, development of existing oil fields is also done under PSA. Some gas field development projects have a combination of agreements, where the upstream is developed under PSA and the downstream is a joint venture.

Basic elements of the exploration and production-sharing agreement (EPSA) or development and production-sharing agreement (DPSA) are:

1. *Title*: Title to the hydrocarbons remains with the host government.

2. *Management*: The host government maintains the management control, and the contractor is responsible to the host government for exe-

cution of petroleum operations in accordance with the fiscal terms of the contract. The contractor's operations are normally monitored by a management committee and a technical committee. These committees have representation for the contractor and the government.

3. *Annual Work Program*: The contractor is required to submit annual work programs and budgets for review and approval by the management and technical committees.

4. *Contract Basis*: The contract is based on production sharing; it is not based on profit sharing.

5. *Financing & Technology*: The contractor provides all the required financing and technology in accordance with the work commitment in the contract and bears all the risk.

6. *Work Commitment*: Work commitment in the exploration phase is generally measured in kilometers of seismic data to be acquired and the number of exploration wells to be drilled. In some cases, the work commitment may involve acquisition of seismic data with an option to drill. These are referred to as seismic options. The duration of the right to explore for hydrocarbons normally ranges from three to six years for the initial exploration period. The exploration phase may be divided into a number of periods (two or three), each having the related work obligation. Linked to the exploration phase or any of its periods, an obligatory work program is stipulated, such as a number of seismic lines and a number of exploration wells within a specified time limit. This obligation may be limited to a certain minimum cost ceiling. However, due to inflation, the budgeted amount may not deliver a desired scope of work. Instead, if the scope of the work is specified, then no matter how many dollars are spent on the project it must be done. Therefore, it is useful to determine the work obligation in terms of scope of work to be performed instead of monetary value. The distinction of the wells to be drilled should be quite specific, indicating the depth or geologic horizons to be penetrated. If the contract covers several blocks, the work program should specify the work in each block, rather than in the area as a whole. On the expiry of the exploration period, if no commercial discovery is made, the contract automatically expires. The terms of work commitments outline penalties for nonperformance.

7. *Relinquishment:* Normally, in almost all countries, there is a require-ment to relinquish certain portion of the exploration area within a stat-ed time limit. The area to be relinquished normally constitutes between 50% and 75% of the original area, and relinquishment is made typi-cally in two or three steps (for example, 25% every two years).

8. *Exploitation and Development:* Exploitation and development duration is usually 20 to 25 years, which can be extended, limit-ed to terms prevailing in the industry at the time.

9. *Bonus Payments:* Cash bonuses are sometimes paid upon finalization of negotiations and contract signing. This bonus is referred to as sig-nature bonus. The amount of bonus depends on the prospectivity of the contract area and competition. Once the field is put on production, pro-duction bonuses are paid when production from a given contract area or block reaches a specified level. For example, the contractor may pay $2 million when the production from the block reaches 10,000 Stb/d and another $2 million when the production reaches 20,000 Stb/d, and so on. Production bonuses may also be tied to the cumula-tive production. For example, $2 million may be paid when five mil-lion barrels are produced and another $2 million may be paid when the cumulative production reaches 10 million barrels. The bonuses are normally not recoverable costs to the contractor. These bonuses become a cost to the contractor and revenue to the host government.

10. *Royalties:* Although rare, some PSAs include provision for royalty pay-ments. Royalties are taken right off the top of gross (wellhead) revenues. Some systems allow a netback of transportation costs. This occurs when there is a difference between the point of valuation for royalty calcula-tion purposes and the point of sale. If royalties are included, they are usu-ally in the range of 8% to 15% of gross revenue. Royalty is paid directly to the host government as oil and gas are produced and sold, irrespective of the level of profit or loss from the contract area.

11. *Cost Recovery:* The sequence of calculations following the bonus and royalty calculations leads to the recovery of costs. Under the concessionary system, these are called deductions; while in the contractual systems these are called *cost recovery*. The gross rev-

enue, after royalty deduction if any, is split into two portions. One portion is called *cost recovery oil* (or simply *cost oil*) and the second is called *profit oil*. The contractor's costs (CAPEX and OPEX), also referred to as *petroleum costs*, are recovered from the cost recovery portion. Any unrecovered costs are carried forward and recovered in the succeeding years.

Any excess cost recovery left after all the costs have been recovered is again split between the contractor and the host government according to the fiscal terms in the contract. Cost recovery limits, also referred to as cost recovery ceilings, typically range from 30% to 60%. The recoverable costs, recovered from the cost recovery oil, normally are:

a. Unrecovered costs carried over from the previous years. These may include (i) tax loss carry forward; (ii) unrecovered depreciation balance, (iii) unrecovered amortization balance, and (iv) cost recovery carry forward.

b. Operating costs. These may include some of contractor home office's general and administrative (G&A) costs. Some contracts allow a percentage of the total petroleum costs to be recovered as G&A costs.

c. Expensed capital costs: Some contracts allow the capital expenditure to be expensed in the year incurred and recovered from the cost recovery. In other cases, these have to be amortized, and then only the amortized amount is allowed for recovery, while the unrecovered balance is carried forward.

d. Current year DD&A: Sometimes depreciation of fixed capital assets is differentiated from the amortization of intangible capital costs. In some contracts, the intangible exploration and development costs are not amortized. They are expensed in the year incurred.

e. Interest on financing (usually with limitations).

f. Investment credits and uplift: These are incentives. Uplift allows the contractor to recover an additional percentage of capital costs through cost recovery. For example, an uplift of 15% on $70 million of capital expenditure allows the contractor to recover $80.5 million.

     g. Abandonment cost recovery fund. Anticipated cost of abandonment is accumulated through a sinking fund that matures at the anticipated time of abandonment of the block.

12. *Profit Oil Split and Taxation:* The oil left after the royalty payment and cost recovery deduction is referred to as profit oil. This is immediately split between the contractor and the host government according to the fiscal terms of the contract. The split in most countries ranges from 10% to more than 55% for the contractor. It is negotiated before the contract is signed and is dependent on geopotential, costs, infrastructure, political stability, and other key factors that may influence the business decisions of the contractor. If the contractor has to pay taxes, these are deducted from the profit oil portion of the contractor. To attract investors, governments usually introduce royalty and tax holidays in the contract. These specify that for a given holiday period, say 15 years, royalty or taxes are not payable. The contractor's share of profit oil, excess cost recovery, and cost recovery are often referred to as the contractor entitlement. The taxes can be as high as 56%, so this is another cash flow to the host government. In some production-sharing contracts, the National Oil Company pays the taxes for the contractor.

13. *Domestic Obligation:* Some host governments have domestic requirements for oil and gas produced from the contract area. These requirements are referred to as the domestic supply requirements or domestic market obligation (DMO). If the contract has such provision, a certain percentage of the contractor's pre-tax profit oil share is sold to the host government, usually at a price lower than the market price.

14. *Sliding Scales:* In order to account for uncertainties in field size, oil price, average daily production, etc., many fiscal terms (royalties, taxes, cost recovery, and profit oil splits) are based on sliding scale. These factors are either tied to the average barrels of oil produced, to the R-factor, crude oil price, or a combination of these. Each increment in the sliding scale is called a tranche.

For example, if average daily production is 10,000 Stb/d, the cost recovery is 40%. If the daily oil production is 20,000 Stb/d, the cost recovery changes to 35%, and so on. Alternatively, on the first 10,000 Stb/d, it is 40% and the second 10,000 Stb/d it is 35%. The objective of the sliding scale fiscal terms is to create an environment to benefit contractors in lower production on marginal fields. As the production increases, the contractor's take flexes downward. This theoretically allows reasonable terms for the contractor to develop both large and small fields. Fixed fiscal terms for a contract area can become regressive when applied to the small and marginal discoveries, and they may even completely prevent their development. Similarly, if the terms are tied to the oil price, the contractor's take is automatically adjusted when the price variations take place. Such terms also restrict the contractor from making excessive profits in case a larger than anticipated field is encountered. Some typical sliding scale factors are given in Table 5–3.

Profit Oil Split (Contractor's Share), %					Cost Recovery Limit, %				
	R-Factor					R-Factor			
Stb/d	1.00	1.25	1.5	2.00	$/Stb	1.00	1.25	1.5	2.00
≤ 10,000	25	23	21	19	≤ 10	50	48	46	44
10,001 – 15,000	20	18	16	14	13	48	46	44	42
15,000 – 20,000	15	13	12	10	16	46	44	42	40
> 20,000	10	10	10	10	19	44	42	40	38
					22	42	40	38	36

Table 5–3 Typical sliding scale factors

15. *R-factor:* Most contracts use this factor for triggering sliding scale factors such as cost recovery, profit oil split, royalty, and taxes, etc. The R-factor is the ratio of the cumulative contractor's revenue after taxes and royalty, and the cumulative contractor's cost from the day contract is signed. The R = 1 implies a breakeven point for the contractor. The R-factor is calculated each year or quarterly and is used as the basis for adjusting the royalty fraction,

cost recovery, profit oil splits, and taxes, etc. in accordance with a predetermined schedule. Thus, as the contractor makes more profit, a larger portion of the gross revenue is paid to the host government in the form of royalty, taxes, profit oil, etc. Mathematically, the R-factor is calculated by the following equations.

(5.1)

$$R = \frac{X}{Y}$$

where

X = Cumulative net revenue actually received by the contractor equals *turnover* (gross revenues) for all tax years less royalties and taxes

Y = Total cumulative expenditure, exploration, and appraisal expenses and operating costs actually incurred by contractor from date contract is signed

A variation of the above equation, typically used by the Colombian Government is given below.

(5.2)

$$R = \frac{X}{[ID + A - B + (\alpha \times C) + GO]}$$

where

X = Accumulated earnings of the contractor

$[ID + A - B + (\alpha \times C) + GO]$ = Accumulated investment + Accumulated Costs of the Contractor

ID = 50% of cumulative gross development costs

A = Cumulative gross successful exploration costs

B = Cumulative successful exploration costs reimbursed by NOC (50% partner)

C = Cumulative gross unsuccessful exploration costs

α = Proportion of dry-hole costs reimbursed by NOC

GO = Contractor cumulative net operating costs including war tax payments and duties on imports

Sample mathematical calculations for a typical production-sharing agreement are shown in Example 5–2. A flowchart showing the sequence of the required mathematical calculations is shown in Figure 5–2.

Example 5–2

Information for a typical EPSA is given in Table 5–4. Calculate the yearly net revenue (net cash flow) for the contractor and the host government. Assume the price of oil to be $14/Stb.

Solution:

Year	Oil Production (Stb/D)	Bonus (MM$)	CAPEX (MM$)	OPEX (MM$)	Cost Rec. (CR) (%)	Contractor's Share ECR (%)	PO (%)
2002	0.0	3.0	15.0		45.0	42.0	42.0
2003	6,986.0		15.0	6.0	45.0	42.0	42.0
2004	13,973.0			10.0	45.0	42.0	42.0

Table 5–4 Data for production-sharing agreement (For Example 5–2)

For 2002:

Since production is zero, $CR=0$, $PO=0$, and $ECR=0$

Contractor's Net Rev. $= (CR - ECR) + PO_c + ECR_c - Bonus - CAPEX - OPEX$
$$= (0 - 0) + 0 + 0 - 3 - 15 - 0 = -18 \text{ MM\$}$$

Government's Net Rev. $= PO_g + ECR_g + Bonus$
$$= 0 + 0 + 3 = 3 \text{ MM\$}$$

Cumulative Cost $= Bonus + CAPEX + OPEX$
$$= 3 + 15 + 0 = 18 \text{ MM\$}$$

Cost to Recover $= CAPEX + OPEX$
$$= 15 + 0 = 15 \text{ MM\$}$$

Cum. Contractor's Rev. $= (CR - ECR) + PO_c + ECR_c = 0 \text{ MM\$}$

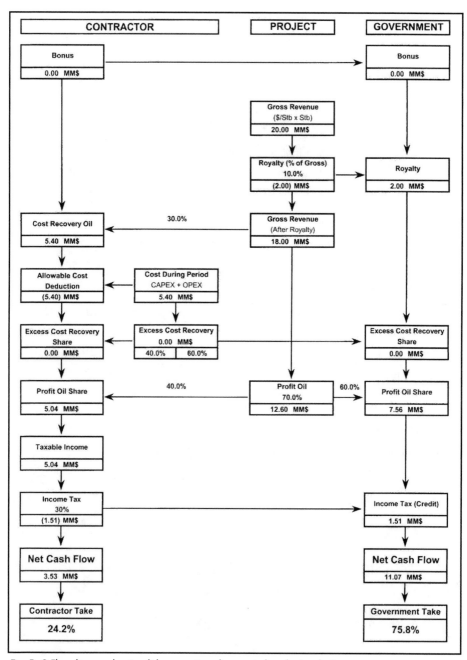

Fig. 5–2 Flow diagram showing disbursements under a typical production-sharing contract.

For 2003:

$$\text{Oil Revenue} = 6{,}986 \times 14.0 \times 365 = 35.698 \text{ MM\$}$$

$$\text{Cost Recovery} = 35.698 \times 0.45 = 16.064 \text{ MM\$}$$

$$\text{Contractor's PO Share, } PO_c = 35.698 \times (1 - 0.45) \times 0.42$$
$$= 8.246 \text{ MM\$}$$

$$\text{Government's PO Share, } PO_g = 35.698 \times (1 - 0.45) \times 0.58$$
$$= 11.388 \text{ MM\$}$$

$$\text{Cumulative Cost} = [\text{Cum. Cost}]_{2002} + \text{Bonus} + \text{CAPEX} + \text{OPEX}$$
$$= 18 + 0 + 15 + 6 = 39 \text{ MM\$}$$

$$\text{Cost to Recover} = [\text{Cost to Recover}]_{2002} + \text{CAPEX} + \text{OPEX} - \text{CR}$$
$$= 15 + 15 + 6 - 16.064 = 19.936 \text{ MM\$}$$

$$\text{Excess Cost Recovery, ECR} = 0 \quad (\text{Since Cost to Recover is} > 0)$$

$$\text{Contractor's Net Rev.} = (\text{CR} - \text{ECR}) + PO_c + \text{ECR}_c - \text{Bonus} - \text{CAPEX} - \text{OPEX}$$
$$= (16.064 - 0) + 8.246 + 0 - 0 - 15 - 6 = 3.31 \text{ MM\$}$$

$$\text{Cum. Contractor's Gross Rev.} = (16.064 - 0) + 8.246 + 0$$
$$= 24.410 \text{ MM\$}$$

$$\text{R-factor} = \text{Cum. Contractor's Gross Rev.} \div \text{Cumulative Cost}$$
$$= 24.31 \div 39 = 0.623$$

$$\text{Government's Net Rev.} = PO_g + \text{ECR}_g + \text{Bonus}$$
$$= 11.388 + 0 + 0 = 11.388 \text{ MM\$}$$

For 2004:

$$\text{Oil Revenue} = 13{,}973 \times 14.0 \times 365 = 71.402 \text{ MM\$}$$

$$\text{Cost Recovery} = 71.402 \times 0.45 = 32.131 \text{ MM\$}$$

$$\text{Contractor's PO Share, } PO_c = 71.402 \times (1 - 0.45) \times 0.42$$
$$= 16.494 \text{ MM\$}$$

$$\text{Government's PO Share, } PO_g = 71.402 \times (1 - 0.45) \times 0.58$$
$$= 22.777 \text{ MM\$}$$

$$\text{Cumulative Cost} = [\text{Cum. Cost}]_{2003} + \text{Bonus} + \text{CAPEX} + \text{OPEX}$$
$$= 39 + 0 + 0 + 10 = 49 \text{ MM\$}$$

$$\text{Cost to Recover} = [\text{Cost to Recover}]_{2003} + \text{CAPEX} + \text{OPEX} - \text{CR}$$
$$= 19.936 + 0 + 10 - 32.131 = -2.195 \text{ MM\$}$$

$$\text{Excess Cost Recovery} = 2.195 \text{ MM\$}$$

$$\text{Contractor's Net Rev.} = (\text{CR} - \text{ECR}) + PO_c + ECR_c - \text{Bonus} - \text{CAPEX} - \text{OPEX}$$
$$= (32.131 - 2.195) + 16.494 + (2.195 \times 0.42) - 0 - 0 - 10$$
$$= 37.352 \text{ MM\$}$$

$$\text{Cum. Contractor's Gross Rev.} = 24.31 + (32.131 - 2.195) + 16.494$$
$$+ (2.195 \times 0.42)$$
$$= 71.662 \text{ MM\$}$$

$$\text{R-factor} = 71.662 \div 49 = 1.463$$

$$\text{Government's Net Rev.} = PO_g + ECR_g + \text{Bonus}$$
$$= 22.777 + (2.195 \times 0.58) + 0$$
$$= 24.05 \text{ MM\$}$$

Government and Contractor Take

The division of net cash flow (based on the agreed fiscal regime) between the contractor and the host government are called *contractor take* and *government take*, respectively. The contractor take provides a good yardstick for comparing the fiscal terms of one contractor to another while competing for the same concession area. It focuses exclusively on the division of profits and correlates directly with reserve values, field size thresholds, and other measures of relative economics.[1]

The government and contractor takes are quantitative indicators that measure the overall effect of a particular fiscal system, thus allowing a meaningful comparison between them. The government take is defined as the amount of money received by the government over the life of a project. It is a percentage of the total net cash flow that the government would have received if the project was done by the government itself. The contractor take is compliment of the government take.[3]

A prerequisite for calculating the contractor or government takes is to first develop a detailed cash-flow model that incorporates (a) intended fiscal terms, (b) exploration and facilities' capital expenditure (CAPEX), (c) estimated operating expenditure (OPEX), and (d) the anticipated production forecast. For exploration projects, the sensitivity of the fiscal terms is normally evaluated at various field sizes. For example, what will be the contractor take if a 20-million-barrel oil field is discovered versus a discovery of a 50-million-barrel field. Once the cash-flow model has been built, the merit of any proposed fiscal terms can be evaluated. Based on these economic evaluations, technical capabilities of the contractors, and contractor's work commitments, the fiscal terms are negotiated. The result of government efforts to arrive at feasible fiscal terms, which are considered appropriate under a variety of unknown circumstances, are sometimes referred to as *fiscal marksmanship*.

Mathematically, the takes are calculated using the following equations.

(5.3)

$$\text{Government Take} = \frac{Government's\ NCF}{Government's\ NCF + Contractor's\ NCF} \times 100$$

(5.4)

$$\text{Contractor Take} = 1 - Government's\ Take$$

The following example clarifies the calculations of government and contractor takes.

Example 5–3

Gross revenue from a field over its economic life is $500 million. The capital and operating costs over the project life is $200 million. The contractor pays $129 million in royalty and tax to the host government. Calculate the government and contractor takes for this concessionary arrangement.

Solution: The calculations are shown in Table 5–5.

Gross Revenue, MM$	500.00	
CAPEX and OPEX, MM$	-200.00	
Net Operating Revenue, MM$	300.00	
Royalty and Taxes, MM$	-129.00	Government Share
Net After-Tax Cash Flow, MM$	171.00	Contractor Share
Government Take	43.00%	=$129/$300
Contractor Take	57.00%	=$171/$300 or (100 – 43.00)

Table 5–5 Calculation of government/contractor take (Example 5–3)

Equations (5.3) and (5.4), used for calculating the government/contractor takes do not account for the time value of money. The disbursements such as signature bonuses, discovery and commercial discovery bonuses, and indirect taxes (sales tax, value-added tax, and import duties) that are levied on the capital items greatly affect the net present value of the contractor's cash flow. Fiscal regime with such up-front disbursements is referred to as a front-end loaded fiscal regime. Therefore, the discounted takes for significantly front-end loaded fiscal regimes is different from the undiscounted takes.

Since the timing of payments to governments can vary widely depending on the structure of fiscal terms, it is important to include the effect of this timing in the calculation of government/contractor takes. Front-end loaded fiscal terms tend to increase government take on a discounted basis. Rapp et. al. has introduced a term called *Front-end Loading Index.*[4]

The Front-end Loading Index (FLI) highlights the spread in the discounted and undiscounted takes. A value of FLI = 0 indicates no front-end loading al all (an ideal condition). The higher the FLI becomes, the more front-end loaded the fiscal regime becomes. The fiscal regime with excessive front-end loading becomes less attractive for the contractor. The FLI is given by the following equation.

(5.5)

$$FLI = \frac{Discounted\ Government\ take}{Undiscounted\ Government\ Take} - 1$$

Applying Equation (5.5) to the fiscal terms in Table 5–2 and Table 5–6 gives

$$FLI\,(Table\ 5-2) = \frac{52.7}{49.6} - 1 = 0.063$$

$$FLI\,(Table\ 5-6) = \frac{79.37}{65.49} - 1 = 0.212$$

The above comparison shows that the fiscal terms in Table 5–2 are less front-end loaded as compared to that of Table 5–6. Although the above concept makes sense, the question is "do the contractor and the government have the same discount rates?"

Sample PSC Cash-Flow Spreadsheet

To start with, the National Oil Company or the Oil Ministry of a host government divides all the prospective exploration areas into concession areas or blocks. Data packages are prepared for each block, and they are advertised so interested international oil companies can bid on them. The bids are normally received in two versions (1) a technical bid and (2) a commercial bid. The technical bids are passed on to the exploration department for technical evaluation, and the legal/financial departments evaluate the commercial bids.

The technical bids are evaluated based on the following criteria:

1. Work commitment the contractor is proposing.

2. The technical standing of the contractor.

3. Experience in the area or similar areas.

4. Financial position of the company.

5. Previous experience and success in exploration, etc.

In some cases, the minimum work commitment is pre-defined in the bid packages and the legal terms outlined. Economists evaluate the commercial bids for the fiscal terms proposed by the contractor.

The economists build a production-sharing cash-flow model as shown in Table 5–6 (an Excel spreadsheet is given on the CD that accompanies Volume 2). This model is then used to test the fiscal terms proposed by each contractor to determine which contractor's terms are more favorable for the

PRODUCTION SHARING ECONOMICS

Ref: XYZ Energy
Offshore Block 708

As of 1st January, 2002

Year	Oil Prod. (MB/D)	EXPL. CAPEX (MM$)	CAPEX (MM$)	OPEX (MM$)	OTHER COSTS (MM$)	TOTAL COST (MM$)	BONUS (MM$)	OIL PRICE ($/Bbl)	COST REC. (%)	HOST GOVT P. OIL (%)	HOST GOVT SHARE ECR (%)	COST TO RECOVER (MM$)	CR (MM$)	PO (MM$)	ECR (MM$)	NET REV. CONT. (MM$)	NET REV. H. GOVT (MM$)	CUM NET REV. CONT. (MM$)	CUM NET REV. H. GOVT (MM$)	R FACTOR
2002	-	6.18				6.18	3.00	12.00	50.00	58.00	58.00	6.18	-	-		(9.18)	3.00	(9.18)	3.00	-
2003	-	6.37				6.37		12.36	50.00	58.00	58.00	12.55	-	-		(6.37)		(15.55)	3.00	-
2004	-		23.49			23.49		12.73	50.00	58.00	58.00	36.04	-	-		(23.49)		(39.04)	3.00	-
2005	-		37.31			37.31		13.11	50.00	58.00	58.00	73.35	-	-		(37.31)		(76.35)	3.00	-
2006	-		60.28			60.28		13.51	50.00	58.00	58.00	133.63	-	-		(60.28)		(136.63)	3.00	-
2007	6.996			6.05	1.53	7.58		13.91	50.00	58.00	58.00	123.47	17.74	17.74		17.61	10.29	(119.02)	13.29	0.17
2008	13.973			6.23	3.06	9.29		14.33	50.00	58.00	58.00	96.22	36.54	36.54		42.60	21.19	(76.43)	34.48	0.50
2009	13.973			6.42	3.06	9.48		14.76	50.00	58.00	58.00	68.07	37.64	37.64		43.96	21.83	(32.47)	56.31	0.80
2010	13.973			6.61	3.06	9.67		15.20	50.00	58.00	58.00	38.98	38.76	37.64		45.38	22.48	12.91	78.79	1.07
2011	13.973			6.81	3.06	9.87		15.66	40.00	61.00	61.00	16.90	31.94	47.91		40.76	29.23	53.67	108.02	1.29
2012	12.301			7.01	2.69	9.70		16.13	40.00	65.00	65.00		28.96	43.44	2.36	32.93	29.77	86.60	137.79	1.45
2013	10.822			7.22	2.37	9.59		16.61	40.00	65.00	65.00		26.25	39.37	16.66	19.61	36.42	106.21	174.20	1.53
2014	9.534			7.44	2.09	9.53		17.11	40.00	69.00	69.00		23.82	35.72	14.29	15.50	34.51	121.71	208.71	1.58
2015	8.384			7.66	1.84	9.50		17.62	40.00	69.00	69.00		21.57	32.36	12.07	13.77	30.66	135.48	239.37	1.61
2016	7.397			7.89	1.62	9.51		18.15	40.00	69.00	69.00		19.50	29.40	10.09	12.24	27.25	147.73	266.62	1.64
2017	6.493			8.13	1.42	9.55		18.70	40.00	69.00	69.00		17.72	26.58	8.17	10.77	23.98	158.50	290.60	1.66
2018	5.726			8.37	1.25	9.62		19.26	40.00	69.00	69.00		16.10	24.15	6.47	9.49	21.13	168.00	311.73	1.67
2019	5.041			8.63	1.10	9.73		19.83	40.00	69.00	69.00		14.60	21.90	4.86	8.30	18.46	176.29	330.20	1.68
2020	4.438			8.88	0.97	9.85		20.43	40.00	69.00	69.00		13.24	19.86	3.39	7.20	16.04	183.50	346.23	1.68
2021	3.918			9.15	0.86	10.01		21.04	40.00	69.00	69.00		12.04	18.05	2.03	6.23	13.66	189.72	360.09	1.68
2022	-					-		21.67	40.00	69.00	69.00		-	-		-	-	189.72	360.09	1.68
2023	-					-		22.32	40.00	69.00	69.00		-	-		-	-	189.72	360.09	1.68
2024	-					-		22.99	40.00	69.00	69.00		-	-		-	-	189.72	360.09	1.68
2025	-					-		23.68	40.00	69.00	69.00		-	-		-	-	189.72	360.09	1.68
2026																				
Total	**49.980**	**12.55**	**121.08**	**112.50**	**29.99**	**278.12**	**3.00**						**356.51**	**469.42**	**80.39**	**189.72**	**360.09**			

PROFIT OIL SPLIT (HOST GOVERNMENT'S SHARE)

MBOD	R - Factor				
	1.00	1.25	1.50	2.00	2.00
15.00	58.0	58.0	61.0	65.0	69.0
25.00	58.0	58.0	65.0	69.0	72.0
35.00	58.0	58.0	65.0	69.0	75.0

COST RECOVERY

OIL PRICE ($/Bbl)	R - Factor				
	1.00	1.25	1.50	2.00	>2.50
10.00	50.0	50.0	40.0	40.0	40.0
15.00	50.0	50.0	40.0	40.0	40.0
20.00	50.0	50.0	40.0	40.0	40.0

BONUS PAYMENTS

Year	BONUS (MM$)	CUM. PROD. (MMBO)	BONUS (MM$)
2002	3.00	5.00	-
		10.00	-
		30.00	-

	NPV 10% (MM$)	IRR (%)	TAKE %
CONTRACTOR	29.75	15.4%	20.63
HOST GOVERNMENT	114.43		79.37
TOTAL PROJECT	144.18	28.9%	

Table 5–6 Typical production-sharing cash-flow model

host government. Based on these evaluations, only the contractors whose terms are favorable to the host government are short listed for further detailed negotiations. Ultimately, a contract is signed with a contractor whose terms give the best return to the host government.

The spreadsheet has to be flexible enough to evaluate the effect of the fiscal terms for different field sizes, work commitment, and pricing scenarios, etc. Description of the various columns of the spreadsheet in Table 5–6 follows.

1. *Column A:* shows the contract period from year 1 to year 25.

2. *Column B:* shows the calendar years of the contract period.

3. *Column C:* expected production forecast in 1000 Stb/d (MB/d) for a successful exploration. The column can also be programmed to utilize decline curve formulas.

4. *Column D:* shows estimated exploration (G&G) costs.

5. *Column E:* estimated facilities costs required if the exploration effort is successful and the field has to be developed.

6. *Column F:* estimated operating expenditure to operate the field when it is developed.

7. *Column G:* other costs, such as tariff or variable operating expenditure. $0.60/Stb used in this spreadsheet.

8. *Column H:* shows total recoverable cost or petroleum cost.

9. *Column I:* shows bonus payments by the contractor. Note the bonuses are normally not considered petroleum costs and therefore cannot be recovered from cost recovery oil. The model accommodates up to three bonus payments tied to a particular year (i.e., 2002, 2003, or 2008, etc.). In addition, it accommodates up to three bonus payments tied to user specified cumulative production limits. When the respective cumulative production is reached, bonus is paid in the corresponding year.

10. *Column J:* shows oil price, the base price of $12/Stb in 2002 and escalated at 3% per year from year 2003 onward.

11. *Column K:* shows the cost recovery split based on the R-factor and the price of oil.

12. *Column L:* shows the profit oil share of the host government based on the R-factor and the oil production during the year.

13. *Column M:* shows the ECR share of the host government. In this spreadsheet, it is assumed that the ECR share of the host government is the same as its profit oil share.

14. *Column N:* shows the balance of recoverable cost each year (i.e., the balance in 2002 is to be recovered from the cost recovery petroleum in year 2003 and so on).

15. *Column O:* shows the amount of cost recovery oil revenue allocated to the contractor, based on the balance in Column N and the cost recovery split in Column K.

16. *Column P:* shows the profit oil portion of the gross revenue, which will be shared between the contractor and the host government according to their allocated shares.

17. *Column Q:* shows the excess cost recovery amount (left after the contractor has recovered its costs from the cost recovery portion of the gross revenue), which will be shared between the contractor and the host government according to their allocated shares.

18. *Column R:* shows the ultimate net revenue share or net cash flow of the contractor. This is its profit oil share + share of the ECR if any + the CR revenue - the bonuses and costs.

19. *Column S:* shows the ultimate net revenue share or net cash flow of the host government. This is its profit oil share + share of the ECR if any + bonuses.

20. *Columns T and U:* show the cumulative net revenue of the contractor and the host government, respectively.

21. *Column V:* shows the contractor's R-factor for each year.

22. *Cells T44–V44.* Show the profitability indicators of the contractor and the host government.

Risk Service Contracts

The countries importing crude oil normally use this approach. According to this type of contract, the contractor provides all the capital required for the exploration and development of petroleum resources. If the exploration and development efforts are successful, the contractor is allowed to recover its costs from the revenues generated by the sale of oil and/or gas. The government keeps the oil. In addition, the contractor is paid a fee based on a percentage of the remaining revenues. The fee may or may not be subject to taxes. The term *risk* implies that if the contractor is not successful in finding oil and/or gas, all his costs of exploration are to his account with no liability to the host government.

On the other hand, some governments have a lot of money but lack the technical know-how. They may get into pure service contracts. According to such contracts, although rare, the host government bears the cost of exploration and development, and the contractor is paid a fee. This type of contract is also referred to as the *Technical Service Agreement (TSA)*.

There is little difference between the risk service contracts and the PSCs. The difference lies in how payments are made to the contractor. Other than that, the arithmetic and terminology are quite similar. Therefore, many service contracts are commonly referred to as the PSCs.

Rate of Return (ROR) Contracts

A rate of return contract is just another version of the PSC where the fiscal terms are on a sliding scale, tied to the ROR rather than the simple R-factor. Some governments have developed progressive taxes or sharing arrangements based on project rate of return. The effective government take in such agreements increases as the project ROR increases. The ROR system takes into account products price, cost of capital, and timing of cash flows (inflows and outflows).

A modest royalty and tax in the beginning characterize these types of contracts, i.e., early production phase. The host government does not receive any other share until the contractor has recovered the initial investment plus a predetermined minimum (threshold/hurdle) rate of return. The host government's share in this type of contract is calculated by accumulating the net cash flows and compounding them at the minimum (threshold) rate of return until the cumulative value becomes positive, i.e., payout time. At this point, additional taxes are levied. The contractor, in some cases, still receives some of the profits in excess of the minimum rate of return. In other cases, the contractor's share is limited only to his predetermined rate of return; and any amounts in excess of this rate of return are made to the host government. However, sharing of the excess encourages the contractor to achieve cost effectiveness and improve hydrocarbon recovery. The additional taxes are typically referred to as the resource rent taxes (RRT) or additional profits tax (APT).

EFFECTS OF VARIOUS FISCAL TERMS

In order for international oil companies to invest in oil-producing countries, their fiscal regime has to be flexible enough and efficient enough to economically encourage the international oil companies. The fiscal regime has to be in balance with many other aspects of petroleum exploration and development in a particular country (i.e., the country's prospectivity, political stability, economic environment, etc). For example, a country with an expected low prospectivity should set lenient fiscal terms as compared to the countries with high expected hydrocarbon prospectivity. Similarly, less politically stable countries should set lenient fiscal terms as compared to the more politically stable countries.

The efficiency of a particular fiscal regime can be judged from the host government's take in a particular situation. There is a large variation in the fiscal severity of different oil producing countries. The effects of various fiscal terms on the host government's take and the contractor's profitability are discussed. The economic effects of petroleum fiscal regimes in more than 100 countries are examined by Petroconsultants Australasia Pty, Ltd. They show how onerous or how severe the regime is in a particular country by comparison with those in other countries.[5]

The discovery of giant or large oil/gas fields is diminishing. Therefore, it is important that more attention is focused on developing marginal fields. The economic development of these marginal fields (being on the borderline of being economic because of size, production rates, costs, etc.) requires flexible fiscal terms. The terms should be flexible enough to provide high levels of government take in case of a profitable development.

Efficient Fiscal Regime

An efficient fiscal regime is the one in which the contractor's net present value (NPV) before the government takes honors the NPV after its takes. Projects that will be profitable before the government takes will also be profitable after the government takes and vice versa. For example, some fiscal regimes tax very profitable projects heavily and marginal projects lightly or not at all. This type of fiscal regime is referred to as a *progressive* fiscal regime.

On the other hand, some fiscal regimes tax marginal projects relatively heavily as compared to the relatively profitable projects. This type of fiscal regime is referred to as a *regressive* or *inefficient* fiscal regime. When a fiscal regime is designed in such way that less profitable projects are taxed relatively lightly and the more profitable projects are taxed relatively heavily, the fiscal regime is referred to as a *flat, stable,* or *efficient* fiscal regime.

The progressive, regressive, or inefficient fiscal regimes may be liable to change in the future as the economic or exploration/field development conditions change. For example, severe fiscal terms may render a new marginal discovery uneconomical for the contractor. These terms may require revision if the host government is interested in the development of this marginal field. On the other hand, if the fiscal terms are very lenient (i.e., giving away too much to the contractor, the government may see a need to revise fiscal terms or renegotiate the contract).

One way to determine if a particular fiscal regime is efficient is to plot the NPV of net cash flow from an oil field development *after* government takes (i.e., net contractor's share or contractor's NPV) versus NPV of the same *before* government takes (i.e., total project NPV) as shown in Figure 5–3.

In Figure 5–3, line *B* represents an efficient fiscal regime. This line shows that if a project is economical (positive NPV) before host government takes, it is also economical after the host government take and vice versa. On the other hand, lines *A* and *C* represent inefficient or less efficient fiscal regimes. For example with line *C*, projects that are profitable for the contractor before host government take become unprofitable after host government take. Such a situation discourages the contractor from further involvement in the project. The contractor may walk away from

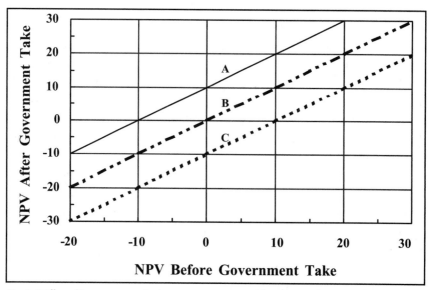

Fig. 5–3 Effect of host government's take on project economics (after Petroconsultants Australasia Pty, Ltd.)[5]

the project, thus leaving petroleum in the ground that could be developed. Alternatively, he could ask for renegotiations of the fiscal terms. Such a regime prevents the development of marginally profitable fields.

The effect in line *C* is mainly due to some components of fiscal terms that are not tied to profitability of the project as a whole. The royalty is one of the culprits. This is because royalty is deducted from the gross revenue without any consideration for the project costs. Marginal developments are particularly affected by such terms. Payment of royalty reduces or even eliminates the positive difference between the revenues and the costs. Taxes, on the other hand, reduce the overall contractor's profitability from a marginal project. Since taxes are deducted only from the contractors' positive net cash flow before host government takes, the results are shown in line *B*.

The line *A* is interpreted opposite in nature to line *C*. In this situation, the project that is not economical before host government take becomes economical after the host government take. Such a situation takes place in projects that are incremental to existing field developments where the host government provides tax relief for additional (incremental) costs incurred within the license area.

The ROR type of production-sharing contracts are considered efficient. These types of fiscal regimes are efficient because they are based on the NPV of the project. The contractor's NPV at the contract ROR is calculated each year, and if it is positive, only then are the incremental benefits allocated to the host government. In other words, positive NPV projects are taxed and negative NPV projects are not taxed. Similarly, high NPV projects are taxed heavily as compared to the low NPV projects.

The Effect of Cost Recovery Ceiling

The PSC provides for cost recovery. The effect of an inappropriate cost recovery ceiling lengthens the costs' recovery time. The efficiency of the PSC also depends on how the excess cost recovery is shared between the host government and the contractor. The excess cost recovery oil can be allocated in two ways: (1) it is entirely attributed to the host government or (2) it is treated as profit oil and shared in the same way between the host government and the contractor. Case 1 does not provide any economic incentive to the contractor to reduce costs by increasing efficiency, introducing new technologies, or by further investments in this direction.

Therefore, it is economically convenient for the host government to regard a portion of the excess cost oil as profit oil and shared with the contractor. In doing so, the contractor strives to reduce costs and ultimately benefits. The sharing of the excess cost recovery oil as profit oil neutralizes any further economic effect for the contractor as the cost recovery oil varies. The changes in the cost recovery percentage will have an insignificant effect on the economics of the contractor. Figure 5–4 shows that the NPV of the contractor after CR=40% is constant even if the CR is raised to 60%.

At the beginning of production, the cost recovery oil is usually insufficient to recover the exploration, development, and operating costs. Consequently, a portion of these costs (not fully recovered through the allocated cost recovery oil) must therefore be carried forward to subsequent years. This mechanism penalizes the contractor since it delays his cost recovery. In principle, the value of the cost recovery oil must minimize or, even better, *prevent* this carrying forward. Some contracts acknowledge this effect in the contracts by either (1) increasing the cost

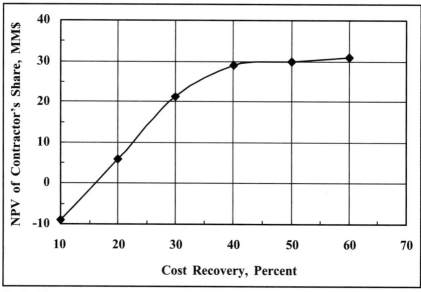

Fig. 5–4 Contractor's NPV versus cost recovery percent.

recovery by a certain percentage (uplift) or (2) allowing interest to be charged on the unrecovered portion. Such mechanisms have a positive economic effect and, if well devised, they benefit both the contractor and the host government.

Another consideration is the effect of *ringfencing*. Ordinarily all costs associated with a given block (concession area) must be recovered from the cost recovery oil generated within that block. This means the block is *ringfenced*. This element may have a significant impact on the recovery of costs of exploration and development. Some countries allow certain types of costs associated with a given field or license to be recovered from cost recovery oil from another field or license operated in the same country by the same contractor. Allowing the contractor's exploration costs to *cross the fence* can be a strong financial incentive, especially on marginal fields.

The production-sharing cash flow in Table 5–6 has been worked out in order to assess numerically the effects of the cost recovery oil variation on the economic indicators. The excess cost recovery oil has been treated as a profit oil, shared between the contractor and the host government in the same way as the profit oil. Figures 5–4 and 5–5 show how the economic indicators change with the change in cost recovery oil percentage.

Figures 5–4 and 5–5 show that as the cost recovery percentage is increased, the contractor's IRR, NPV, and percentage of costs recovered increase up to a maximum cost recovery percentage of approximately 40%. This occurs when all the costs are recovered according to the allocation allowed by the contract. Since the excess cost recovery oil is treated as profit oil and shared between the contractor and the host government, the economic indicators remain relatively constant after the 40% cost recovery percentage. If the excess cost recovery oil was entirely allocated to the host government, the economic indicators start to decline as the cost recovery percentage increases beyond the 40%. Therefore, any cost recovery percentage in excess of 40% are disproportionate to the need for the recovery of the costs.[6]

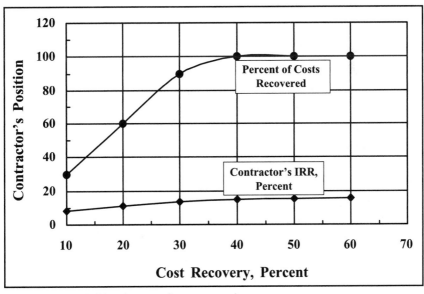

Fig. 5–5 Contractor's IRR and percent of costs recovered versus cost recovery percent

QUESTIONS and PROBLEMS

5.1   An international contractor signs an EPSA on 1/1/2001 for a block in Nigeria. On signing the contract, the contractor pays $5 million in bonus. During the first two years, the contractor conducts exploration activities at a cost of $8 million each year. If a commercial oil field is discovered, it will take another two years to develop the field at a cost of $35 million in year one and $28 million in year two. Production from the field starts at a rate of 15,000 Stb/day in 2005 declining exponentially at a rate of 15% each year. The yearly operating expenditure is 5% of the total development cost. If the oil price is $15 per barrel, calculate the net cash flow of the contractor and the host government for the next five years. The fiscal terms of the contract are CR=30%, PO share of the contractor is 25%, and the excess cost recovery oil is shared between the contractor and the host government in the same way as the profit oil.

5.2   Evaluate Problem 5.1 if the contractor has to pay another $6 million when the cumulative production from the field reaches 10 million barrels and the contractor has to pay 5% royalty to the host government out of the gross production.

5.3   Data on a prospective exploration concession is given in Table 5–7. Build a production-sharing economics model and then design fiscal terms in such a way that the contractor will receive a rate of return of approximately 15% no matter what field size he discovers. Assume the oil price of $15 per barrel, escalating at 3% per year. The costs are in $2000, assume the costs will be escalating at 3% per year. The operating cost in each case is 5% per year of the total development cost in each case. The contractor has to pay a tariff of $0.45 per barrel to the host government for using their oil storage and handling facility. The contractor pays a signature bonus of $6 million on 01/01/2002 and pays production bonuses of $5 million and $4 million when the cumulative reaches 10 million and 25 million barrels, respectively.

5.4   Repeat Problem 5.3 if the contractor has to pay 5% royalty and 35% tax to the host government. Assume a tax holiday of 10 years from the first production and ignore depreciation and depletion.

	Production Forecast, Stb/day				CAPEX for each Case, MM$			
	A	B	C	D	A	B	C	D
2002					6.00	6.00	6.00	6.00
2003					6.00	6.00	6.00	6.00
2004					19.4	20.8	27.6	23.6
2005					14.5	32.2	43.3	40.4
2006					22.6	50.3	79.1	82.3
2007	3,493	6,986	13,973	20,959			30.9	44.2
2008	6,986	13,973	13,973	20,959				42.9
2009	6,986	13,973	27,945	45,000				
2010	6,986	13,973	27,945	43,000				
2011	6,986	13,973	27,945	41,918				
2012	6,151	12,301	27,945	41,918				
2013	5,411	10,822	27,945	41,918				
2014	4,767	9,543	27,945	41,918				
2015	4,192	8,384	16,986	41,918				
2016	2,822	7,397	14,411	34,608				
2017		6,493	12,192	31,147				
2018		5,724	10,329	21,600				
2019		5,041	9,590	16,240				
2020		4,438	7,425	14,616				
2021		3,973	7,425	13,154				
2022				11,839				
2023				10,655				
2024				9,589				
2025				8,630				
2026				7,767				
2027				6,990				
2028				6,292				
2029				5,662				
2030				5,096				
2031				4,587				

Table 5–7 Estimated production and cost data for a prospective exploration concession (Problem 5.3)

REFERENCES

1. Bindemann, K., *Production-Sharing Agreements: An Economic Analysis*, Oxford Institute for Energy Studies, WPM 25, 57 Woodstock Road, Oxford OX2 6FA, England, October 1999.
2. Johnston Daniel, *International Petroleum Fiscal Systems and Production-Sharing Contracts*, PennWell Publishing Co., Tulsa, Oklahoma, 1994.
3. Smith, D.E., "True Government Take (TGT): A Measurement of Fiscal Terms," *SPE Paper 16308*, presented at SPE Hydrocarbon Economics and Evaluation Symposium held in Dallas, Texas, March 2–3, 1987.
4. Rapp, W.J., Litvak, B.L., Kokolis, G.P., and Wang, B., "Utilizing Discounted Government Take Analysis for Comparison of International Oil and Gas E&P Fiscal Regimes," *SPE Paper 52958*, presented at SPE Hydrocarbon Economics and Evaluation Symposium held in Dallas, Texas, March 20–23, 1999.
5. Petroconsultants Australasia Pty, Ltd., *Economics of Petroleum Exploration and Production* course notes, 1996.
6. Muscolino, Riccardo, Rizzo, C.A., and Mirabelli, Giuseppe, "The Cost Recovery Oil in a Production-Sharing Agreement, *SPE Paper 25844*, paper presented at SPE Hydrocarbon Economics and Evaluation Symposium held in Dallas, Texas, U.S.A., 29–30 March, 1993.

chapter SIX

Capital Budgeting Techniques

The term *capital* refers to expenditure for the purchase or expansion of physical assets, such as property, plants, and equipment. The term *budget* refers to a plan that details projected inflows resulting from projected outflows. Thus, the *capital budget* is an outline of planned capital investments, and *capital budgeting* is the whole process of analyzing the projects and deciding whether they should be included in the capital budget. Capital budgeting is the deliberate allocation of present resources with the expectation of future returns. Through the capital budgeting process, an investor is able to answer three main questions:

1. How large the budget should be?
2. Which projects/investments should be included in the portfolio?
3. How should the required budget be financed?

Although we are referring to property, plants, and equipment, the parameters presented here may also be used in other investment situations.

Prudent capital investment decision-making is an important and critical managerial responsibility. The long-term survival, profitability, value, and growth of a business are dependent on these decisions. Capital budgeting decisions also play an important role in providing a mechanism for the implementation of business strategies.

Capital projects normally entail large commitments of funds and their impact on the financial well-being of the organization extending over relatively long time spans. The investments once made are difficult to amend or retrieve. An ill-advised decision concerning capital investments frequently cannot be reversed before it seriously affects the financial health of the organization. Because of its importance, systematic procedures are essential for effective planning of these investments. Each investment proposal should be viewed as an identifiable incremental project having its own unique time dimension and reward structure. The term incremental refers to all those costs or investments that otherwise would not be incurred in the absence of the project/investment

An important part of the planning process is to define and lay down rules and techniques to form what is called *profitability analysis*. It is essential for the management to define what is meant by a *profitable project* or *investment*. In order to achieve this objective, management must provide a way to choose between alternative schemes of carrying out a given investment or project. Unless these guidelines are provided clearly, it is difficult to delegate the responsibility of evaluating investment projects to the lower levels of management.

The overall capital expenditure plan of an oil company consists of a series of unique capital projects/investments. These may include:

1. Exploration for oil and gas

2. New oil and gas fields' development

3. Infill drilling

4. Facilities replacements/upgrades

5. Installation of new facilities

6. Secondary and enhanced oil recovery projects

7. A variety of downstream projects

Major capital additions should be accorded special analysis, management evaluation, and judgment. Approaches to determine their investment worth should loom large in the decision-making process.

To judge the attractiveness of any investment, three main elements are considered. These are (a) *investment amount*, (b) the *operating benefits*, and (c) the *economic life*. The economic life of an investment is the time period where positive net benefits are expected from the investment alternative. For example, it is technically possible to produce a certain reservoir down to 10 Stb/day at the end of 15 years. However, at the end of year 10, costs incurred to produce this reservoir exceed the revenues generated from 50 Stb/day. Therefore, the economic life is only 10 years and not 15. Similarly the economic life of equipment may be shorter than its physical life. Therefore, all investment analysis must combine these three elements in a logical manner in order to provide a clue whether the investment is worthy of consideration or not. These basic conditions are true of all investment proposals under consideration.

Capital budgeting, in practice, involves understanding an integrated use of various techniques presented in

1. Managerial and corporate finance

2. Industrial economics

3. Strategic planning (i.e., developing a sustainable competitive edge over other investors in the industry)

4. Decision theory

Considerable amount of literature on the subject of capital budgeting is available in the publications of finance, economics, accounting, and oil industry trade journals. Some selected references are given at the end of this chapter.[1-13]

Therefore, capital budgeting is an exercise that requires estimating the net value of future cash flows and other benefits as compared to the initial investment required. Many financial analyses entail the search for an answer to the question: "Is the investment worthwhile considering potential future returns?"

For the capital budgeting, management needs objective measures of the economic worth of investment proposals. They should be able to rank, accept, reject, compare, or choose among them and select those most beneficial to the company's long-term prosperity. The parameters used to facilitate the above decisions are frequently called *measures of profitability, profit indicators, profitability yardsticks, economic yardsticks, decision criteria, or measure of investment worth*. The investment evaluation techniques should have the capability of estimating whether the cash returns from the investment will be large enough to make the initial investment worthwhile.

One of the main difficulties in capital budgeting is the large number of economic evaluation yardsticks used. These criteria have different properties and are used in various ways. Studying the mathematical properties of these criteria, as well as working through examples, is an effective way to put them into focus.

This chapter considers the meaning, mathematics, and properties (advantages and disadvantages) of the most commonly used measures of profitability. In the course of our discussion, the methods are compared in order to (1) highlight their relative strengths and weaknesses and (2) evaluate performances in terms of identifying investments that will maximize the corporate worth. At this point, no attempt is made to rank the desirability of these measures. The measures of profitability presented in this chapter do not include any explicit statements of risks and uncertainty. *Both the accounting measures and the time-adjusted measures of profitability are presented. However, common time-adjusted measures are emphasized and recommended for use.*

No unique profitability measure accounts for all possible decision factors or dimensions of a capital investment. Economists should select profitability measures and assumptions related to each particular financial environment. Ideally, profitability measures should be backed up by experience and sound economic judgment. The ideal measures of profitability should have the following characteristics:

1. It must be suitable for comparing and ranking the profitability of available investment alternatives.

2. It should account for the time value of money.

3. It should provide a means for telling whether profitability exceeds some minimum *cut-off* (threshold) requirement of the organization.

4. It should be able to include probability estimates to generate expected values.

5. If possible it should reflect other factors such as corporate goals, decision makers' risk preferences, and corporate asset position.

6. It should reflect the size of the initial investment. Otherwise there might be an inappropriate bias towards small investments. Such a situation may strain the company resources essential for the implementation of the available projects.

The following capital budgeting techniques/approaches are discussed in this chapter.

- Net present value (NPV)
- Payback period
- Internal rate of return (IRR)
- Profitability index
- Unit technical cost
- Cost benefit ratio

In Chapter 7, these parameters are used in arriving at economic decisions in a variety of investment situations. Note that all subsequent techniques for ranking projects are no better than the data input—the old saying, "garbage in, garbage out," is certainly applicable to capital budgeting analysis.

Today, computers are used to analyze virtually all capital budgeting decisions of importance, and therefore it is easy to calculate and list all the measures of profitability. As mentioned in the previous chapter, the prerequisite to adequate investment analysis is the realistic estimates of cash flows. Once the cash flow estimates are generated, the calculation of the measures of profitability is then easy. Throughout most of this chapter, the Table 3–18 cash flow is used for discussion. The second half of Table 3–18 is reproduced in Table 6–1 for convenience. The last three columns are used to calculate most of the profitability indicators.

	A	I	J	K	L	M	N	O
7		Expenditure			Operating Revenue			Cum. NCF
8		LOE	Taxes	TOTAL	Gross	Net	Cum. NCF	Disc. @10%
9	Year	(M$)	(M$)	(M$)	(M$)	(M$)	(M$)	(M$)
10	2002	0.00	0.00	185.00	0.00	(185.00)	(185.00)	(176.39)
11	2003	14.40	14.81	29.21	185.11	155.90	(29.10)	(41.26)
12	2004	14.40	7.29	21.69	91.07	69.39	40.28	13.41
13	2005	14.40	5.39	19.79	67.34	47.55	87.83	47.48
14	2006	14.40	3.56	17.96	44.50	26.54	114.37	64.76
15	2007	14.40	2.85	17.25	35.67	18.42	132.79	75.66
16	2008	14.40	2.38	16.78	29.77	12.99	145.78	82.65
17	2009	14.40	2.04	16.44	25.55	9.10	154.88	87.11
18	2010	14.40	1.85	16.25	23.11	6.86	161.74	90.16
19	2011	14.40	1.77	16.17	22.09	5.92	167.66	92.55
20	2012	14.40	1.65	16.05	20.69	4.63	172.29	94.25
21	2013	14.40	1.60	16.00	20.02	4.02	176.31	95.60
22	2014	14.40	1.59	15.99	19.92	3.92	180.23	96.79
23	2015	14.40	1.59	15.99	19.85	3.86	184.09	97.85
24	2016	14.40	1.57	15.97	19.60	3.63	187.72	98.76
25	2017							
26	Sub	201.60	49.94	436.54	624.26	187.72		
27	Rem	0.00	0.00	0.00	0.00	0.00		
28	Total	201.60	49.94	136.54	624.26	187.72		
29							NPV Profile	
30		Net Present Value @10% (M$)			98.76		Percent	NPV (M$)
31		Rate of Return (ROR)			37.00%		5%	136.26
32		Profitability Index			1.56		15%	70.37
33		Payback (Disc. @10%), Years			2.75		20%	48.22
34		Technical Cost, $/Stb			27.90		25%	30.52
35		Technical Cost, $/BOE			14.81		30%	16.10
36		Technical Cost, $/Stb (Disc.)			30.68		35%	4.19
37		Technical Cost, $/BOE (Disc.)			16.23		40%	(5.77)

Table 6–1 Data reproduced from Table 3–18

ACCOUNTING APPROACHES

This section deals with often-used simple capital budgeting techniques, their key elements, and their advantages and disadvantages. The next section addresses more advanced but increasingly popular methods that employ the discounted cash flow concepts, namely: adjustment for the timing of cash flows and the recognition of economic opportunity costs.

Payback Period

The *payback period*, also referred to as the *breakeven point*, is defined as the expected number of years required for recovering the original investment. At this point, the cash receipts exactly equal the cash disbursements. This yardstick is used along with at least one other measure of profitability, since it does not provide meaningful decision criterion by itself.

The only question the calculated payback period answers is "How long will it take to get my money back?" From an economic viewpoint this is not enough, of course, since one would also hope to earn a profit on the investment. When related to the useful economic life of an investment, the payback figure is used as an indication of whether the investment is repaid within the economic life.

The payback period is calculated from the net cash flow by two different methods. The first method requires accumulating the negative net cash flow each year until it turns positive as shown in Column N of Table 6–1 (between Cells N11 and N12). The payback period is then the *cumulative time* (each year with negative cumulative net cash flow from time zero) to a point between the negative and positive net cash flow. The partial payback period in the year when the NCF turns positive is calculated by interpolating between the two values, the following equation is used.

(6.1)

$$\text{Payback Period} = \textit{Cum.} - \textit{ve NCF Years} + \frac{1}{+\textit{ve NCF} - (-\textit{ve NCF})} \times (-\textit{ve NCF})$$

$$= 2 + \frac{1}{40.28 - (-29.10)} \times (-29.10)$$

$$= 2.42 \ \text{years}$$

The second method involves plotting the cumulative net cash flow versus time as shown in Figure 6–1. The payback period is read at the intersection of the time line at zero net cash flow, the point at which the cumulative net cash flow turns from the negative quadrant into the positive quadrant.

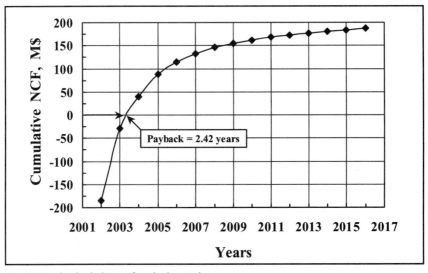

Fig. 6-1 Graphical calculation of payback period.

The payback period does not provide any idea of the benefits to follow. The method is not concerned with profitability. For an investment to provide profit, the useful economic life beyond the payback period is important. For example, there are two investments of $150,000 each and both have equal payback periods of three years (the net cash flow is $50,000 each year). Furthermore, Project A does not generate any cash flow after the payback period, while Project B generates $60,000 in three years after the payback period. Therefore, Project B is the preferred choice. The payback period fails to highlight this fact.

In fact, if economic life and payback period are equal, then an opportunity loss occurs, since the same capital invested elsewhere would presumably have earned some return. For example, in Table 6–1 the 185 M$ if invested in a bank at an interest rate of 10% per year accumulates to approximately 343.74 M$ by the end of 2008 as shown in

Figure 6–2. On the other hand, the *positive net revenue* generated each year if reinvested at 10% accumulates to 504.82 M$ by the end of 2008 as shown in Figure 6–3. By plotting the yearly cumulative position from Figures 6–2 and 6–3 as shown in Figure 6–4, the breakeven point or the payback period is approximately 2.75 years. Thus the 2.42 years previously calculated is not correct.

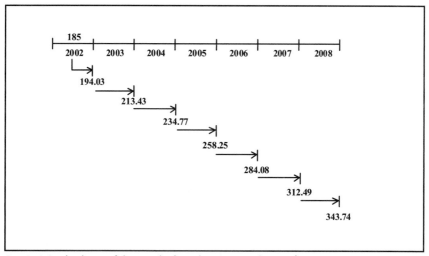

Fig. 6–2 Graphical view of the growth of initial investment of 185 M$ at 10%

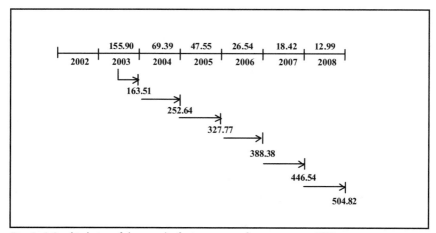

Fig. 6–3 Graphical view of the growth of reinvestment of net revenue at 10%

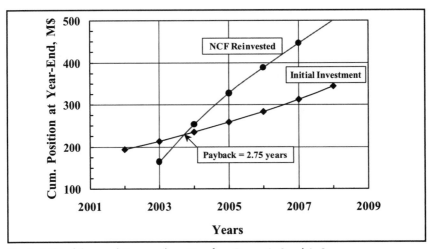

Fig. 6–4 Plot of the cumulative growth positions from Figures 6–2 and 6–3

In Figure 6–2, it is assumed the 185 M$ earns interest over a partial year of 2002. Therefore, 194.03 M$ = $[185 \times (1 + 0.1)^{0.5}]$ is taken in 2002, 213.43 M$ = (194.03 x 1.1) in 2003, and so on. On other hand, in Figure 6–3, it is assumed the revenues received each year are reinvested at 10%.

The mid-year compounding assumption is used for the first year of reinvestment since the revenues are received monthly. Therefore, it does not earn interest for the whole year. The calculations are shown below.

Cumulative at end of 2003 = $155.90 \times (1 + 0.1)^{0.5}$ = 163.51 M$

Cumulative at end of 2004 = $69.39 \times (1 + 0.1)^{0.5} + 163.51 \times (1 + 0.1)$ = 252.64 M$

Cumulative at end of 2005 = $47.55 \times (1 + 0.1)^{0.5} + 252.64 \times (1 + 0.1)$ = 327.77 M$

and so on.

The method as outlined above does not account for the time value of money. The payback period is useful because it provides information on how long funds are tied up, i.e., the shorter the payback period (other things held constant) the greater the liquidity. Also, the future expected cash flows are generally believed to be riskier than near-term cash flows. Thus payback may indicate aspects of a project's riskiness (i.e., the longer the payback period, the higher the risk exposure). This is particularly true if the investment is taking place in

1. An industry where the rate of technological change is high (i.e., technological advances quickly make state-of-the-art products obsolete)

2. An environment where the produced product's price is highly volatile such as the oil price, or

3. A politically and/or economically unstable country.

Average Return on Investment (AROI)

This method is also referred to as the Return on Investment (ROI) or Accounting Rate of Return (ARR). The method simply relates the average annual cash inflow to the average investment. The formula is:

$$(6.2)$$

$$\text{Average Return on Investment} = \frac{Annual\ Average\ Cash\ Inflow\ or\ Savings}{Net\ Investment\ Outlay}$$

Substituting the data from Table 6–1,

$$\text{Average Return on Investment} = \frac{\dfrac{(Gross\ Revenue - Taxes - LOE)}{Economic\ Life}}{Investment}$$

$$\text{Average Return on Investment} = \frac{\dfrac{624.26 - 49.94 - 201.60}{15}}{185}$$

$$= 0.1343\ or\ 13.43\%$$

The ROI method shares most of the technical problems associated with the payback method discussed in the previous section. Following are the properties of the ROI method.

1. The technique does not account for the time value of money.

2. The averaging process ignores the length of the life of the alternatives being evaluated.

3. It does not give any indication about the size of the initial investment.

4. It does not give any indication of the value of the project (i.e., no contribution to wealth maximization effort).

5. The technique is not additive (i.e., if one project has an ROI of 10% and another project has an ROI of 15%, the total ROI does not become simply 25%). The average annual cash inflows from the two projects have to be first added together, then divided by the total investment of the two projects to arrive at the ROI of the total investment in the two projects.

6. It does not provide any indication of capital's exposure to risk and uncertainty.

7. The ROI is not comparable with the cost of capital of the investment (i.e., opportunity cost or interest rate).

DISCOUNTED CASH-FLOW APPROACHES

The discounted cash flow methods are widely accepted and used in the industry for all types of capital investment evaluations. The discounted cash flow methods recognize the time value of money. This is critical when assessing the profitability of long-term investments. Future and past values of money can be converted into their present value equivalent by using the time value of money concepts presented in Chapter 2.

In this section, mathematics of the various discounted cash flow methods and their utility in practical investment evaluations are discussed. The various methods presented are (1) discounted payback period, (2) net present value, (3) internal rate of return, (4) profitability index, (5) unit technical cost, (6) modified internal rate of return, and (7) modified net present value. At the end of this chapter the effect of the (a) frequency of discounting/compounding and (b) flow of funds (continuous or discrete) on these measures of profitability is presented.

Discounted Payback Period

The discounted payback period is calculated in exactly the same way as presented in the previous section. The exception here is accounting for the time value of money. Referring to Table 6–1, the cumulative discounted NCF of Column O instead of the cumulative NCF of Column N is used for computing the discounted payback period. A weighted cost of capital of i_d=10% and the mid-year assumption to calculate the discounted NCF of Column M and the following equation is used

$$Cell\ O12 = Cell\ M12 \times \frac{1}{\left(1+i_d\right)^{n-0.50}}$$

$$= -185 \times \frac{1}{\left(1+0.10\right)^{1-0.50}} = -185 \times 0.9535 = -176.39$$

The n for the first year is 1, for the second year is 2 and so on. If the year-end assumption is used, then the 0.5 in the power is omitted. Each year the present value of the net revenue is added to the discounted NCF of the previous year to compute the cumulative. This cumulative discounted NCF is then used to calculate the payback period in the same way as in the previous case. Figure 6–5 illustrates the plot of the cumulative discounted NCF of Column O and the discounted payback period.

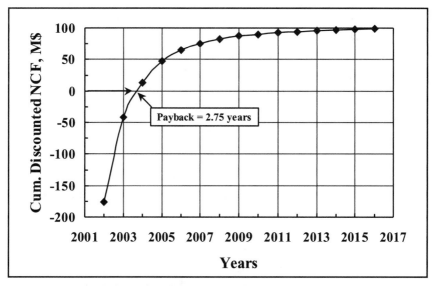

Fig. 6–5 Graphical calculation of the discounted payback period

Figures 6–5 and 6–3 show that it takes longer to breakeven in discounted terms as compared to the previous case (2.75 years versus 2.42 years). This is due to the recovery of the 10% interest on the initial investment. Therefore, this method removes the time value of money limitation from the previously calculated payback period. The rest of the properties are the same in both cases. The payback period is a subjective measure and depends on project type and the preference of the investor. Some investors may reject projects if their payback period is more than 5 years even if they are otherwise profitable. Others may limit their choice to only 3-year payback projects, while some may not mind even longer payback projects. In most cases it may be a strategic decision more than a financial decision.

Net Present Value (NPV)

The net present value (NPV), also referred to as the present value of *cash surplus* or *present worth*, is obtained by subtracting the *present value* of periodic cash outflows from the *present value* of periodic cash inflows. The present value is calculated using the *weighted average cost of capital* of the investor, also referred to as the *discount rate* or minimum *acceptable rate of return.*

The discount rate should reflect the value of the alternative use of funds. What is an alternative use of funds? Money has value regardless of how it is utilized. If it is kept in a bank savings account, it earns interest; if it is kept in a mattress, it loses *real* value with time because of the missed opportunity of earning interest. For example, if $100,000 invested in a bank earning 5% interest is withdrawn for investing it in another project, the 5% becomes the cost of capital or the opportunity cost of the $100,000 that is forgone by investing it in another project. The bank account is the alternative use of funds. Therefore, when evaluating the project it must generate at least 5% to breakeven with the returns from the bank account. The risk factor also comes into play (if return from the project is riskier than the return on the bank account, then some risk premium more than the 5% return is desired).

When NPV of an investment at a certain discount rate is positive, it pays for the cost of financing the investment or the cost of the alternative use of funds. The *investment generates revenue that is equal to the positive present value.* It also implies the rate of return on the investment is at least equal to the discount rate. Conversely, a negative NPV indicates the investment is not generating earnings equivalent to those expected from the alternative use of funds, thus causing opportunity loss. The net present value (NPV) method of evaluating the desirability of investments is mathematically represented by the following equation.

(6.3)

$$NPV = \frac{S_1}{(1+i_d)} + \frac{S_2}{(1+i_d)^2} + \frac{S_3}{(1+i_d)^4} + \cdots\cdots + \frac{S_n}{(1+i_d)^n} - I_o$$

OR   **(6.3a)**

$$NPV = \sum_{t=1}^{n} \frac{S_t}{(1+i_d)^t} - I_o$$

where
S_t = the expected net cash flow (gross revenue − LOE − taxes) at the end of year t
I_o = the initial investment outlay at time zero, i.e., 1/1/2002
i_d = the discount rate, i.e., the required minimum annual rate of return on new investment
n = the project's economic life in years

Since the capital outlay may stretch longer than one period, a more general formulation would be to define I_o as the present value of the capital outlays. On the other hand, to further simplify the calculations, a net cash flow (NCF) is calculated as shown in Table 6–1. The NPV of this NCF stream is then calculated. Therefore, Equation (6.3) is modified as:

(6.4)

$$NPV = \sum_{t=1}^{n} \frac{NCF_t}{(1+i_d)^t}$$

The above equations assume cash flows are received or disbursed at the end of the year. In reality this is not a valid assumption because cash flow transactions take place continuously or at the most monthly.

To account for this, it is assumed all cash flow transactions occur in mid-year (average over the year). To do this the t in Equations (6.3) and (6.4) is changed to $(t - 0.5)$.

Example 6–1

Calculate NPV of the NCF stream (Column M) in Table 6–1 using a 10% discount rate and mid-year cash flow assumption.

Solution: The calculations for Example 6–1 are shown in Table 6–2.

Year	NCF M$	t	$\dfrac{1}{(1+0.10)^t}$	NPV M$
2002	(185.00)	0.50	0.9535	(176.39)
2003	155.90	1.50	0.8668	135.13
2004	69.39	2.50	0.7880	54.68
2005	47.55	3.50	0.7164	34.06
2006	26.54	4.50	0.6512	17.28
2007	18.42	5.50	0.5920	10.90
2008	12.99	6.50	0.5382	6.99
2009	9.10	7.50	0.4893	4.45
2010	6.86	8.50	0.4448	3.05
2011	5.92	9.50	0.4044	2.39
2012	4.63	10.50	0.3676	1.70
2013	4.02	11.50	0.3342	1.34
2014	3.92	12.50	0.3038	1.19
2015	3.86	13.50	0.2762	1.07
2016	3.63	14.50	0.2511	0.91
TOTAL	187.72			98.76

Table 6–2 Calculations of NPV for Example 6–1

The NPV of 98.76 M$, at 10% discount rate and mid-year cash flow assumption is calculated in Table 6–2. Combining the analysis with the payback period calculation, the initial capital investment is recovered in 2.75 years and 10% is earned on the declining outstanding NCFs during the investment's economic life. Moreover, a cushion of 98.76 M$ of extra dollars in present value can be counted on if the project lives out its economic life and the cash flow estimates are correct.

Spreadsheets have built-in function for NPV calculation. In MS Excel, the =NPV(rate, NCF_1:NCF_n) function calculates the NPV of an investment by using a discount rate and a series of future net cash flows. The =NPV function assumes year-end cash flows. The NPV calculated by Excel is adjusted to the mid-year cash flow assumption by multiplying it by the factor $(1 + i_d)^{0.5}$. For example, the NPV in Cell L30 of Table 6–1 is calculated by using the function =NPV(0.1,M10:M25)*(1+0.1)^0.5.

Once the NPV of the investment alternative is calculated, the following decision rules apply.

If the NPV is positive, accept the proposal.
If the NPV is negative, reject the proposal.

If the NPV is zero, the analyst will be indifferent because the proposal is generating the same return as the alternative use of funds will generate (assuming both alternatives have the same risk). The NPV decision criterion follows directly from the assumption that the analyst is required to maximize the worth of the firm. This criterion results in *optimal* choice of projects.

The size of a project's NPV depends, among other things, on the discount factor. A plot showing this is called the NPV profile. Figure 6–6 illustrates the *NPV profile* for the NCF generated in Table 6–1. The NPV profile shows the sensitivity of the NCF to the discount rate and gives a range of the discount rates below which the project generates a positive NPV. Therefore, if one is not sure of the firm's cost of capital, this profile gives a useful range. When the discount rate is equal to zero (at the intercept with the vertical axis), the NPV equals the algebraic sum of the periodic *undiscounted* NCFs.

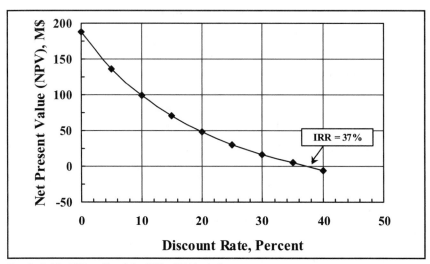

Fig. 6–6 The NPV profile of the NCFs of Table 6–1

Main features of this method are summarized below.

1. The technique accounts for the time value of money.

2. It considers cash flows over the economic life of the investment.

3. It does not give any indication about the size of the initial invest-ment (i.e., the NPV of $100 investment may be $100, and the NPV of $10,000 investment may also be $100).

4. It gives direct indication of the value of the investment (i.e., contributes to the wealth maximization effort—when a firm takes on an investment with a positive NPV, its value increases by the amount of the NPV).

5. The NPVs are additive (i.e., if there are 10 projects each with an NPV of $10, the total NPV will be $100).

6. The NPV method implicitly assumes all cash flows are reinvest-ed at the weighted average or opportunity cost of capital.

7. The same discount rate does not have to be used for the entire period of cash flows.

8. NPV is suitable for use with probabilities, i.e., for calculating the expected monetary value (see Chapter 3 of Volume 2 in this series).

Internal Rate of Return (IRR)

Internal rate of return (IRR) is another important and widely reported measure of profitability. IRR is reported as a percentage rather than a dollar figure such as NPV. The internal rate of return (IRR) is also referred to as the discounted cash flow rate of return (DCFROR), rate of return (ROR), internal yield, marginal efficiency of capital, and the investors method. IRR is the discount rate at which the net present value is exactly equal to zero, or the present value of cash inflows is equal to the present value of cash outflows. Another definition of IRR is the interest rate received for an investment consisting of payments (negative values) and income (positive values) that occur at regular periods. The equation for calculating IRR is

(6.5)

$$\sum_{t=1}^{n} \frac{NCF_t}{(1+IRR)^t} = 0$$

In Equation (6.5) the net cash flows at time t are known, but the IRR (fraction) is unknown. Some value of IRR causes the discounted NCFs of the project to equal zero; this value of IRR is then called the internal rate of return. IRR resembles the interest rate paid on financial investments or debts.

The IRR formula, Equation (6.5), is simply the NPV formula, Equation (6.4), solved for the value of i_d that causes the NPV equal zero. The only difference is that in the NPV method i_d is known and NPV is calculated; in the IRR method NPV is known (equals zero) and the value of IRR that forces the NPV to equal zero is calculated. Therefore, the calculation of IRR requires an iterative solution.

IRR can be calculated manually in one of two ways (a) by trial-and-error and (b) graphically. The IRR calculation by trial-and-error requires at least two interest rates that when substituted for IRR in Equation (6.5) give a positive and a negative NPV. The first step is to make a best guess of the IRR for the investment. If a positive NPV is calculated, the IRR should be increased and NPV calculated again. The trial-and-error is repeated until a negative NPV is calculated. The IRR is then between the two adjacent interest rates that gave positive and negative NPVs, which is determined by linear interpolation using the following equation:

(6.6)

$$IRR = \frac{NPV_A}{NPV_A - NPV_B}\left(IRR_B - IRR_A\right) + IRR_A$$

where
NPV_A = positive net present value
NPV_B = negative net present value
IRR_A = interest rate associated with NPV_A
IRR_B = interest rate associated with NPV_B

As shown in Figure 6–6, the relationship between interest rate and NPV is not linear; therefore, linear interpolation is not recommended over more than 5 or at the most 10 percentage points.

To determine the IRR graphically, three to five NPVs are calculated at different interest rates. These NPVs are then plotted versus their respective interest rates on Cartesian coordinate graph paper. A line is drawn through these points. The intersection of this line at NPV of zero gives the IRR.

Example 6–2

A net present value profile for the NCFs in Table 6–1 follows. Using the methods discussed previously, calculate the internal rate of return for the project. Note that the NPV at $i_d = 0$ is equal to the cumulative undiscounted net cash flow.

NPV Profile									
Percent	0	5	10	15	20	25	30	35	40
NPV, M$	187.72	136.26	98.76	70.37	48.22	30.52	16.10	4.19	(5.77)

Solution: From the NPVs profile above, it is obvious the IRR is between 35% (+ve NPV) and 40% (-ve NPV). Using Equation (6.6), the IRR is calculated as

$$IRR = \frac{4.19}{4.19 - \left(-5.77\right)}\left(40 - 35\right) + 35 \cong 37.10\%$$

The "approximately equal to" (symbol, $\cong$), is used rather than the equality (=) sign because interpolation provides an approximate solution, especially when the relationship is not linear. To determine IRR graphically, the NPV profile is plotted as shown in Figure 6–6 and the IRR read at the point where the NPV profile intersects the NPV at zero.

The spreadsheet programs (Lotus 1-2-3 and Microsoft Excel) have built-in functions for the IRR calculation. In Microsoft Excel the "=IRR(values, guess)" function returns the internal rate of return for a series of cash flows represented by the numbers in values. *Values* are an array or a reference to cells that contain desirable numbers for the internal rate of return. A corresponding function in Lotus 1-2-3 is "@IRR(guess, values)." For example, the IRR in Cell L31 (Table 6–1) is calculated using the NCFs in Column M by entering the formula =IRR(M10:M25). Microsoft Excel uses an iterative technique for calculating IRR. Starting with *guess*, IRR cycles through the calculation until the result is accurate within 0.00001 percent. If guess is omitted, it is assumed to be 0.1 (10 percent).

The rule for making the investment decision when using IRR is:

- *Accept* the investment if its calculated IRR is greater than the return on the alternative use of funds or cost of capital.
- *Reject* the investment if its calculated IRR is less than the return on the alternative use of funds or cost of capital. If the investment is financed 100% by borrowed capital, then the rate of return should at least exceed the interest rate being paid on the loan. A company could also set a minimum required rate of return or hurdle rate.

If the calculated IRR is (1) greater than the required rate of return, the NPV is positive; (2) less than the required rate of return, the NPV is negative; and (3) equal to the required rate of return, the NPV is zero.

Dual Rate of Return

It is mathematically possible to have multiple rates of return in a complex project, which adds to the problem of interpreting IRR. Multiple rates of returns occur when there are multiple sign changes (i.e., multiple payback periods or negative, positive, negative and positive cash flows) in the net cash flow. The second or third sign reversal, however, is not sufficient to result in multiple rate sof return. It also depends on when the second or third reversals take place and the magnitude of the negative cash flow causing the reversal.[10]

Such situations may occur whenever a proposal calls for advanced payment or high terminal costs. Also, rate acceleration projects (which attempt to increase production in early years at the cost of decreased production in the later years) and projects requiring a large expenditure at a later point in the project life (such as abandonment costs related to the removal of production facilities) generate multiple rates of return.

When analyzing alternative measures of profitability, it is important to keep in mind the type of cash flow. The forecasted cash flows of a project are classified as either *conventional* or *nonconventional*. A conventional cash flow is the one where the initial capital investment outlay is followed by a stream of positive net revenues of the form: $- + + + +$ .....; or if the initial outlay takes place over a number of years, the cash flow has the form: $- - - + + + +$. The cumulative net cash flow of such conventional cash flows shows only one sign change from negative to positive. The nonconventional cash flows are the ones in where more than one sign change as $+ - - + + +$ or $- + + + -$. Many oil field investments may follow nonconventional cash flows. They have initial negative capital outlays, followed by positive cash flows, and finally negative cash flow for the abandonment of the facilities preceding the terminal year.

Stermole has presented some useful observations regarding the interpretation of IRR resulting from nonconventional cash flows, such as:[10]

- income or savings precedes costs
- investment—income—investment situation, and
- income—investment—income situation

In the dual IRR situation, the calculated IRR has a combination rate of return and rate of reinvestment meaning. In such situations, other profitability yardsticks should be used. The following rules of thumb can be used to determine if dual rates of return exist.

Capital Budgeting Techniques

When the undiscounted net cash flow (i.e., NPV at i_d=0%) is negative for an investment followed by income followed by an investment situation, dual positive IRRs exist if any real interest rate solutions exist for the NPV equation. On the other hand, if the undiscounted net cash flow (i.e., NPV at i_d=0%) is positive, the dual IRR values exist with one being negative and the other positive. Further, if significant income follows the second investment such as investment—income—investment—income, a dual rate of return situation may not exist depending on the magnitude and timing of the income following the second investment.

In an income—investment—income situation, dual rates of return occur for the conditions opposite to the investment—income—investment situation. In this situation, dual IRRs exist if the undiscounted net cash flow is positive, and positive dual IRRs do not exist if it is negative. When the dual IRR does not exist, an investment is acceptable for i_d greater than the investment's IRR because in this region the NPV is positive. When the dual IRRs exist, an investment is acceptable only for i_d values outside the region between the dual rates because in this region the NPV is positive.

Example 6-3

A strip mining company invests $70,000 at time zero to generate net revenue of $40,000 per year for the following five years. During the sixth year, the company has to spend $140,000 in order to restore the land to its original condition. Calculate the IRR of this investment. Assume year-end discounting assumption.

Solution: The total undiscounted net cash flow (i.e., NPV at 0%) is −$10,000. The NPV at 5% discount factor is calculated as follows. Since the net revenue of $40,000 is an annuity, Equation (2.14) is used

273

to calculate its present value. The present value of $140,000 is calculated using Equation (2.10).

$$NPV \ @5\% = -\$70,000 + \$40,000\frac{\left(1+i_e\right)^t - 1}{i_e\left(1+i_e\right)^t} - \$140,000\left(\frac{1}{\left(1+i_e\right)^t}\right)$$

$$= -\$70,000 + \$40,000\frac{\left(1+0.05\right)^5 - 1}{0.05\left(1+0.05\right)^5} - \$140,000\left(1+0.05\right)^{-6}$$

$$= -\$70,000 + \$40,000\left(4.3295\right) - \$140,000\left(0.7462\right)$$

$$= -\$1,288$$

Similarly, the NPV at other discount rates is calculated as shown below and in Figure 6–7.

Rate, %	NPV	Rate, %	NPV
5	–$1,288	25	$871
10	$2,605	30	–$1,582
15	$3,560	35	–$4,329
20	$2,739	40	–$7,187

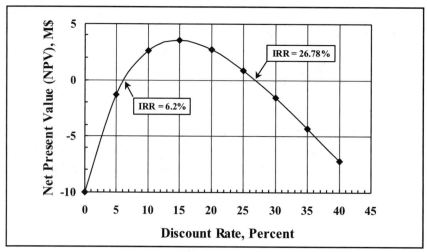

Fig. 6–7 NPV Profile for the data of Example 6–3

Figure 6–7 shows the NPV profile crosses the NPV=0 line at approximately 6.2% and 26.78%, or dual rate of returns of 6.2% and 26.78%. These rates cannot be used directly for decision-making purposes. However, they do provide useful information by providing a range of i_e when the investment's NPV is positive. Thus the investment is accepted if i_e is between 6.2% and 26.78%. Whenever a dual IRR situation exists, it is recommended to use NPV for decision-making. If the "=IRR(values, guess)" function of MS Excel is used to calculate IRR of the cash flows, it calculates an IRR of only 6.2%. It does not show if a dual rate of return has occurred unless the NPV profile of the cash flow is looked at.

Reinvestment in the IRR Calculation

To achieve the calculated IRR, the IRR method implicitly assumes the generated cash flows are *reinvested* at the calculated IRR. However, in the views of most authors and evaluators, a question whether the IRR calculation involves the reinvestment of income still remains.[13–20]

Some feel that inherent in the calculation procedure is a reinvestment of income at the computed IRR. Others argue there is no reinvestment implied and it does not matter what is done with the interim revenue generated by the investment. Many authors state categorically that reinvestment at the IRR is implied in the calculation procedure. Others state just as emphatically that no reinvestment is implied. Collarini states "the discounted cash flow (or internal) ROR is simply a measure of project efficiency that is more useful in the banking industry than in the petroleum business."[16]

Stermole[10] states *reinvestment is not implied or required to achieve the calculated project rate of return when investment precedes income or savings*. The statement is further mathematically proven by Dougherty[13,15] and Aguilera[18].

The authors arguing against the reinvestment assumption requirement state the calculated IRR gives the rate of return on the unamortized investment (unpaid principal) at the end of each year and is not the rate of return on the initial investment for the life of the project. The confusion is caused due to the lack of understanding of the difference between *project rate of return* and *overall growth rate*.

Weston and Brigham state the reinvestment requirement in the following way, which does not explicitly say that without the reinvestment the calculated IRR or NPV values are not valid.

> *Suppose the cash flows from a project are not reinvested but are used for current consumption. No reinvestment is involved; yet an IRR for the project could still be calculated. Does this show that the reinvestment assumption is not always implied in the IRR calculation? The answer is no; reinvestment itself is not necessarily assumed, but the opportunity of reinvestment is assumed. Because that assumption is made in the very construction of the NPV equations and because calculation of both NPV and IRR is based on those equations, we simply could not define or interpret the concepts of NPV and IRR without assuming reinvestment.*[5]

To show how the internal rate of return is unrelated to reinvestment of incomes derived from the particular investment, consider a person deposits $100,000 in a bank saving account at an annual interest of 8%. At the end of each year, he withdraws the earned interest of $8000 to meet his expenses, i.e., the money is not reinvested. At the end of year 5 he withdraws all his money (the $8000 for the 5th year and his initial deposit of $100,000). This generates an IRR of 8% over the 5-year period while the interim cash flows are not reinvested at all (Option A in the following table).

From the above example it is evident the 8% return received on this investment (bank account) is not related to reinvestment of the $8000 annual interest dividends or the $100,000 principal received at the end of year 5. Whether the earned interest is spent or reinvested at the same or larger rate of return does not change the fact that this is an 8% IRR investment. However, what is done with the earned interest does affect the overall individual or corporate *growth rate*. For example, assume the $8000 interest earned each year is left in the account. Its accrued interest would give $146,933 at the end of 5 years, which also results in an IRR of 8% as shown below (Option B in the following table).

Year	Option A	Option B
0	−$100,000	−$100,000
1	$8,000	0
2	$8,000	0
3	$8,000	0
4	$8,000	0
5	$108,000	$146,933
IRR	8.00%	8.00%

The above example is valid for bank accounts. Is it really applicable to other capital investments where the initial investment is not recovered at the end of the project rather, it is recovered from the revenues generated by the project every year? Assume $100,000 is invested in a capital project that will generate a net yearly cash flow of $33,400 for the next 5 years. The IRR for this will be about 20%. On the other hand, instead of receiving $33,400 per year for 5 years, $167,000 ($33,400 x 5 = $167,000) is received at the end of year 5. The IRR for this option is 10.8%. The difference is obviously due to the time value of money, hence the reinvestment. If the $33,400 is received each year and reinvested at 20%, it accumulates to $248,549 in 5 years to yield a rate of return of 20% as shown below.

Year	OPTION A	OPTION B	OPTION C
0	−$100,000	−$100,000	−$100,000
1	$33,400	0	0
2	$33,400	0	0
3	$33,400	0	0
4	$33,400	0	0
5	$33,400	$167,000	$248,549
IRR	20.0%	10.8%	20.0%

Terry states:

> *Those that argue that the rate of return calculation does not imply reinvestment say that the incomes can be removed without affecting the calculation. While this may appear to be true on the surface, the IRR calculation does not allow the removal of incomes without assigning a value to them. Since all incomes in the IRR calculation are brought back to the present at the IRR, the calculation is placing a worth on them. By removing the incomes without stating that they are worth the IRR, then the problem has been changed.*[12]

The above discussion is provided for academic interest. For the purpose of economic evaluation, due to the unresolved controversy of reinvestment assumption, IRR is losing its credibility as a decision yardstick. However, it is suggested not to worry too much about the issue of reinvestment. If properly used, IRR can still provide meaningful results. The investment situations where IRR can be successfully used are discussed in Chapter 7.

Specific Characteristics of IRR

Following are the salient features of the internal rate of return (IRR).

1. It accounts for the time value of money.

2. It considers cash flows over the economic life of the investment (i.e., it has a built-in economic earnings requirement beyond the recovery of the original investment). Thus an IRR higher than the minimum desired rate of return provides an incremental economic gain beyond satisfying a normal earnings standard.

3. Since it is a percentage measure, it does not give any indication about the size of the initial investment. Under a constrained budget situation, it is desirable to invest in a lower-yielding larger-size project rather than a higher-yielding, smaller-size project. Generation of the largest addition to total portfolio remains the ultimate objective.

4. It does not give direct indication of the value of the investment.

5. The IRRs are not additive (i.e., if there are three projects with an IRR of 10%, 12%, and 18%, the total IRR will not be 40%). The only valid procedure is to combine the cash flows of the projects under consideration and then determine the IRR for the combined cash flow. In joint venture partnerships, the IRR for each partner is the same as the IRR of the total investment. On the other hand, the NPV is proportional to the share of the individual partners.

6. IRR cannot be calculated for the following situations:
   a. When cash flows are all negative.
   b. When cash flows are all positive, i.e., investment is paid out of the future revenues.
   c. Total undiscounted revenues are less than the investment (i.e., a marginal producing well or field depleted before reaching payback).
   d. When cumulative cash flow stream goes negative more than once.

7. To achieve the calculated IRR, the IRR method implicitly assumes the generated cash flows are *reinvested* at the calculated IRR, which may not be possible for the higher IRR investments. For example, if a project's IRR is calculated at 35%, it achieves this rate of return only if all monies received from this project are reinvested at 35%. If at the time, a reinvestment opportunity at a lower than 35% rate is available, then the project IRR is between this lower rate and the 35%. This argument is frequently used against the use of this concept.

8. The timing of cash flows is especially significant to accuracy of the IRR, as IRR is usually more sensitive to the assumptions of timing than other profitability measures.

9. IRR is not affected by delay in project start dates. If a project starts several years in the future, then the net present value of the project is reduced because its annual net cash flows must be discounted more. For example, if NPV of a project is $100 million, a 2-year delay in the project start date would mean a reduction in the NPV to $100(1 + IRR)^{-2}$. However, the IRR does not change because of the delay. This is then a disadvantage of the IRR, as it cannot dis-

tinguish between projects that start late as compared to the ones that start early. This limitation of IRR is applicable only when the cash flows of the delayed project are identical to the cash flows of the original project. If the cash flows change due to inflation or price escalation, then the IRR also changes.

10. The method gives conflicting ranking when used for ranking mutually exclusive investments or selecting non-mutually exclusive investments. This problem is generally attributed to the reinvestment assumption. This author feels it is due to the pattern of particular cash flows and that discounting favors the early cash flows over the cash flows received later in the economic life of the investment.

11. Risk (probability) cannot be mathematically incorporated in the IRR equation.

12. IRR can be computed for after-tax and before-tax cash flows.

Profitability Index (PI)

The discussion of NPV and IRR shows how these two methods fail to reflect the size of the initial investment. These yardsticks pose problems when an analyst has to make a choice among several alternative investments of different sizes. For example, the NPV and IRR for two investments may be equal or close; but the amount of investment required by the two alternatives may vary widely. Measures like the NPV tend to emphasize the adoption of larger capital investments since such investments tend to have higher NPVs. Therefore, NPV as an investment criterion frequently comes under attack because it does not measure the efficiency of an investment.

To overcome this efficiency problem, *profitability index* (PI) is introduced as a profitability criterion. PI is a dimensionless ratio obtained by dividing the present value of future operating cash flows by the present value of the investment. Mathematically, the PI is given by the following equation. [21,22]

(6.7)

$$PI = \frac{Present \ Value \ of \ Future \ Operating \ Cash \ Flow}{Present \ Value \ of \ Capital \ Investment}$$

The PI simply answers the question: How much in present value benefits is created per dollar of investment? The PI shows the relative profitability of an investment, or the present value of benefits per the present worth of every dollar invested (i.e., higher net return for each dollar invested). Consider the following two investments being mutually exclusive (i.e., only one of the investments can be selected).

	Option A	Option B
PV of Investment, M$	$100	$1,000
Net Present Value, M$	$100	$100

The two options cited above, therefore, give PIs as follows.

$$PI_A = \frac{\$100 + \$100}{\$100} = 2.00$$

$$PI_B = \frac{\$100 + \$1,000}{\$1,000} = 1.10$$

Note both the numerator and denominator are discounted by using the same discount rate. Investment A is generating more PV dollars for every dollar invested as compared to Investment B. The PI = 2.00 means total return on the investment dollars is $2 per dollar, where $1 is the cost and $1 per every dollar invested is the net gain in PV terms. The definition of PI implies that projects with the largest PI values generate the largest cumulative NPV that can be accumulated from the available present worth investment dollars (i.e., the higher the PI, the better the investment).

A variation to the definition of the profitability index is the *Present Value Ratio (PVR), Present Value Index (PVI), Discounted Profit-to-Investment Ratio (DPIR),* or *Investment Efficiency.* The PVR is the ratio of the NPV to the present value of capital investment rather than the ratio of the PV of future operating cash flows to the PV of capital investment. Mathematically, this relationship is represented by the following equation.

(6.8)

$$PVR = \frac{NPV}{PV \ of \ Capital \ Investment}$$

According to Equation (6.8), the above calculations become

$$PVR_A = \frac{\$100}{\$100} = 1.00$$

$$PVR_B = \frac{\$100}{\$1,000} = 0.10$$

As shown in the above calculations, the PI is equal to PVR+1. The PVR shows net PV dollars generated per the PV of every capital investment dollar (i.e., the capital investment is already recovered and the value of the PVR is the net gain over every dollar invested). *Sometimes the two definitions are reversed. Therefore, the analyst needs to be careful when interpreting these values.* The PI for the data in Table 6–1 is calculated as follows

$$PI = 1 + \frac{98.76}{176.39} = 1.56$$

The PI generates a number greater than one for investments with a positive NPV and a number less than one for investments with a negative NPV. The decision rules for use of the PI are:

- *Accept* all independent investment proposals with PI greater than 1.
- *Reject* all independent investment proposals with PI less than 1.

A PI = 1.0 means the project breaks even (i.e., it neither makes money nor losses money). Similarly, accept all investments with PVR greater than zero and reject those with PVR less than zero. Following are properties of the profitability index.

1. It shares all the advantages of NPV (such as realistic reinvestment rate, no multiple rates, not a trial-and-error solution, etc.).

2. It provides a measure of profitability per dollar invested. This is a particularly important consideration when faced with the selection of investments from a list containing more opportunities than the available funds can cover.[10]

3. It is the most representative measure of true earning potential of an investment, thus contributing to the portfolio maximization effort.

4. As a ranking criterion, it can be used in capital allocation.

Unit Technical Cost (TC)

The Unit Technical Cost (TC), also referred to as the finding cost, is another useful indicator for screening capital investment projects. The unit technical cost is defined as the ratio of the total cost (CAPEX and OPEX) over the economic life of a project to the total expected reserves from the project. The indicator is thus reported in $/barrel. If other products such as gas, NGLs or condensate are also recovered along with oil, then the indicator is reported in dollar per barrel of oil equivalent ($/BOE).

The conversion from any other units to BOE can be either done through BTU content, physical constants, or revenue basis. For example, when using physical constants, 5.615 cubic feet of gas is equivalent to one barrel of oil equivalent or one metric ton of NGLs is equivalent to 0.1342 barrels of oil equivalent. The revenue conversion involves product prices. For example, if the oil price is $14/Stb and the gas price is $2.25/Mscf then 6.222 Mscf are equal to one barrel of oil equivalent. Similarly, if the price of a ton of NGL is $139/ton then one ton of NGL is 9.929 barrels of oil equivalent. The revenue conversion gives a more realistic and meaningful cash flow evaluation as compared to the other conversions.

The Technical Cost (TC) may be undiscounted and/or discounted. The calculation of discounted TC requires both yearly costs and production be discounted to the present value by using the same discount rate used for the calculation of NPV.

The positive point about TC is that it is independent of the prices of the products involved. It gives an indication of what the product is costing to develop and produce. It provides a measure of the cushion available when compared to the actual estimated product prices. For example, the profit margin is $7/Stb if the discounted (at 10%) TC for an oil project is $5/Stb and the anticipated oil price over the life of the project is $12/Stb. The project breaks even if the price of oil, over the life of the project, remains at $5/Stb.

Technical Costs for the data in Table 3–18 and Table 6–1 are calculated as shown below. The total cost (CAPEX and LOE) over the productive life of the lease (Table 3–18) is $386.60 M. The net oil and gas reserves (net of Severance tax) are 13.858 MStb and 119.751 MMScf, respectively. The product prices are $22/Stb and $2.25/Mscf. The gas production is converted to its barrel of oil equivalent by revenue basis, i.e., 9.778 MScf ($22/$2.25=9.778) is equivalent to one barrel of oil equivalent. The following steps are followed to calculate the TCs.

1. Convert the 119.751 MMScf to its BOE as:

$$\text{Total Reserves} = 13,858 + \frac{119,751}{9.778} = 26,104.983 \text{ BOE}$$

2. Calculate the undiscounted Technical Cost as:

$$\text{Technical Cost in BOE} = \frac{\$185,000 + \$201,600}{26,104.983} = \$14.81 \text{ per BOE}$$

3. If it was only an oil producing well, then the $/Stb and $/BOE are equal. If it is predominantly a gas well, then the technical cost should be calculated in $/MScf. The technical cost in $/Stb for the same cash flow is:

$$\text{Technical Cost in Stb} = \frac{\$185,000 + \$201,600}{13,858} = \$27.90 \text{ per Stb}$$

4. To calculate *discounted* Unit Technical Cost, the product stream and the total cost are discounted using the 10% discount factor (the same discount factor used for discounting cash flow is used for technical cost calculation). The rest of the calculations are the same as shown above.

5. Discounted oil production (net of severance tax) = 8,624.29 Stb
    Discounted gas production (net of severance tax)= 75,134.316 MScf
    Discounted cost (LOE + CAPEX) = $264,618.45

$$\text{Discounted TC in BOE} = \frac{\$264{,}618.45}{8{,}624.29 + \dfrac{75{,}134.316}{9.778}} = \frac{\$264{,}618.45}{16{,}308.307} = \$14.81 \text{ per BOE}$$

$$\text{Discounted TC in Stb} = \frac{\$264{,}618.45}{8{,}624.29} = \$30.68 \text{ per Stb}$$

The technical cost in Stb, in this particular cash flow, is high (higher than the oil price of $22/Stb) because it is predominantly a gas well with high oil yield. The decision rule for the use of technical cost is:

- *Accept* the project if its discounted technical cost in $/BOE (or $/MScf for gas lease) is less than the expected oil price (or gas price for gas lease) over the economic life of the project.
- *Reject* the project if its discounted technical cost in $/BOE (or $/MScf for gas lease) is higher than the expected oil price (or gas price for gas lease) over the economic life of the project.

If the barrel of oil equivalent replaces the oil production in Table 3–18 and the oil price is replaced by the discounted technical cost of $16.23/BOE, the measures of profitability are (a) NPV = 0, (b) PI = 1.0, (c) IRR = 10%, and (d) TC = $16.23/BOE. Remember this is the breakeven case. The NPV = 0 means the present value of net revenues equals the present value of CAPEX. The PI = 1.0 means all the costs are recovered, and the IRR = 10% means the project's rate of return offsets the cost of capital.

If the *undiscounted* TC ($14.81/BOE) replaces oil price, the cash flow results in negative NPV and the IRR less than the discount rate. This means the project is loosing in PV terms. The TC can be obtained graphically from a graph of NPV (calculated at various prices) versus the respective prices. The product price at the intersection of NPV=0 is the desired technical cost.

Some analysts have problem reconciling the idea of discounting production when calculating the discounted TC. An engineer once said, "I don't believe in discounting production." Therefore, the mathematical derivation of the TC is given here. As per our definition, TC is the product price (oil, gas, or BOE) at which the present value of costs equals the present value of gross revenues. Therefore

$$PV\ of\ Costs = PV\ of\ Gross\ Revenue$$

OR
$$\sum_{t=1}^{n}\frac{(Costs)_t}{(1+i_d)^t} = \sum_{t=1}^{n}\frac{(Gross\ Revenue)_t}{(1+i_d)^t}$$

$$= \sum_{t=1}^{n}\frac{(Production\cdot Price)_t}{(1+i_d)^t}$$

By assuming constant price over the economic life of the project

(6.9)

$$= Price\sum_{t=1}^{n}\frac{(Production)_t}{(1+i_d)^t}$$

Therefore,
$$Price(TC) = \frac{\sum_{t=1}^{n}\frac{(Costs)_t}{(1+i_d)^t}}{\sum_{t=1}^{n}\frac{(Production)_t}{(1+i_d)^t}}$$

Growth Rate of Return (GRR)

The PI does not have much meaning to most managers who are accustomed to using IRR or some other rate-of-return measure. On the other hand, the IRR is not a reliable profitability indicator in all cases. This leads to introducing a new term called *growth rate of return (GRR)*, also referred to as the *Equity Rate of Return* or *Modified Internal Rate of Return (MIRR)*. The GRR resolves the shortcomings of the IRR (i.e., multiple rates of return, reinvestment rate assumption, and trial-and-error calculation).

The GRR is calculated by first compounding all the positive net cash flows forward to some time horizon, t years in the future. For the GRR comparison, it is recommended that the same time horizon be used for all projects under consideration. Any cash flow beyond that time is discounted back to this point. Secondly, all the negative cash flows (capital investments) are discounted to time zero to get the present value of investment, I. The rate at which the positive cash flows are compounded and the negative investments are discounted is the reinvestment rate or opportunity rate of the organization. The GRR implies total growth from the investment at time t, counting the revenue from the investment plus the interest earned by reinvesting in future projects. Let us call the total growth as B (FV of positive net cash flows).

The investment promises a return of B dollars at time t if the equivalent of one dollar is invested now. If these investment dollars were put in a bank instead, what interest rate would they have to earn to do as well? That interest rate is the project's GRR. It shows the investor is just as well off investing in this project and reinvesting the proceeds at his/her opportunity rate as he/she would if the money was put in a bank and earned the GRR.[4]

If the available reinvestment rate is the same as the project's IRR, then the GRR is equal to IRR. If the available reinvestment rate is less than the project's IRR, then the GRR is somewhere between the project's IRR and the reinvestment rate. In this case, the GRR is a weighted average of a project's IRR and the reinvestment rate. Thus in GRR, the worth of a project plus the reinvestment opportunities are calculated (i.e., total growth) rather than the worth of a project alone. Mathematically the GRR is represented by the following equations.

For Annual Compounding:

(6.10)

$$GRR = \left(\frac{B = FV \ of \ Positive \ Cash \ Flow}{I = PV \ of \ CAPEX} \right)^{1/t} - 1$$

For Continuous Compounding:

(6.11)

$$GRR = \frac{1}{t} \ln \left(\frac{B = FV \ of \ Positive \ Cash \ Flow}{I = PV \ of \ CAPEX} \right)$$

In terms of the PVR and PI, for annual compounding:

(6.12)

$$GRR = (PVR + 1)^{1/t}(1 + i_d) - 1$$

(6.13)

$$GRR = (PI)^{1/t}(1 + i_d) - 1$$

For Continuous Compounding:

(6.14)

$$GRR = \frac{1}{t}\ln(PVR + 1) + i_d$$

(6.15)

$$GRR = \frac{1}{t}\ln(PI) + i_d$$

where
$\quad i_d$ = the reinvestment rate, fraction

The GRR yields the same accept/reject decisions as the net present value (NPV), it yields the same ranking of projects as the profitability index (PI) or present value ratio (PVR), and it is expressed as a rate of return. In addition, as previously mentioned, the calculation of GRR is straightforward (i.e., it does not require trial-and-error calculations as the IRR), and it does not result in multiple solutions. Accept the project if its GRR is greater than the minimum acceptable rate of return and reject the project if its GRR is less than the minimum acceptable rate of return.

If NPV is negative, the GRR $< i_d$. If NPV is positive, the GRR $> i_d$. Thus, GRR is equivalent to NPV as an accept/reject criterion. If one project has a higher PI or NPV than another, it also has a higher GRR provided i_d and t are the same for both projects.

Example 6–4

The cash flows for two projects are given in Table 6–3. Calculate the IRR and GRR for each project assuming the reinvestment rate is 10%. Comment on the difference between the IRR and GRR of the two projects.

Solution: The calculations in Table 6–3 were performed using Excel, the detailed calculations are shown below.

The future value of positive net cash flow, each year, is calculated as

$$FV_A \text{ in Year } 1 = \$210(1+0.10)^9 = \$495.17$$
$$FV_A \text{ in Year } 2 = \$210(1+0.10)^8 = \$450.15 \text{ and so on}$$

Similarly, for Option B the future value of positive net cash flow, each year, is

$$FV_B \text{ in Year } 1 = \$750(1+0.10)^9 = \$1,768.46$$
$$FV_B \text{ in Year } 2 = \$750(1+0.10)^8 = \$1,607.69$$

	A	B	C	D	E	F
3		**Reinvestment**	**PROJECT A**		**PROJECT B**	
4	**Year**	**Years**	**NCF, $**	**FV @10%**	**NCF, $**	**FV @10%**
5	0		−1,000		−1,000	
6	1	9	210	495.17	750	1,768.46
7	2	8	210	450.15	750	1,607.69
8	3	7	210	409.23		0
9	4	6	210	372.03		0
10	5	5	210	338.21		0
11	6	4	210	307.46		0
12	7	3	210	279.51		0
13	8	2	210	254.10		0
14	9	1	210	231.00		0
15	10	0	210	210.00		0
16				3,346.86		3,376.15
17	**IRR**		**16.4%**		**31.9%**	
18	**GRR @ 10%**		**12.8%**		**12.9%**	
19	**PVR = NPV/PV of I**		**0.29**		**0.30**	

Table 6–3 Project cash flows for example 6–4

Using Equation (6.10), the GRR is

$$GRR_A = \left[\left(\frac{3{,}346.86}{1{,}000}\right)^{1/10} - 1\right] \times 100 = 12.84\%$$

$$GRR_B = \left[\left(\frac{3{,}376.15}{1{,}000}\right)^{1/10} - 1\right] \times 100 = 12.94\%$$

Using Equation (6.13) and the PVR in Table 6–3, the GRR is

$$GRR_A = \left[(1 + 0.29)^{1/10}(1 + 0.29) - 1\right] \times 100 = 12.84\%$$

$$GRR_B = \left[(1 + 0.30)^{1/10}(1 + 0.10) - 1\right] \times 100 = 12.92\%$$

From the above, both projects have GRR greater than 10%. There-fore, both are accepted. If a choice has to be made between the two proj-ects, Project B will be selected over Project A since $GRR_B > GRR_A$. According to IRR, Project B seems to be much better than Project A. On the other hand, GRR ranks Project B only slightly higher than Project A. To judge which criterion gives a more realistic comparison between the two projects, compare the total worth (assuming reinvestment opportu-nity of 10% per year) of each project at the end of 10 years. The posi-tive cash flows reinvested from Project A gives the future worth of $3,346.86 as compared to the $3,376.15 of Project A. These values sug-gest there is hardly any difference (less than 1%) between the two. Yet, IRR suggests Project B is almost "twice as good" as Project A. Note a project that looks far superior to another in terms of IRR may have only a slightly higher GRR as shown in Table 6–3. In such cases, as shown above, the IRR can be misleading.

The GRR calculated for a project depends on the time horizon cho-sen. As the time horizon is moved further beyond the end of the project, the reinvestment rate becomes more heavily weighted in calculating GRR. However, the relative ranking of the projects do not change as the time horizon changes.

Adjusted Net Present Value (ANPV)

This method can be used to evaluate capital investment projects when the investment and financing decisions cannot be separated. The method is particularly suitable for evaluating projects in a multinational setting. The traditional NPV, which is calculated by using the weighted average cost of capital of the corporation, may be inadequate in a multinational setting in view of the following.[23]

1. International variations exist in capital structure type and the widespread use of subsidized project-specific financing, loan guarantees, and insurance against political risks.

2. Political and currency risks may be unsystematic in nature for a capital budgeting proposal in a multinational firm.

3. Project systematic risk may not reflect the systematic risk of the parent company.

Thus the adjusted net present value approach has been widely suggested as being more appropriate for the capital budgeting process in a multinational corporation. In this method, each element of the investment is explicitly accounted for. It uses an all-equity discount rate that reflects local inflation and interest rates and a systematic part of the business risk of a particular project. In addition, (1) it uses the value-additivity approach and (2) adds to the present value of the operating cash flows the present value of after-tax amounts of any subsidies inherent in project-specific financing, as well as the present value of debt-related tax shields reflecting the capital structure appropriate for the particular project being evaluated.

As an example, consider the following for the adjusted net present value of a project being considered by a foreign affiliate of a multinational company.[24]

(6.16)

$$ANPV = -I_o + \sum_{t=1}^{n} \frac{CF_t}{(1+k_e)^t} + \sum_{t=1}^{n} \frac{T_t}{(1+k_d)^t} + \sum_{t=1}^{n} \frac{S_t}{(1+k_d)^t} + \sum_{t=1}^{n} \frac{O_t}{(1+k_e)^t} + \sum_{t=1}^{n} \frac{TV_t}{(1+k_e)^t}$$

where

I_0 = Initial investment

k_e = all-equity cost or discount rate reflecting the riskiness and diversification benefits of the project

k_d = cost of debt

n = number of periods in the investment horizon

CF_t = after-tax net cash inflows for period t

T_t = ax shield on debt service payments for period t reflecting the capital structure of the affiliate undertaking the project

S_t = after-tax value of special financial or other subsidies associated with the project for the period t

O_t = estimated value in period t of any options, such as the ability to enter a new business created by the project

TV_t = estimated terminal value in period n at the end of the investment horizon, which also can be the estimated present value of compensation received for an expected government takeover.

In Equation (6.16), the first term covers the initial investment at time zero. The second term reflects the present value of the net after-tax cash inflows the project is expected to generate, which are discounted at the all-equity cost of capital. The third term reflects the present value of the tax savings with the use of debt in the capital structure. By explicitly accounting for the tax shields, it is possible to account for the unique capital structure being used by the affiliate undertaking the project. The fourth term reflects the present value of any financial or other subsidies often received by international projects from home, host, or other governments. The fifth term reflects the value of any options, such as the ability to enter a new business, whether exercised or not, generated by the project. These values may be zero or very small, at least for the first few years, and may often be difficult to estimate. The last term reflects the estimated terminal value at the end of the investment horizon. Although there are many ways to estimate the terminal value, one approach commonly used is to set it equal to the present value of all future cash flows, that is, equal to CF/(k – g), where CF is the annual cash flow after the investment horizon, k is the discount rate, and g is the expected growth rate for these cash flows.[23]

Effect of Discounting Frequency

The objective of this section is to show how the discounting frequency and the funds flow assumption, as presented in Chapter 2, affect the profitability indicators discussed in the preceding sections and how to account for these differences. In Chapter 2, various assumptions were presented that can be used for discounting future cash flows.

As discussed in the preceding sections, various profitability indicators (such as NPV, IRR, PI, TC, GRR, etc.) are often calculated to evaluate most investment opportunities. The magnitude of the profitability indicators is highly dependent on the assumptions used to calculate them. Blindly dealing with the profitability indicators without knowing the assumptions used to calculate them leads to costly and hazardous decisions. For an investor, it is essential to not only use an appropriate discount rate but also to make sure consistent funds flow and discounting frequency assumptions are used for the alternative investments under consideration.

Table 6–4 provides five cash flow and discounting methods assumptions and their corresponding formulas used to calculate present value factors. These five cases (Cases A and B being the most common) are frequently encountered in the oil industry. Any one of these assumptions, if consistently used, yield consistent investments choices. However, if at any time, different investment opportunities are evaluated using different assumptions, the decisions will be hazardous. The differences also result in considerable confusion when two negotiating companies use different methods and assumptions.

Case	Funds Flow Assumptions	Discounting Frequency	Present Value Factor
A	Year-End	Periodic	$(1 + i_d)^{-t}$
B	Mid-Year	Periodic	$(1 + i_d)^{-(t-()}$
C	Continuously	Periodic	$[i/\ln(1+i)](1+i)^{-t}$
D	Year-End	Continuous	e^{-rt}
E	Continuously	Continuous	$(e^r - 1)/(re^{rt})$

Table 6–4 Funds flow and discounting frequency assumptions[25]

Note the @NPV and @IRR functions of Lotus1-2-3 and the corresponding =NPV and =IRR functions of Microsoft Excel use the Case A assumptions. Two hypothetical investment profiles as shown in Table 6–5 are used to
highlight the significance of the various assumptions used. All cash flows are
assumed to be lump sum payments/receipts at the end of each year.

Table 6–5 shows the three profitability indicators calculated for the two
investments using the five cash flow assumptions and discounting methods.
Note the NPV of Investment A varies from a low of $112,378 to a high of
$123,075 and Investment B varies from a low of $117,445 to a high of
$131,212. Similar differences exist between other two profitability indica-
tors. The differences in NPV are even higher at higher discount rates.

Year		Investment A	Investment B
1		−$268,600	−$345,000
2		132,900	132,900
3		132,900	112,965
4		97,600	96,020
5		69,200	81,617
6		23,500	69,375
7		28,600	58,968
8		15,900	50,123
9		9,400	40,098
10		5,600	30,073
11		1,900	18,044
CASE A	NPV @ 10%	$117,303	$125,059
	IRR	29.46%	22.15%
	PVR=NPV/PV of I	0.480	0.399
CASE B	NPV @ 10%	$123,028	$131,163
	IRR	29.47%	22.15
	PVR=NPV/PV of I	0.480	0.399
CASE C	NPV @ 10%	$123,075	$131,212
	IRR	29.47%	22.15%
	PVR=NPV/PV of I	0.480	0.399
CASE D	NPV @ 10%	$112,378	$117,445
	IRR	25.82%	20.01%
	PVR=NPV/PV of I	0.462	0.376
CASE E	NPV @ 10%	$118,189	$123,518
	IRR	25.82%	20.01%
	PVR=NPV/PV of I	0.462	0.376

Table 6–5 Hypothetical investment profiles and their profitability indicators

If 10% is the minimum acceptable rate of return, both investments are acceptable yielding higher IRR regardless of the assumptions used. However, if the investments are mutually exclusive, the selection will be different. For example, if Investment A has used Case C assumptions and Investment B has used Case D assumptions, Investment A will be selected since NPV of Case C for Investment A is higher than NPV of Case D for investment B. However, under most assumptions, Investment B is the preferred investment out of the two alternatives.

To avoid such misleading decisions, the profitability indicators (if not calculated using consistent assumptions) need to be adjusted to a common cash flow assumption and discounting method for each investment and then compared. This can be achieved using the following relationships.

The adjustment of IRR is based on Equation (2.5) because Case A through C give *effective* IRR and Cases D through E give *nominal* IRR. The IRRs of Case D and E can be converted to effective IRR by using Equation (2.5). For example

$$i_e = e^r - 1 \tag{2.5}$$

$$IRR_A = IRR_B = IRR_C = i_e$$

$$IRR_A = e^{IRR_D} - 1 = e^{0.2582} - 1$$

$$= 0.2946 \ or \ 29.46\%$$

The net present values are adjusted using the following relationships.

$$NPV_A = \frac{NPV_B}{(1+i_d)^{0.50}} \tag{6.17}$$

$$NPV_A = NPV_C \left[\frac{\ln(1+i_d)}{i_d} \right] \tag{6.18}$$

$$NPV_E = NPV_D \left(\frac{e^{i_d} - 1}{i_d} \right) \tag{6.19}$$

$$NPV_B \cong NPV_C \tag{6.20}$$

Another assumption commonly used in many economic evaluations, textbooks, and technical articles is the *time zero* investment assumption, which introduces further significant variation in most profitability indicators calculated using different discounting methods.

The complication arises due to the mixed cash flow assumption in the 1st year, i.e., for year 1, investment is treated as occurred at the beginning of the year (instantaneous cash outflow), and the cash inflow in this year is treated as year-end cash flow. Also all other cash flows after the 1st year are assumed as being received at the end of each year. So the cash flow assumption in year 1 is not consistent with the future years.

For example, rearranging Investments A and B as shown in Table 6–6, the profitability indicators calculated using these profiles changes. Comparing the net present values (NPV) for the investments given in Table 6–5 are significantly different from those in Table 6–6. The IRR and PI for Cases A, D, and G are similar; but there is significant difference in IRR for Case A and Case B (in Table 6–6), and the difference is dependent on the magnitude of the time zero investment as shown in Figure 6–8. The data used to generate the graph in Figure 6–8 is given in Table 6–7.

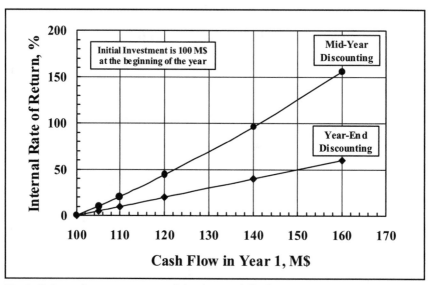

Fig. 6–8 Rates of return comparison with lump sum cash flow[8]

Year		Investment A	Investment B
0		–$268,600	–$345,000
1		132,900	132,900
2		132,900	112,965
3		97,600	96,020
4		69,200	81,617
5		23,500	69,375
6		28,600	58,968
7		15,900	50,123
8		9,400	40,098
9		5,600	30,073
10		1,900	18,044
CASE A	NPV @ 10%	$129,033	$137,564
	IRR	29.46%	22.15%
	PVR=NPV/PV of I	0.480	0.399
CASE B	NPV @ 10%	$148,441	$161,118
	IRR	39.98%	27.43%
	PVR=NPV/PV of I	0.553	0.467
CASE C	NPV @ 10%	$148,599	$161,309
	IRR	40.41%	27.57%
	PVR=NPV/PV of I	0.553	0.468
CASE D	NPV @ 10%	$124,197	$129,796
	IRR	25.82%	20.01%
	PVR=NPV/PV of I	0.462	0.376
CASE E	NPV @ 10%	$144,508	$154,348
	IRR	33.94%	24.35%
	PVR=NPV/PV of I	0.538	0.447

Table 6–6 Hypothetical investment profiles and their profitability indicators

	Year	A	B	C	D	E
	0	−$100,000	−$100,000	−$100,000	−$100,000	−$100,000
	1	$105,000	$110,000	$120,000	$140,000	$160,000
IRR – Year End CF		5.0%	10.0%	20.0%	40.0%	60.0%
IRR – Mid Year CF		10.3%	21.0%	44.0%	96.0%	156.0%

Table 6–7 Data used to generate the graph of figure 6–8[8]

When using the time zero assumption for cash flows, the IRR and NPV cannot be easily converted from one method to another as previously shown. The time zero investment has to be known in order to achieve the NPV conversions. For IRR conversion, the NPV profile at various discount rates has to be known. For example, converting NPV_B to NPV_A in Table 6–6 using Equation (6.6) is

$$NPV_A = \frac{NPV_B + I_o}{(1 + i_d)^{0.50}} - I_o$$

$$= \frac{148,441 + 268,600}{(1 + 0.10)^{0.50}} - 268,600$$

$$= 129,033$$

TREATMENT OF FINANCING MIX

The approach used for the analysis of the interactions of corporate financing and investment decisions is reviewed in this section. In the preceding sections, it was assumed all investment decisions are tied to the *weighted average cost of capital (WACC)*. This is the classical approach presented in most finance textbooks. However, the literature of finance does not give full analysis of the use of the weighted average cost of capital as a standard for capital budgeting. Most of us are probably not aware of the limitations/assumptions inherent in the calculations when using the WACC. The common understanding regarding the use of WACC is:

1. Use *total cash flows* and *pre-tax* cost of capital (pre-tax weighted average cost of capital), or

2. Use *operating cash flows* and *after-tax* cost of capital (after-tax weighted average cost of capital).

Both these approaches should result in the same answer. Although this statement is true, it is true only under special circumstances. If the *special circumstances* are not met, the two approaches will result in numerically different net present values (NPVs). These may occasionally result in conflicting signals to decision makers. *If the special circumstances are met, only the NPVs calculated through each method will be same but the rest of the profitability indicators and the cash available (as depicted from the cash flows) for reinvestment will still be different.*

The total cash flow approach explicitly includes in its cash flow estimates the reduction in corporate income taxes resulting from the deductibility of interest payments generated by debt used in financing the investment. The discount rate (pre-tax cost of capital) used with this type of cash flow recognizes the total cash returns expected from the organization by various groups of capital providers, i.e., banks, stock holders, etc.

On the other hand, the classic NPV uses operating cash flows that do not require the estimates of tax deduction on the interest payments. The discount rate (after-tax cost of capital) used with this type of cash flow recognizes the cash flows that the firm must actually generate from its operations (after-tax) in order to service its capital claims. Thus the cash flows have to exclude nonoperational subsidies, such as the tax deduction on interest.[26]

In the following pages, numerical examples are presented to show if the two approaches are equivalent and under what conditions. Four standard methods that incorporate the interaction of investment and financing decisions in evaluating investment opportunities are presented. Various features of these four methods are compared to explore the implications of using them. The four methods reported are:[27]

- The After-Tax Weighted Average Cost of Capital method
- The Equity Residual method
- The Arditti-Levy Weighted Average Cost of Capital method
- The Mayers Adjusted Present Value method

Pattern of Project Debt Repayment Schedule

Most standard approaches to the analysis of prospective capital investment projects attempt to take into account the method of financing the investment. Theoretically, the investment and financing decisions are interdependent. Firms obtain financing in relatively large blocks. Although a given financing decision may be made to support a particular investment, the decision of what percentage of the investment should be financed by debt and what percentage by equity varies from company to company. Each company determines its own capital structure to fit its investment environment. In the following discussion, 60% debt and 40% equity are assumed.

For the capital investment evaluation, it is important to know that once the projects are implemented, how the debts relate to a particular investment will be paid back. Debt repayment schedule is the key issue in the discussion of the proceeding four methods. In practice, the standard term loans are serviced in a variety of ways as:

- equal periodic payments such as mortgage or car loan payments (principal and interest)
- equal principal payments and the resulting interest on outstanding loan balance
- level debt schedule that assumes all issued debt remain outstanding until the end of the project's life and thus implies more average project debt than the first two
- constant debt ratio schedule, which implies the debt weight is constant over the life of the project

In the constant debt ratio schedule, project debt at time t is the present value of all net operating cash flows in periods beyond t discounted at the weighted average cost of capital i_w, and multiplied by the debt weight W_d. Consequently, project debt remains a constant percentage of the market value of the project. The principal payment each year is the difference between the present values of two adjacent periods.

The constant debt schedule implies more debt is initially issued as compared to the above-mentioned debt schedules. On the other hand, the constant ratio schedule has project debt declining as cash flows from the project are realized (i.e., the debt value decreases in constant proportion to total value across time). As debt value decreases, so do the tax savings due to interest deduction. This means the i_w discount rate and the classic NPV calculation adjust for these decreased tax savings due to interest across time, because i_w is calculated in constant value ratio of debt to total capital.

The following example illustrates how the various debt schedules are calculated.

Example 6–5

A capital investment project involves initial investment, at time zero, of $1000 financed $400 by equity and $600 by debt, i.e., the debt to investment ratio is 0.6. Interest on debt is 12% with a repayment schedule of 5 years. The corporate tax rate is 46%. The project generates after-tax operating cash flows $[R_t - C_t - D_t)(1 - T_c) + D_t]$ of $300 per year for the next 5 years. Calculate (a) equal periodic debt payment schedule, (b) equal principal payment debt schedule, (3) level debt schedule, and (4) constant ratio debt schedule.

Solution: The equal periodic payment debt schedule, the equal principal payment debt schedule, and the constant ratio debt schedule are presented in Tables 6–8, 6–9, and 6–10, respectively. The calculations are performed using an Excel spreadsheet. The respective spreadsheets are given on the CD-ROM accompanying Volume 2 of this series.

The level debt schedule is calculated as follows

Level Debt Schedule $= \$600 \, (1 + 0.12)^5 = \$1,057.41$

Out of the $1,057.41, $600 is the principal payment, and $457.41 is the interest.

In Tables 6–8 and 6–9, interest is the previous year's outstanding loan balance multiplied by the interest rate per period. Note the present value of the year-end payments at an interest rate of 12% are equivalent to the total debt of $600. In these schedules, initial debt issued is equal to the debt ratio W_d times the investment outlay (i.e., W_d times the total investment) on the grounds this is likely what the analysts would do in practice.

	A	B	C	D	E
3	PV of Loan				600
4	Total Number of Payments for Loan				5
5	Interest Rate Per Period				12.00%
6					
7					Year-End
8				Year-End	Loan
9	Period	Interest	Principal	Payment	Balance
10	0				$600.00
11	1	$72.00	$94.45	$166.45	$505.55
12	2	$60.67	$105.78	$166.45	$399.77
13	3	$47.97	$118.47	$166.45	$281.30
14	4	$33.76	$132.69	$166.45	$148.61
15	5	$17.83	$148.61	$166.45	0.00

Table 6–8 Calculation of equal periodic debt payment schedule

	A	B	C	D	E
3	PV of Loan				600
4	Total Number of Payments for Loan				5
5	Interest Rate Per Period				12.00%
6					
7					Year-End
8				Year-End	Loan
9	Period	Interest	Principal	Payment	Balance
10	0				$600.00
11	1	$72.00	$120.00	$192.00	$480.00
12	2	$57.60	$120.00	$177.60	$360.00
13	3	$43.20	$120.00	$163.20	$240.00
14	4	$28.80	$120.00	$148.80	$120.00
15	5	$14.40	$120.00	$134.40	0.00

Table 6–9 Calculation of equal principal payment debt schedule

The calculation of equal periodic payment debt schedule is presented in Chapter 2 as "Loan Amortization Schedule."

The following steps are to be followed for generating the constant ratio debt schedule as shown in Table 6–10.

1. The weighted average cost of capital (WACC) is calculated as

$$i_w = W_d i_d (1 - T_c) + (1 - W_d) i_e$$
$$= 0.60(0.12)(1 - 0.46) + (1 - 0.60)(0.70)$$
$$= 0.0669 \quad or \quad 6.688\%$$

2. Using the after-tax weighted average cost of capital (discussed in the following section), calculate the present value of the periodic net cash flows.

$$PV_o = 300(1 + 0.06688)^{-1} + 300(1 + 0.06688)^{-2} + 300(1 + 0.06688)^{-3}$$
$$+ 300(1 + 0.06688)^{-4} + 300(1 + 0.06688)^{-5}$$
$$= 281.19 + 263.57 + 247.04 + 231.56 + 217.04$$
$$= 1,240.40$$

	A	B	C	D	E	F	G
3	Total Number of Payments	5					
4	Interest Rate per Period	12.00%					
5	Tax Rate	46.00%					
6	Return on Equity	7.00%					
7	Debt Weight	60.00%					
8	WACC	6.688%					
9							
10		0	1	2	3	4	5
11	Net Operating Cash Flow		$300	$300	$300	$300	$300
12	Value of Net Cash Flow	1,240.40	1,023.3	791.80	544.76	281.19	–
13							
14	Debt Financing of Investment	744.24	614.02	475.08	326.86	168.72	–
15							
16	Interest on Outstanding Loan		89.31	73.68	57.01	39.22	20.25
17	Principal Payment		130.23	138.93	148.23	158.14	168.72
18	Total Payment		**219.53**	**212.62**	**205.24**	**197.36**	**188.96**

Table 6–10 Calculation of Constant Ratio Debt Payment Schedule

$$PV_1 = 300(1+0.06688)^{-1} + 300(1+0.06688)^{-2} + 300(1+0.06688)^{-3}$$
$$+ 300(1+0.06688)^{-4}$$
$$= 281.19 + 263.57 + 247.04 + 231.56$$
$$= 1{,}023.36 \text{, and so on}$$

3. The debt each year is then calculated by multiplying the debt weight by each year's present value of the cash flows.

   $Debt_0 = 1{,}240.40 \times 0.6 = \$744.24$
   $Debt_1 = 1{,}023.36 \times 0.6 = \$614.02$ and so on

4. Interest each year is the previous year's outstanding debt times the interest rate (cost of debt) of debt, i.e., interest at end of year one is $744.24 \times 0.12 = \$89.31$, and so on.

5. The principal payment each year is the difference between the current year's outstanding debt and the previous year's outstanding debt, i.e., principal payment in year 1 is $744.24 - \$614.02 = \$130.22$, and so on.

It would be possible for an analyst, in analyzing investment alternatives, to assume debt schedules consistent with the theoretical requirements of the models. Practitioners are unlikely to do this because most firms do not manage their financial structures in this way. The constant ratio debt schedule is not in common use. In practice, due to the way corporate funds are raised and the way equity values rise and fall (for a variety of reasons), maintaining constant debt ratios for individual projects would be next to impossible. Once the pattern of project debt is determined, it has to be evaluated in line with the other costs and benefits of the project. The basic question is, should net loan proceeds, principal payments, and interest rate or tax savings due to the interest be included in the cash flows? In practice it is typically assumed the repayment of interest and principal exactly offsets the market value of the net proceeds.

After-Tax Weighted Average Cost of Capital Method

The after-tax weighted average cost of capital (WACC) method is discussed in most major textbooks of corporate finance. It is well known and widely used in the industry. However, the method does not give a true picture of the available cash flows generated by an investment. This results in calculation of varying profitability indicators, depending on which method is used.

In this method, the NPV is calculated by discounting the after-tax operating cash flows of an investment alternative at a rate i_w. The i_w reflects both the equity and debt required rates of return. The cash flow combination is represented by the following equation.

(6.21)

$$NPV_{WACC} = \sum_{t=1}^{n} \frac{(R_t - C_t - D_t)(1 - T_c) + D_t}{(1 + i_w)^t} - I_o$$

(6.22)

$$i_w = W_d i_d (1 - T_c) + (1 - W_d) i_e$$

where

R_t = pre-tax operating cash revenues generated by the investment during period t

C_t = pre-tax operating cash expenses due to the investment during time period t

D_t = additional depreciation due to the investment during period t

T_c = corporate tax rate, fraction

I_o = initial after tax cash outlay to undertake the investment

i_w = weighted average cost of capital, fraction

i_e = required rate of return on equity over the investment life, fraction

i_d = cost of debt, fraction

W_d = weight of debt to total capital investment I_o, fraction

The key point to note in Equation (6.21) is that the *financial flows* (*interest and principal payments on debt*) do not appear in the cash flows. The effects of financing flows, on the other hand, rather than being treated explicitly in the cash flows are handled implicitly via the discount rate i_w. Thus i_w takes into account (1) the debt/equity mix used to finance the project, and (2) the tax deductibility of interest. In theory, this weight is to be expressed in market value terms with the assumption the market value debt-equity mix of the firm remains constant over time. In practice, it is assumed i_w is constant over the life of the investment.

Some authors over-extend the assumptions of discounting and claim depreciation is also accounted for in the discounting process. Therefore, they say, it should not be included in the cash flows: "Fundamentally, the analysis of present value must exclude depreciation as a cost because the present value concept *automatically* provides for the return of the initial investment over its useful life."[28] This statement is not correct; depreciation is not added because it is a non-cash item. However, since depreciation is deducted for tax purposes, the tax outflow savings achieved due to depreciation shall be accounted for in the cash flows. This is shown in Equation (6.21) and in Chapter 4. The following example clarifies the use of Equations (6.21) and (6.22).

Example 6–6

A capital investment project involves initial investment of $1000, financed $400 by equity and $600 by debt. The corporate tax rate is 46%, interest on the debt is 12%, and the minimum acceptable rate of return on equity is 7% (assuming the equity can be invested elsewhere at a rate of return of 7%). The project will generate after-tax operating cash flows $[R_t - C_t - D_t)(1 - T_c) + D_t]$ of $300 per year for the next five years. Calculate the NPV, IRR, PI, and GRR for the investment.

Solution: The cash flow for Example 6–6 is shown in Table 6–11.

Year	0	1	2	3	4	5
Investment	–$1,000					
Operating CF		$300	$300	$300	$300	$300
NCF	–$1,000	$300	$300	$300	$300	$300

Table 6–11 Cash flow for the data in example 6–6

Using Equation (6.22), the after-tax weighted average cost of capital is

$$i_w = \frac{600}{1,000} \times 0.12(1-0.46) + \left(1 - \frac{600}{1,000}\right) \times 0.07$$

$$= 0.60 \times 12 \times 0.54 + (1-0.60) \times 0.07$$

$$= 0.0669 \quad or \quad 6.688\%$$

The NPV is calculated as

$$NPV_{WACC} = -1,000 + \frac{300}{(1+0.06688)^1} + \frac{300}{(1+0.06688)^2} + \frac{300}{(1+0.06688)^3}$$

$$+ \frac{300}{(1+0.06688)^4} + \frac{300}{(1+0.06688)^5}$$

$$= -1,000 + 281.19 + 263.57 + 247.04 + 231.56 + 217.04$$

$$= \$240.40$$

Similarly, the IRR, PI, and GRR are

IRR = 15.24%

Roesnt this underestimate IRR?

PI = 1 + 240.40/1,000 = 1.24

GRR @ 7% = 11.70%

Note the cash flow in Table 6–11 does not include tax savings due to interest (interest tax shield) and principal payments on debt in the cash flow. These are implicitly incorporated in the calculation of the i_w. The other three methods, presented in the following pages, do account for the tax savings on interest payments and/or the principal payments in the cash flows. The objective here is to formulate all the methods in such a way they all calculate the same NPV.

Equity Residual Method—NPV$_{ER}$

The objective of pursuing any investment project is to maximize the shareholder's interest in the firm. According to the Equity Residual Method, the value of these shareholder interests, NPV_{ER}, can be expressed by the following equation.

$$NPV_{ER} = \sum_{t=1}^{n} \frac{\overbrace{\left[\left(R_t - C_t - D_t - i_d B_t\right)\left(1 - T_c\right) + D_t\right]}^{\text{AFTER TAX CASH FLOW}} - \overbrace{\left(B_t - B_{t+1}\right)}^{\text{PRINCIPAL}}}{\left(1 + i_e\right)^t} - \left(I_o - NP\right) \quad \overset{\text{NET EQU}}{} \quad (6.23)$$

where

B_t = the project debt outstanding from time $t-1$ to time t

NP = the net proceeds (time zero) of issuing B_t of project debt, which is outstanding from time 0 to time t.

The first term in Equation (6.23) is the present value of the after-tax cash income less repayment from equity sources. Therefore, Equation (6.23) is the present value of the residual cash flows to equity owners matched against their initial equity outlay. A positive NPV_{ER} means a desirable investment from the viewpoint of the equity holders. In applications where the project specific financing scheme is known, the shareholder interests in the project could be calculated directly by Equation (6.23). The cash flows generated and calculations under the equity residual method are shown in Table 6–12. Note the constant ratio debt schedule of Table 6–10 is used in Table 6–12.

Year	0	1	2	3	4	5
Investment	–$1,000.00					
Loan Proceeds	$744.24					
Operating CF		$300.00	$300.00	$300.00	$300.00	$300.00
Principal Payment		–$130.23	–$138.93	–$148.23	–$158.14	–$168.72
Interest (Net of Tax)		–$48.22	–$39.79	–$30.79	–$21.18	–$10.94
Net Cash Flow	–$255.76	$121.55	$121.28	$120.98	$120.68	$120.34

Table 6–12 Cash flow for the equity residual method (data of Example 6–6)

The NPV is calculated by using the rate of equity as

$$NPV_{ER} = 255.76 + \frac{121.55}{\left(1+0.07\right)^1} + \frac{121.28}{\left(1+0.07\right)^2} + \frac{120.98}{\left(1+0.07\right)^3} + \frac{120.68}{\left(1+0.07\right)^4} + \frac{120.34}{\left(1+0.07\right)^5}$$

$$= -255.76 + 113.60 + 105.93 + 98.76 + 92.07 + 85.80$$

$$= \$240.40$$

Similarly, the IRR, PI, and GRR are

$$IRR = 37.86\%$$
$$PI = 1 + 240.40/255.76 = 1.94$$
$$GRR @ 7\% = \left[(1.94)^{1/5} \times 1.07 - 1\right] \times 100 = 22.16\%$$

Arditti-Levy Method—NPV$_{AL}$

Because interest payments are tax-deductible, the cash flow estimates used in the Weighted Average Cost of Capital (WACC) model overstates (by the amount $T_c i_d B_t$) the corporate taxes actually paid by the corporation. The model proposed by Arditti and Levy accounts for the cash flows actually received by both the debt and equity claimants. Their model is represented by the following equation.

(6.24)

$$NPV_{AL} = \sum_{t=1}^{n} \frac{\left[(R_t - C_t - D_t - i_d B_t)(1 - T_c) + D_t\right] + i_d B_t}{(1 + i_{AL})^t} - I_o$$

where **(6.25)**

$$i_{AL} = W_d i_d + (1 - W_d) i_e$$

The Arditti-Levy approach presented in Equations (6.24) and (6.25) differ from the WACC approach represented by Equations (6.21) and (6.22) in two fundamental aspects. The cash flows in the numerator of Equation (6.24) are the sum of flows to both the equity and debt owners. Comparison of Equations (6.24) and (6.21) show the cash flows in the numerator of Equation (6.24) exceed those in Equation (6.21) by the amount of the tax savings due to interest on debt ($i_d B_t T_c$). Thus, Equation (6.24) shows lower taxes paid to the government than those paid by the WACC method. The comparison of Equations (6.22) and (6.25) shows the i_{EL} has no adjustment for the tax savings due to interest payments instead, this arrangement has been accounted for in the cash flows. The cash flows generated and calculations under the equity residual method are as shown in Table 6–13 (the constant ratio debt schedule of Table 6–10 is assumed).

Year	0	1	2	3	4	5
Investment	−$1,000.00					
Operating CF		$300.00	$300.00	$300.00	$300.00	$300.00
Interest Tax Saving		$41.08	$33.89	$26.22	$18.04	$9.32
Net Cash Flow	−$1000.00	$341.08	$333.89	$326.22	$318.04	$309.32

Table 6–13 Cash flow for the Arditti-levy method (data of Example 6–6)

The cost of capital for the Arditti-Levy method is calculated using Equation (6.25) as

$$i_{AL} = \frac{600}{1,000} \times 0.12 + \left(1 - \frac{600}{1,000}\right) \times 0.07$$

$$= (0.60 \times 0.12 + 0.40 \times 0.04) \times 100 = 10.0\%$$

The NPV is calculated using the Arditty-Levy before-tax weighted average cost of capital as

$$NPV_{AL} = -1,000 + \frac{341.08}{(1+0.10)^1} + \frac{333.89}{(1+0.10)^2} + \frac{326.22}{(1+0.10)^3} + \frac{318.04}{(1+0.10)^4} + \frac{309.32}{(1+0.10)^5}$$

$$= -1,000 + 310.07 + 275.94 + 245.09 + 217.23 + 192.06$$

$$= \$240.40$$

Similarly, the IRR, PI, and GRR are

$$IRR = 19.19\%$$
$$PI = 1 + 240.40/1,000 = 1.240$$
$$GRR @ 7\% = 11.72\%$$

Adjusted Net Present Value—NPV$_A$

Unlike the other three methods, this method treats operating cash flows and financing in two separate steps as shown in the following equation. The first term in the Equation (6.26) discounts the after-tax operating (without any effects due to interest payments on debt) cash flows at the discount rate, ρ, that would be appropriate if the project was entirely financed by equity. The last term of Equation (6.26) accounts for the value of the projects' financing, which is the discounted value of the tax savings due to the interest payments on the debt.

$$(6.26)$$

$$NPV_A = \sum_{t=1}^{n} \frac{\left[(R_t - C_t - D_t)(1-T_c) + D_t\right]}{(1+\rho)^t} - I_o + \sum_{t=1}^{n} \frac{T_c i_d B_t}{(1+i_d)^t}$$

where (6.27)

$$\rho = \frac{i_w}{(1-T_c W_d)}$$

The cash flow streams generated in Table 6–13 for the Arditti-Levy method are used to calculate the NPV_A as follows.

Using Equation (6.27), the discount rate used to discount the after-tax operating cash flow is

The NPV_A is calculated as given below

$$\rho = \frac{0.06688}{1 - 0.46 \cdot 0.60} = 0.0924 \quad or \quad 9.24\%$$

$$NPV_A = -1,000 + \frac{341.08}{(1+0.0924)^1} + \frac{333.89}{(1+0.0924)^2} + \frac{326.22}{(1+0.0924)^3} + \frac{318.04}{(1+0.0924)^4} + \frac{309.32}{(1+0.0924)^5}$$

$$+ \frac{41.08}{(1+0.12)^1} + \frac{33.89}{(1+0.12)^2} + \frac{26.22}{(1+0.12)^3} + \frac{18.04}{(1+0.12)^4} + \frac{9.32}{(1+0.12)^5}$$

$$= -1,000 + 274.62 + 251.40 + 230.13 + 210.67 + 192.85 + 36.68 + 27.02 + 18.66 + 11.46 + 5.29$$

$$= \$258.78$$

Similarly, the IRR, PI, and GRR are

$$IRR = 19.19\%$$
$$PI = 1 + 258.78/1,000 = 1.259$$
$$GRR @ 7\% = 12.04\%$$

Comparison of the Four Methods

The application of the four methods to a simple numerical example is illustrated in the preceding pages. In these analyses, the *constant ratio debt schedule* and a tax rate of 46% is used. Further analyses were done based on (1) constant ratio debt schedule and zero tax rate, (2) equal periodic debt payment on $600 debt and zero tax rate, and (3) equal periodic payment on $600 debt and a tax rate of 46%. The results of all these different scenarios are presented in Table 6–14 for discussion.

When the four methods are applied to projects with cash flow patterns and debt repayment schedules typically encountered in practice, they yield different results. The four methods yield similar results only under special conditions. The conclusions are:

1. Under the constant ratio debt schedule and $T_c>0\%$ assumption, NPV_{WACC}, NPV_{ER}, and NPV_{AL} are equal. However, all other profitability indicators are different.

2. Under the constant ratio debt schedule and $T_c=0\%$, the profitability indicators in most of the methods are the same.

3. Under the conventional debt schedules (constant periodic payments, constant principal payments, or level debt) and $T_c>0\%$, the profitability indicators in most of the methods are different. Thus, if the project debt ratio is not kept constant, NPV_{WACC}, NPV_{ER}, and NPV_{AL} are not equivalent.

4. Under the conventional debt schedules and $T_c=0\%$, most methods yield same profitability indicators except for the equity residual method.

5. If the tax rate is zero or no consideration is given to the tax savings due to interest payments on debt, any debt payment schedule yields the same profitability indicators in most of the methods.

The analyst has to be careful when dealing with the profitability indicators generated by the different methods. The reason why these methods yield different profitability indicators is due to the implicit assumption each makes as to the treatment of tax savings due to interest payments.

	WACC	Equity Residual	Arditti-Levy	Adjusted NPV
Constant Debt Ratio, $T_c = 46\%$				
Net Present Value	$240.40	$240.40	$240.40	$258.78
Internal Rate of Return	15.24%	37.86%	15.24%	19.19%
Profitability Index	1.24	1.94	1.24	1.26
Growth Rate of Return @ 7.0%	11.71%	21.16%	11.71%	12.04%
Constant Debt Ratio, $T_c = 0\%$				
Net Present Value	$137.24	$137.24	$137.24	$137.24
Internal Rate of Return	15.24%	21.73%	15.24%	15.24%
Profitability Index	1.14	1.43	1.14	1.14
Growth Rate of Return @ 7.0%	9.79%	14.97%	9.79%	9.79%
Equal Periodic Payment, $T_c = 46\%$				
Net Present Value	$240.40	$238.63	$222.69	$241.79
Internal Rate of Return	15.24%	27.97%	18.50%	18.50%
Profitability Index	1.24	1.60	1.22	1.24
Growth Rate of Return @ 7.0%	11.7%	17.50%	11.39%	11.74%
Equal Periodic Payment, $T_c = 0\%$				
Net Present Value	$137.24	$147.60	$137.24	$137.24
Internal Rate of Return	15.24%	19.93%	15.24%	15.24%
Profitability Index	1.14	1.37	1.14	1.14
Growth Rate of Return @ 7.0%	9.79	13.94%	9.79%	9.79%

Table 6–14 Comparison of profitability indicators from the four methods

There is a reasonable intuitive appeal to the use of the equity residual method because it accounts for the total dollars generated to service capital at each point in time. From the viewpoint of the net cash flow, the equity residual method gives a more realistic picture of the cash flows available for distribution as dividend or reinvestment. The cash flows in the other methods are overstated (i.e., they are subject to the payment of the principal on the debt). As long as the equity residual method is consistently used from project to project, the selection of any practical (close to reality) debt payment schedule may be adopted. NOTE: This author recommends using the equity residual method as against the weighted average cost of capital method.

QUESTIONS and PROBLEMS

6.1 Define the profitability measures payback period, NPV, IRR, PI, PVR, TC, and GRR. What is the logic behind each method?

6.2 Which payback period (discounted or undiscounted) is appropriate to be used in investment analysis and why?

6.3 What are the three most important indications provided by the payback period?

6.4 Briefly list the advantages and disadvantages of (a) payback period, (b) net present value, (c) internal rate of return, (d) profitability index, and (e) growth rate of return.

6.5 What is the technical cost of development? How would you interpret the technical cost of $12/Stb calculated at 10% discount factor?

6.6 For the calculation of discounted technical cost, the production stream and the total costs have to be discounted at the desired discount rate. An engineer once said, "I don't believe in discounting the production." Comment on this statement.

6.7 List three different ways of converting gas production into its barrel of oil equivalent (BOE). Which method is the most appropriate for calculating technical cost of development for an oil and gas project?

6.8 List the accept/reject criteria for (a) payback period, (b) net present value, (c) internal rate of return, (d) profitability index, (e) present value ratio, (f) technical cost of development, and (g) growth rate of return.

6.9 For independent projects, is it true that if PI>1, then NPV will also be greater than zero, and IRR>i_d?

6.10 The IRR of a project with a constant cash flow S for n years is positive. Hence the NPV of the project at a zero discount rate must be positive. Do you agree? Prove your answer.

6.11 In what sense is a reinvestment rate assumption embodied in NPV and IRR calculations? What is the assumed reinvestment rate of each method? Which assumption is correct and why?

6.12 What is the significance of the GRR and how it differs from the IRR.

6.13 For a project with 5 years of useful economic life, the PI is 1.5, and the available reinvestment rate is 7%. Calculate its growth rate of return.

6.14 Given the following cash flow:

0	1	2	3	4	5
–$3,352	$1,000	$1,000	$1,000	$1,000	$1,000

(a) Calculate the NPV of the project using the following discount rates: 5%, 10%, 15%, 20%, and 25%.
(b) Graph the NPVs of the project as a function of the discount rates.
(c) Find the IRR, mathematically and graphically.
(d) Calculate the NPV and IRR of the project using Excel spreadsheet.

6.15 For each of the following investment projects, calculate:
(a) The net present value (NPV) using a 15% discount rate.
(b) The Internal Rate of return.
Based on the two profitability measures calculated, which project(s) should be accepted?

	0	1	2	3	4	5	6	7
A	–4,564	1,000	1,000	1,000	1,000	1,000	1,000	1,000
B	–2,000	524.7	524.7	524.7	524.7	524.7	524.7	524.7
C	–21,000	3,000	3,000	3,000	3,000	3,000	3,000	3,000

6.16 Two projects are considered for evaluation. Project A has a cost of $10,000 and is expected to produce benefits of $3000 per year for

5 years. Project B costs $25,000 and is expected to produce cash flows of $7500 per year for 5 years. Calculate the payback period, NPV, IRR, PI, PVR, and GRR for the 2 projects. Assume the minimum acceptable rate of return and the available reinvestment rate of 8%. Should both projects be accepted if they are independent?

6.17 Calculate the NPV, IRR, and GRR for the cash flows given in the following table. Assume the minimum acceptable rate of return of 8%. Which projects should be accepted if they are independent projects? Would the selection of the projects change if the cost of capital were 12%?

	Expected Net Cash Flow	
Year	Project A	Project B
0	($10,000)	($10,000)
1	6,500	3,500
2	3,000	3,500
3	3,000	3,500
4	1,000	3,500

6.18 A company is deciding whether or not it should develop a strip mine at an initial cost of $4.5 million. Net cash inflows are expected to be $9 million for each of the first 3 years of operations. In the 4th year, the land must be returned to its natural state at a cost of $23 million. Develop and plot the NPV profile for the project. Should the project be accepted at a rate of return of 8%? Should it be accepted at a rate of return of 15%? What are the project GRRs if the available reinvestment rate is (a) 8% and (b) 15%?

6.19 Revisit Problem 3.7 of Chapter 3. Calculate the NPV for the first 5 years (1/1/1999 to 12/31/2003) cash flow generated by this problem. Assume the minimum acceptable rate of return is 8%.

6.20 Revisit Problem 3.11 of Chapter 3. Calculate the NPV of the net cash flows generated by the lease. Assume the after-tax weighted average cost of capital of 8%.

6.21 Develop a simple spreadsheet to enable calculation of payback period (discounted), NPV, PI, PVR, IRR, TC, and GRR for the data in Problem 3.16 Assume the cost of capital and the reinvestment rate is 8%, and it is constant throughout the economic life of the investment.

6.22 Suppose there is an investment proposal requiring $16,000 outlay now (time zero) and returning a constant cash flow of $7000 per period before tax savings due to interest payments for the next 3 years. The proposal is to have a market debt proportion of 50% (i.e., 0.50). The capital market requires per period rate of return on equity of 27% and on debt of 9%. The corporate tax rate is 40%, and interest is deductible for the calculation of income tax. Calculate the NPV and IRR based on (a) weighted average cost of capital method, (b) Arditty-Levy method, (c) Equity residual method, and (d) Adjusted Net Present Value method.

6.23 Rework Problem 6.22, assuming the corporate tax rate is not applicable.

6.24 Rework Problem 6.22, assuming the loan is paid in 3 equal periodic year-end payments. Comment on the outcomes as compared to the outcomes in problem 6.22.

6.25 Two investment alternatives are to be economically evaluated. Both projects require initial capital outlay of $1000 (in time zero). Project A generates a net before income tax cash flow of $300 per year for the next 5 years. Project B generates a net before tax cash flow of $200 per year for the next 4 years and $792.58 in year 5. The rate of equity is 7%, the interest rate on debt is 11%, the corporate tax rate is 46%, and the debt weight is 30% (i.e., equity = $700 and debt = $300). Using the methods of (a) weighted average cost of capital, (b) Arditti-Levy, and (c) Equity Residual; calculate the NPV, IRR, and GRR (assuming reinvestment rate of 7%). Assume the debt repayment follows a constant ratio debt schedule, and the loan is paid back in 5 years.

6.26 Rework Problem 6.25, assuming the loan is serviced in (a) 5 year-end equal principal payments of $60, and (b) 5 year-end equal payments. Comment on the profitability measures in comparison the ones calculated in Problem 6.25.

REFERENCES

1. Newendorp, P. D., *Decision Analysis for Petroleum Exploration*, PennWell Books, PennWell Publishing Company, Tulsa, Oklahoma, 1975.

2. Lyon, J.R., "Using Multiple Cutoff Rates for Capital Investments," *Journal of Petroleum Technology*, July 1975, pp. 822–826.

3. Capen, E.C., Clapp, R.V., and Phelps, W.W., "Growth Rate—A Rate-of-Return Measure of Investment Efficiency," *Journal of Petroleum Technology*, May 1976, pp. 531–543.

4. Bowlin, O. D., Martin, J. D., and Scott, D. F., *Guide to Financial Analysis*, McGraw-Hill Book Company, 1980.

5. Weston, J.F., and Brigham, E.F., *Managerial Finance, Seventh Edition*, The Dryden Press, Hinsdale, Illinois, 1981.

6. Stanley, Lyn T., "Petroleum Engineering Economics Today," *Journal of Petroleum Technology*, April 1982, pp. 691–695.

7. Helfert, E. A., *Techniques of Financial Analysis, Fifth Edition*, Richard D. Irwin, Inc., Homewood, Illinois 60430, 1982.

8. Cotton, F. E., "Investment Indicators for Profitability Analysis Must Reflect Recent Economic Developments," *Oil & Gas Journal*, October 17, 1983, pp. 113–122.

9. Reobuck, F., " Minimum-Interest Rate of Return Optimizes ROI," *Oil & Gas Journal*, February 20, 1984, pp. 69–70.

10. Stermole, F. J., *Economic Evaluation and Investment Decision Methods, 10th Edition*, Investment Evaluations Corporation, Golden, Colorado, 2000.

11. Cotton, F. E., "Three Strategic Improvements in Petroleum Investment Analysis," *SPE Paper 13106*, presented at the 59th Annual Technical Conference and Exhibition held in Houston, Texas, September 16–19, 1984

12. Terry, R.E., "Internal Rate of Return: Friend or Foe?" *SPE Paper 13771*, presented at the SPE 1985 Hydrocarbon Economics and Evaluation Symposium held in Dallas, Texas, March 14–15, 1985, pp. 117–122.

13 Dougherty, E.L., "Guidelines for Proper Application of Four Commonly Used Investment Criteria," *SPE Paper 13770*, presented at the SPE 1985 Hydrocarbon Economics and Evaluation Symposium held in Dallas, Texas, March 14–15, 1985, pp. 101–115.

14 Wolff, Martin and Van Rensburg, W. C. J., " Computing the Internal Rate of Return," *Journal of Petroleum Technology*, May 1986, pp. 577–582.

15 Dougherty, E. L., "What Discounted Cash Flow Rate of Return Never Did Require," *Journal of Petroleum Technology*, January 1986, pp. 85–87.

16 Collarini, C. R., "Discussion of What Discounted Cash Flow Rate of Return Never Did Require," *Journal of Petroleum Technology*, June 1986, pp. 674–675.

17 Wanssbrough, R. S., "Discussion of What Discounted Cash Flow Rate of Return Never Did Require," *Journal of Petroleum Technology*, June 1986, pp. 675.

18 Aguilera Roberto, "Discussion of What Discounted Cash Flow Rate of Return Never Did Require," *Journal of Petroleum Technology*, June 1986, pp. 676–678.

19 Wolf, M. and Van Rensburg, W. C. J., "Discussion of What Discounted Cash Flow Rate of Return Never Did Require," *Journal of Petroleum Technology*, June 1986, pp. 678.

20 Dougherty, E. L., "Author's Reply to Discussion of What Discounted Cash Flow Rate of Return Never Did Require," *Journal of Petroleum Technology*, June 1986, pp. 679–681.

21 Seba, R.D., "The Only Investment Selection Criterion you Will Ever Need," *SPE Paper 16310*, presented at the SPE Hydrocarbon Economics and Evaluation Symposium held in Dallas, Texas, March 2–3, 1987, pp. 173–180.

22 Levy, Haim and Sarnat, Marshall, *Capital Investment and Financial Decisions, Fifth Edition*, Prentice Hall International Ltd., 1994.

23 Aggarwal, R., *Capital Budgeting Under Uncertainty*, Prentice-Hall, Inc. Englewood Cliffs, NJ, 1993.

24 Folks, W. R., and Aggarwal, R., *International Dimensions of Financial Management*, PWS-Kent Publishing, Boston, MA, 1988.

25 Essley, P.L., Jr., "The Difference Between Nominal and Effective Interest Tables and Nominal and Effective Rates of Return," *SPE Reprint Series*, No. 16, 1982, pp. 105–114.

26 Boudreaux, K. J., and Long, H. W., "The Weighted Average Cost of Capital as a Cutoff Rate: A Further Analysis," *Financial Management*, Summer 1979, pp. 7–14.

27 Chambers, D. R., Harris, R. S., and Pringle, J. J., "Treatment of Financing Mix in Analyzing Investment Opportunities," *Financial Management*, Summer 1982, pp. 24–41.

28 Welsh, G. A., *Budgeting: Profit Planning and Control, Fourth Edition*, Prentice-Hall, Inc., Englewood Cliffs, New Jersey, 1976, p. 370.

chapter SEVEN

Investment Selection Decision-Making

The data requirement for each investment alternative under evaluation and the methods used to forecast relevant factors is presented in Chapters 3 and 4. In Chapter 6, the data organized in Chapters 3 and 4 were combined and translated into meaningful profitability/decision measures. In this chapter, the information gathered/calculated in Chapters 3 to 6 is used to make a decision whether to select the proposed investment and to rank the selected investment if a number of investment alternatives available.

Capital expenditure plans must be consistent with the cash position and financing considerations created. Both the timing of the capital expenditures and the amount of funds to invest in projects involve serious policy decisions. Capital additions should be analyzed in terms of their probable effect on return on investment. Prudent management should not undertake a capital addition unless its analysis indicates it will yield a return equal to, or greater than, the long-range company objective for return on investment.

A basic assumption of microeconomics is that the primary objective of a firm is to maximize profits throughout some planning horizon. To achieve this objective, what particular capital investments out of a number of available alternatives should the firm acquire? The simple answer is, the firm should invest only in those capital projects that will maximize its worth.

The investment evaluation process is comprised of two components, namely screening and ranking investment opportunities. Screening of all known investment opportunities identifies those projects that meet or exceed a predetermined standard (i.e. opportunities of value to the investor warranting further detailed evaluation). Screening criteria are based upon the investors' long-term goals and objectives. The criteria set the minimum acceptable profitability standard for potential investment opportunities. If the profitability of a potential investment exceeds the screening criteria, it may be accepted. A screening criterion is necessary for every economic evaluation. The screening ensures only investments projected to achieve the desired goals of the investing organization are considered.

Once an array of investment opportunities has fulfilled the screening criteria, the second step is to rank them in some order for a systematic evaluation. Ranking places these screened projects in order of most desirable to least desirable. Ranking criteria are only needed to allocate resources when they are in short supply. Selection of projects from the investment opportunities being considered, in accordance with proper ranking criterion will yield the maximum return possible within the limited resources (capital requirement) available. If the investor has unlimited resources, all projects (even those that exceed the screening criteria) may be approved.

The investments are normally grouped according to their nature and requirement. Although practices vary from firm to firm, investment proposals are frequently grouped according to the following categories:

1. Routine replacements and/or upgrades of service-producing assets,

2. Expansion providing additional capacity in existing facilities or introduction of new product lines,

3. Acquisitions of producing properties,

4. Infill/development drilling—primary recovery,

5. Infill/development drilling—secondary and enhanced recovery, and

6. Exploration activities.

While evaluating capital investments, it is recommended they be classified into groups. This will help in developing standardized estimation and administration procedures for handling particular classes of proposals. A few of the many possible ways of classifying investment proposals are:

1. *By project size* (i.e. the amount of cash resources required for implementing the project). Three general classes of project sizes are major projects, regular capital expenditures, and small proposals.

2. *By type of benefit* (i.e. benefits can arise from either cost reduction, expansion of existing product lines, risk reduction, or social overhead investment).

3. *By degree of dependence or interdependence* between two or more investment proposals. These can arise for several reasons such as:
   a. *Proposals are mutually exclusive*: The acceptance of one precludes the acceptance of the other. The early identification of these investments is crucial for a logical screening of investments.
   b. *Proposals are complements*: Decision to execute one investment increases the expected benefit from another investment.
   c. *Proposals are substitutes*: The acceptance of one investment decreases the profitability of another investment.
   d. *Proposals are independent or dependent*: Two investments are considered statistically dependent when increase (decrease) in the benefits from one investment is accompanied by an increase (decrease) in the benefits of the second, or vice versa.

In using the various measures of profitability discussed in Chapter 6 and applied in this chapter, the role of *sound management judgment and experience* must not be overlooked. Most evaluations are based on estimates of their potential. Therefore, the results cannot be better than the estimates. The estimates themselves may be subjective, and there may be other numerous unquantifiable factors related to a proposal. Therefore, a keen appreciation of the assumptions underlying the computations in each technique is essential.

SERVICE-PRODUCING INVESTMENTS

In this section, the profitability yardsticks discussed in Chapter 6 are used to select the economic service-producing investment alternative. The service-producing investments are mainly the facilities required for oil and gas production. These include separators, pumps, tanks, engines, turbines, flowlines, etc. These capital additions, replacements, or upgrades are assumed to provide the same revenue contribution but at different costs. For example, a decision has to be made to install one of four artificial lift systems out of (1) gas lift, (2) beam pumping unit, (3) hydraulic pump, or (4) electrical submersible pump. The beam-pumping unit may have three additional alternatives of whether it should be primed by electric motor, gas engine, or diesel engine. Each of these pumps will produce the same amount of oil but at different initial and annual maintenance/replacement costs.

The selection of service-producing investments is mutually exclusive (i.e. the selection of a beam pumping unit precludes the selection of the other three artificial lift systems). If the revenue contribution differs from one alternative to the other, then it should be considered as a revenue-producing investment (i.e. accounting for the revenue contribution along with the costs). A decision whether to install any type of artificial lift system, by itself, is revenue-producing investment proposal.

Ordinarily, replacement decisions are the simplest to make. Facilities wear out or become obsolete, and they must be replaced if production efficiency is to be maintained. The firm has a good idea of the cost savings obtained by replacing an old equipment/facility, and it knows the consequences of non-replacement. Overall, the outcomes of most replacement decisions can be predicted with a high degree of confidence.

Equivalent Cost Analysis

In this section, it is assumed the alternatives considered will be of equal economic life, will be technically comparable, and will provide the same service. The selection will be based on the equivalent cost basis, i.e. the (1) equivalent present value of costs, (2) equivalent annual value of costs, or (3) equivalent future value of costs. Comparison of either of the equivalent costs will assist in selection of the most economical and cost-effective alternative.

The equivalent costs will be calculated at a discount rate equivalent to the opportunity cost of investing the funds elsewhere. The following example will clarify the computation. Once the equivalent costs of each of the alternatives are calculated, the following decision yardsticks will be applied.

1. Select the alternative with the lowest present value (PV) of cost, or

2. Select the alternative with the lowest annual value (AV) of cost, or

3. Select the alternative with the lowest future value (FV) of cost.

Example 7–1

A choice has to be made between a diesel engine and a secondhand gasoline engine for a service expected to last seven years. Minimum attractive rate of return is 8%. Select the most economical alternative using (a) PV of costs, (b) AV of costs, and (c) FV of costs. The two alternatives are diagrammatically presented in Figure 7–1.

	A Diesel	B Gasoline
Initial Cost	$15,000	$5,000
Salvage value after seven years	5,000	0
Annual fuel cost	2,500	6,000
Annual maintenance cost	500	1,000

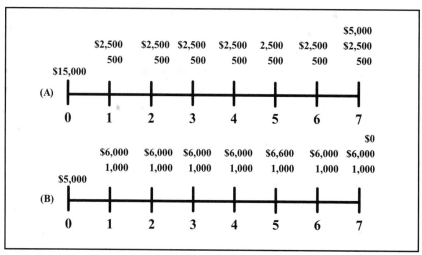

Fig. 7–1 Cash-flow diagram for the data in Example 7–1

Solution: Present values of costs for each alternative are:

(a) PV_A = $15,000 + $2,500(P/A_{8,7}) + $500(P/A_{8,7}) - $5000(P/F_{8,7})$
    = $15,000 + $2,500(5.2064) + $500(5.2064) - $5000(0.5835)$
    = $27,701.70$

PV_B = $5,000 + $6,000(P/A_{8,7}) + $1,000(P/A_{8,7}) - $0(P/F_{8,7})$
    = $5,000 + $6,000(5.2064) + $1,000(5.2064) - $0(0.5835)$
    = $41,444.80$

Select Alternative A, i.e. diesel engine with the lowest PV_{cost} of $27,701.70.

(b) AV_A = $15,000(A/P_{8,7}) + $2,500 + $500 - $5,000(A/F_{8,7})$
    = $15,000(0.19207) + $2,500 + $500 - $5,000(0.11207)$
    = $5,320.70$

AV_B = $5,000(A/P_{8,7}) + $6,000 + $1,000 - $0(A/F_{8,7})$
    = $5,000(0.19207) + $6,000 + $1,000 - $0(0.11207)$
    = $7,960.35$

Select Alternative A, i.e. diesel engine with the lowest AV_{cost} of $5,320.70.

(c) FV_A = $15,000(F/P_{8,7}) + $2,500(F/A_{8,7}) + $500(F/A_{8,7}) – $5,000
    = $15,000(1.7138) + $2,500(8.9228) + $500(8.9228) – $5,000
    = $47,475.40

  FV_B = $5,000(F/P_{8,7}) + $6,000(F/A_{8,7}) + $1,000(F/A_{8,7}) – $0
    = $5,000(1.7138) + $6,000(8.9228) + $1,000(8.9228) – $0
    = $71,028.60

Select Alternative A, i.e. diesel engine with the lowest FV_{cost} of $47,475.40.

The preceding example shows that regardless of which method is used, an appropriate alternative will be selected.

Rate of Return Analysis

Using this profitability measure for the selection of economical service-producing investments will give infinite rate of return (IRR). This is because of the negative cash flow (costs) and no positive cash flow to offset these costs. Remember, one of the limitation of IRR is it cannot be calculated when cash flows are either all positive or all negative.

This limitation of IRR can be avoided by performing incremental IRR analysis for selecting among service-producing investment alternatives. This is done by subtracting the costs of one alternative from the costs of the other alternative. The difference between the two costs is the savings (positive and negative) one alternative generates over the other. The IRR analyses are then performed on these incremental costs.

If the *incremental* IRR is greater than the minimum acceptable IRR, select the high initial cost alternative, and vice versa. If there are more than two alternatives, the survivor of the two is then compared with the next alternative. This is repeated until the entire available alternatives are exhausted. Remember the negative incremental costs are treated as positive savings, and vice versa.

Example 7–2

Using the IRR analysis on the investments presented in Example 7–1, which alternative will be the economic choice? Is the selection consistent with the selection made in Example 7–1? The incremental cash-flow diagram for the investment is shown in Figure 7–2.

Solution: Calculate the PV_{cost} at $i = 8\%$.

$$
\begin{aligned}
PV_{(A-B)} &= -\$10,000 + \$3,500(P/A_{8,7}) + \$500(P/A_{8,7}) - \$5,000(P/F_{8,7}) \\
&= -\$10,000 + \$3,500(5.2064) + \$500(5.2064) - \$5,000(0.5835) \\
&= \$7,908.10
\end{aligned}
$$

Since the present value of the incremental costs is positive at $i = 8\%$ (minimum acceptable rate of return), the incremental IRR will be greater than 8%. Therefore, select Alternative A. The selection is consistent with the selection made in Example 7–1. The incremental IRR is calculated as follows.

Try $i=30\%$

$$
\begin{aligned}
PV_{(A-B) \,@\, i=0.30} &= -\$10,000 + \$3,500(P/A_{30,7}) + \$500 \,(P/A_{30,7}) \\
&\quad -\$5000(P/F30,7) \\[6pt]
&= -\$10,000 + \$3,500(2.8021) + \$500(2.8021) \\
&\quad -\$5000(0.1594) \\[6pt]
&= \$411.40
\end{aligned}
$$

Similarly, for $i=35\%$, the $PV_{(A-B) \,@\, i=0.35} = -\$582.00$

Therefore, IRR by interpolation is,

$$
\begin{aligned}
IRR_{(A-B))} &= \frac{411.40}{411.40 + 582.00}(35 - 30) + 30 \\
&= 32.07\%
\end{aligned}
$$

Since the incremental IRR is greater than the minimum acceptable rate of return of 8%, the alternative with the higher initial cost (Alternative A) is selected.

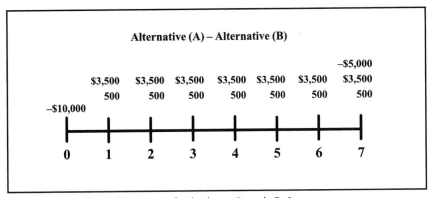

Fig. 7-2 Incremental cash-flow diagram for the data in Example 7–1.

Present Value Ratio or PI Analysis

The PVR and PI can be used in the same way as IRR is used. If PVR of the incremental cash flow is greater than zero, the alternative with the higher initial cost is selected and vice versa. On the other hand, if PI of the incremental cash flow is greater than 1, the alternative with the higher initial cost is selected and vice versa. The calculations of the PVR and PI for the data in Example 7–2 follow.

From Example 7–2, the present value of the incremental costs, $PV_{(A-B)}$, at the minimum acceptable rate of return of 8% is $7,908.10, and the incremental investment over Alternative B is $10,000. Therefore, the PVR and PI are,

$$PVR_{(A-B)} = \frac{7,908.1}{10,000} = 0.791$$

$$PI_{(A-B)} = \frac{7,908.10 + 10,000}{10,000} = 1.791$$

Both the PVR and PI confirm the selection of Alternative A.

Service Life Breakeven Analysis

The use of this method gives the same selection obtained by using the methods (PV, AV, FV, IRR, PVR, or PI) discussed in the preceding sections. The following steps should be followed for service life breakeven analysis.

1. Select one alternative and calculate the AV of its costs.

2. For the second alternative, compute n (service life) that gives the AV equal to the AV calculated in Step 1.

3. If n in Step 2 is less than the service life of the first alternative, select the alternative in Step 2. If n in Step 2 is greater than the service life calculated in Step 1, select the alternative in Step 1. The following example will clarify the calculations.

Example 7–3

Use service life breakeven analysis to select the least costly investment alternative out of the alternatives given in Example 7–1.

Solution: $AV_A = \$5,320.7$ (From Example 7–1)
$n = 7$ years

Compute n for Alternative B (by trial-and-error), which will make the $AV_A = AV_B$. For $n=10$ years,

$$AV_B = \$5,000(A/P_{8,10}) + \$6,000(P/A_{8,7})(A/P_{8,10})$$
$$+ 1,000(P/A_{8,7})(A/P_{8,10})$$

$$= \$5,000(0.14903) + \$6,000(5.2064)(0.14903)$$
$$+ \$1,000(5.2064)(0.14903)$$

$$= \$6,176.52$$

Since the $AV_B = \$6,176.52$ for $n=10$ years is greater than the $AV_A=\$5,320.7$ for $n=7$ years, another trial is needed.

For $n = 15$ years,

$$AV_B = \$5,000(A/P_{8,15}) + \$6,000(P/A_{8,7})(A/P_{8,15})$$
$$+ 1,000(P/A_{8,7})(A/P_{8,15})$$

$$= \$5,000(0.11683) + \$6,000(5.2064)(0.11683)$$
$$+ \$1,000(5.2064)(0.11683)$$

$$= \$4,842.00$$

For $n=15$ years, the $AV_B=\$4,842.00$ is less than the $AV_A=\$5,320.7$. Therefore, the required n is calculated by linear interpolation as shown below.

$$n = \frac{\$5,320.70 - \$4,842.00}{\$6,176.52 - \$5,320.70}(15-10)+10$$

$$= \frac{\$478.70}{\$855.82} \times 5 + 10 = 12.8 \ or \ 13 \ \text{years}$$

The service life of Alternative B (13 years) is greater than the service life of Alternative A for the same annual costs. Therefore, Alternative A is selected. This selection is again consistent with the selection made using the other methods discussed above.

Unequal Life Service-Producing Alternatives

In the examples above, the selection of service-producing investment alternatives with *equal service life* was assumed. The same techniques are used for selecting the economical service-producing investment alternatives with unequal lives, provided the lives of the alternatives are made equal for comparison purposes. In general, the methods presented here are not valid for comparing unequal life income or service-producing investments that do not result in the same service (these methods are presented in the next section).

To get a meaningful comparison of unequal life alternatives that provide the same service, assumptions or estimates must be made to permit comparison of the alternatives on an equal life (or equal study period) basis. Comparing project costs for unequal periods will mean comparing different total costs.[1]

A common service life is obtained by first carefully defining the time span required for the service, for instance, 10 years. Assume there are two alternatives, one with 10-year life and the other with 5-year life. To make the lives common, it is assumed the 5-year alternative will be replaced by another (like-for-like) 5-year alternative and then compared. Alternatively, it may be assumed the life of the 5-year alternative will be extended for another 5 years with a major overhaul at the end of Year 5.

The situation can be the other way around (i.e. the service is required for only 5 years). In this case, the extra 5 years of the 10-year life alternative are ignored and its salvage value at the end of Year 5 is considered. The alternative may be either sold at the end of Year 5, or it will be used elsewhere. If it is used elsewhere, it will have opportunity cost. In either case, it will have an alternative value.

If capitalized cost analysis is used for comparison, the life of the permanent life (perpetual) alternative is used as a common life and the preceding assumptions are not required.

Example 7–4

Two conveyors are being considered to handle ore in a smelting operation. Conveyor A will cost $15,000 with annual maintenance/operating costs of $2,000 and an expected salvage value of $10,000 at the end of its expected useful life of 6 years. Conveyor B will cost $4,500 with annual operating/maintenance costs of $4,000 and an expected salvage value of $2,500 at the end of its expected useful service life of 3 years. Both conveyors are technically compatible. If the minimum acceptable rate of return before taxes for investments of this type is 8%, determine the most economical alternative by PV_{cost} comparison if the (a) service is required for six years and (b) service is required for only three years.[1]

Solution: The useful life of Conveyor A is 6 years and Conveyor B is only 3 years. In the first case, it is assumed that at the end of three years, Conveyor B can be replaced (like-for-like) with another conveyor so the total

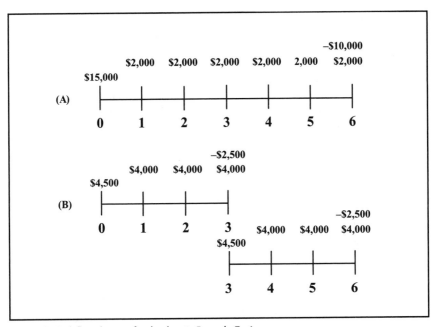

Fig. 7–3 Cash-flow diagram for the data in Example 7–4

service life of 6 years is achieved. The cash-flow diagram for this situation is as shown in Figure 7–3.

(a) $PV_A = \$15,000 + \$2,000(P/A_{8,6}) - \$10,000(P/F_{8,6})$
$= \$15,000 + \$2,000(4.623) - \$10,000(0.6302)$
$= \$17,944$

$PV_B = \$4,500 + \$4,000(P/A_{8,3}) - \$2,500(P/F_{8,3})$
$+ \$4,500(P/F_{8,3}) + \$4,000(P/A_{8,3})(P/F_{8,3})$
$- \$2,500(P/F_{8,6})$
$= \$4,500 + \$4,000(2.577) - \$2,500(0.7938)$
$+ \$4,500(0.7938) + \$4,000(2.577)(0.7938) - \$2,500(0.6302)$
$= \$23,002.6$

Therefore, Alternative A with $PV_A < PV_B$ should be selected.

(b) For this option, the life of the 6-year conveyor is shortened to 3 years, and it is assumed its salvage value will be $12,000 as compared to $10,000 after 6 years.

$$PV_A = \$15,000 + \$2,000(P/A_{8,3}) - \$12,000(P/F_{8,3})$$
$$= \$15,000 + \$2,000(2.577) - \$12,000(0.7938)$$
$$= \$10,628.4$$

$$PV_B = \$4,500 + \$4,000(P/A_{8,3}) - \$2,500(P/F_{8,3})$$
$$= \$4,500 + \$4,000(2.577) - \$2,500(0.7983)$$
$$= \$12,812.25$$

For the 3-year requirement, Alternative A is the economical choice. Cost estimates (both initial cost, annual operating/maintenance costs and salvage value) will increase due to inflation and tax consequences due to depreciation, if any, for the alternative to be replaced later. If replacement happens at the end of the initial 3-year period, its cost 3 years from now may be higher due to inflation so this should be accounted for rather than assuming that even after 3 years, the machine can be replaced at the same cost as today.

Lease Versus Buy Decision Analysis

For a business to use equipment for providing a product or service, it does not have to be owned. It can be leased. Equipment leasing provides customized financing with potentially unique tax features. J.S. Schallheim gives a detailed treatment of lease versus buy decisions in a very well-written book.[2]

In general, an asset is leased from a leasing company for a fixed duration of time at predetermined periodic lease payments during the lease period. Lease contracts can be written to provide the *lessee* with great flexibility in terms of the amount and timing of the lease payments. The ownership of the leased asset remains with the *lessor* in most leases (i.e. the lessee does not own the asset after completing all the contracted payments). However, the ownership does not affect the use of the asset by a lessee.

The economics of lease versus buy decisions are dependent on the tax rules applicable to a particular class of leases. The IRS specifies rules for tax-oriented leases. If a lease qualifies under the tax guidelines, it is called a *true lease*. Otherwise, the lease is a *conditional sales* contract under the IRS rules. Therefore, it is important to know the tax laws applicable for the leased asset under evaluation. Some of the major advantages of leasing are as follows.[2]

1. Leasing offers tax savings, thus advantageous for the firms with:
2.
   a. Excess tax shields
   b. Low earnings and/or low tax rates
3. Leasing offers financial cost savings.
   a. Permits 100% financing (i.e. it does not tie up capital and may, in some cases, require lower initial capital outlay thus freeing working capital for more productive use)
   b. Avoids restrictions inherent in debt contracts
   c. Increases a firm's ability to acquire funds, thus leaving normal line of bank credit undisturbed
4. Leasing offers transaction and information cost savings.
   a. Avoids the purchase transaction and may be tailored to the lessee's needs
   b. All costs related to the leased asset are known with certainty
   c. Requires less record keeping
5. Leasing provides risk sharing.
   a. Avoids the sale of asset no longer required in the lessee's operations
   b. Provides protection against asset obsolescence
   c. Provides a hedge against inflation and business risk

In leasing, the lessee is saving the upfront cost of purchasing the asset and in return commits to a series of periodic lease payments that are generally tax deductible. On the other hand, the lessee gives up depreciation tax shields and any other tax credits associated with ownership. Since lessee is saving the cost of purchasing the asset and is subject to tax swaps from tax shields, the Net Present Value (NPV) or Internal Rate of Return (IRR) can be used for the lease versus buy decision-making. The NPV in this context is also referred to as the |Net Advantage to Leasing (NAL).|The following equation is a general NPV or NAL formula used for lease versus buy analysis.

(7.1)

$$NPV = A_o - \sum_{t=0}^{n-1} \frac{L_t}{(1+r_1)^t} + \sum_{t=0}^{n-1} \frac{L_t(T)}{(1+r_2)^t} - \sum_{t=1}^{n} \frac{D_t(T)}{(1+r_3)^t} - \sum_{t=1}^{n} \frac{I_t(T)}{(1+r_4)^t}$$

$$+ \sum_{t=1}^{n} \frac{O_t(1-T)}{(1+r_5)^t} - \frac{S_n}{(1+r_6)^n} - TC$$

where

A_o = price of the asset, if purchased, at present time ($t = 0$)

L_t = lease payment at time t

D_t = depreciation charge, if owned, at time t

I_t = interest charge on the equivalent loan, if purchased with debt, at time t

O_t = operating expenses that are higher if the asset is purchased but not if the asset isleased

S_N = expected after-tax salvage value of the asset, if purchased, at time N

r = appropriate discount rate for each of the cash flows above

T = marginal corporate tax rate of the lease

n = number of time periods covered by the lease

T_C = tax credits applicable to the asset that are taken by the lessor and not the lessee

As discussed in Chapter 6, the asset cost A_o may be included in Equation (7.1) and the after-tax weighted average cost of capital used as a discount rate. On the other hand, the principal and interest payments and the cost of debt used as the discount rate may replace the A_o term. The two approaches—asset cost versus loan payments—are equivalent if the total cost of the asset is borrowed (100% financing) and the discount rate is the after-tax cost of debt. If the borrowing is not 100%, then the weighted average cost of capital can still be used provided constant ratio debt payment schedule is used.

Mayers, Dill, and Bautista (MDB) present another model. The MDB model simultaneously solves the problem of the proper discount rate for the cash flows and the equivalent amount of borrowing. This approach treats the amount of borrowing equivalent to the lease as the present value of the after-tax lease payments and depreciation tax shields, all discounted at the after-tax cost of debt. The following equation is proposed by MDB.[3]

(7.2)

$$NPV = A_o - \sum_{t=1}^{n} \frac{L_t(1-T) + D_t(T)}{[1+r_B(1-T)]^t} + \sum_{t=1}^{n} \frac{O_t(1-T)}{(1+r_1)^t} - \frac{S_n}{(1+r_2)^n}$$

where
r_B = the cost of debt
r_1, r_2 = represent the discount rates appropriate for the operating expenses and salvage value, respectively.

If the before-tax cost of debt is used as the discount rate, Equation (7.2) becomes,

(7.3)

$$NPV = A_o - \sum_{t=1}^{n} \frac{L_t(1-T) + D_t(T) - I_t(T)}{(1+r_B)^t} + \sum_{t=1}^{n} \frac{O_t(1-T)}{(1+r_1)^t} - \frac{S_n}{(1+r_2)^n}$$

Example 7–5

An oil company is either leasing or purchasing a pumping unit for a well. The purchase price of the unit is $40,000 with an estimated economic life of 5 years. The unit may be leased for annual year-end lease payments of $10,000 for 5 years. Calculate the Net Value of Leasing if (a) the salvage value of the unit is zero, (b) the operating costs for both options are same, (c) depreciation is straight line over 5 years, (d) the cost of before-tax cost of capital is 10%, and (e) the corporate tax rate is 35%.

Solution: The cash flow for Example 7–5 is shown in Table 7–1
Lease payment (net of taxes) = $10,000 x (1 – 0.35) = $6,500
Depreciation = 40,000/5 = $8,000
Tax saving due to depreciation = $8,000 x 0.35 = $2,800
After-tax cost of debt = $r_B(1 - T)$ = 10.0 x (1 – 0.35) = 6.5% OR 0.065

		1	2	3	4	5
Lease Payment	$L_t(1 - T)$	6,500	6,500	6,500	6,500	6,500
Depreciation Tax Shield	$D_t(T)$	2,800	2,800	2,800	2,800	2,800
Cost of Leasing	$L_t(1 - T) + D_t(T)$	9,300	9,300	9,300	9,300	9,300

Table 7–1 Cash flow for Example 7–5

Using Equation (7.2), the Net Advantage of Leasing (NAL) is,
$$\text{NAL} = \$40,000 - 9,300(1 + 0.065)^{-1} - 9,300(1 + 0.065)^{-2}$$
$$- 9,300(1 + 0.065)^{-3} - 9,300(1 + 0.065)^{-4}$$
$$- 9,300(1 + 0.065)^{-5}$$
$$= \$40,000 - 8,732.39 - 8,199.43 - 7,699.00 - 7,229.10$$
$$- 6,787.89$$
$$= \$1,352.19$$

Since the NAL is positive (+ve), the leasing option is the preferred choice.

Example 7–6

Rework Example 7–5, assuming the lease payment includes maintenance by the lessor, which will otherwise cost $1,000 per month. Also, assume the residual (salvage) value of the unit at the end of 5 years is 20% of the initial cost (i.e. $40,000 x 0.2 = $8,000).

Solution: The cash flow for this Example 7–6 is shown in Table 7–2. Note the new terms in the third line of the table show the after-tax operating cost savings (positive) and the fourth line captures the after-tax residual value lost (negative). The residual value *lost* is because the unit is fully depreciated (zero book value) at the end of Year 5. Therefore, the $8,000 will be considered as a capital gain, which will be fully taxed.

Using Equation (7.2), the Net Advantage of Leasing (NAL) is,
$$\text{NAL} = \$40,000 - 8,090(1 + 0.065)^{-1} - 8,090(1 + 0.065)^{-2}$$
$$- 8,090(1 + 0.065)^{-3} - 8,090(1 + 0.065)^{-4}$$
$$- 13,290(1 + 0.065)^{-5}$$
$$= \$2,585,18$$

Since the NAL is positive (+ve), the leasing option is the preferred choice.

		1	2	3	4	5
Lease Payment	$L_t(1-T)$	6,500	6,500	6,500	6,500	6,500
Depreciation Tax Shield	$D_t(T)$	2,240	2,240	2,240	2,240	2,240
Operating Cost Savings	$O_t(1-T)$	–650	–650	–650	–650	–650
Residual Value	$S_N(1-T)$					5200
Cost of Leasing	$L_t(1-T)+D_t(T)$	8,090	8,090	8,090	8,090	13,290
	$+ O_t(1-T)$					
	$- S_N(1-T)$					

Table 7-2 Cash flow for Example 7–6.

To calculate the internal rate of return (IRR) or yield for lease contracts, the before-tax cost of capital is calculated by trial-and-error that
will result in NAL = 0. The following equation is used.

(7.4)

$$A_o - L_t \frac{\left(1 + IRR_{leasing}\right)^t - 1}{IRR_{leasing}\left(1 + IRR_{leasing}\right)^t} = 0$$

Using Equation (7.4), the before-tax lease yield for Example 7–5 is calculated as follows.

For $IRR_{Leasing}$ = 10%, Equation (7.4) becomes,

$$\$40,000 - \$10,000\frac{\left(1 + 0.10^5\right) - 1}{0.10\left(1 + 0.10\right)^5} = \$2,092.13$$

For $IRR_{leasing}$ = 5%, Equation (7.4) becomes,

$$\$40,000 - \$10,000\frac{\left(1 + 0.05\right)^5 - 1}{0.05\left(1 + 0.05\right)^5} = -\$3,294.77$$

Therefore, $IRR_{Leasing}$ by linear interpolation is

$$IRR_{leasing} = \frac{3,294.77}{3,294.77 + 2,092.13}(10 - 5) + 5 = 8.06\%$$

The before-tax yield is about 8.06%, compared to the before-tax cost
of capital of 10%. According to this criterion, leasing is preferred. If the

before-tax yield were higher than the before-tax cost of capital, the purchase option would be the preferred choice.

INCOME-PRODUCING INVESTMENTS

In the preceding section, profitability measures were applied to the investment analysis of service-producing investments. In this section, the same profitability measures will be applied to the analysis of income-producing investment alternatives. The alternatives to be discussed include:

1. Project screening economics (single/independent investment analysis).
2. Mutually exclusive investment analysis.
3. Non-mutually exclusive investment analysis.
4. Economics of rate acceleration projects.

Most of the profitability measures presented in the previous chapter, if properly used, will result in the same investment decision. The objective is to maximize the total worth of the investing organization.

Project Screening Economics

In this type of analysis, each investment alternative, whether it is a part of mutually exclusive alternatives or non-mutually exclusive alternatives, will be screened. A decision is made whether the alternative is economical or not, i.e. accept or reject decision. If the alternative is not economical, it is rejected and not considered for analysis as part of the mutually exclusive or non-mutually exclusive alternatives. All the economically accepted investments will then be further analyzed as part of either mutually exclusive alternatives or non-mutually exclusive alternatives. As mentioned previously, if funds are unlimited, all investment alternatives that survive the screening criteria will be undertaken.

In this case, the first step is to carefully select screening criteria based on which alternatives will be screened (i.e. the minimum acceptable rate of return or cost of capital and the desired payback period). Benchmarks should be in place. For example, a company may not accept any project with payout greater than 3 years or with a rate of return less than 15% and so on. Using this minimum acceptable rate of return, compute the various profitability measures discussed in Chapter 6. As mentioned above, any one of the profitability measures if properly used, will result in the same accept or reject decision. The decision rules are summarized in Table 7–3. The following example will clarify the use of profitability measures as applied to revenue-producing investment alternatives.

Profitability Measure	ACCEPT IF	REJECT IF
Payback Period @ i_d	<= Desired	>= Desired
Net Present Value (NPV) @ i_d	> 0	< 0
Internal Rate of Return (IRR)	> i_d	< i_d
Profitability Index (PI) @ i_d	> 1	< 1
Present Value Ratio (PVR) @ i_d	> 0	< 0
Technical Cost @ i_d	< Average Product Price	> Average Product Price
Growth Rate of Return (GRR) @ i_d	> i_d	< i_d

Table 7–3 Summary of profitability measures and decision rules

Example 7–7

A company has an opportunity to invest money. Two investment alternatives are considered with estimated initial investment and expected cash inflows given below. If the company's minimum acceptable rate of return is 8% and the company has enough funds to invest in both alternatives, should the investments be accepted? Base your decision on (a) NPV analysis, (b) IRR analysis, (c) PI analysis, (d) PVR analysis, and (e) GRR analysis.

	0	1	2	3	4	5	6	7	8
A	-1,000	700	600	500	300	200	0	0	0
B	-1,500	750	650	550	450	300	250	150	100

Solution:

(a) $NPV_A = -1,000 + 700(1 + 0.08)^{-1} + 600(1 + 0.08)^{-2}$
$+ 500(1 + 0.08)^{-3} + 300(1 + 0.08)^{-4} + 200(1 + 0.08)^{-5}$
$= \$916.10$

$NPV_B = -1,500 + 750(1 + 0.08)^{-1} + 650(1 + 0.08)^{-2}$
$+ 550(1 + 0.08)^{-3} + 450(1 + 0.08)^{-4} + 300(1 + 0.08)^{-5}$
$+ 250(1 + 0.08)^{-6} + 150(1 + 0.08)^{-7} + 100(1 + 0.08)^{-8}$
$= \$1,022.35$

Both investment alternatives have positive NPV ($NPV_A > 0$ and $NPV_B > 0$). Therefore, both of them are acceptable, provided there are enough funds to implement the two investments.

(b)   For the calculation of IRR, NPVs at various discount rates are calculated as shown below.

Discount Rate	NPV_A	NPV_B
0.05	$1,046.32	$1,245.08
0.10	836.98	890.61
0.15	662.10	608.91
0.20	514.40	381.10
0.25	388.42	193.99
0.30	279.98	38.19
0.35	185.88	-93.15
0.40	103.62	-205.09
0.45	31.21	-301.44
0.50	-32.92	-385.12

By linear interpolation, the IRR for each project is,

$$IRR_A = \frac{31.21}{31.21 + 32.92}(0.50 - 0.45) + 0.45 = 0.4743 \ or \ 47.43\%$$

$$IRR_B = \frac{38.19}{38.19 + 93.15}(0.35 - 0.30) + 0.30 = 0.3145 \ or \ 31.45\%$$

Since the $IRR_A > i_d = 8\%$ and $IRR_B > i_d = 8\%$, both investments are acceptable.

(c) The PI and PVR are calculated as follows,

$$PVR_A = \frac{NPV_A}{(I_o)_A} = \frac{916.10}{1,000} = 0.9161$$

$$PVR_B = \frac{NPV_B}{(I_o)_B} = \frac{1,022.35}{1,500} = 0.6816$$

Since $PVR_A > 0$ and $PVR_B > 0$, both investments are accepted.
(d) For the PI analysis, $PI_A = 1 + PVR_A = 1.9161 > 1$ and $PI_B = 1 + PVR_B = 1.6816 > 1$, therefore both the projects are accepted according to the PI decision criterion.

(e) For the calculation of GRR, we assume the available reinvestment rate will be the same as the minimum acceptable rate of return of 8%. The GRR has to be calculated for the same project life (eight years) for both projects, even though Project A's life is 3 years shorter than Project B.

$$GRR_A = \left[(1 + PVR_A)^{1/8} \times (1 + i_d) - 1\right] \times 100$$
$$= \left[(1 + 0.9161)^{1/8} \times (1 + 0.08) - 1\right] \times 100$$
$$= (1.0847 \times 1.08 - 1) \times 100 = 17.15\%$$

$$GRR_B = \left[(1 + PVR_B)^{1/8} \times (1 + i_d) - 1\right] \times 100$$
$$= \left[(1 + 0.6816)^{1/8} \times (1 + 0.08) - 1\right] \times 100$$
$$= (1.0671 \times 1.08 - 1) \times 100 = 15.25\%$$

Based on the GRR, since $GRR_A > 8\%$ and $GRR_B > 8\%$, both the projects are economical and therefore accepted.

Mutually Exclusive Investment Analysis

In this type of investment alternative, several opportunities will exist, but only one investment alternative is selected. The other alternatives are abandoned. The first step, as discussed previously, is to screen each alternative and consider which are economically and technically acceptable. Therefore, the first step is always to apply "accept or reject" criteria. The accepted projects are then further analyzed against each other. Once again, any of the profitability yardsticks discussed in the previous chapter, if properly used, will provide selection of the most economical alternative out of the available alternatives. The following rules will result in the selection of the economic choice.

1. *Select the alternative with the highest NPV.* The NAV and NFV may be used in the same way except for unequal life investments, in which case the life of the longest life alternative should be used as a common life. The disadvantage in using NPV criterion is it does not provide the magnitude of the return per dollar invested.

2. *The use of PI, PVR, IRR or GRR will give conflicting selections.* For example, if the investments given in Example 7–7 are mutually exclusive, then the following selections will result.
   a. NPV will select Alternative B, since $NPV_B > NPV_A$.
   b. On the contrary, the IRR, PI, PVR, and GRR will select Alternative A since $IRR_A > IRR_B$, $PI_A > PI_B$, $PVR_A > PVR_B$, and $GRR_A > GRR_B$. However, in order to maximize net worth, Alternative A with the higher NPV will be the most economical choice.

3. *To avoid this conflicting selection situation, the IRR, PI, PVR or GRR must be applied to the incremental cash flows of any two mutually exclusive alternatives.* For example, perform incremental IRR analysis on two alternatives at a time. If the incremental IRR is greater than the minimum acceptable rate of return, select the investment with the higher initial cost, or vice versa. If there are more than two mutually exclusive alternatives, the survivor of the first two sets of alternatives is then compared with the third alternative, and so on. Similarly, if the

PI of the incremental cash flow is greater than zero, then select the investment with the higher initial cost, and vise versa.

Selection of the lower initial cost alternative will mean that it is not worth it to make the incremental investment in the higher initial cost investment alternative (i.e. it will be better to invest the incremental capital elsewhere at the minimum acceptable rate of return).

Example 7-8

Rework Example 7–7, keeping in mind the alternatives are mutually exclusive (i.e. only one of the alternatives has to be selected). Based on the appropriate profitability analysis, (using NPV, IRR, PI, PVR, and GRR), which of the two alternatives will result in the most economical choice if only $1,500 are available for investment?

Solution:

(a) $NPV_A = \$916.10$ (from Example 7–7)
$NPV_B = \$1,022.35$ (from Example 7–7)

Since NPV_B is greater than NPV_A; therefore, select Investment B
(b) To use IRR, PI, PVR and/or GRR, the incremental analysis are as follows. The incremental cash flows for the two investments follow.

	0	1	2	3	4	5	6	7	8
A	1,000	700	600	500	300	200	0	0	0
B	1,500	750	650	550	450	300	250	150	100
B – A	500	50	50	50	150	100	250	150	100

The NPV, IRR, PI, PVR and GRR for the incremental cash flow (B – A) are:

$NPV_{(B - A)} @ i_d = 8\%$ is,

$$
\begin{aligned}
NPV_{(B - A)} &= -500 + 50(1 + 0.08)^{-1} + 50(1 + 0.08)^{-2} \\
&\quad + 50(1 + 0.08)^{-3} + 150(1 + 0.08)^{-4} + 100(1 + 0.08)^{-5} \\
&\quad + 250(1 + 0.08)^{-6} + 250(1 + 0.08)^{-7} + 100(1 + 0.08)^{-8} \\
&= -500 + 46.30 + 42.87 + 39.69 + 110.25 + 68.06 \\
&\quad + 157.54 + 145.87 + 54.03 \\
&= \$164.61
\end{aligned}
$$

Since the $NPV_{(B - A)} > 0$, Alternative B with the higher initial cost is selected. This selection is consistent with the selection made in "(a)" above. To calculate the IRR of the incremental cash flow, calculate the $NPV_{(B - A)}$ at another discount rate (i.e. $i_d = 15\%$).

$NPV_{(B - A)} @ i_d = 15\%$ is,

$$
\begin{aligned}
NPV_{(B - A)} &= -500 + 50(1 + 0.15)^{-1} + 50(1 + 0.15)^{-2} + 50(1 + 0.15)^{-3} \\
&\quad + 150(1 + 0.15)^{-4} + 100(1 + 0.15)^{-5} + 250(1 + 0.15)^{-6} \\
&\quad + 250(1 + 0.15)^{-7} + 100(1 + 0.15)^{-8} \\
&= -500 + 43.48 + 37.81 + 32.88 + 85.76 + 49.72 \\
&\quad + 108.08 + 93.98 + 32.69 \\
&= -\$15.60
\end{aligned}
$$

Therefore, $IRR_{(B - A)}$ by linear interpolation is,

$$
IRR_{(B-A)} = \frac{164.61}{164.61 + 15.60}(15 - 8) + 8
$$

$$
= 0.9134 \times 7 + 8 = 14.39\%
$$

Since $IRR_{(B - A)} = 14.39\% > i_d = 8\%$, Alternative B with the higher initial investment is accepted. Similarly, the PI, PVR and GRR of the incremental cash flow at a discount rate of 8% are:

$$
PVR_{(B-A)} = \frac{NPV_{(B-A)} @ 8\%}{500} = \frac{164.61}{500} = 0.329
$$

$$
PI_{(B-A)} = 1 + PI_{(B-A)} = 1.329
$$

$$
\begin{aligned}
GRR_{(B-A)} &= \left[1 + PVR_{(B-A)}\right]^{1/t} \times (1 + i_d) - 1 \\
&= (1.329)^{1/8} \times 1.08) - 1 = 0.1191 \ or \ 11.91\%
\end{aligned}
$$

Since $PVR_{(B-A)} = 0.329 > 0$, $PI_{(B-A)} = 1.329 > 1.0$, and $GRR_{(B-A)}$ = 11.91% > i_d = 8%; select Alternative B. If the $NPV_{(B-A)} < 0$, $IRR_{(B-A)}$ < i_d, $PVR_{(B-A)} < 0$, $PI_{(B-A)} < 1.0$, and/or $GRR_{(B-A)} < i_d$ then Alternative A will be selected and the remaining \$500 will be invested in the alternative providing a return of i_d = 8%. This combination will maximize the return on total investment of \$1,500.

The NPV profile is used to find out if incremental analyses are required. NPV profile of an investment under consideration is a graphic presentation of its NPVs at various discount rates. If several investment alternatives are under consideration, their NPVs are plotted versus their respective discount rate (i.e. NPV vs. i_d) on the same graph paper as shown in Figure 7–4. Figure 7–5 shows the NPV profiles for the investment alternatives in Example 7–8. The NPV profile is a useful graphic illustration having the following advantages:

1. The profile shows sensitivity of each investment alternative to the timing and discount rate. In Figure 7–5, Investment B is more sensitive to discounting than Investment A. In Figure 7–4, the two investments have similar behavior.

2. The profile tells if a unique decision can be made by using any of the regular *(non-incremental)* investment analysis techniques. If the investments' NPV profiles are as shown in Figure 7–4 (the profiles do not intersect), then using any of the regular investment analysis techniques will provide consistent selections. When the profiles intersect each other as shown in Figure 7–5, then incremental analysis are required. The intersection is referred to as the Fisherian intersection.

3. The NPV profile shows the range of minimum acceptable rate of return in which each investment alternative is preferred. If there is no fixed minimum guideline (not sure of the cost of capital), the profile provides a range. In Figure 7–5, if the cost of capital is less than 12.33% (the intersection of two profiles for investments A and B), then Investment B is preferred. If the cost of capital is between 31.37% (IRR_B) and 47.36% (IRR_A), then Investment A is preferred. At the Fisherian intersection (i.e. if the cost of capital is 12.33%), the investor will be indifferent (i.e. selection of either alternative will give same result).

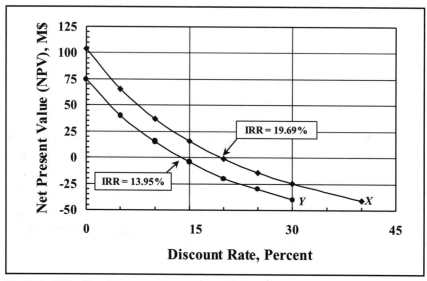

Fig. 7–4 NPV profiles of two investments, without Fisherian intersection

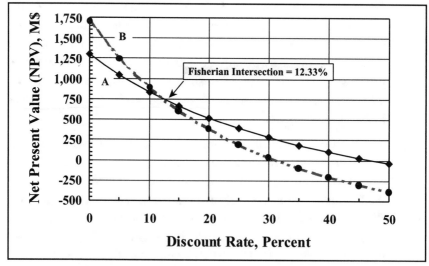

Fig. 7–5 NPV profiles (with Fisherian intersection) for the investments in Example 7–8

4. If Fisherian intersection exists, one investment can have an IRR superior to the other, yet have an inferior NPV over one or more ranges of discount rate. Therefore, if an investment is selected according to the IRR only, the selection will be sub-optimal if the actual discount rate falls below the Fisherian intersection. Investment selection using IRR is appropriate only if it can be proven the Fisherian intersection does not exist between zero and the IRR of the lower of the two investments' IRRs.

Example 7–9

A company has an opportunity to invest $1,500,000. Three mutually exclusive investment alternatives are considered with the investments and expected cash flows as given below. If the company's cost of capital is 15%, which of the three investment alternatives should be selected in order to maximize the net worth of the company? Base your decision on (a) NPV analysis, (b) IRR analysis, and (c) PI analysis.

	Investment A	Investment B	Investment C
Initial investment	$500,000	$800,000	$1,000,000
Annual revenues	100,000	150,000	200,000
Annual expenses	10,000	13,000	30,000
Investment life (years)	20	20	20
Salvage value	50,000	75,000	100,000

Solution: First the NPV at $i = 15\%$ is calculated for each investment.

(a) $NPV_A = -\$500,000 + (100,000 - 10,000)(P/A_{15,20})$
$+ 50,000(P/F_{15,20})$
$= -\$500,000 + 90,000(6.2593) + 50,000(.0611)$
$= \$66,392.00$

$NPV_B = -\$800,000 + (150,000 - 13,000)(P/A_{15,20})$
$+ 75,000(P/F_{15,20})$
$= -\$800,000 + 857,524.10 + 4,582.5$
$= \$62,106.60$

$$NPV_C = -\$1,000,000 + (200,000 - 30,000)(P/A_{15,20})$$
$$+ 100,000(P/F_{15,20})$$
$$= -\$1000,000 + 1,064,081 + 6110$$
$$= \$70,191$$

(b) For the calculation of IRR, NPV at $i = 20\%$ is calculated for each investment.
$$NPV_A = -\$500,000 + 90,000(P/A_{20,20}) + 50,000(P/F_{20,20})$$
$$= -\$500,000 + 90,000(4.8696) + 50,000(0.0261)$$
$$= -\$500,000 + 438,264 + 1,305$$
$$= -\$60,431.00$$

Similarly,
$$NPV_B = -\$130,907.30$$

$$NPV_C = -\$169,558.00$$

Therefore, IRR for each investment alternative (by linear interpolation) is,

$$IRR_A = \frac{66,392}{66,392 + 60,431}(20 - 15) + 15 = 17.62\%$$

$$IRR_B = \frac{66,106}{66,106 + 130,907.3}(20 - 15) + 15 = 16.61\%$$

and
$$IRR_C = 16.46\%$$

The PVRs for each investment are,

$$PVR_A = \frac{NPV_A @15\%}{I_A} = \frac{66,392}{500,000} = 0.133$$

$$PVR_B = \frac{NPV_B @15\%}{I_B} = \frac{62,106}{800,000} = 0.078$$

$$PVR_C = \frac{NPV_C @15\%}{I_C} = \frac{70,191}{1,000,000} = 0.070$$

The profitability indicators show all the investments are economical. Since the investments are mutually exclusive, only one of them has to be selected. Note the *NPV of each investment shows Investment C should be selected while the IRR shows Investment A should be selected.* The NPV profiles as shown in Figure 7–6 intersect each other, therefore, incremental analyses are required.

First, incremental analysis of Investments A and B are done,

$$NPV_{(B-A)} = -\$300,000 + 47,000(P/A_{15,20}) + 25,000(P/F_{15,20})$$
$$= -\$300,000 + 47,000(6.2593) + 25,000(0.0611)$$
$$= -\$4,285.40$$

Since the $NPV_{(B-A)}$ is less than zero, Investment A with the lower initial investment is selected. Similarly, since the $NPV_{(B-A)}$ at 15% is less than zero, the $IRR_{(B-A)}$ is less than i_d=15%. This also means Investment A should be selected. Now the survivor (Investment A) will be compared with Investment C.

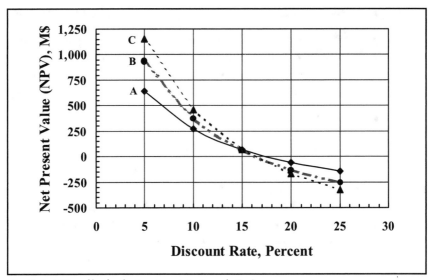

Fig. 7–6 NPV profiles for the investments in Example 7–9

$$NPV_{(C-A)} = -\$500,000 + 80,000(P/A_{15,20})$$
$$+ 50,000(P/F_{15,20})$$
$$= -\$500,000 + 80,000(6.2593) + 50,000(0.0611)$$
$$= \$3,799$$

Since $NPV_{(C-A)}$ is greater than zero, Investment C with the higher initial cost is selected.

Example 7–10

A company is producing crude oil and associated gas from one of its offshore locations. The crude oil is transported to the tank farms through a dedicated flowline. The gas is stripped at the station into gas and raw NGL. The gas and raw NGL are transported to onshore gas processing facility through 89-kilometer, 24-inch, and 12-inch pipelines, respectively. However, the 12-inch NGL line is old and not reliable. The company is considering the following options.

1. Spike the stripped NGLs into the crude line and sell as crude oil.

2. Replace the 12-inch NGL pipeline with a new pipeline of the same diameter. This option will cost $37 million. It will take approximately 30 months (starting 01/01/2003) to install the new line. The NGLs will be spiked into crude until the pipeline is replaced.

The resulting production streams for Option 1 and Option 2 are given in Table 7–4. The raw NGL if transported to gas processing facility is split into Ethane (C_2) and LPG (C_{3+}). Assume the price of crude (net of operating expenses) to be $17/Stb, the price of C_2 as $22/Ton, and the price of C_{3+} as $175/Ton. The capital expenditure is phased as 30% in 2002, 60% in 2003, and 10% in 2004. If the company's minimum acceptable rate of return is 10%, which option should be selected?

Solution: The cash flows for each option are shown in Table 7–5. Since the NPV of Option 1 is higher than the NPV of Option 2, Option 1 is recommended for implementation.

	2002	2003	2004	2005	2006	2007	2008	2009	2010
Crude, Stb/d	1,807	1,580	2,174	2,045	1,988	1,889	1,785	1,669	1,540
Ethane, T/d	80	76	80	73	70	68	62	55	50
LPG, T/d	321	279	340	323	316	299	272	242	238

Table 7–4 Production forecast for the problem in Example 7–10

	OPTION 1			OPTION 2						
	Crude	Crude	Net	Crude	C_2	C_{3}+	Product Price			Net
	Prod.	Price	Rev.	Prod.	Prod.	Prod.	C_2	C_{3}+	CAPEX	Rev.
Year	Stb/d	$/Stb	MM$	Stb/d	T/d	T/d	$/T	$/T	MM$	MM$
2002	1,807	17.00	11.21	1,807			22	175	10.50	0.71
2003	1,580	17.00	9.80	1,580			22	175	21.00	(11.20)
2004	2,174	17.00	13.49	1,087	40	170	22	175	3.50	14.42
2005	2,045	17.00	12.69		73	323	22	175		21.22
2006	1,988	17.00	12.34		70	316	22	175		20.75
2007	1,889	17.00	11.72		68	299	22	175		19.64
2008	1,785	17.00	11.08		62	272	22	175		17.87
2009	1,669	17.00	10.36		55	242	22	175		15.90
2010	1,540	17.00	9.56		50	238	22	175		15.60
TOTAL			102.24						35.00	114.93
NPV			65.94							63.90

Table 7–5 Economics of pipeline replacement (Example 7–10)

Non-Mutually Exclusive Investment Analysis

In most firms, there are more proposals for investments than the firm is able or willing to finance (i.e. budget constraint). Some proposals are good, others are bad, and methods must be developed for distinguishing between the good and the bad. Essentially, the result is ranking of the proposals and a cutoff point for determining how far down the ranked list to go. In this type of investment analysis, several investment alternatives will be available and more than one may be selected, depending on the availability of funds. The investments have to be selected in such a way the total worth of the investor is maximized within the budget constraint (i.e. available investment dollars).

The ranking criterion is only necessary when the investment funds are in short supply or are limited by management strategy/policy. The first step is the same as in the previous section, i.e. apply accept or reject criteria. Only the economically acceptable investments are then considered. The following rules apply.

1. Select the investments that will yield the highest cumulative NPV within the budget constraint. When there are several alternatives, the NPV criterion becomes cumbersome because several different combinations will have to be tried in order to arrive at the maximized net worth.

2. IRR analysis, due to its limitations and conflicting results, cannot be applied to this type of decision analysis.

3. Investments are selected in order of decreasing PI, PVR, or GRR until the desired budget level is reached. The GRR has to be calculated based on equal economic life of the investments, the economic life of the longer life investment has to be used. Some analysts overlook this requirement of GRR, which leads to inconsistent results.[4]

Some analysts suggest the investor should assemble all its investment opportunities into a capital demand schedule. This is a table showing the total investment available to the investor for any given IRR cutoff. Similarly, the investor prepares a capital supply schedule tabulating the total capital funds it can obtain below any given cutoff rate. If both the schedules are plotted on the same graph paper, the intersection simultaneously determines how much to invest and what the cutoff rate should be. This type of graph is shown in Figure 7–7 (projects' IRR data taken form Table 7–6).

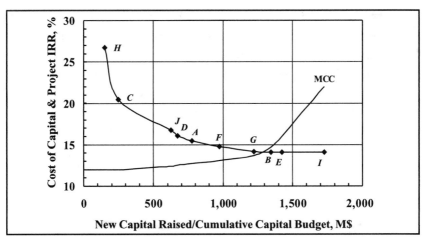

Fig. 7–7 Interfacing the MCC and IRR curves to determine the total capital budget

Year	A	B	C	D	E	F	G	H	I	J
0	−100	−120	−100	−50	−80	−200	−250	−150	−300	−375
1	45	35	35	17	24	60	80	60	100	150
2	35	30	30	15	20	55	70	55	85	120
3	25	25	25	12	17	50	60	50	75	100
4	20	22	22	10	15	45	50	45	60	80
5	15	21	21	8	13	40	40	40	45	45
6		19	19	6	11	35	30	35	35	35
7		15	15	5	9	30	20	30	20	20
8		13	13	4	7		15		13	13
9		12	12	3	6		12		12	12
10		11	11	3	5		10		10	10
11				2	5		8		8	8
12					3		6		6	6
13					2					
14					2					
NPV, M$	11.6	17.3	37.3	9.6	11.8	28.3	32.5	78.3	36.2	68.0
IRR, %	15.48	14.12	20.44	16.10	14.12	14.75	14.20	26.73	14.08	16.75
GRR , %	10.87	11.06	12.52	11.39	11.09	11.04	10.96	13.35	10.9	11.32
PI	1.116	1.144	1.373	1.192	1.148	1.141	1.130	1.522	1.121	1.181

Table 7–6 Cash flows for 10 different investments for Example 7–11

The method implies the cost of capital of the incremental funds required to finance the incremental investments increases (i.e. the marginal cost of capital increases with increased leverage). Therefore, an investor will take on investments to the point where the marginal returns from investment are just equal to their estimated marginal cost of capital (MCC).

Remember, in the selection of non-mutually exclusive investments, not all of the available cash may be evenly invested in the available alternatives. The remaining cash will be invested elsewhere at the minimum acceptable rate of return, i.e. cost of capital. The following example shows the ranking of non-mutually exclusive investments.

Example 7–11

The cash flows of 10 different investment alternatives are given in Table 7–6. Calculate the NPV, IRR, PI, and GRR for each investment. If the available funds are limited to $1.2 million, select the investments that will maximize the net worth of the investor. The minimum acceptable rate of return and the reinvestment rate of the investor are 12%.

Solution: The ranking of the projects based on NPV, IRR, PI, and GRR are shown in Table 7–7. To maximize the net worth of the investor within the budget constraint, the PIs of the investments are plotted against the cumulative investments as shown in Figure 7–8. The investments falling below the capital constraint of $1.2 million are selected. The selected investments will yield a net worth of $250.56 million for a total investment of $1.075 million. The balance of $0.125 million will be invested elsewhere at the investor's minimum acceptable rate of return. Ranking the projects, using descending order of IRR, will give a net worth of $233.06 million for a total investment of $0.975 million.

NPV	H	J	C	I	G	F	B	E	A	D
IRR	H	C	J	D	A	F	G	B	E	I
PI	H	C	D	J	E	B	F	G	I	A
GRR	H	C	D	J	E	B	F	G	I	A

Table 7–7 Ranking investments of Table 7–6 (Example 7–11)

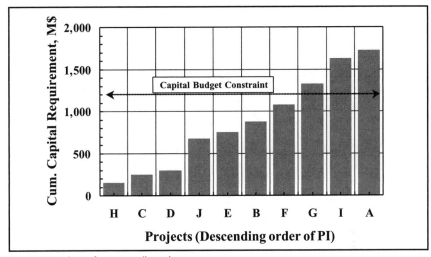

Fig. 7–8 Ranking of non-mutually exclusive investments

QUESTIONS and PROBLEMS

7.1 Give two examples of (a) mutually exclusive projects, (b) non-mutually exclusive projects, (c) complementary projects, and (d) substitute projects.

7.2 How would the NPV, IRR, GRR, and PI be used to select among mutually exclusive investment alternatives?

7.3 How would the NPV, IRR, GRR, and PI be used to rank non-mutually exclusive investment alternatives?

7.4 How the NPV, IRR, GRR, and PI screen investments?

7.5 After using a Machine A for 5 years, the company has an opportunity to purchase Machine B, which would replace Machine A. Machine B would have a 5-year life, cost $80,000, have a salvage value of $20,000, generate gross revenue of $150,000 per year, and reduce operating expenses by $10,000 per year. If investing in Machine B replaces Machine A, the amount realized on the sale of Machine A would be $30,000.
   a. What change in cash flow does replacing Machine A create?
   b. Calculate the NPV for the investment in Machine B.
   c. Compare the NPV of Machine B to the NPV of Machine A. Should Machine A be replaced by Machine B if the cost of capital is 12%?
   d. Rework Part C above using IRR as a decision criterion.

7.6 Two investment alternatives are under consideration, both require $20,000 each. Investment Alternative A will generate net cash flow of $9,000 in each of the first two years and $2,500 in the third year. Investment B will generate $2,500 in each of the first two years and $7,000 in each of the last three years. Calculate the payback period and NPV for each investment. If the alternatives are mutually exclusive and the opportunity cost of the investor is 8%, which alternative should be selected based on (a) payback period and (b) net present value?

7.7 A small independent oil company is considering investing some money in a drilling prospect. Two prospects are under consideration out of which only one will be drilled this year. The initial drilling and completion costs and net revenues (revenues – expenses) are provided below.

	Prospect A	Prospect B
Drilling and Completion Cost	-$800,000	-$1,500,000
Net Revenue, Years 1 to 5	$200,000	$300,000
Net Revenue, years 6 to 10	$70,000	$120,000

a. Compute the payback period for each investment.
b. Based on NPV analysis, which prospect should be selected if the company's minimum acceptable rate of return is 12%?
c. Compute the IRR for each investment, if the investment with the highest IRR is the economic choice, which prospect should be selected? Is the selection consistent with the selection made using NPV analysis? Why?

7.8 Assume an investor has to evaluate the following three projects:

	Cash flow					
	0	1	2	3	4	5
Project A	-1,200	150	150	150	150	150
Project B	-1,200	280	280	280	280	280
Project B	-1,200	-	-	-	-	2,000

a. Calculate the NPV of each of the above projects, assuming a 10% discount rate, and rank the projects.
b. Calculate the IRR for each of the above projects and rank the projects.
c. Calculate the NPV of each of the above projects based on 6% discount rate and rank the projects.
d. Calculate the NPV of each of the above projects based on 15% discount rate and rank the projects.
e. Compare and explain the ranking obtained in parts (a) to (d) above, using a diagram that graphs the NPV as a function of discount rate.

7.9   Three mutually exclusive investment alternatives are under consideration. The initial capital outlays and the pattern of the net annual cash benefits (revenues – expenses) for each alternative are presented in the table below. Based on NPV analysis, if the company's minimum acceptable rate of return is 10%, which alternative should be the best economic choice?

	Investment		
	A	B	C
Initial Cost, M$	-200	-350	-500
Net Revenue (Yr 1 to 3)	80	105	85
Net Revenue (year 4)	60	90	150
Net Revenue (year 5)	40	80	250
Net Revenue (year 6)	20	75	350

7.10

	0	1	2	3	4	5
Project A	-48,675	17,000	17,000	17,000	17,000	17,000
Project B	-31,575	12,000	12,000	12,000	12,000	12,000

    Consider the following two mutually exclusive investment opportunities:

a.   Calculate each investment's NPV and IRR (assume the cost of capital is 8%).

b.   Which of the two investments would be chosen according to the IRR criterion? Which according to the NPV criterion?

c.   Explain the differences in rankings given by the NPV and IRR methods in each case.

7.11   Calculate the IRR, PI, and GRR for the three investments in Problem 7.9. Do all these indicators give the same selection? If the selection using these profitability yardsticks is not consistent with the selection in Problem 7.9, then use appropriate incremental analysis to defend your finding in Problem 7.9.

7.12 A small independent oil company has $2,000,000 to invest in 2002. The company has four drilling prospects, all of which are considered of equal risk but their initial drilling and completion costs and the patterns of their generated benefits are different. The cash-flow pattern for each prospect is given below. Using the various profitability indicators presented in this chapter, which one or more of the available prospects should be drilled to maximize the investment worth of the company. The money can be invested elsewhere at a rate of 8%.

Prospect	2002	2003	2004	2005	2006	2007	2008	2009	2010	2011
A	-450	150	150	150	150	150				
B	-550	300	210	147	103	72				
C	-1,000	400	350	300	250	200	150	100	50	
D	-1,500	500	475	450	425	400	350	300	250	200

7.13 Consider the investment of Problem 7.12. Use PVR analysis to select the best economic combination of prospects that will maximize the profit within the budget constraint of $2,000,000.

7.14 The XYZ oil company has recently drilled an oil well. The company has tested two productive formations approximately 1000 feet apart. According to state regulations, only one formation can be produced at a time. This means dual or commingle completions are not allowed. The lower formation will be put on production at a rate of 1500 barrels/month declining exponentially at a rate of 30% per year to economic limit of 252 barrels/month. To produce the other formation, the company has two alternatives (A) to complete the behind pipe formation after the lower formation is depleted, or (B) drill a twin well now to produce the upper formation. The recompletion cost of Alternative A would be $80,000. The drilling of twin well will cost $850,000 now. In either case, the formation will produce at a rate of 1500 barrels/month and declining exponentially at a rate of 25% per year to the economic limit of 150 barrels/month. In each case, the operating expenses are estimated to be $3,900 per month, and the oil price would be $22 per barrel. Using an appropriate technique, select the best economic choice (assume the discount rate to be 15%).

7.15   Three mutually exclusive investment alternatives are available. Alternative A costs $400,000—it will generate net revenue of $200,000 per year for the next 5 years. Alternative B costs $850,000—it will generate $400,000 in year 1 and then decrease by a constant gradient of $50,000 for each of the next four years. Alternative C will cost $1,500,000—it will generate net revenue of $500,000 in each of the first 3 years and $300,000 per year in the remaining two years. The opportunity cost of capital is 15%. Basing your decision on NPV analysis, which alternative should be selected? Use appropriate IRR analysis to double-check your selection.

7.16   A gas well at a cost of $450,000 has just been completed. Due to the poor gas market, the pipeline companies will not purchase gas at deliverability. If they do purchase the gas at deliverability, they will pay only half the regular price of $6/MScf for 4 years and then pay the regular price thereafter. Alternatively, they will pay the regular price but take half the deliverability for 2 years and starting the 3rd year, they will purchase gas at the deliverability and pay $7/MScf for the remaining life of the well. The well's deliverability is $10,000 MScf/month declining exponentially at 30% per year to the economic limit of 575 MScf/month. If the well is curtailed, it will produce at 5000 MScf/month for the next 2 years, starting the 3rd year, the rate will be back to normal at 6400 MScf/month declining at 20% to the economic limit of 575 MScf/month. The operating expenses and taxes in each case amount to $3,500/month. If the opportunity cost of capital of the company is 15%, which alternative should be selected?

7.17   A company is considering acquisition of proved reserves worth a total of $3,000,000. Four properties are being considered. Alternative A will cost $500,000—it will generate net revenue of $200,000 for each of the next 5 years. Property B costs $800,000—it will generate net revenue of $500,000 in the 1st year and declining by $50,000 from 2nd year for each of the next 4 years. Property C will cost $1,700,000—it will generate net revenue of $600,000 in the 1st year and then declining thereafter by $25,000 per year for the next 3 years, in the 5th year it will generate $300,000 and declining thereafter by $50,000 per year for each of the next 3 years. Property D will cost $2,500,000—it will generate net revenue of $1,100,000 in the 1st year and declining thereafter by 25% per year until the economic limit of $147,000 per year. If the company has opportunity to invest all or part of the money elsewhere at 15% per year, which projects, if any, should be selected in order to maximize its investment worth?

7.18 Consider the initial costs and net revenue profiles of the following 4 investments. Use the appropriate techniques of investment analysis to select the most economic investment alternative. Carefully study the results obtained by each technique. Which techniques have given consistent selection of the investments? For all cases assume the opportunity cost of capital of 15%

	A	B	C	D
Initial Cost, M$	1,000	2,500	4,000	7,000
Net Revenue, M$				
Year 1 through 4	350	800	1,300	2,300
Year 5 through 8	210	400	500	700
Year 9 through 12	60	160	250	420

7.19 Rework Problem 7.18, assuming the alternatives are non-mutually exclusive and we have capital budget of $6,500,000. All or any part of this money can be invested elsewhere at an interest rate of 15%. Which alternatives, if any, should be selected to optimize net worth?

7.20 Rework Problem 7.19, assuming the money can be invested elsewhere at an interest rate of 20%. Does this change your selection of the investments?

7.21 A company is examining cost of some of its maintenance equipment. Its present equipment is costing $20,000 per year to operate, and an additional $5,000 expense is expected during the 3rd year. The company estimates a salvage value of $3,500 after 6 years of operation. The equipment can be upgraded at a cost of $13,500. After upgrade, operating costs are expected to be $17,000 per year, with no other costs. Salvage value after 6 years is expected to be $8,500. Determine if it is feasible to upgrade the equipment, assuming the $13,500 required for upgrade is earning interest at a rate of 8% per year.

First Cost	$90,000	$170,000
Life	5 Years	5 Years
Salvage Value	$15,000	$50,000
Operating/Maintenance Cost per year	$44,000	$70,000

7.22   A firm must decide between two models of a machine. The following estimates apply.
The firm evaluates all equipment purchases based on 8% rate of return. Which is the preferred model based on (a) equivalent annual cost, (b) present value of cost, (c) future value of cost, and (d) internal rate of return?

7.23   Evaluate and compare the operating expenses of the 456D Mark II pumping units currently in use in a 6000 ft waterflood and a planned hydraulic lift system for the same waterflood. The cost data for the two alternatives is given as follows.

456D API Beam Pumping Units	Hydraulic Pumping Equipment
Maintenance expense for one-year show surface well equipment cost $20,403; pump repair costs $15,319; and well service expense costs $32,723. Ninety percent of these costs are allocated to the producing wells. The waterflood has 26 x 228 API pumping units with 25 hp electric motors and 13 456D Mark II pumping units with 60 hp electric motors. Maintenance expenses are allocated to the producing wells based on electric motor horsepower. Electric power costs $0.11/KWH	The planned hydraulic system will utilize one 115 hp Ajax engine for every two wells. The Ajax engine's maintenance will cost an average of $22 per hp-year. The other surface hydraulic equipment per two well unit costs $1,88/year in maintenance. Hydraulic bottomhole pump repairs average $600/repair. Three such pumps are repaired per year per well. Other service costs $600 per year per well. Gas costs $0.14/Mscf.

Calculate:

a. The separate monthly maintenance cost for the Mark II Beam Pumped wells and the hydraulic pumped wells (on a per well basis).

b. The separate monthly power costs per well for the two systems. Assume electric motors use $3/4$ KWH/hp-hr. Assume 65% utilization rate for the time clock controlled Mark II units. The Ajax engines use 13 cu ft of gas per hp-hr. The hydraulic surface equipment averages a utilization rate of 95% on any power system.

c. The power cost of a 100 hp electric powered hydraulic surface pump ($/month/well).

7.24 Rework Example 7–10 if a 3rd, technically feasible, option of replacing the 12-inch NGL line with an 89-kilomer 6-inch pipeline is available. The 6-inch pipeline will cost $31 million. Timing of the capital expenditure is the same as the 12-inch line.

REFERENCES

1   Stermole, F. J., *Economic Evaluation and Investment Decision Methods, 10th Edition*, Investment Evaluations Corporation, Golden, Colorado, 2000.

2   Schallheim, J.S., *Lease or Buy? Principles for Sound Decision Making*, Harvard Business School Press, Boston, Massachusetts, 1994.

3   Myers, S.C., Dill, D.A., and Bautista, A.J., "Valuation of Financial Lease Contracts," *Journal of Finance*, 31(3), 1976, pp. 799–819.

4   Seba, R. D., "The Only Investment Selection Criterion You Will Ever Need," *SPE Paper 16310*, presented at the SPE Hydrocarbon Economics and Evaluation Symposium held in Dallas, Texas, USA, March 2–3, 1987, pp. 173–180.

Appendix A

t	Single Payment		Equal Payment Series				Uniform
	Compound Amount Factor, F/P	Present Worth Factor, P/F	Compound Amount Factor, F/A	Sinking Fund Factor, A/F	Present Worth Factor, P/A	Capital Recovery Factor, A/P	Gradient Series, A/G
1	1.0100	0.9901	1.0000	1.0000	0.9901	1.0100	0.0000
2	1.0201	0.9803	2.0100	0.4975	1.9704	0.5075	0.4975
3	1.0303	0.9706	3.0301	0.3300	2.9410	0.3400	0.9934
4	1.0406	0.9610	4.0604	0.2463	3.9020	0.2563	1.4876
5	1.0510	0.9515	5.1010	0.1960	4.8534	0.2060	1.9801
6	1.0615	0.9420	6.1520	0.1625	5.7955	0.1725	2.4710
7	1.0721	0.9327	7.2135	0.1386	6.7282	0.1486	2.9602
8	1.0829	0.9235	8.2857	0.1207	7.6517	0.1307	3.4478
9	1.0937	0.9143	9.3685	0.1067	8.5660	0.1167	3.9337
10	1.1046	0.9053	10.4622	0.0956	9.4713	0.1056	4.4179
11	1.1157	0.8963	11.5668	0.0865	10.3676	0.0965	4.9005
12	1.1268	0.8874	12.6825	0.0788	11.2551	0.0888	5.3815
13	1.1381	0.8787	13.8093	0.0724	12.1337	0.0824	5.8607
14	1.1495	0.8700	14.9474	0.0669	13.0037	0.0769	6.3384
15	1.1610	0.8613	16.0969	0.0621	13.8651	0.0721	6.8143
16	1.1726	0.8528	17.2579	0.0579	14.7179	0.0679	7.2886
17	1.1843	0.8444	18.4304	0.0543	15.5623	0.0643	7.7613
18	1.1961	0.8360	19.6147	0.0510	16.3983	0.0610	8.2323
19	1.2081	0.8277	20.8109	0.0481	17.2260	0.0581	8.7017
20	1.2202	0.8195	22.0190	0.0454	18.0456	0.0554	9.1694

Table A–1 Interest factors for annual interest compounding, i=1.0%

t	Single Payment		Equal Payment Series				Uniform
	Compound Amount Factor, F/P	Present Worth Factor, P/F	Compound Amount Factor, F/A	Sinking Fund Factor, A/F	Present Worth Factor, P/A	Capital Recovery Factor, A/P	Gradient Series, A/G
1	1.0200	0.9804	1.0000	1.0000	0.9804	1.0200	0.0000
2	1.0404	0.9612	2.0200	0.4950	1.9416	0.5150	0.4950
3	1.0612	0.9423	3.0604	0.3268	2.8839	0.3468	0.9868
4	1.0824	0.9238	4.1216	0.2426	3.8077	0.2626	1.4752
5	1.1041	0.9057	5.2040	0.1922	4.7135	0.2122	1.9604
6	1.1262	0.8880	6.3081	0.1585	5.6014	0.1785	2.4423
7	1.1487	0.8706	7.4343	0.1345	6.4720	0.1545	2.9208
8	1.1717	0.8535	8.5830	0.1165	7.3255	0.1365	3.3961
9	1.1951	0.8368	9.7546	0.1025	8.1622	0.1225	3.8681
10	1.2190	0.8203	10.9497	0.0913	8.9826	0.1113	4.3367
11	1.2434	0.8043	12.1687	0.0822	9.7868	0.1022	4.8021
12	1.2682	0.7885	13.4121	0.0746	10.5753	0.0946	5.2642
13	1.2936	0.7730	14.6803	0.0681	11.3484	0.0881	5.7231
14	1.3195	0.7579	15.9739	0.0626	12.1062	0.0826	6.1786
15	1.3459	0.7430	17.2934	0.0578	12.8493	0.0778	6.6309
16	1.3728	0.7284	18.6393	0.0537	13.5777	0.0737	7.0799
17	1.4002	0.7142	20.0121	0.0500	14.2919	0.0700	7.5256
18	1.4282	0.7002	21.4123	0.0467	14.9920	0.0667	7.9681
19	1.4568	0.6864	22.8406	0.0438	15.6785	0.0638	8.4073
20	1.4859	0.6730	24.2974	0.0412	16.3514	0.0612	8.8433

Table A–2 Interest factors for annual interest compounding, i=2.0%

t	Single Payment		Equal Payment Series				Uniform
	Compound Amount Factor, F/P	Present Worth Factor, P/F	Compound Amount Factor, F/A	Sinking Fund Factor, A/F	Present Worth Factor, P/A	Capital Recovery Factor, A/P	Gradient Series, A/G
1	1.0300	0.9709	1.0000	1.0000	0.9709	1.0300	0.0000
2	1.0609	0.9426	2.0300	0.4926	1.9135	0.5226	0.4926
3	1.0927	0.9151	3.0909	0.3235	2.8286	0.3535	0.9803
4	1.1255	0.8885	4.1836	0.2390	3.7171	0.2690	1.4631
5	1.1593	0.8626	5.3091	0.1884	4.5797	0.2184	1.9409
6	1.1941	0.8375	6.4684	0.1546	5.4172	0.1846	2.4138
7	1.2299	0.8131	7.6625	0.1305	6.2303	0.1605	2.8819
8	1.2668	0.7894	8.8923	0.1125	7.0197	0.1425	3.3450
9	1.3048	0.7664	10.1591	0.0984	7.7861	0.1284	3.8032
10	1.3439	0.7441	11.4639	0.0872	8.5302	0.1172	4.2565
11	1.3842	0.7224	12.8078	0.0781	9.2526	0.1081	4.7049
12	1.4258	0.7014	14.1920	0.0705	9.9540	0.1005	5.1485
13	1.4685	0.6810	15.6178	0.0640	10.6350	0.0940	5.5872
14	1.5126	0.6611	17.0863	0.0585	11.2961	0.0885	6.0210
15	1.5580	0.6419	18.5989	0.0538	11.9379	0.0838	6.4500
16	1.6047	0.6232	20.1569	0.0496	12.5611	0.0796	6.8742
17	1.6528	0.6050	21.7616	0.0460	13.1661	0.0760	7.2936
18	1.7024	0.5874	23.4144	0.0427	13.7535	0.0727	7.7081
19	1.7535	0.5703	25.1169	0.0398	14.3238	0.0698	8.1179
20	1.8061	0.5537	26.8704	0.0372	14.8775	0.0672	8.5229

Table A–3 Interest factors for annual interest compounding, i=3.0%

	Single Payment		Equal Payment Series				Uniform
	Compound Amount Factor, F/P	Present Worth Factor, P/F	Compound Amount Factor, F/A	Sinking Fund Factor, A/F	Present Worth Factor, P/A	Capital Recovery Factor, A/P	Gradient Series, A/G
t							
1	1.0400	0.9615	1.0000	1.0000	0.9615	1.0400	0.0000
2	1.0816	0.9246	2.0400	0.4902	1.8861	0.5302	0.4902
3	1.1249	0.8890	3.1216	0.3203	2.7751	0.3603	0.9739
4	1.1699	0.8548	4.2465	0.2355	3.6299	0.2755	1.4510
5	1.2167	0.8219	5.4163	0.1846	4.4518	0.2246	1.9216
6	1.2653	0.7903	6.6330	0.1508	5.2421	0.1908	2.3857
7	1.3159	0.7599	7.8983	0.1266	6.0021	0.1666	2.8433
8	1.3686	0.7307	9.2142	0.1085	6.7327	0.1485	3.2944
9	1.4233	0.7026	10.5828	0.0945	7.4353	0.1345	3.7391
10	1.4802	0.6756	12.0061	0.0833	8.1109	0.1233	4.1773
11	1.5395	0.6496	13.4864	0.0741	8.7605	0.1141	4.6090
12	1.6010	0.6246	15.0258	0.0666	9.3851	0.1066	5.0343
13	1.6651	0.6006	16.6268	0.0601	9.9856	0.1001	5.4533
14	1.7317	0.5775	18.2919	0.0547	10.5631	0.0947	5.8659
15	1.8009	0.5553	20.0236	0.0499	11.1184	0.0899	6.2721
16	1.8730	0.5339	21.8245	0.0458	11.6523	0.0858	6.6720
17	1.9479	0.5134	23.6975	0.0422	12.1657	0.0822	7.0656
18	2.0258	0.4936	25.6454	0.0390	12.6593	0.0790	7.4530
19	2.1068	0.4746	27.6712	0.0361	13.1339	0.0761	7.8342
20	2.1911	0.4564	29.7781	0.0336	13.5903	0.0736	8.2091

Table A–4 Interest factors for annual interest compounding, i=4.0%

	Single Payment		Equal Payment Series				Uniform
	Compound Amount Factor, F/P	Present Worth Factor, P/F	Compound Amount Factor, F/A	Sinking Fund Factor, A/F	Present Worth Factor, P/A	Capital Recovery Factor, A/P	Gradient Series, A/G
t							
1	1.0500	0.9524	1.0000	1.0000	0.9524	1.0500	0.0000
2	1.1025	0.9070	2.0500	0.4878	1.8594	0.5378	0.4878
3	1.1576	0.8638	3.1525	0.3172	2.7232	0.3672	0.9675
4	1.2155	0.8227	4.3101	0.2320	3.5460	0.2820	1.4391
5	1.2763	0.7835	5.5256	0.1810	4.3295	0.2310	1.9025
6	1.3401	0.7462	6.8019	0.1470	5.0757	0.1970	2.3579
7	1.4071	0.7107	8.1420	0.1228	5.7864	0.1728	2.8052
8	1.4775	0.6768	9.5491	0.1047	6.4632	0.1547	3.2445
9	1.5513	0.6446	11.0266	0.0907	7.1078	0.1407	3.6758
10	1.6289	0.6139	12.5779	0.0795	7.7217	0.1295	4.0991
11	1.7103	0.5847	14.2068	0.0704	8.3064	0.1204	4.5144
12	1.7959	0.5568	15.9171	0.0628	8.8633	0.1128	4.9219
13	1.8856	0.5303	17.7130	0.0565	9.3936	0.1065	5.3215
14	1.9799	0.5051	19.5986	0.0510	9.8986	0.1010	5.7133
15	2.0789	0.4810	21.5786	0.0463	10.3797	0.0963	6.0973
16	2.1829	0.4581	23.6575	0.0423	10.8378	0.0923	6.4736
17	2.2920	0.4363	25.8404	0.0387	11.2741	0.0887	6.8423
18	2.4066	0.4155	28.1324	0.0355	11.6896	0.0855	7.2034
19	2.5270	0.3957	30.5390	0.0327	12.0853	0.0827	7.5569
20	2.6533	0.3769	33.0660	0.0302	12.4622	0.0802	7.9030

Table A–5 Interest factors for annual interest compounding, i=6.0%

	Single Payment		Equal Payment Series				
	Compound Amount Factor, F/P	Present Worth Factor, P/F	Compound Amount Factor, F/A	Sinking Fund Factor, A/F	Present Worth Factor, P/A	Capital Recovery Factor, A/P	Uniform Gradient Series, A/G
t							
1	1.0600	0.9434	1.0000	1.0000	0.9434	1.0600	0.0000
2	1.1236	0.8900	2.0600	0.4854	1.8334	0.5454	0.4854
3	1.1910	0.8396	3.1836	0.3141	2.6730	0.3741	0.9612
4	1.2625	0.7921	4.3746	0.2286	3.4651	0.2886	1.4272
5	1.3382	0.7473	5.6371	0.1774	4.2124	0.2374	1.8836
6	1.4185	0.7050	6.9753	0.1434	4.9173	0.2034	2.3304
7	1.5036	0.6651	8.3938	0.1191	5.5824	0.1791	2.7676
8	1.5938	0.6274	9.8975	0.1010	6.2098	0.1610	3.1952
9	1.6895	0.5919	11.4913	0.0870	6.8017	0.1470	3.6133
10	1.7908	0.5584	13.1808	0.0759	7.3601	0.1359	4.0220
11	1.8983	0.5268	14.9716	0.0668	7.8869	0.1268	4.4213
12	2.0122	0.4970	16.8699	0.0593	8.3838	0.1193	4.8113
13	2.1329	0.4688	18.8821	0.0530	8.8527	0.1130	5.1920
14	2.2609	0.4423	21.0151	0.0476	9.2950	0.1076	5.5635
15	2.3966	0.4173	23.2760	0.0430	9.7122	0.1030	5.9260
16	2.5404	0.3936	25.6725	0.0390	10.1059	0.0990	6.2794
17	2.6928	0.3714	28.2129	0.0354	10.4773	0.0954	6.6240
18	2.8543	0.3503	30.9057	0.0324	10.8276	0.0924	6.9597
19	3.0256	0.3305	33.7600	0.0296	11.1581	0.0896	7.2867
20	3.2071	0.3118	36.7856	0.0272	11.4699	0.0872	7.6051

Table A–6 Interest factors for annual interest compounding, i=6.0%

	Single Payment		Equal Payment Series				
	Compound Amount Factor, F/P	Present Worth Factor, P/F	Compound Amount Factor, F/A	Sinking Fund Factor, A/F	Present Worth Factor, P/A	Capital Recovery Factor, A/P	Uniform Gradient Series, A/G
t							
1	1.0700	0.9346	1.0000	1.0000	0.9346	1.0700	0.0000
2	1.1449	0.8734	2.0700	0.4831	1.8080	0.5531	0.4831
3	1.2250	0.8163	3.2149	0.3111	2.6243	0.3811	0.9549
4	1.3108	0.7629	4.4399	0.2252	3.3872	0.2952	1.4155
5	1.4026	0.7130	5.7507	0.1739	4.1002	0.2439	1.8650
6	1.5007	0.6663	7.1533	0.1398	4.7665	0.2098	2.3032
7	1.6058	0.6227	8.6540	0.1156	5.3893	0.1856	2.7304
8	1.7182	0.5820	10.2598	0.0975	5.9713	0.1675	3.1465
9	1.8385	0.5439	11.9780	0.0835	6.5152	0.1535	3.5517
10	1.9672	0.5083	13.8164	0.0724	7.0236	0.1424	3.9461
11	2.1049	0.4751	15.7836	0.0634	7.4987	0.1334	4.3296
12	2.2522	0.4440	17.8885	0.0559	7.9427	0.1259	4.7025
13	2.4098	0.4150	20.1406	0.0497	8.3577	0.1197	5.0648
14	2.5785	0.3878	22.5505	0.0443	8.7455	0.1143	5.4167
15	2.7590	0.3624	25.1290	0.0398	9.1079	0.1098	5.7583
16	2.9522	0.3387	27.8881	0.0359	9.4466	0.1059	6.0897
17	3.1588	0.3166	30.8402	0.0324	9.7632	0.1024	6.4110
18	3.3799	0.2959	33.9990	0.0294	10.0591	0.0994	6.7225
19	3.6165	0.2765	37.3790	0.0268	10.3356	0.0968	7.0242
20	3.8697	0.2584	40.9955	0.0244	10.5940	0.0944	7.3163

Table A–7 Interest factors for annual interest compounding, i=7.0%

	Single Payment		Equal Payment Series				
	Compound Amount Factor, F/P	Present Worth Factor, P/F	Compound Amount Factor, F/A	Sinking Fund Factor, A/F	Present Worth Factor, P/A	Capital Recovery Factor, A/P	Uniform Gradient Series, A/G
t							
1	1.0800	0.9259	1.0000	1.0000	0.9259	1.0800	0.0000
2	1.1664	0.8573	2.0800	0.4808	1.7833	0.5608	0.4808
3	1.2597	0.7938	3.2464	0.3080	2.5771	0.3880	0.9487
4	1.3605	0.7350	4.5061	0.2219	3.3121	0.3019	1.4040
5	1.4693	0.6806	5.8666	0.1705	3.9927	0.2505	1.8465
6	1.5869	0.6302	7.3359	0.1363	4.6229	0.2163	2.2763
7	1.7138	0.5835	8.9228	0.1121	5.2064	0.1921	2.6937
8	1.8509	0.5403	10.6366	0.0940	5.7466	0.1740	3.0985
9	1.9990	0.5002	12.4876	0.0801	6.2469	0.1601	3.4910
10	2.1589	0.4632	14.4866	0.0690	6.7101	0.1490	3.8713
11	2.3316	0.4289	16.6455	0.0601	7.1390	0.1401	4.2395
12	2.5182	0.3971	18.9771	0.0527	7.5361	0.1327	4.5957
13	2.7196	0.3677	21.4953	0.0465	7.9038	0.1265	4.9402
14	2.9372	0.3405	24.2149	0.0413	8.2442	0.1213	5.2731
15	3.1722	0.3152	27.1521	0.0368	8.5595	0.1168	5.5945
16	3.4259	0.2919	30.3243	0.0330	8.8514	0.1130	5.9046
17	3.7000	0.2703	33.7502	0.0296	9.1216	0.1096	6.2037
18	3.9960	0.2502	37.4502	0.0267	9.3719	0.1067	6.4920
19	4.3157	0.2317	41.4463	0.0241	9.6036	0.1041	6.7697
20	4.6610	0.2145	45.7620	0.0219	9.8181	0.1019	7.0369

Table A–8 Interest factors for annual interest compounding, i=8.0%

	Single Payment		Equal Payment Series				
	Compound Amount Factor, F/P	Present Worth Factor, P/F	Compound Amount Factor, F/A	Sinking Fund Factor, A/F	Present Worth Factor, P/A	Capital Recovery Factor, A/P	Uniform Gradient Series, A/G
t							
1	1.0900	0.9174	1.0000	1.0000	0.9174	1.0900	0.0000
2	1.1881	0.8417	2.0900	0.4785	1.7591	0.5685	0.4785
3	1.2950	0.7722	3.2781	0.3051	2.5313	0.3951	0.9426
4	1.4116	0.7084	4.5731	0.2187	3.2397	0.3087	1.3925
5	1.5386	0.6499	5.9847	0.1671	3.8897	0.2571	1.8282
6	1.6771	0.5963	7.5233	0.1329	4.4859	0.2229	2.2498
7	1.8280	0.5470	9.2004	0.1087	5.0330	0.1987	2.6574
8	1.9926	0.5019	11.0285	0.0907	5.5348	0.1807	3.0512
9	2.1719	0.4604	13.0210	0.0768	5.9952	0.1668	3.4312
10	2.3674	0.4224	15.1929	0.0658	6.4177	0.1558	3.7978
11	2.5804	0.3875	17.5603	0.0569	6.8052	0.1469	4.1510
12	2.8127	0.3555	20.1407	0.0497	7.1607	0.1397	4.4910
13	3.0658	0.3262	22.9534	0.0436	7.4869	0.1336	4.8182
14	3.3417	0.2992	26.0192	0.0384	7.7862	0.1284	5.1326
15	3.6425	0.2745	29.3609	0.0341	8.0607	0.1241	5.4346
16	3.9703	0.2519	33.0034	0.0303	8.3126	0.1203	5.7245
17	4.3276	0.2311	36.9737	0.0270	8.5436	0.1170	6.0024
18	4.7171	0.2120	41.3013	0.0242	8.7556	0.1142	6.2687
19	5.1417	0.1945	46.0185	0.0217	8.9501	0.1117	6.5236
20	5.6044	0.1784	51.1601	0.0195	9.1285	0.1095	6.7674

Table 9–1 Interest factors for annual interest compounding, i=9.0%

	Single Payment		Equal Payment Series				
	Compound Amount Factor, F/P	Present Worth Factor, P/F	Compound Amount Factor, F/A	Sinking Fund Factor, A/F	Present Worth Factor, P/A	Capital Recovery Factor, A/P	Uniform Gradient Series, A/G
t							
1	1.1000	0.9091	1.0000	1.0000	0.9091	1.1000	0.0000
2	1.2100	0.8264	2.1000	0.4762	1.7355	0.5762	0.4762
3	1.3310	0.7513	3.3100	0.3021	2.4869	0.4021	0.9366
4	1.4641	0.6830	4.6410	0.2155	3.1699	0.3155	1.3812
5	1.6105	0.6209	6.1051	0.1638	3.7908	0.2638	1.8101
6	1.7716	0.5645	7.7156	0.1296	4.3553	0.2296	2.2236
7	1.9487	0.5132	9.4872	0.1054	4.8684	0.2054	2.6216
8	2.1436	0.4665	11.4359	0.0874	5.3349	0.1874	3.0045
9	2.3579	0.4241	13.5795	0.0736	5.7590	0.1736	3.3724
10	2.5937	0.3855	15.9374	0.0627	6.1446	0.1627	3.7255
11	2.8531	0.3505	18.5312	0.0540	6.4951	0.1540	4.0641
12	3.1384	0.3186	21.3843	0.0468	6.8137	0.1468	4.3884
13	3.4523	0.2897	24.5227	0.0408	7.1034	0.1408	4.6988
14	3.7975	0.2633	27.9750	0.0357	7.3667	0.1357	4.9955
15	4.1772	0.2394	31.7725	0.0315	7.6061	0.1315	5.2789
16	4.5950	0.2176	35.9497	0.0278	7.8237	0.1278	5.5493
17	5.0545	0.1978	40.5447	0.0247	8.0216	0.1247	5.8071
18	5.5599	0.1799	45.5992	0.0219	8.2014	0.1219	6.0526
19	6.1159	0.1635	51.1591	0.0195	8.3649	0.1195	6.2861
20	6.7275	0.1486	57.2750	0.0175	8.5136	0.1175	6.5081

Table 10–1 Interest factors for annual interest compounding, i=10.0%

Appendix B

A CD-ROM is included in Volume 2 of this series. The CD contains Excel spreadsheets with all the tables and example problems solved in Chapter 2 to Chapter 7 of this volume. Once the CD is installed, the following MAIN MENU appears. This menu links the various spreadsheets and provides easy access to them.

Project Economics and Decision Analysis

MAIN MENU

VOLUME 1		VOLUME 2	
Chapter 2	Chapter 6	Chapter 2	Chapter 6
Chapter 3	Chapter 7	Chapter 3	Appendix A Probability Tables
Chapter 4	Appendix A Interest Tables	Chapter 4	Probability Graph Paper
Chapter 5	Economics Spreadsheets	Chapter 5	QUIT

In addition to the spreadsheets, two comprehensive economics spreadsheets are included. These spreadsheets are installed in a directory called ECONPAC, created in the root directory (i.e. C\ECONPAC\). The spreadsheets are designed for use by investors, analysts, engineers, or anyone else interested in knowing more about the value and vitality of oil and gas property. The following three spreadsheets are presented in this option.

1. **ECONOIL** – performs economic evaluation of oil and associated gas wells/lease for production life of up to 30 years.

2. **ECONGAS** – Same as ECONOIL but used to evaluate gas and associated oil or condensate wells/lease.

3. **ECONSUM** – this is a utility spreadsheet used for creating summaries of individual cash flows that are created by ECONGAS and ECONOIL.

4. **ECONPSA** – this comprehensive spreadsheet can be used to evaluate economics of production-sharing deals. The spreadsheet is flexible in terms of handling various tranches linked to R-factor, production volumes, product price, etc.

ECONOIL / ECONGAS — ECONOMIC EVALUATION SPREADSHEETS

The ECONOIL and ECONGAS are the same as far as functional capabilities are concerned. Following are the detailed functional capabilities of these two models.

1. Once the ECONOIL or ECONGAS file is retrieved, a main data input screen appears. This screen is used for inputting all data.

2. The model uses exponential decline rate to schedule oil or gas (major phase) production, gas–oil ratio or oil or condensate yield, which is specified to calculate the associated gas, oil or condensate production,

respectively. The user has to specify initial the monthly production rate of the major phase and the percent exponential decline rate per year.

3.   The model is capable of calculating the economic limit of the production, based on product prices, working interest, net revenue interest, monthly operating costs, severance, and ad valorem taxes, and gas–oil ratio or yield. Production of the major phase will be scheduled to the economic limit or up to 30 years whichever comes first.

4.   Oil and gas severance taxes may be specified in $/Stb, $/MScf or in percentages. In the former case, input the taxes with a minus (negative) sign.

5.   In case of escalated economics or when evaluating overriding royalty interest only, the model will not calculate economic limit, therefore, the user has to specify the ending rate (ERATE in the menu).

6.   The models are capable of handling up to three escalation scenarios for oil price, gas price, and operating cost.

7.   The presentation format of the cash flows is typical of many such cash flow formats encountered in the industry. The bottomline profitability indicators and economic parameters calculated/used by the models are listed at the bottom of the printout.

ECONSUM — CREATING SUMMARIES OF EVALUATIONS

Economic evaluations are normally performed for oil and gas properties classified into different reserve categories, locations (such as state, etc.), and operator, etc. In order to get composite cash flows summarizing each group and the total of all groups (total portfolio), the individual cash flows generated by using ECONOIL and ECONGAS have to be added together in the respective categories as required.

ECONSUM is a utility spreadsheet that can be used to perform this task. Once the cash flows for individual properties are generated, this spreadsheet can then be used to create their summaries. The spreadsheet requires that the ECONSUM and the cash flows to be added together be on the same disk and in the same directory.

ECONSUM adds up to 30 files together at a time. However, there is no upper limit to this. If more than 30 files are to be added together in any one category, the summary file created for the first 30 wells is then used with file names of another 29 wells. This process is repeated until all the files in a specified category are added.

The following steps are to be followed when using this spreadsheet.

1. Open file ECONSUM. The following statement will appear
   a. ? This document contains links. Re-establish Link ?
   b. Click on **NO**

2. A menu will appear, enter the file names to be added together in the empty Cells (up to 30 files can be added at a time).

3. Click on **Tools** in the Excel toolbar. At the bottom of this drop-down menu the following commands appear.
   a. SUMMARISE
   b. NAME CHECK
   c. SAVE AS NEW FILE
   d. MAIN MENU

4. Before creating summary, Click at NAME CHECK to enter the file name where the summary (i.e. PROVEPR for proved pro-ducing) will be stored. <u>This should be done only if you want to add together another 29 files to the 30 files already added in PROVEPR</u>, or else specify file name ECONSUM. Only ECON-SUM can be printed.

5. Click on SUMMARISE to start adding the files.

6. Click at SAVE AS NEW FILE to save the PROVEPR.

Index

B

D

G

H

J

K

L

N

O

Q

T